SIMPLER LIVING HANDBOOK

SIMPLER LIVING HANDBOOK

A Back to Basics Guide to Organizing · Decluttering · Streamlining · and More

Jeff Davidson

**Foreword by Mark Victor Hansen,
co-author of *Chicken Soup for the Soul***

Skyhorse Publishing

SIMPLER LIVING HANDBOOK

Skyhorse Publishing books may be purchased in bulk at special discounts for sales promotion, corporate gifts, fund-raising, or educational purposes. Special editions can also be created to specifications. For details, contact the Special Sales Department, Skyhorse Publishing, 307 West 36th Street, 11th Floor, New York, NY 10018 or info@skyhorsepublishing.com.

Skyhorse® and Skyhorse Publishing® are registered trademarks of Skyhorse Publishing, Inc.®, a Delaware corporation.

Visit our website at www.skyhorsepublishing.com.

10 9 8 7 6 5 4 3 2 1

Library of Congress Cataloging-in-Publication Data is available on file.

Cover photos courtesy of Thinkstock.

Print ISBN: 978-1-62914-361-3

Ebook ISBN: 978-1-63220-126-3

Printed in China

To all of those people in my life—past, present, and future—who have shown me the path toward simplicity. To the authors, journalists, and speakers who stress the vital importance of simplicity in each of our lives. To my wonderful, now-departed parents, Emanuel and Shirley Davidson, for imbuing me with the sense to figure things out for myself. And to Valerie Davidson—every little thing she does is magic.

Contents

Acknowledgments

I'd like to thank the professional team at Skyhorse Publishing for all of their support. Thanks, in particular, to my key contact point and day-to-day manager Bill Wolfsthal and to publisher Tony Lyons.

Thanks also to the editors of such top publications as *Men's Health* and *Prevention* for the countless tips, tidbits, and minor gems that they gleaned over the years, which helped to round out this text.

A big thank you to Tammy Bristow for her remarkable assistance in originally identifying research materials and helping me assemble several chapters, and upgrading and refining chapters as needed. Thanks also to Ashley Pittman and Christine Truesdale for their endless rounds of research, fact-checking, and editing, and to Skyhorse staff members Julie Matysik, Kaylan Connally, and Abigail Gehring, for their able editing and production.

Foreword

There is a fascinating book by Benard Grun called *The Timetables of History: A Horizontal Linkage of People and Events*. Beginning in 5000 BC and proceeding to the present, the book chronicles the development of humankind in areas such as history and politics, literature and the arts, music, religion, philosophy, education, science, technology, and daily life. Grun starts out covering 1,000 years at a time then narrows the increments to 500 years, 100 years, and—by AD 500—50 years. From that point on, he goes a year at a time.

Grun had good reason for using ever-decreasing intervals. The number of noteworthy events has risen with each passing year. These days, they're occurring at a feverish pace. And why not? After all, this planet has more inhabitants to generate more breakthroughs and milestones. The Connecticut of today has a larger population than the entire world of 200 BC.

The global population is now approaching seven billion—all of us connected by economics, ecology, technology, communication, and transportation. The environment is ripe for more innovations. Consider that 85 percent of all scientists who have ever lived are alive today.

Of course, with new discoveries and developments come new opportunities for complexity. Now more than ever, simplicity is crucial to our sanity—and our survival.

In writing Simpler Living, Jeff Davidson has successfully filled a void in information on the science and art of simplification. In his research for this book, Jeff came across scores and scores of other publications on the general topic of simplicity, dating from the mid-1970s right through to 2010. Virtually every book he encountered had some glaring omission or other shortcoming. For example:

- Books written before 1995 contain little—if any—information about the dramatic impact of the Internet, cell phones, and e-mail, among many other technological breakthroughs.
- Books relying on affirmations or a one-tip-per-day format lack the comprehensive approach necessary to simplify all aspects of life.
- Some books focus on solely personal issues or professional issues rather than on both.
- Some books advise readers to withdraw from certain aspects of their lives, if not from society as a whole.
- Some books propose changes that might simplify some aspects of life but complicate others.

Jeff's mission, then, became one of going where no book has gone before. He decided to take a room-by-room, space-by-space look at what the typical man and woman in the United States—and anywhere in the postindustrial world, for that matter—could do to make their lives simpler.

The sheer amount of territory that Jeff covers is staggering and, in a sense, paradoxical. After all, with more than 1,500 tips, this book may at first seem less like a guide to simplicity than yet another vehicle for complexity.

As Jeff says, you needn't read this book from cover to cover. In fact, he advises against it. Instead, peruse those chapters that are of most relevance or interest to you, glean those tips that make the most sense for you, and act on them. If you take even a few of the steps suggested in any of the 24 chapters, you're likely to benefit significantly.

I found *Simpler Living* to be enjoyable, illuminating reading. The tips are practical and sensible (something you'd expect in a book such as this), and they're presented in a logical, easy-to-follow sequence. This is a book to be retained, to be referred to whenever you notice the level of complexity in your life edging upward. It is a book to share with a spouse, a friend, a co-worker. It is a book whose message will guide you toward a more relaxed, rewarding, fulfilling lifestyle.

The reality of our times is that life has become far too complex. Fortunately for you, you hold the antidote in your hands. May your reading experience be as pleasurable and compelling as mine has been.

—Mark Victor Hansen
co-author of *Chicken Soup for the Soul*

Introduction

Take a look around your home and office. What do you see? More paper, more piles, and more clutter than you can comfortably handle. When you take a big-picture approach to the current state of your life, an obvious reality confronts you. Complexity has become the hallmark of human existence.

Would you like to be in a committed relationship, to raise children, to have a full-time career? These days, any major undertaking of a personal or professional nature seems to have its own built-in set of rules, regulations, protocols, and instructions.

As a professional speaker and an author, I see people all around me leading increasingly hectic lives, hoping to get through each day with their sanity intact. With all of the changes that have occurred in the past decade, and with even more changes on the way, I'm not surprised that so many folks are searching for an off-ramp from the rat race. More and more of us are taking the time to reassess how we run our lives, searching for ways to create simpler, more efficient lifestyles without sacrificing what is truly important.

You or someone you know is feeling overwhelmed or stressed or frustrated by a particular aspect of life. That's why I've written this book: to help you find and maintain balance in an increasingly hectic and demanding world. Is this balance possible? I, for one, am convinced that it is.

Each of the 24 chapters that follow offers dozens of practical how-to solutions for eliminating unnecessary trappings and leading a more peaceful, pleasurable, and productive life. Some of the advice comes directly from experts on a variety of subjects relevant to simplifying home, career, and lifestyle. Other advice is drawn from my own experience helping people like you live and work at a more comfortable pace in a high-speed world.

Most of the tips cost nothing or next to nothing to implement. I believe that making a change is far more palatable when you don't have to dip into the till time and time again. Sometimes, however, paying someone to do a job for you is much more efficient—in terms of money and time—than tackling it yourself. Where you're asked to spend, it is truly your best and easiest option.

As you read through the chapters, keep in mind that to achieve simplicity in your life you needn't do everything that I suggest. Choose only those strategies that seem right for you and that will benefit you most. If you adopt only eight to ten strategies per chapter, you'll be doing great.

Do you want to make your quest for simplicity even simpler? Start by picking one to three tips that you can readily and easily implement. With a few victories under your belt, you may be prompted to go back and try some more tips.

Each chapter concludes with a special feature called "The Simplest of the Simple." It summarizes the easiest changes that will produce the greatest results. If you do only what is highlighted in these sections, you'll make your life much simpler.

One final bit of advice: Treat this book as a reference. Rather than wading through it from cover to cover (a daunting task for even the speediest readers), turn to it on an as-needed basis. If you find yourself referring to certain passages again and again, you may want to mark those pages with self-stick notes, paper clips, bookmarks, or whatever else suits your fancy. In your quest for simplicity, use this book in the manner that serves you best.

PART ONE   # A World Gone Complex

Chapter 1

The Quest for Simplicity

Yes, You Can Achieve Sanity in a Crazed World

This book is going to make your life simpler—no kidding—in a world that grows increasingly complex. It's not going to tell you to change your personality or to run to the store and spend a lot of money to do so. The observations, tips, and strategies throughout this book come in the form of friendly advice that will help virtually anyone to have a simpler time of things.

Remember that any changes you make to have a simpler life need to come naturally and easily so that they will take hold. If you try to make too many changes at once, or if the changes are too radical or too rigorous to maintain, chances are high that they will not take effect—you'll forsake them in a nanosecond. As you consider any advice you encounter, here or anywhere else, be sure to measure it against the all-embracing notion of what is right and what feels comfortable for you.

More and more people are taking the time to reassess how they run their lives and are searching for ways to achieve a simpler, more effective lifestyle without sacrificing what is vital to them. That's what "making things simpler" will mean throughout this book—having a more effective lifestyle without giving up what is truly important to you.

Achieving simplicity in your life starts with the simple notion that you are in control. You steer the rudder, flip the switch, pull the lever, call the shots, and have the power within you to take steps to make your life simpler. Even if you work in a highly demanding job and have oodles of professional and personal responsibilities, take heart because there are ways to make your life simpler.

In this chapter, we'll first take a look at simplicity from both historical and modern perspectives, and then we'll explore ways to achieve the attitude and motivation you'll need to effectively streamline your existence and find the serenity you deserve.

A Movement Centuries in the Making

Believe it or not, wanting to have a simpler life is not some new millennium phenomenon. It's not a New Age fad and it didn't start in California. The desire for simple living has been around for hundreds of years. "From the earliest days of the American experience, advocates of simple living have challenged consumerism and materialism," says Jerome Segal, PhD., of the Institute for Philosophy and Public Policy at the University of Maryland in College Park, "although simple living, or plain living, as it was sometimes called, has meant different things to different groups."

Dr. Segal explains that Puritans were known for their hard work, religious devotion, plain dress, plain homes, and plain lives. Their economy and culture reinforced the notion of limited consumption and limited possessions. Elsewhere, Quakers admonished one another to work a fair day but not an excessively long day. They maintained simple homes, simple churches, and simple lives.

Throughout the 1800s, writers and philosophers from Ralph Waldo Emerson and Henry David Thoreau to the lesser known but sharp-tongued John Ruskin advocated various forms of simpler living for their inherent virtue and the larger benefits to society in general. Thoreau believed that consuming and owning less freed one up for the pursuit of the arts and development of one's intellect.

For another century, the growing nation—facing war, boom times, depression, and social movements—teetered back and forth between conspicuous consumption and the seemingly nobler pursuit of voluntary simplicity, which included ecological notions like reduced consumption, recycling, conservation, and a generally simple lifestyle.

Today, this movement is so widespread that the term *simplicity* means many things to many different people. Among the many definitions are the following: more time, less stress, more leisure, fewer bills to pay, less clutter, less to clean and maintain, greater peace of mind, and spirituality. Your quest for simplicity may encompass one or all of these notions.

How Complex Can It Get

Breakthroughs at Breakneck Speed: In the twenty-first century, significant technological breakthroughs —in software, medicine, and communications, for instance—will occur at an initial rate of 17 per second, which equates to more than 1.4 million daily.

How Did Things Get So Complex Anyway?

You were born into an era in which complexity is the hallmark of our existence. Let's take a look at the contributing factors.

Never in history has a generation been besieged by more items competing for time and attention. Think of it—in his entire life, George Washington never spent a second watching CNN.

With each passing year, each day, hour, minute, and second, an accelerating amount of information is generated on Earth and an accelerating number of technological breakthroughs are achieved. From a capability standpoint, all the high-tech products on your desk and in your home will be antiques (and not high-priced antiques either) five years from this day, observes futurist Lowell Catlett, PhD, of the University of New Mexico in Albuquerque, an author and lecturer on the topic of technology and change. Moreover, technology manufacturers themselves are bent on putting their own products out to pasture in shorter and shorter cycles.

For example, Sony's shelf life, or market life span, for high-tech products is 90 days. When Sony sells a product to an electronics or office supply store, within 90 days on average, Sony itself has an updated product that exceeds the capability or design function of what it previously shipped. Sony estimates that its shelf life will soon be 18 days. Its mission is to make

its own products obsolete because its newer products will be so superior.

Why would the company do this? Doesn't continually coming out with new products wreak havoc on its employees, its distribution systems, and you as a consumer? The answer is a big, fat yes. At the same time, if Sony doesn't constantly improve what it is offering, then it will be done in by the competition. Every major manufacturer feels the same pinch. Consumers have no idea what is hitting them.

The Incredible Shrinking Technology

The almighty computer microprocessing chip, as you may know, grows ever smaller and more powerful. Thanks to advancing technology, the chip size is dwindling to the thickness of less than a human hair—a couple of microns, for you technophiles. Indeed, microscopic *motors* now exist that are no thicker than a hair.

Gizmos that were once the stuff of science fiction movies and Superman comics will actually soon be headed for the shelves at your local department store. Here are a handful of miraculous devices that exist now or soon will, according to industry reports (although at last word, these items were still too costly for mass production).

- Sunglasses that pick up television channels and display images on the lenses, enabling you to watch any show while you're wearing them, wherever you are
- Laser-enhanced glasses that enable Air Force pilots to fire missiles or operate plane controls with their eye movements
- A disc the size of a silver dollar that enables you to watch up to thousands of movies
- "Smart books" that sense when you're lingering over a particular word, indicating that you don't understand it, and insert an appropriate synonym in its place

Well-funded fire and police departments could equip their officers with special sunglasses that instantaneously give them updated images from the field. A firefighter entering a burning building could be told to turn left to safety, rather than right, which would spell certain doom. A police officer in the midst of a blinding snowstorm could be told that the bridge is out 50 yards ahead.

Similar technological advances will have more social than practical implications. One type of high-tech eyewear, for example, will identify people by the irises of their eyes or some other physical feature. About 30 seconds after you look at someone across a room, you'll be able to have his name spelled out in the corner of one of your lenses. No more forgetting old what's-his-name.

Think of it: You'll walk into a new company, not knowing a soul, but you'll be able to greet everyone by first name. Until the technology is widely known, you'll be regarded as some type of wizard (or demon).

Your Tax Dollars at Work

Government does its part to make your life complex. It's a paradox that has become particularly prominent since the mid-1970s in the United States: The population grows and resources diminish. As matters grow increasingly complex in society, the government tries to respond with regulations. Those regulations, of course, add another layer of complications. And so the complexity of life snowballs. The same scenario is being played out around the world.

Federal agencies in the United States now examine nearly all aspects of nearly all companies' operations. The Occupational Safety and Health Administration patrols the factory floor. The Equal Employment Opportunity Commission oversees hiring and firing. The Environmental Protection Agency prevails over everything from construction materials to indoor atmosphere to sanitation systems to the use of natural resources. The IRS looms omnipotent. It's getting more and more complex to start a business, grow a business, maintain a business, and even work for a business.

And all the while, government intrusion into private lives has evoked angry responses among many groups and individuals in society, and not just crazed hermits. The most obvious intrusion, of course, is that hefty tab you pay to fund all of that government complexity. By 2010 the cost of federal regulations was well over $10,000 per American household, estimates economists with the Rochester Institute of Technology in New York.

Beware: This World Bites Back

Before you start depending on expensive gizmos and widgets to simplify matters for you, think carefully. Nature may abhor a vacuum, but it also seems to abhor technological solutions. "The Revenge Effect is the curious way the world has of getting even, defeating our best efforts to speed it up and otherwise improve it," says historian Edward Tenner, PhD of Princeton University. The failure of technology to solve problems, Dr. Tenner says, can often be traced to the interaction between machine and man.

An example: In his book *Why Things Bite Back: Technology and the Revenge of Unintended Consequences,* Dr. Tenner notes that corporations had hoped automation would produce the "paperless office." They put a personal computer on every desk and a copier at the end of every hall. Yet, for the first 20 years of the personal computer revolution (starting in 1985), the use of paper in the workplace more than tripled.

With the advent of the Internet, people are getting online, zapping messages around the world at the speed of electricity. So pundits concluded, "Ah-hah, *now* we will see a decline in the use of paper." Yet the paper that gluts the work-a-day world has not declined. You only have to look at the blizzard of mail, interoffice memos, and corporate trash bins each evening to know that the American economy rips through paper like starving raccoons in a garbage heap.

Meanwhile, those electronic message enthusiasts are driven bananas by a growing phenomenon that was unimaginable just a few years ago: junk e-mail.

Prepare for Advances to Backfire

The research of historian Edward Tenner, PhD of Princeton University, reveals that nearly every technological breakthrough invariably backfires in some way.

An example: Equipment was engineered to make playing football safer, but the added protection actually prompted players to try more reckless plays. The result was more injuries per player and per team than in previous years, when players had to suffer with inferior equipment.

Another example is "miracle drug" antibiotics, dispensed in the early twentieth century by a health care industry that forecast the elimination of ancient maladies. Today, a new generation of drug-resistant microbes leaves us hoping for new "miracle" cures.

Here are some tips to consider in light of Dr. Tenner's research, to make sure some of your best intentions don't turn into complex monsters in your household.

Rethink your subscriptions. Maybe you subscribed to a travel-and-leisure magazine with the honorable goal of putting more travel and leisure in your life. Now, however, the magazines are mounting up, and you've taken fewer trips than before you subscribed. Perhaps you can chuck the issues, clear some space, and begin to think about travel closer to the time you're going to actually hit the road. Maybe you can even do without the magazine. The next time you're going to travel, simply bone up on your destination with one swift trip to the library a couple of weeks beforehand.

Keep technology in its place. There are some things that computers and other high-tech devices handle remarkably well. And there are some things that still go more smoothly with paper and pencil or similarly low-tech implements. Until voice recognition technology is part of all computers and until powerful computers are so tiny they can be built into the handle of your kitchen cabinet, it makes sense to keep your file of recipes right where they are in your card file box, not on a computer disk. Someday, home computers may be slick enough to produce recipes as quickly as you can say "chicken curry with noodles." For now, entering recipes into your computer and retrieving them each time you want to use them is definitely more bother than it's worth. Chances are, you won't use them.

Make your own rules. View each new technological tool as both beneficial and detrimental. That way you'll be in a far better position to keep things simple. For example, before buying a cellular phone, you could establish rules for its use: only making calls to loved ones and for crucial appointments, for instance, or limiting calls to less than three minutes and not listing your cellular phone number on business cards or brochures. The crucial element is that you define your personal set of rules for using each tool. Naturally, your rules can change, but they're still your rules.

Avoid unnecessary tinkering. Computer repair experts will testify that most of the breakdowns and downtime that computer users endure are the result of people's tinkering unnecessarily with their own systems. Much of the time, if you let things be, they work just fine.

Look for thin manuals. Did you trade in your old microwave with the simple dial for one with a new digital touch pad with multiple functions, most of which you've never explored? Consider that, and then look at your television set and DVD player, iPod, and perhaps even your car. All of the technological devices in your life have far more capabilities than their predecessors. Many of them come with thick instruction manuals (so thick you still can't figure out how to set the clock). Why not buy the item with the simplest instructions? Maybe the device doesn't do everything the more involved versions do, but if it does what you want—simply—that's all you need.

Standing Up for Yourself

The regulations, laws, information, and technology that we're expected to abide by are leaving many of us overwhelmed and exhausted. The very infrastructure that now holds society in place—the computer systems, the highways, the buildings, and the energy that runs them all—are based on ever-more-sophisticated systems.

If you look around and see that the world is getting more complex each day, and if you feel as if your own life is overly intricate, relax—you're probably quite rational. It is not a figment of your imagination. It is not because you're aging. It is not because you have more responsibility, a bigger mortgage, higher rent, or more children. Even if you've done nothing more that sit on the curb and twiddle your thumbs, life is becoming more complex.

How to Wrestle with Complexities and Win

Subsequent chapters in this book are brimming with specific ways to simplify your life. Before you start implementing those, here are some general strategies for preserving your sanity and steering yourself toward solutions.

Acknowledge the reality of the times

Merely being born into this world at this time all but guarantees that you will face a never-ending stream of complexity—inside your home, when you step outside, on the highway, at work, and everywhere in between. Acknowledging this reality is one of the most basic and effective steps for achieving redress. If you can firmly and conclusively identify the root causes of the problems that you face, you're in a far better situation to take control. Some people won't get to this level of understanding in their entire lives. Sadly, they'll blame themselves or someone else.

View your problems as challenges

The Nobel Prize–winning physicist Richard Feynman, PhD, would amaze his colleagues and students when he first encountered a complex physics problem. He would dive in with disarming enthusiasm, saying, "Well, what have we here?" To him, a problem was an opportunity dressed up in disguise. Complexity was a challenge to be solved. He thought it was good fun to tackle and solve what baffled others. Dr. Feynman didn't resist what he found; he used it to flourish. He recognized that by

identifying and accepting the problem, he was already that much closer to resolution.

Look for the answer alongside the problem.

A generation before Dr. Feynman, Charles Kettering pursued problems with an equally ingenious and innovative approach. Kettering, a founder of the Sloan-Kettering Institute for Cancer Research in New York City, was among the most brilliant inventors in the last hundred years, perhaps on par with Thomas Edison but barely known today. Kettering perfected the diesel engine, automobile ignition systems, chrome-painting procedures, and a host of other innovations that virtually transformed the auto industry in the 1920s and 1930s. His approach to problem solving was unsurpassed.

The major distinction between a problem and a solution, according to Kettering, was that people more readily understood a solution. Kettering said that solutions involved merely a change in perception—are you ready for this?—since the solution to the problem must have existed all along, within the problem itself. He believed it was the role of the problem-solver simply to understand where within the problem the solution lay.

Hereafter, in your pursuit of making your life simpler, recognize that the solution to a problem may be right there, right alongside the problem itself.

Turn the question around

If you're facing a tough challenge, employ language that will help you rather than leave you in a quandary. When beset by complexity, rather than asking yourself "What can I do?" ask yourself "What *will* I do?" Then, get out a piece of paper and start writing down whatever answers come to you.

Rather than asking how you *can* make time for both your family and your work, ask yourself how you *will* make time for your family and your work. Even a generic question such as "What can I do about this issue?" can be converted into a more powerful inquiry: "How will I handle this issue?"

Try Not to Go Overboard

A *Time* magazine article entitled "Perils of the Simple Life" opened with the observation that the gurus who promote "the pleasures of unadorned living" are discovering that success brings unexpected complexities. One of the most celebrated of these simplicity sages apparently downsized her wardrobe to the point where she had two pairs of slacks, two blazers, two skirts, five T-shirts, and six turtlenecks. You can get away with this malarkey, perhaps, if you're a best-selling author making millions of dollars and you do not have to maintain a professional wardrobe, because you don't go into work five days a week. For most of us, however, going to extremes will have the reverse effect, making life harder. So as you proceed through this book's recommendations for achieving greater simplicity, remember Dr. Tenner's Revenge Effect. No one is immune.

"By definition, you can't buy simplicity," writes publisher Larry Roth in his newsletter, *Living Cheap News*. "You can't make simplicity. Simplicity comes from within. It's a human quality. It's not a product, for heaven's sake!" So with Roth's admonition in mind, here are some ideas that will keep you from going overboard in your effort to streamline your lifestyle.

Hold on to a reasonable amount of your stuff

For most people, reducing their wardrobes to subsistence levels will yield only a temporary experience of simplicity. Initially, it will feel good when you look in your closet and see it uncluttered, with only the few clothes that you truly enjoy wearing hanging there. Soon enough, one item will get torn, another will be in the wash, and an event will pop up that requires you to look your best. Paring down your clothes, credit cards, or other elements of life below a sensible level is not an act of simplicity but an emergency waiting to happen.

Hold on to your standards of cleanliness and order

Some advice givers say that the road to simplicity is to do less, as in: Don't make your bed each morning. That's fine if you live alone and if no one ever glances into your bedroom. For many people, however, making the bed is an initiation to the day. It's an official completion of sleep, providing energy, direction, and focus for moving on to what comes next.

Beds are a great place to relax and contemplate the quest for simplicity.

Leaving things undone, even if you save a few minutes in your day, does not support the notion of simplicity. Forsaking order and decorum is not simplicity. Leaving things incomplete all around you is not simplicity. Ignoring simple tasks will save you negligible time and could erode your sense of balance.

Beware of absurd advice

Some simplicity gurus would have you toss all your plates into a dumpster and eat right out of pots and pans. Others would have you skip baths to save on water, energy, and soap. (Hey, as a simple person you'll be entertaining less, so who needs pristine hygiene anyway?) You can see where this kind of absurd logic is heading: You become a hermit or a Howard Hughes–style eccentric, alienated from the world, leading a cold, boring, shallow existence earmarked by a conspicuous lack of consumption. No, don't let your quest for simplicity take on zealous and tragicomic dimensions.

Get the Right Frame of Mind

If your life is complex now, chances are it would be even more complex if your days were longer. Ken Dychtwald, PhD, founder of Age Wave, a Berkeley, California, research firm that tracks the aging of the population, has devised what he calls the more-so theory. The more-so theory holds that if you're a crabby, harried, joyless person, in 10 years, you're likely to be the same—but more so. Unless you take specific measures to make your life simpler, magically getting 48- or 72-hour days would only get you more of what you have now.

> ### Simply Stated
>
> *If I had eight hours to chop down a tree, I'd spend six hours sharpening my ax.*
>
> **—Abraham Lincoln,**
> **16th president of the United States**

These ideas will get you mentally prepared to make your life truly simpler:

Acknowledge your goal as worthy

If you've resolved to make your life simpler, then you're well on the road to achieving less. Some people, however, mistakenly believe that simplicity means having less of a life—and not being as happy, independent, or comfortable as they once were. Those who scoff at the notion of making their lives simpler might believe that

the sacrifices are too great. Yet the opposite is true. If you've resolved to make your life simpler, you're likely to be happier, more independent, and ultimately more comfortable. It's not necessarily less of a life—it's a different life.

Let your mind take you places

So what if you don't fly to the Newport Jazz Festival in Rhode Island once a year like you used to? Perhaps you can catch the 2 pm Sunday jazz festival a block from the town hall. If you close your eyes and the breeze is just right, you could be in Newport; or Monterey, California; or Montreux, Switzerland, along with the jet-setters. Besides, it's free, the crowds are manageable, and when the concert is over, you can be home within 20 minutes.

Make happiness a priority

Happiness is underrated. The quest for happiness ought to be the underpinning of everything that you do, believes management guru and author Brian Tracy, based in Solana Beach, California. Tracy explains in his lectures that unless you do work that makes you happy, have relationships that make you happy, and engage in hobbies and activities that make you happy, you're unmercifully consuming the time in your life. By striving for the things that make you happy, you're more productive, energetic, focused, and directed. You're able to give more of yourself to others. You're able to have more fulfilling experiences and maintain the feeling of being in control of your life. What a deal.

Make your own declaration of independence

The feeling of independence is a key component of happiness, whether you work for a large corporation, are self-employed, or don't have a job outside the home, and whether you're part of a large family with extensive responsibilities, you have a small family, or you live alone. Would you rather be a relatively small fish in a large pond or a large fish in a small pond? For those who choose to make their lives simpler, the answer is often the latter. When you're dependent, you must wait for others, get the approval of others, count on others, and be beholden to others. Small-business entrepreneurs, even those who work gargantuan workweeks, often report that they feel happier than their corporate counterparts because of their independence.

Forget the symbols of success

Attempting to keep up with the Joneses is inherently complex. At its worst, it means always having the latest model car, the fastest computer with the biggest hard drive, the largest house, and the most chic vacation home. It means maintaining a killer

Events with smaller crowds are more manageable and cause less stress.

Taking the Noise with You

Virtually every luxury car commercial in the last quarter of the twentieth century has highlighted the ability of the driver to raise the push-button windows and screen out all the external sounds in the overly noisy environment. Yet, at the same time, the manufacturers put in the finest stereo systems, mp3 players, and even televisions, and all other forms of electronic information dissemination ever to be invented.

You can drive off to the hills looking for solitude, but if you're not careful, you'll invite along as much noise and distraction as if you had pitched a pup tent in the middle of New York City's Grand Central Station.

and long ago developed the habit of living within their means while saving at least 15 percent of their annual incomes.

wardrobe, sending your children to exclusive schools, joining the right clubs, paying the large initiation fees, and making appearances. Chasing after such symbols of achievement can be an all-consuming, hollow existence.

Choose comfort over fashion

If you can muster the mental and emotional strength to let go of the trappings of success and instead focus on what is comfortable, rewarding, and enjoyable, your life will be that much simpler. A study of millionaires, for example, reported that most are unpretentious people who drive older cars, dress plainly,

Above all else, choose good health

Poor health is complexity; good health is simplicity. Most people deplete their health in pursuit of wealth, and then spend that wealth trying to regain their health, according to Wayne Pickering, a health and nutrition trainer based in Daytona Beach, Florida. If ever there was a vicious circle, this is it. So if you want a simpler life, stay healthy. You'll have fewer trips to the hospital, fewer doctor visits, fewer bills, fewer needs for medication, fewer days away from work, and fewer restrictions on how you live your life. Get in the habit of choosing what's good for you. Eat low-fat foods—fruits, vegetables, and grains are a good bet. (If you have a choice between a baked potato or french fries, for instance, take the baked spud every time. And if you can stand it, hold the butter.) Exercise, too. Fitness experts say it's best to establish a routine that includes both aerobic exercise (like running, swimming, or cycling) and resistance training (like weight lifting).

Also, give up destructive habits. Your body has a miraculous ability to bounce back. For instance, if you quit smoking now—even after years of abuse—your lungs will feel remarkably better in as little as a few months. In as little as a year, you'll have erased many of the harmful effects of long-term smoking. You'll have a shot at becoming one of the healthiest people you know.

Carve out personal time for yourself

Having some personal time for yourself is part and parcel of having a sense of independence and feeling in control of your life. Undoubtedly, you've heard this before, but have you done anything about it? No matter how complex your job or domestic situation may be, there are periods throughout the day and the week and the month and the year in which you can make some time for yourself. The simplest way to do it is also the most effective: Literally schedule time for yourself in your personal calendar, scheduler, or appointment book.

Score Some Early and Easy Wins

Behavior that is rewarded is repeated. That's a fundamental principle of modern psychology. It's even true of self-generated behavior—things you decide to do all by yourself. If you follow these tips to achieve some immediate measure of simplicity, the rewards may give you the motivation to keep going and undertake others. So here are some easy wins to get you rolling.

Reevaluate your required reading

If you truly enjoy reading the daily newspaper, that's fine. Keep reading anything that's useful or brings you

Reading the nutrition information label on food items can help you eat healthy.

enjoyment. Consider giving up anything you read on a regular basis just because you've always done so. This may include anything from magazines you no longer enjoy to reports at work that never divulge useful information. Also, give up anything that you think you have to read just to keep up socially.

Which would you rather have: less expense, less clutter, and a few more moments of rest and relaxation, or the nagging feeling that you have to read a publication because it's in front of you? Declare your freedom.

Inventory what needs fixing

Take inventory of everything in your home that needs to be fixed or updated. Examine your house or apartment room by room, and jot down everything that needs to be done. Should you fix a leaky faucet? Write it down. Clear out a closet? Write it down. Sweep the garage floor? Write it down. When you're done, you'll have a to-do list that will make your home the kind of place you want it to be.

Determine who will accomplish each item on the list and when. Don't burden yourself with everything. Per-

Cloning Yourself Might Not Even Help

In the clever little movie Multiplicity, Michael Keaton stars as a construction supervisor, husband, and father who struggles with too many commitments and seemingly not enough time. He meets a research scientist who has cloned himself. The scientist offers Keaton the same opportunity. Clone number one volunteers to assume Keaton's professional role, thereby freeing up the original to have a life at home.

As time passes, Keaton decides that he could use a second copy of himself. Clone number two spends time around the house, plays with the kids, and fixes everything that the original never had time to handle.

Meanwhile, the original rediscovers himself. He works on his golf game, has time for his wife, catches up on his sleep, tones up his body, and, in general, has a life once again. Ultimately, however, the clones are not sufficient to fulfill all the obligations and desires of the one original soul.

So it is with many people in society today. Even if you enjoyed double the hours per day (which is, in effect, like having a clone of yourself), it's still not likely you would be able to tend to everything that screams out for your attention. Instead, with the one life you have, look for opportunities all day long to avoid complexity and keep things simple.

Choose to spend more active hours outdoors.

any of the other express delivery services. You don't have to be in business, and you don't have to be a high-volume user. Increasingly, in every community, product and service providers are recognizing the value of capturing your business by offering pickup and delivery services. Why not put a reminder near your phone that says, "Ask if they pick up or deliver"? Every time you make a call, you'll be prompted to ask this labor-saving question.

Go for a walk without your wallet

You read it correctly. A master stroke of making your life simpler is to take a walk without any credit cards or money in your pocket. If it's around your neighborhood, you don't need to have these items with you anyway. A revealing test of character is to walk past a row of stores without having the means to stop in and buy anything. Walking without your wallet enables you to discover the simple pleasure of, well, walking.

If you see something on your sojourns that you simply must have, relax. It will still be there if you choose to return. Often, however, to your extreme benefit, the impulse to buy will subside, and you'll arrive at the happy conclusion that you can well do without the item. Meanwhile, your stroll is helping you burn calories, stay in shape, and see a little bit of the world at close range.

Delivery services can simplify your errand list.

haps others in your household can help. Perhaps you can get part-time help at affordable rates. The point is that finally, instead of having a half-baked approximation of what needs to be done, you now have the real McCoy. Knowledge is power. Having the whole list is a form of simplicity in itself. At least now you know what you're up against and can plan accordingly.

Learn to live with less television

A decision to watch one fewer television show per week, say from 8 to 9 PM on Mondays, would yield 52 hours a year—hours when you can take a walk, work on your list of household repairs, write poetry, play basketball, sew, meditate, actually talk to your kids, go bowling, and do all the things you say you never have time for. Come to think of it, why not take *two* hours off from TV every Monday?

Get it delivered

Do you realize that there are dry cleaners who are willing to pick up and deliver if you do enough business with them? Federal Express will come to your door to pick up a package, as will the United Parcel Service or

Besiege your tailor

Round up every stitch of clothing you own that needs to be taken up, taken out, stitched, sewn, mended, or otherwise altered. Unless you're an absolute whiz with a sewing machine, take all of these to the tailor in one fell swoop. Ask for your tailor's best volume rate. Then, take your ticket and leave. For far less money than it would have cost you to buy new goods, you just updated your wardrobe in grand fashion and made your life a whole lot simpler.

Round up everything you won't use again

Early some Saturday morning, following a wonderful night of sleep, arise and go through your home from top to bottom on a reconnaissance mission. Your goal is to gather up every item that's been taking up space but that you're not likely to use again. What kinds of items? Clothes, books, magazines, CDs, knickknacks, souvenirs, toys, appliances, equipment, and anything else you haven't touched in a year or more that you can part with unemotionally.

Then get these items out of your life once and for all. Hold a garage sale if you have the time and energy. Otherwise, turn them over to secondhand stores, church bazaars, or Goodwill. Don't let these items just loiter around your house in boxes—your home needs the breathing space.

Make a list of items in your home that you no longer need.

Keep It or Toss It?

Books, clothes, business cards, reports, magazines. Those vexing little possessions you let accumulate over the years will be spilling out the second-floor windows if you don't keep them under control. This table will help you with the weeding-out process. To paraphrase Kenny Rogers, you gotta know when to hold 'em—and when to discard 'em.

Items	Feel Free to Toss or Recycle if . . .	Feel Free to Retain if . . .
Business cards and assorted notes	You have many cards and never call anyone; you can't recall the person or his goods or services.	You have an organized way of collecting them; you know or believe you'll use them.
Papers, files, and documents	They're old, outdated, or uninformative; they've been transferred to a computer disk; they no longer cover your derriere.	You refer to them often; they have future value; they comfort you.
Reports and magazines	They're old, outdated, or stacking up; you think you have to retain them to "keep up"; you fear a quiz on them.	They're vital to your career or well-being; there definitely will be a quiz on them.
Books, guides, and directories	You've copied or scanned the pages of interest; you've made notes; they are obsolete or have been updated.	They're part of a life collection; you refer to them monthly; they have sentimental value.
CD and videos	You never play them, or if you do, they don't evoke any feelings or memories; they play poorly. You own an iPod.	You play them; you like them; you couldn't bear to not have them in your collection; they're keepsakes.
Clothes, shoes, and linens	You know who would like them as a donation; you can sell them; they're collecting moths; they're in the way.	They're worth using; they serve a specific purpose; they can be mended or repaired.
Mementos and knickknacks	They no longer hold meaning; you have many similar items; you do not have room.	They still evoke strong memories; you will hand them down someday; they look good on display.
Gifts	They're never used or not wanted, and the provider won't notice or be concerned if you toss them.	You use them often; you are glad you have them; you are saving them for some special reason.

Practice doing less but enjoying it more

As society all around you grows more complex, that's all the more reason for you to practice the high art of simplicity. Watch fewer DVDs and make them more enlightening or entertaining DVDs. Read fewer professional publications, and make them more informative publications. Spend time with fewer friends, if the situation fits, and make them your closest friends. Eat less, and eat healthier and more delicious foods. In nearly every aspect of your life, you have the opportunity to turn less into more by choosing to focus on higher-quality experiences.

The Simplest of the Simple

Here's a recap of the best techniques for achieving early and easy wins in the quest to make your life simpler.

- Make sure that any changes you make to have a simpler life come naturally and easily, so they will take hold. At least at first, attempt changes that don't represent a major stretch.
- Acknowledge that this is a truly complex time you were born into (you're not nuts). Keeping this simple reality in mind is one of the most basic and effective steps for achieving redress.
- When you encounter a problem, recognize that the solution may be right there alongside the problem itself.
- Don't shortchange simple tasks that take but a few seconds, such as making your bed each morning. Don't be lured by the false promise of significant time savings by giving up decorum in your life.
- Pursue happiness in every corner of your life. You'll be more productive, energetic, focused, and directed.
- Let go of the trappings of social status and financial success. Instead, focus on the things in life that are the most comfortable, rewarding, or enjoyable to you.
- Go for some early and easy wins in your effort to simplify. When you reap those rewards, you'll be motivated to keep going.

How Complex Can It Get

Anything on the Tube Tonight? If you have your own satellite dish or a service like DirecTV, in the course of one month you will have access to a minimum of 61,000 television programs, encompassing news, sports, movies, sitcoms, soap operas, dramas, and more.

| Chapter 2 | # Some General Principles |

Master the Science of Piles and Priorities

One of the wonderful things about making your life simpler is that it need not cost much or require a great deal of time. You can chip away at the complexity in your life a little bit at a time and still achieve fabulous results. As with any worthwhile endeavor, some general, proven guidelines are worth learning. These principles work whether you're in your home, in your office, or in Timbuktu. But the home is where you have the greatest measure of control, the most possessions, and the ability to put these ideas into practice late at night or on weekends.

While the principles in this chapter and tips throughout the book will help you, it is important to understand something: Just as Albert Einstein was not able to devise a unified theory of the universe, there is no absolute unified theory of simplicity. What is simple and easy for one person may be onerous and involved for you. So evaluate every simplicity tip that you encounter in terms of what will work for you.

No Ad Hoc Piles

In every life, some piles will accumulate. A basic step in making your life simpler is to confront the piles in your life head-on with a take-no-prisoners attitude. These piles include stacks of magazines, newspapers, bills, reports, documents, certificates, notices from your child's school, homework, photographs, and much more. If you haven't noticed already, such piles can accumulate in a hurry. A couple of issues of a magazine, some coupons you clipped from the newspaper, a single day's worth of mail, some flyers left by your door, the electric bill that came in a couple days ago, and poof—you have a pile.

Piles, by their nature, represent complexity. The higher the stack and the more diverse the elements composing it, the more complexity the pile represents. Don't be surprised if some researcher finds a link between the incidence of heart disease and the number of piles one accumulates. Piles represent unfinished business and, therefore, a lack of completion of one's affairs. Each pile that you encounter registers in your brain, if only for a nanosecond at a time, as more stuff that you haven't handled.

Shovel Out from under Those Piles

Organizational specialists say that an accumulation of things represents a lack of decision making. Merely adding something to a heap of other stuff consumes space and reduces your psychic freedom. Fortunately, there are many ways to handle the ad hoc piles that materialize a little too frequently in your life. If your piles are rivaling the Grand Tetons, get a good night's rest before you launch your assault—you'll need the energy. Then take the following steps to drive those piles into the ground.

1. Round up a pen, some file folders, paper clips, rubber bands, and a stapler. Now, grab up those offending piles (use a wheelbarrow, if necessary) and haul them over to a work area like your kitchen table or a desk. Stack up all of them in front of you in a temporary pile. Check your watch, and allow yourself 30 minutes or less to dismantle and reallocate this simplicity-threatening mountain into four smaller stacks: one for stuff that's important, one for stuff that's urgent, one for stuff that's interesting, and one that's destined for the recycling bin (where most items will go).

2. Don't fret very long about what pile to place each item in. Allocate to the best of your ability. If an item is urgent and important, place it near the top of the important pile. If it's simply urgent, place it in the urgent pile. If you are unsure about any particular item, place it at the bottom of the original large stack. Do this no more than once for each item. Next time through the original stack, make a decision. In 30 minutes or less, the voluminous pile should be gone, and you'll be left with four semi-neat little piles. Dispose of the recycle pile. Then rank the items in the remaining piles, with the most important at the top. Downgrade or toss anything you can. Finally, you'll be left with three small, precisely arranged piles of important, urgent, and interesting stuff. You probably feel better already.

3. As you study and rearrange the three piles of tasks that you have created, remember that you can always get meaner, leaner, and more focused. What else can you chuck? What items can be combined, ignored, delayed, delegated, hired out, automated, systemized, or used for kindling? The more items you can downgrade to interesting, the further ahead you'll be because you can deal with these items whenever you feel like it.

4. When you've pared down your piles to the lowest possible volume and gotten them into slim, trim shape, keep the like items together. Use a stapler, paper clips, rubber bands, or other organization tools. In general, the more like items you can fasten together, the easier it will be for you to find any particular item that you need.

5. Starting with the important pile, estimate how long it will take to complete each item. Add all of your estimates together, and multiply that number by 1.5. (This will allow for most people's habitual underestimation.) Do the same with the other piles. As the task hours climb to alarming heights, you will see how problematic the pile-building habit is. Your new approach to the work in front of you will vary based upon what you want to accomplish, the help available, and other particulars of your situation.

Become a Task Master

Once the piles that haunted your household have been reduced to a few carefully sorted stacks, you're ready to attack the tasks that survived the weeding-out process. Here's some advice to help you accomplish that.

Tackle items one by one

After you've identified the most important project or task (the one at the top of the important folder), begin working on it to its completion. If you can't complete it—maybe it requires help from others—proceed with it as far as you can go. Then place it back in the stack, either on top or wherever you determine it now belongs. Similarly, begin on the next-most-important item and proceed as far as you can go.

Mix it up

When you need a break from working on the important tasks, flip to the urgent stack for a change of pace. Review the interesting pile only intermittently, perhaps every couple days or weeks. It's okay if the interesting pile grows exceedingly thick. Eventually, you'll reclassify or chuck its contents.

Lower the volume

A small stack of material is easier to manage than a monstrous pile. Always strive to keep only the bare minimum information that you believe is necessary. Strive to reduce the size, weight, and volume of each pile. Rather than keeping a five-page report, retain only the single page that you actually need. Rather than retaining an entire page, clip the paragraph, address and phone number, or key item of information that you actually need, and chuck the rest of the page. Tape the small clipping you've retained to a sheet that contains other relevant tidbits.

items. For example, perhaps everything in a stack is related to your child's education, or the pile is temporary and you fully intend to organize it within an identified time frame. Even in these circumstances, a pile can still be pared down. Go on a search-and-destroy mission. Look for duplicate information and chuck the excess.

Reexamine everything in a new light

Even after you've pared down a particular pile to a smaller, more concise pile, review it with this question in mind: What am I continuing to retain that adds unnecessary complexity? Perhaps you are already familiar with the issue an item represents and you don't need to retain printed information relating to it. From that viewpoint, you may be able to chuck a third or more of the documents remaining in your already-stripped-down pile.

Draw up a list of key words

If you are keeping items in your pile that merely serve as reminders to you, maybe a list of key words would work better instead. Such simple words and phrases written on a single slip of paper can substitute for pages and pages of items. The key words used to devise the writing of this chapter, for example, included "ad hoc piles," "unfinished business," "information crutches," "key words," "holding bins," and "giveaway boxes," among others.

On rare occasions, let piles accumulate

Mirror, mirror, on the wall, when is it okay to let some piles grow? The answer is when they represent like

---

Multiple Stations, Greater Simplicity

Using multiple stations means stocking your desk, locker, car, or other convenient location with items you may need there, freeing you from lugging paraphernalia around with you. These before-and-after examples illustrate the point.

Without Multiple Stations	With Multiple Stations
You take out one of your contact lenses, but are in a bind because you don't have a storage case and saline solution handy.	You easily pop out the lens because you routinely keep cases and saline in your desk, glove compartment, and gym locker.
You get a great idea at 3 AM, then drift back to sleep and forget it.	You get a great idea at 3 AM, jot it down on the notepad that you keep by your bed or record it on a pocket memo, then act upon it later that day.
You head home from work prepared to make several stops, but forget one of them.	You head home from work and make all your stops because you had a note attached to your dashboard that listed all your stops in sequence.
You have a pounding headache at work and scrounge around to see who has some aspirin.	You have a pounding headache at work and open the desk drawer where you keep personal items to get two aspirin.
You lose your wallet, but are not able to readily identify your credit card numbers and fear that your whole day is ruined.	You lose your wallet and you quickly identify your credit card numbers because you have a photocopy of them safely hidden in your car.
You have to traipse up two flights of stairs when the phone rings and sometimes miss a call.	You have a portable phone that enables you to answer the phone whenever you want to, wherever you are.

Arrange your piles for easy access

If you have slimmed down several piles, try arranging them in a cascading or stair-step manner down one side of your desk or table. Each would have the top inch visible before being covered by the next. This kind of arrangement allows you to draw upon any one of the piles while keeping the others in order.

Get them out of sight

Many people insist they'll lose track of their piles of papers if they stash them away. You don't have to spread out your piles to know where they are. Use file cabinets, desk drawers, and so forth to store things where they're out of sight yet easily retrievable. Use a visible arrangement of your piles on a desktop only when you will deal with the piles shortly.

Put Your Possessions on Hold

Stuff accumulates. You don't have to be rich to quickly gather possessions. Society is awash with material things. In any household today, particularly one with kids, you're likely to have more stuff in more rooms than you could have witnessed at any other time in history. One way to forestall the avalanche of material things in your life is to adopt the idea of holding bins.

In its simplest form, a holding bin can be a file that is simply labeled "Review these items on January 1." Or a holding bin can be a shoe box, a plastic bag, a packing box, or a shipping crate. Whether large or small, thin or voluminous, holding bins afford you the opportunity to park items for later review.

When in Doubt, Toss It in a Bin

These tips for holding bins will dramatically simplify your life.

Let a folder hold it

Any time you receive printed information that you suspect may be worth retaining but cannot determine where it ought to go, the answer is evident—put it in a holding

bin. In this case, the holding bin could actually be a file folder with a creative label such as "Check again next month," "Review after Tom graduates," "Read before leaving for trip to the mountains," and so on. Recognize the value and power of using creatively labeled file folders to house materials that you would otherwise not know what to do with but sense that you cannot chuck.

Put unused clothes in a box

If you haven't worn something in at least a year or two, put it in a box so you have at least freed up your dresser drawers and closets. Close the box and label it as you see fit. You might write "Check again next spring," "Open after I've dropped 10 pounds," or "Examine contents after June 1." The mere act of freeing up the space in your dresser drawers and closets yields a feeling of simplicity and enables you to more easily find and wear current clothing.

Exercise your options

When you review the contents of the clothes you've boxed, you have several options. These include reinserting them into your wardrobe, and this time wearing the darned things; continuing to keep them boxed, which guarantees that you'll have to go through this process again (ugh); ripping them to shreds and using them as rags; or the preferred strategy, giving them away.

Dealing with Knickknacks, Bric-a-Brac, and Collections

For some people, it's porcelain figurines. For others, it's souvenir plates or licensed merchandise like beer steins that say "Go Red Sox." Regardless of what's taking up valuable space in your house, perhaps it's time for you to round up the excess, box it, and see where that leads. Take a gander at the stuff populating your mantles, shelves, tables, ledges, and other furniture. If you've been in your present home for as little as two years, and certainly if you've lived there more than three to four, chances are you've already begun to accumulate more things than you are comfortable with. Here's how to deal with such accumulations.

Get real about what you need to display

You don't need a memento or knickknack for every event in your life. Sure, some items had their moments, but that was then, this is now. Box up the excess and live without it in your visual field for several months. You'll breathe easier, having reclaimed the open spaces in your home. This is an early and easy win in your effort to simplify.

Make a timed revisit

After several months, revisit your boxed-up knickknacks and critically examine each item. If you can't bear to part with it, consider this written permission to reinsert it back into your home. Otherwise, you have the option of keeping the items boxed up and out of the way, having a yard sale, or simply giving them away.

Seek out the best of the best

Suppose you're a stamp collector or a coin collector whose collection has gotten unduly large. What if you were to focus on the most rare, most valuable, most beautiful, or most pleasing items in your collection—the best of the best—with an eye on retaining those while selling, trading, or donating the rest? In every collection, there are some items that you can remove without sentiment. Make like a hit man: Do the task and be gone.

Consolidate your trinkets

Can you gather the mundane parts of your collection and trade them for something valuable? In coin collecting, it's likely that fewer than 20 percent of your coins represent the greatest value anyway. Why not pool together many of your most common coins and sell or swap them for a single, rare, more valuable coin? The value of your collection would remain the same, while its volume would extraordinarily decline. The same is true of stamp collections, baseball cards, old magazines, or whatever else you've chosen to collect.

Send the Pack Rats Packing

In a culture that speeds off in all directions, it's understandable that now and then you want to hang on to pieces of the past. Joining the pack-rat contingent is not the answer. Here are some suggestions to keep pack-rat tendencies under control. The judgment calls are yours to make, but regard anything you retain as potentially hazardous to a simpler life.

Separate your possessions by seasons

There's no need to have all of your clothes crammed into your closets all year long. If spring is coming, pack away all of your winter clothes. With the first frost, it's a safe bet that you can stow all of your summer clothes. This is also true of garden utensils, athletic equipment, toys, and anything else that you only use during particular seasons. The hour or so that it takes to put your possessions into seasonal storage is more than offset by the freed-up space and the sense of simplicity you gain thereafter.

Store frequently used items in multiple locations

If you wear contact lenses, you know the value of using multiple stations. Lens wearers know to keep extra storage solution and cases at the various stations in life: their desks, cars, and health club lockers as well as their medicine cabinets at home. Hence, they are always prepared without having to carry these materials.

What else can you store at multiple stations, freeing yourself from worry and freeing your purse, briefcase, or gym bag from clutter? Consider items that are

inexpensive, often used, and easily missed, such as combs, brushes, note pads, pens, calendars, and even medicine. Think of yourself as a squirrel stashing away choice acorns for later.

Controlling Collections

Here are before-and-after descriptions of what it's like to proceed in life with and without the replacement principle.

Without Replacement Policy	With Replacement Policy
Your child's collection of DVDs grows to beyond 24 as you buy or record the classic and latest hits.	You and your child decide in advance on a total number of DVDs he can have; each new one means replacing an old one.
Your file cabinet keeps growing until you need to buy another.	Your files stay the same size because for each item you add, you discard one.
You've collected books since you were a teenager, and now you have overflowing shelves with no hope of reading most of what you've collected.	You retain only books of continuing interest or sentimental value; you quickly scan most books or copy the pages that are most important to you, then give them away.
Your clothes drawers and closets are overfilled, mostly with items you haven't worn in years.	There is more than sufficient space to house the clothes that you actually use, because you give the rest to charities.
You have a ton of brochures and memorabilia from your last trip and many previous trips as well.	You have several choice mementos from your last few trips; you display some of them and store the rest.
Your record collection spans many shelves, is covered with dust and is hardly ever played.	You sell, trash, or donate those albums covered with dust and buy a few greatest hits compact discs that you know you will play and enjoy.

Forget appearances

Set up your home, car, office, or any other space to accommodate the way you sleep, eat, drive, work, and live. Never mind how your arrangement appears to someone else. The noted psychoanalyst Erich Fromm once remarked that it's important not to jump too hastily to the conclusion that you're mentally ill, when indeed it may be the society around you that is ill. When you manage your environment, it may not look conventional or normal to others. Big deal. Which would you rather have? Simpler ways of doing things, or more involved ways of doing things merely to meet the expectations of others?

Rotate and replace what you use

One of the easiest ways to control the spaces in your life is to pay homage to the replacement principle. You probably have a collection of 24 knickknacks that you've accumulated over the years. Some are undoubtedly no longer of interest to you. When you happen to acquire another, decide which of your existing collection must go.

As long as you keep your collection at 24 or whatever you deem to be a reasonable number, you'll control one of the spaces in your life, and you'll even be a role model to people who are being overrun by their collections.

Focus on small items that accumulate quickly

The replacement principle works best when the items are small, relatively inexpensive, tend to accumulate quickly, and contain no one item of particular importance to you. Some examples include batteries, office supplies, and cosmetics. The principle also works well when you can readily reuse existing items, relabel them, and restore them, without taking a lot of time and effort, making additional purchases, or relying on others.

There but for the Grace of God . . .

Here's an effective method for paring down your excess holdings: Identify people who would revel in what you're starting to take for granted. Whether it's clothes, books, games, toys, sports equipment, appliances, or knickknacks (and paddywacks), there's somebody right in your own community who would greatly appreciate some of the stuff that's inundating your home.

As you go through your closets, drawers, shelves, and storage areas, it's far easier to fill up a giveaway box if you've already identified who will be receiving it. A home for the elderly? A school? Street people? Joe the bartender? Some charities will provide you a gift letter or receipt suitable for including in your income tax returns, which means you benefit doubly.

To help you distribute your excess stuff, get a list of all of the groups in your community that accept donations of household goods. The local branch of the United Way often maintains a roster of community groups, including addresses and phone numbers. Some newspapers publish a special issue listing such groups as well. Search the Web and see if you can come up with a list.

Put Your Excess to Good Use

Here's a reminder about tried-and-true places to deposit your excess goods.

Support the Salvation Army and Goodwill

A branch of the Salvation Army or Goodwill can be found in nearly every community. Both organizations are routinely listed in the local telephone book and through directory assistance. If you haven't made a donation before, it's as simple as boxing or bagging up old clothes or items and dropping them off. Just drop off your box of goods and be gone, although you may want to ask for a gift receipt to use when completing your taxes.

Donating can not only de-clutter your life, but can greatly benefit others.

Help someone see

The Lion's Club collects old glasses, with or without the lenses intact. If your prescription has changed in the last couple years and you're still holding on to an older pair of glasses that you never use, donate them. Sure, you're only freeing up a tiny portion of some drawer, but you're achieving another easy win on the road to simplifying your life. You're conveying to your subconscious that you don't need to steep yourself in excess. You can be happy with fewer possessions in your life.

Get thee to a nunnery

Churches, synagogues, and mosques can all use the most mundane and ordinary donations such as cleaning supplies, sheets, pillowcases, towels, and even rags. Places of worship can directly use the items themselves, hold rummage sales to raise money, or donate items to needy people in the community. Remember that churches can also use gardening and lawn supplies and equipment.

As you survey your attic, basement, garage, and tool shed, don't worry about whether the recipients will have a use for your donation. Grab everything you know you're not going to use and donate it. Let them dispense and allocate the items however they want.

No Thank-Yous Necessary

We know a Delaware man who routinely sends his old clothes up to New Hampshire to his brother and sister-in-law. The couple live in the semiwilderness and care little about fashion. They need lots of clothes for two reasons: because the layered effect is necessary in winter and because those who lead the outdoor life so often rip and tear clothing as they traverse about the woods. The recipients of these packages have never asked for them. At the same time, they have never requested that the clothes not be sent. And they've been spotted on frequent occasions making good use of such offerings.

Remember your relatives when giving away clothes. Does your brother have children younger than yours who would benefit from a big box of toddler clothing? Does your second cousin once removed have an elderly parent who would greatly appreciate your five old cardigan sweaters?

Prepare a bundle for the Red Cross

At any given moment, some region of the world is experiencing a flood, earthquake, hurricane, tornado, tidal wave, drought, famine, or epidemic. The Red Cross is always in need of sheets, blankets, pillows, pillowcases, towels, washcloths, bathrobes, pajamas, and anything else you can prune from your overloaded collection. The Red Cross can use all types of games, toys, and gadgets. If you were eight years old and your home had been wiped out by a natural disaster, even the smallest toy from some well-wishing stranger halfway around the globe could bring comfort.

How to Dig Even Deeper

Here are some other ways of decluttering your home that might not have occurred to you.

Stock your local library

Do you have a stack of books that you received as gifts years ago—books that you have never touched and probably won't in the future? Are there books that you have read but that are no longer important to you? Many libraries face severe budget crunches. The cost of new books can be onerous. Therefore, the books you donate to your local library are most welcome. The books don't need to be in top condition, but if they are, it helps. Ask if the library can issue you a letter acknowledging the gift, which you can use when compiling your taxes.

Give learning a lift

Virtually all schools today face budget challenges. The elementary school in your neighborhood could use a helping hand in the form of books, magazines, paper, pens, pencils, rulers, and any type of writing or desk equipment. Do you have wall posters suitable for a school building? How about charts, maps, or historical memorabilia? Schools could also use globes and educational puzzles or games.

You may not realize it, but there's a battle going on over control and influence in the classroom. As reported at length in *U.S. News and World Report* and *Newsweek*, major corporations are making substantial donations of branded audiovisual materials and supplies to classrooms across America. If you're concerned about the commercialization of the classroom, donating your excess holdings is one small way you can help stem the tide.

Make a direct donation to a homeless person

The fastest way to make a donation is to simply hand an item to the very person who needs it. Toward that

end, you could keep some old clothes or shoes in the trunk of your car. Then if you see someone in need, you could politely ask him if he would like to have the item you have to offer. Many needy people will eloquently express their appreciation. Some might mutter something incoherent. In either case, you will have helped someone quickly and easily.

If you're not comfortable approaching a homeless person directly, make a donation to your local shelter for the homeless. Often, the staff there know who could use a new pair of shoes, a belt, or clothes, and they will dispense your gift for you.

Make a food bank deposit

In many communities, the fire department, community shelter, or another charitable organization maintains a food bank. Considering all the stuff stashed away in your pantry, there surely is some canned item that you haven't used and can donate. The same applies to other nonperishable, packaged, never-opened goods you have on hand. So take three minutes to peruse your kitchen cabinets, drawers, and pantry shelves right now. Round up everything you're not likely to consume in the near future, and donate it to your local food bank.

How Complex Can It Get?

At Least There's No Overhead: Some people are reluctant to personally approach homeless people with money or gifts. Still, consider this: When you make a monetary donation, or even a gift donation, to a charitable organization, anywhere from 15 to 90 percent of your donation may be applied to the organization's overhead. Hence, giving a useful item directly to a homeless person is an extremely efficient charity vehicle.

Boot out your old computer gear

Someplace in your community there is an art center, youth center, visitors' center, historical society, or some other group that can use your old computer, printer, modem, or monitor. Such groups can also put to great use an old TV, telephone, or any similar gear that's still in good working condition. (Once again, you can get a tax write-off, although this is the least compelling reason for paring down the excess you're retaining.)

Create Clearings in Your Life

As you begin to clear out portions of your home, car, and office, magical and mystical things occur. You gain a feeling of space, ease, control, and simplicity. What do you do with the space you've created? What you *don't* do is fill it up again with more clutter or things that will recomplicate your life. Here's what you can do to keep a wealth of clearings in your life.

Resist restocking

Given the inherent complexity of society in general, it makes sense for you to maintain some slack in your file cabinets, desk drawers, closets, kitchen cabinets, and pantry, and on the shelves, mantles, and ledges of your life. There's no trick to filling up these spaces. But keeping them unencumbered requires a discipline all but unknown to a great many people. Over the next several months and years, resist the inclination to restock the areas you just "destocked."

Rearrange your furniture

Arrange your furniture so that less covers more. Experiment with moving furniture around so the few items you have kept in the room provide nearly the same coverage that you once had with a greater number of items.

Where is it written that every square yard of floor space has to be covered or that every wall has to have something in front of it? One obvious place to keep clear

is in front of windows. Others are near doorways and entrances. You can get used to having less in each room, just as you were once used to having your rooms filled.

Your file system can quickly get out of control if it's overstocked.

Stop clutter at the border

Hereafter, to keep your holdings simple, evaluate—and then reevaluate—every new item that crosses your threshold. Whether it's paper and documents, knick-knacks, kitchen utensils, clothing, or larger items like furniture, be vigilant about what you acquire. By keeping watch over what enters your personal kingdom, you avoid having to initiate these possession-purging exercises.

Talk to yourself

Each time you encounter a new item, ask yourself questions like: What impact will this have on my life? Will this make a difference in my life? Do I need to have this at all? Is this easily retrievable if I decide to have it in the future? Are there any consequences of not retaining it? Will this make things simpler for me?

The Simplest of the Simple

If you do nothing else after reading this chapter, use these easy tips for keeping accumulations from engulfing you:

- Dismantle piles. Get ready with a pen, file folders, paper clips, rubber bands, and a stapler. Now collect everything on your desk or table that needs attention. Sort this pile into four stacks, categorizing them as important, urgent, interesting, and recycle. Rank the important items, putting the most important at the top. Then work on the single most important item first. If you can't complete it because it requires help from others or for some other reason, proceed with it as far as you can.

- Strive to reduce the size, weight, and volume of your paperwork. Rather than keeping a five-page report, retain only the single page that you actually need.

- Use holding bins to stem the tide of things accumulating in your life. In its simplest form, a holding bin can be a file that is simply labeled, "Review these items on January 1." Or a holding bin can be a shoe box, a plastic bag, a packing box, or a shipping crate.

- Separate your possessions according to the seasons.

- Store frequently used items in multiple locations.

- Maintain some slack in your file drawers, desk drawers, closets, kitchen cabinets, and pantry, and on the shelves, mantles, and ledges.

- Zealously defend the borders of your personal kingdom. Let no items enter that are frivolous or that will needlessly complicate your life.

Chapter 3

Anticipating Complexity

Preventive Measures
Will Cure a Tangled Lifestyle

Complexity abounds, and your ability to spot it will be one of the key tools in your arsenal for minimizing its effects. Let's examine some everyday types of situations, with an eye on identifying entanglements, pressure points, and complex webs you're likely to encounter if you're not careful.

Free Up Four Hours a Month

It's been said that people spend more time planning a party than they do planning for the coming year. Likewise, most people spend more time engaging in complex interactions than they ever spend contemplating how to make things simpler. It is easy to get so caught up in the busyness of life that you never pause to reflect on ways to not be so busy.

There are umpteen ways you can find an extra hour a week, the most obvious of which is to watch one fewer hour-long television show per week. During this golden 60 minutes, recall what transpired over the last seven days. Where did bottlenecks occur in your life? When were you frustrated? What long lines did you stand in? What did you have to finish even though you knew it was an utter waste of time?

What ideas about making life simpler popped into your head? What tools for getting organized could you acquire? Hereafter, if you spend one 60-minute period per week (perhaps on a Sunday evening) contemplating how to make the coming week go smoother, the chances are you will succeed. Here's how to go about it.

Take a Walk through Your Week

Let's take a walk through seven days to identify potential opportunities to have greater simplicity in your life. On Sunday evening, devote an hour to this exercise. Have a pen and paper ready or, if it suits you, a blank computer screen.

Arrange your affairs for Monday morning

That same Sunday evening, assemble by the front door whatever you need to take with you on Monday. If you're heading to work, this could involve papers, reports, or a new coffee mug. If you have a doctor's appointment, perhaps you need records or a claim form. If you have school-age children, they may need to have papers, books, school supplies, or certain articles of clothing by the front door. Obviously, anything that needs refrigeration can't be stashed there for now, but do post a note reminding yourself to retrieve such foods from the kitchen.

How Complex Can It Get?

Ever Heard of Carpooling? The U.S. Department of Transportation says there are nearly two times as many motorized vehicles in America as there are registered drivers. This equates to far more than 300 million vehicles. This figure seems impossible, until you add up all the vans, tractor trailers, taxis, military vehicles, government vehicles, motor homes, motorcycles, and such. Some days, it seems as if everyone is on the road at the same time.

Get a head start

To make Monday morning go more simply, consider getting out of bed 10 or 15 minutes earlier than usual. This is particularly crucial if there are more activities on Monday morning than on other weekday mornings, such as gathering a week's worth of snack items and putting gas in the car. While it may seem as if you're dramatically shifting your day, a 15- or 30-minute jump on Monday can make a world of difference. You will saunter into the day unrushed and at ease. And once you've had a taste of the benefits that extra morning time provides, you won't want to give it up.

Make that one bagel to go

If it's not practical to eat breakfast before you have to head out the door in the morning, then take a piece of fruit or other easily packed food with you. If you are part of a car pool (and it's not your turn to drive), you could eat during the commute. If you take a subway or train you may be able to eat there—depending on the rules of the carrier and how crowded the car is. Otherwise, pick a quiet place once you arrive at work.

Simply Stated

If you're not changing constantly, you're probably not going to be accommodating the reality of your world.
—William G. McGowan, American business executive and founder of MCI Communications

Make time to read books and magazines—whether at home or in the bookstore.

Do not eat while you're driving. Doing so draws your attention away from the road, and it prevents you from being in total control of your vehicle at all times.

List your stops on a notepad

If you have many stops to make, list them in chronological order on a sticky note. Post it inside the front door of your home before leaving, take it to your car when you go, and stick it on your dashboard. Use a different color notepad for each day if it helps.

Clear Away Some Mental Space at Work

When you arrive at work in the morning, particularly if you've arrived before the rest of the office, you have the best opportunity for structuring your day. Envision how you would like your day to go. Review your appointment calendar and plot out the few critical elements that will make your day a success. Keep flat surfaces as clear as you can.

If you don't work outside the home, when everyone else has departed, give yourself a few minutes to undertake the same type of visualization. How would you like your day to be? What are the critical elements or critical tasks you want to complete? If you have stayed home with children or other household occupants, carving out a few minutes for yourself during the early morning is even more crucial.

Have a pat on the back before lunch

At an outside job, at home, and everywhere in between, take a few minutes before lunch to acknowledge what you've accomplished that morning. Sit down, relax, take some deep breaths, and contemplate how good it will be to eat lunch. Once you're actually eating lunch, carefully and slowly chew your food. What was it your mother said—to chew 22 times?

Don't rush your tummy

How you eat your food is as important as what you're eating. If you wolf down your food, you'll miss many of the benefits of what you're eating, even if you're eating high-quality, highly nutritious food, says Susan Barrus, R.N., a therapist and nutritionist in Chapel Hill, North Carolina. So eat at a comfortable, unhurried pace.

Linger a little after lunch

Don't hop to your feet the moment the last morsel of lunch is gone. No matter how hectic your day is, you can always find a couple of extra minutes after lunch to give your digestive system a little bit more help, visualize how you'd like your afternoon to go, and maintain a relatively sane pace.

Twice a day, stop the world

Perhaps the biggest obstacle to making life simpler is the unwillingness to allow it to occur. Many people simply do not give themselves permission to achieve a sense of balance, take a deep breath, and then proceed. Paradoxically, every shred of wisdom about simplification indicates that you will be more effective if you simply pause for a minute a couple of times each day. Choosing specific times of the day will help you establish the habit. Try for one respite in the morning and one in the afternoon—say, when you return to your desk from the watercooler, after visiting the rest room, just before lunch, just after lunch, or precisely at 2:30 PM.

Before departing, tie up loose ends

Before you stop work for the day, see how much order you can restore to your work area so that you will have a fresh start in the morning. Can you put away several file folders? Can you return one key phone call? Can you get tomorrow's project notes ready? Can you discard junk mail and other unnecessary documents? The more little things you complete before departing, the more focused and energized you'll be when you return the next day. Not only will your office be more visually appealing, but you'll also become more productive.

If you work at home all day, do the same thing for the various workstations in your house—the laundry room, the home office, the den, or the kitchen table—before other family members arrive home for the evening.

Going Home: Shifting Gears

When you leave work and go back home to your family, readjust. Sure, you've put in a tough day, and in many ways some of the things you endured were nothing less than heroic. To reintegrate yourself into family life at least for the rest of the evening, however, you have to leave the workday behind. Here are some ways to do that.

Clock out, tune in

Leave as close to your official quitting time as possible. Then, before getting to your car or other mode of transportation, give yourself one more minute of mindful meditation. This will prepare you for the urban madness called commuting, and you'll have a decent chance of arriving home with a sense of balance. Do mini-meditation while you're riding the elevator, descending the steps, or strolling through the parking lot.

Be your own cheerleader

Once you get to your car or other transportation, acknowledge what you've completed that day and that week. Treat the very act of getting to the car as a completion of sorts.

> ### Pause Before Your Alertness Wanes
>
> The lowest time for alertness for most people—even folks accustomed to night shifts—is between 2 AM and 5 AM, says Martin C. Moore-Ede, MD, PhD, in his book *Twenty-Four-Hour Society*. Highest alertness is between 9 AM and noon, and 4 PM to 8 PM. A person's alertness will vary due to hours of consecutive duty, hours of duty in the preceding week, irregular hours, monotony on the job, timing and duration of naps, environmental lighting, sound, aroma, temperature, sleep deprivation over the past week, and more. Make the effort to figure out when you are highly alert versus hardly alert during your typical workday so that you can better schedule tasks that require a sharp mind.

Let your work engine cool down

If you are a gung ho career-climber who arrives home still mentally revving at the pace of business, members of your family may have difficulty relating to you. Let your internal engine "rev down" after work before you interact with your family. After all, you're not talking to Jennifer in production, Ted in personnel, or Seth in shipping. A brief nap, shower, or stroll will help. If you work at home, you may still need to readjust before other family members return.

Before dinner, feed your soul

Do something mentally or physically rewarding before dinner. If you only have five minutes, simply sit in a chair and reflect on the day, play with a child, take deep breaths, or take a long, cool drink of water. Any one of these activities could make all the difference in your having an enjoyable dinner and evening. Avoid flipping on the television or radio, surfing the Web, or reading the newspaper or a magazine if these activities divert your attention away from your family.

Reclaim Your Weekends

Remember when weekends were actually restful, fun, and rewarding? Somehow, for too many people, they've become an extension of the workweek. Rather than having relaxing and titillating experiences, weekends often seem like one long set of errands followed by some excessive eating and late night television. Then, before you know it, it's Monday. Are there ways to savor the weekend and return to work fit and rested? You bet.

Start the weekend early

Do something rewarding on Friday evening. You may like to whoop it up or take it easy. You may like to go out with your one and only or spend a quiet evening at home.

Whatever you do, don't overdo it. Many people who let loose on Friday evening actually steal time from Saturday morning—even the entire weekend—and are not fully prepared to return to work on Monday. This could be called the Oh-no-it's-Monday-again blues.

Avoid the IDIOS trap

IDIOS stands for "I'll do it on Saturday." Do you let errands pile up and then spend the weekend completing them? Instead of tying up Saturday, designate Monday

evening from 7 PM to 10 PM or Thursday evening from 5 PM to 9 PM as errand night. Most businesses are open for extended hours. While already dressed and in your car, there is no better opportunity to make the rounds.

Beware the big sleep

On Saturday morning, feel free to sleep a little later, but not too late. Research reveals that sleeping too much will actually deplete your energy, leaving you feeling even more tired. So if you traditionally sleep eight hours, but you get up on Saturday morning after nine hours of sleep, you may feel just fine. If you extend that sleep to ten hours, however, you may only yield the benefit of seven or eight hours. In that last hour, researchers say, lingering in bed too long may contribute to the buildup of various toxins that otherwise would dissipate as you move about.

Knock off those errands by noon

If you've avoided the I'll-do-it-this-weekend syndrome, then you have a relatively clear, uncluttered weekend. Nevertheless, some domestic tasks and errands may arise. Strive to complete these before noon on Saturday, when most of the rest of the world still hasn't gotten out the door. After noon, the congestion in many metro and suburban areas is actually worse than during workweek rush hour. The only difference is that, on the weekend, people are going every which way, whereas during the workweek the commute is in one general direction in the morning and in the opposite direction in the evening.

Make sure you leave work at work when you return home for the evening.

> ## Put Everyday Items within Reach
>
> One secret of clutter control is developing a clear idea of what items around the house you need instant access to and which items deserve deep storage. Here are a few helpful rules of thumb:
> - If you use an item as often as once a day, it probably belongs on a tabletop or somewhere within easy reach.
> - If you use it once a week, keep it in a top drawer.
> - If you use it once a month, put it in a lower drawer or on shelves.
> - If you use it less than once every three months, it may be a seasonal item, and it can be socked away in a box, closet, or storage room.

Take a nap if you need to

Where is it written you can't lie in the hammock, on the couch, or even in your bed in the middle of the day on a weekend and let your body renew itself? Don't overdo it, however. Remember that sleeping too late in the morning can leave you groggy, and the same goes for naps.

Listen to your rhythm

Your body likes routines, regularity, and predictability. When you change your sleeping hours dramatically from one day to the next, your internal mechanisms must work overtime. Your daily cycles of sleep and your body chemistry—in other words, your circadian rhythm—determine how well you think and move, and even how interested you are in sex, at different times of the day and night. So if you stick to a regular sleep pattern, you'll feel better and be more alert.

Living in the Material World

Most Americans today are awash in material things. From skateboards to Frisbees, DVD players, inline skates, iPods, microwave ovens, designer sunglasses, aerobics outfits, and electric toothbrushes, even the moderate-income families tend to have more and more rooms filled with stuff.

Nowhere is the contemporary focus on materialism more acute than in a typical shopping mall. Take a walk through any shopping mall and you'll see such a vast array of enticing items that it boggles the mind. Let's mentally walk through a mall with an eye on keeping your life simple.

A Stroll through Alluring Anchor Stores

Malls are constructed so that there is an anchor store—a large department store such as Nordstrom, Macy's, Belk Stores, JCPenney, Bloomingdale's, or Sears—that you can't help but notice. Many malls are designed so that you have to enter through one of these stores and walk 25 to 50 yards before you get to the common mall area. From the first minute on, you're subjected to swimwear, lingerie, perfume, men's socks, luggage, and more.

You'll notice that most of the notions in the anchor stores are located closest to the middle aisles, particularly along the path from the outside entrance to the common mall area. This is so you'll be attracted as you walk by. However, consider what's already on your shelves and in your medicine cabinet. Do you need any more perfumes, colognes, or sprays? Aren't most of the multitudinous bottles you already have half to three-quarters full? Do you have more room in your bathroom or supply closet for yet more toiletries, more cosmetics, or more smell-sweet, look-young, feel-better products designed largely to take your money?

No matter where you shop, every store you walk into is designed with one objective in mind: to get you to spend, spend, spend. These tips can help you navigate the aisles and get only what you need at a reasonable price.

Sidestep the specialty stores

Unless you plainly need a particular item, avoid specialty stores like the plague. These include map stores, luggage stores, tobacco shops, cutlery stores, jewelry stores, the myriad shoe stores, and more. If you came into the mall specifically for an item in one of these stores, fine—proceed to the store and do your shopping. On the other hand, if you're walking by and happen to be attracted by this or that, perform a quick mental exercise: Think about what you already have in your closet, on your shelves, in your drawers, and throughout your home. Do you need yet another item that largely duplicates something you haven't used in many moons anyway?

Stop paying top dollar

Even if you need a specific item, do you need to pay top dollar for it? No, no, no.

Bathed in showroom lighting, products look good. They have to. Because they pay such high rents, merchants must

Shopping at flea markets and garage sales can save you money.

sell their wares for high prices in order to stay in business. The same merchandise is often available at a fraction of the cost in discount stores. Yard sales, garage sales, flea markets, church bazaars, and the like can also supply you with goods at a fraction of the cost if you are patient and willing to attend a couple sales before finding the item you're seeking.

Maria Shriver's Simple Solution

Years ago, when TV news anchor Maria Shriver was co-hosting a morning talk show in New York City, she would fly in each week from her home in California and return home at the end of the week. Crisscrossing the United States nearly 100 times a year is a considerable amount of travel, not to mention disruption.

Shriver minimized the effects of thousands of miles in the air and maintained balance in her daily life. Each Friday evening, when heading back to California, she booked the same flight, from the same airport, on the same airline, usually leaving from the same gate, at the same hour. She even reserved the same seat. She often flew with the same pilots, the same flight crew, and occasionally the same passengers.

She felt at home when she boarded the plane. She didn't have to wait until she was physically back at her house or touching down at the Los Angeles International Airport. In essence, she minimized the effects of a rigorous schedule by transforming her seat in the sky into a welcome sanctuary. She was home in that seat.

Resist the impulse

Before you buy anything that you did not specifically come to the mall to buy, stop and think for a second. How often will you use the item starting one week from now? How often will you look at it, play with it, pick it up, touch it, or even refer to it? What would your life be like if you took that $10, $15, or $20 and put it into a long-term retirement account where it would double in value within ten years, quadruple within 20 years—and, added to all the other small contributions that you're going to make, grow to a sizeable sum? What would happen if you put that sum in a fund for your child's higher education?

Ponder where you're going to put the item and how many other items you already have in your living room, den, dining room, bathroom, or kitchen. Isn't your house already strewn with stuff? Are you starting a collection? Where else could you possibly put it?

What would your life be like if you could take back 50 or 100 items you bought on impulse over the years—items costing between $10 and $50 dollars apiece that, cashed in en masse, would yield a small fortune? Think in these terms if you want to keep your house relatively clutter-free. Remember: Less clutter equals greater simplicity.

When Your Olfactory Glands Betray You

Chances are, your local mall includes a food court. Even before you get there, you'll be subject to high-priced, heavily sugared, fat-laden, indescribably delicious chocolate chip cookies. The science of modern retailing is such that purveyors of fast food know how to blow the scent of this stuff into the air so it reaches you before you even approach the storefront.

You'll smell these highly pleasurable cookie aromas in enough time for you to be fully hooked by the time you step up to the counter. Your salivary glands will be activated. Every fiber of your being will be convinced that you want a cookie or, hey, why not half a dozen? You're hungry, aren't you? What damage will one little cookie, or maybe two or three, really do?

Hold on! Before you give in to the urge to splurge, give these tactics a try.

Rally your resistance

When you find yourself in a shopping mall, turn your resistance dial up to full power. Remember how passing up that chocolate chip cookie will keep your life simpler. You will save money and avoid unwanted calories and cholesterol. Without getting personal, take a good look around the mall. Do you see at least a few slender, in-shape people? They're living simpler lives.

Defend yourself in the food court

Once you get by the cookie stands, the candy stores, the oversalted-nut shops, the cotton candy kiosk, and the like, you'll hit the food court. This ring of food stands routinely will include a wiener vendor, a Chinese food vendor, an Italian food vendor, a Mexican food vendor, ad infinitum. Generally, you want to avoid these places. If you have no other choice, at least track down something healthful. A salad of dark leafy greens is good, but beware of high-fat add-ons like hard-boiled eggs and bacon bits. Or order a slice of pizza—light on the cheese, heavy on the vegetable toppings—or a grilled chicken sandwich sans mayonnaise and special sauce. A good rule of thumb: the plainer, the better.

Take your own food

This is no misprint. It may sound like a little extra work, but you would be far better off during your mall visit if you simply took an apple, a banana, or a sandwich with you when shopping. That way you could pause, have a light lunch, and keep going. You could always get a glass of water, milk, coffee, or even a nice herbal tea. You'll spend less money and have a calmer stomach later. Plus, you'll be more energetic, so you'll be able to walk around the mall briskly, passing stores more quickly, spending less money, and leaving with your wallet and sanity intact.

Put Up Your Guard in Those Mall Side Shows

Someplace in the mall there will be a quick-photo kiosk where you and a friend can have your photo taken. (These are always overpriced and frequently lack the quality that you could attain with your own camera.) Someone will be selling gold chains, someone else will be hawking beaded jewelry or jewelry you can make yourself, and another will be offering decorative items for the home. When you think about it seriously, the chances are astronomically high that you'll realize you don't need any of these items. Here are tips for protecting yourself from impulse buys.

Inventory your jewelry box

The next time you're tempted to snap up some mall jewelry, ask yourself these questions: Don't you already have a lot in your jewelry box? Don't you already have several rings, necklaces, and earrings? For men, don't you already have cufflinks, pendants, and pins? Sure, you can support your local economy by shelling out your hard-earned dollars for more baubles to add to your mounting collection. Isn't it more important for you to retain your money, display personal discipline, keep your life clutter-free, and lead a simpler existence?

Test those magazines

Walk by nearly any mall bookstore and you'll notice a huge rack of enticing magazines. Before shelling out $3 to $5 a pop for them, test how essential each one is to your life. Ask yourself, "Will this magazine truly help me maintain my health and well-being?" If the answer is no, walk on by.

If you're in the mood for sampling different magazines, you can probably do so for free. Practically any magazine you'd care to read is available in mint condition from your local recycling bins around town. There's no harm in taking them from recycling bins because, after all, if you read them after someone else has, that in itself is a form of recycling. Besides, you intend to recycle them once you're done.

Pass up the light reading

Elsewhere in the bookstore, you'll find all types of true confessions by celebrities, exposés of political blunders, and the usual assortment of techno-thrillers. Leave them all behind. They cost too much, and you probably don't have the time to read them. Sure, reading is a worthwhile pastime, but you can more than meet your reading needs by visiting your local library and taking out a few well-chosen volumes.

Don't dally at the dollar store

Maybe your mall has one of those bargain stores where every single piece of merchandise is sold at a ridiculously low price. Often, this is because the merchandise is ridiculously low quality. If you see something that you perceive as a supreme bargain and you simply can't resist, okay, make your day. Plunk down your money, pick up the item, and then get out.

Remember: When you stray from the straight and narrow path, every harmless item that you collect adds to the mass of stuff in your life—stuff that you have to house, dust, look at, and store. Even if you're good at stripping your home of the excess stuff you collect, why collect it in the first place? The simplest practice of all is preventing "collectibles" from entering your home to begin with.

Six Simplifying Questions

If you adopt a simplicity mindset, you can get from here to the end of your days with far less complexity than you might have imagined. The next time you confront something that could potentially complicate your life, ask yourself this basic set of questions.

Do I need this?

This is a crucial question whether you're in a mall, thumbing through a catalog, or otherwise confronted by an enticing offer. Often, the answer is, "No, I don't need it."

Do I want it?

Make sure it's something you *really* want—something that's of vital importance or that would bring you great joy. The answer may actually be, "No, it would be of passing interest."

Will this make a difference in my life?

If you're confronted with an item of discernable value, ask yourself whether it would save labor or time or yield peace of mind.

Will it pay for itself shortly?

If an item will pay for itself the first, second, or third time you use it, and you will use it several times within a few months, go ahead and buy it. If it's a high-priced item, if it will pay for itself within a year, and if there are immediate recognizable benefits, take the plunge.

What are my options?

Often, the alternative to buying something new is using something that you already have and that costs you nothing more.

What else accomplishes the same ends?

Before you buy an electric can opener, for example, consider whether you have tested new mechanical can openers. Some are available for $3 or less and work so well that lids practically glide off. If you have arthritis, the electric

---

That Killer Third Shift

No one knows how many people suffer from insomnia, but the Better Sleep Council, based in Alexandria, Virginia, estimates that the problem affects 60 million Americans. Second- and third-shift workers are particularly prone to insomnia, as are older adults. Women also seem to be more susceptible than men. If you work a second- or third-shift job, undoubtedly you've experienced the ways in which your body rebels as you attempt to shift back to traditional waking and sleeping patterns at the end of your workweek. Often, you may feel as if you are "wasted" without ever having touched a drop of alcohol, without having stuffed yourself to the gills with food, or without having otherwise exerted yourself in any way.

Taking Stock of Gridlock

You're already familiar with traffic gridlock, but did you know that traffic is simply one of the arenas in which things are slowing down?

Airlock. Airline passenger traffic has more than tripled in one generation, according to the Federal Aviation Administration. Concurrently, there are fewer nonstop flights, particularly on cross-continental trips. Airport expansion trails behind the increased passenger loads. Worse, all airlines pad their scheduled departure and arrival times—extending them more than 50 percent since decades ago—to appear as if they're not late, while actual air time remains about the same. When you're scheduled to board for a 10:10 AM flight, that time is merely when you're supposed to be seated in the plane. Taxiing from the gate is always much later. The net result is that they're as slow and late as they ever were, but now they're within the promised limits.

Camplock. On an average summer day, Yellowstone National Park has thousands of visitors. Other national parks across the country face swarms of visitors, putting campsites in high demand. While the federal government is making progress in restoring the parks, in the meantime, vacationers have to contend with traffic lines to get into the parks, lines for concessions, and waiting lists for campsites. It won't be long before you have to get in line to have your food scavenged by bears.

Shoplock. By 2009 there was more retail space in America than ever before—28 square feet for each man, woman, and child in the country. Despite the dramatic increase in catalog, TV, and Internet shopping, shopping malls still always appear to be crowded. Finding a parking space can take 15 minutes, unless you are willing to park in the farthest reaches of some lots. Once inside you may have to jostle through crowds to get to shops, theaters, and restaurants. During the holidays, expect the worst.

alarm/snooze button/phone and who knows what else? So many gadgets, so many instructions, so little time. Identify your major need—perhaps a good-quality alarm clock with a large, lighted display so that you can see the time without your glasses, and nothing more. If so, pay less, sleep as soundly, and make your life simpler.

Spread the Word

Sometimes, you need to give other people around you need a polite nudge to simplify your surroundings. Posting a simple message in the right place will often do the trick. Here's how.

Address your letter carrier

Suppose your postal carrier frequently delivers the wrong mail to your house. It belongs to previous tenants or to someone down the street. Why not put the names of all the residents of your home on the inside of your mailbox? The next time a postal carrier is about to deliver someone else's mail, he or she will know better. Hence, there will be one fewer item in your day that you need to encounter.

Post reminder labels

If lights or appliances need to be turned off at certain times of the day but household members or co-workers frequently forget this, post a label on the spot to increase the probability that the proper action will be taken. Near the coffeepot at work, leave a note that says, "Turn off by 5 PM." Similarly, around your home, write notes to help other occupants remember little chores.

Occasionally, change the appearance of the labels to keep the message fresh. After a while, the notes will become part of the environment, and people won't notice them anymore. In that case, change their colors or use gold stars or flare pens to draw attention to them.

Get to know your mail carrier and address him or her by name.

models make perfect sense. If your hands are unencumbered, the low-cost, simple substitute does the job well.

The same principle applies when shopping for an alarm clock. Do you really need a souped-up, overloaded, large-display clock with a combination radio/double

---

The 20-Minute Miracle

Sleep researchers say that a nap of 20 minutes or less is ideal because you arise without having engaged in REM sleep and you feel refreshed. (REM stands for "rapid eye movement," a deeper stage of sleep.)

The average person lying down for a nap takes six to eight minutes to doze off, notes Jack Edinger, PhD, of the Center for Sleep Studies at Duke University in Durham, North Carolina. Therefore, if you allot 20 minutes for nap time, you'll sleep for 12 to 14 minutes. In any case, you're likely to awake feeling better than when you first put your head down.

Timers, available at electronics and kitchen stores, are handy for waking you after a 20-minute lie-down. Cell phone apps or common alarm clocks will do, too, although resetting the alarm on some models can be a bother.

Go electric

Timers are a helpful tool for reminding people of little responsibilities like turning off appliances. They are available for a nominal fee and offer a wide variety of options. As the almighty microchip gets smaller and more powerful, more appliances will have built-in automatic shutoff features. For now, simple timers, either with hand dials or digital keypads, are widely available.

Recruit some allies

Everywhere you go, let others in on your campaign to make living simpler. At first, some people may scoff or not take the idea seriously. Your actions, however, will speak louder than words. With many people, you'll win silent, if not vocal, approval. After all, they have to make their way in this overly complex world, too.

Co-workers, family members, and other people who interact as a group can greatly simplify each other's lives by keeping communications concise, maintaining clutter-free work or living spaces, and giving one another a moment now and then to pause and reflect.

home before you leave, and then take it with you and put it on the dashboard of your car. Or, key the list on your cell phone.

- Before concluding your workday, tie up loose ends. The more little things you complete before departing, the more focused and energized you'll be when you return to a clear and clean environment the next day.
- Instead of tying up a Saturday or Sunday with errands, designate Monday evening from 7 PM to 10 PM or Thursday from 5 PM to 9 PM as errand night.
- Avoid changing your sleeping hours dramatically from one day to the next. Your body likes routines, regularity, and predictable times.
- Keep pens and paper at every station in your life.
- Before buying an item, ask yourself these basic questions: Do I really need this? Will this make a difference in my life? Will it pay for itself shortly? What are my options?
- Let others in on your simplicity campaign.

The Simplest of the Simple

Here is the essence of the preceding chapter, to help make each day less complex and more enjoyable:

- Each week, watch one fewer hour-long television show. During these 60 minutes, recall what transpired over the last seven days, what ideas about making life simpler popped into your head, and what tools for getting organized you could acquire.
- On Sunday evening, contemplate how you'd like your week to go, and assemble by the front door whatever you need to take with you on Monday.
- List your stops in chronological order on a notepad, put the list inside the front door of your

Stash Some Cash

Having a modest amount of money—say, $50—stashed somewhere in the house can save you minor anguish and embarrassment. Having this cash on hand will help you complete transactions swiftly and easily. For instance, when the neighbor's daughter comes to the door selling Girl Scout cookies, you'll be able to make a purchase on the spot. You won't have to explain what you did with the last 10-spot in your wallet, and you won't have to dig under the sofa cushions for change.

PART TWO **Simplify Your Castle**

Chapter 4

Cooking Up Solutions

If You Can't Stand the Clutter, Simplify Your Kitchen

Now we switch from global, all-encompassing observations to more pin-pointed ideas for making your life simpler. The next nine chapters take you through each room in your home, helping you go from pack rat to Jack Sprat. We'll start by examining all the ways you can have an easier time cooking, cleaning, storing items, and in general keeping your kitchen in tip-top shape.

Remember: Be reasonable with yourself—don't attempt to follow every suggestion. Proceed with what you can do for now, or stick to matters that are pressing issues for you. Also, look for easy and early wins. One act can lead to another, and if you only follow a few of the ideas here, you'll still be likely to realize significant benefits.

You've heard the old saying, "If you can't stand the heat, get out of the kitchen." What do you do if you can't stand the clutter in your kitchen and the task of reorganizing seems hopeless? Divide and conquer.

If you can only tackle one drawer for now, hey, that's a start. One drawer can lead to another, and another. Then, if you actually whip your whole kitchen into shape, there will be no stopping you.

Recipes for Smart Storage

Whether you live in a mansion on an estate or in the smallest mobile home in a trailer park, the kitchen is unique among the rooms in your home. In addition to food preparation, the kitchen has a variety of purposes. It's an area for family meetings, storage, studying, and at times, even playing.

Traditionally, television shows use the kitchen as a background for many of their most emotional scenes. From *The Honeymooners* to *Everybody Loves* Raymond, most of the major feel-good (and not-so-feel-good) scenes occur in the kitchen. Many of your family's decisions probably occur there, too.

In fact, "you will spend more time working in and cleaning your kitchen than in any other room in the house. The average homemaker will spend a total of 15 years there," according to one of America's prominent cleaning experts, Don Aslett. Whoa, seems like a life sentence. With so much activity in one place, it's important that your kitchen be organized, safe, and practical.

Today's kitchen can be overwhelming if you don't have time (and you don't) to study a 20- to 60-page instruction manual for each appliance. To make your kitchen simpler, stay with what you know and with what makes you and your family comfortable. Whether your kitchen is the size of an Applebee's restaurant or more like a Tom Thumb cubbyhole, there are many ways to make the most of what you have, save time, and stay in control.

If you've recently moved into a new home, you have the opportunity to start from scratch and organize your kitchen to make it efficient and to prevent the accumulation of clutter. If you haven't, pretend that you have and review your kitchen with a fresh eye. Is there anything about your kitchen you would change? Is this household focal point arranged for simplicity? Were things once arranged more efficiently than they are now?

Find creative ways to store your pots, pans, and trays in your kitchen.

There are many areas to focus on in your kitchen. The underlying goal in all of these areas is improvement in organization. Whether you store your kitchen items in the cupboard, in the pantry, or on shelves, there are simple ways to optimize your storage space. Drawers and refrigerators are also used as storage areas, and there are plenty of ways to save space and money there, too. You can also lower your expenses by timing your purchases effectively. Finally, helpful ideas for cleaning can ease your journey to the well-organized kitchen you desire.

So let's get cooking with some ideas for making your kitchen work for you, not against you.

Cupboards and Shelves: A Closed-Door Session

Here's step number one for making the most efficient use of the cupboards and shelves in your home: Identify all of the kitchen necessities, the things you and your family absolutely must have close at hand for efficient food preparation. These necessities get first priority. Such items will include pots, pans, dishes, and cups, of course. And if you don't have a pantry, you may need to use your cupboard or shelves for food storage: the cereal, crackers, macaroni and cheese, snacks, cookies, and soft drinks all take up huge amounts of space and can be a stacking nightmare.

Still, many things commonly kept in the kitchen aren't actually needed in the room. Infrequently used

china, elaborate serving trays, and unusual utensils (the proper use of which you are not sure) take up valuable cupboard and shelf space. Then there are the duplicate electric can openers and hand mixers that you received as wedding gifts and the many casserole dishes that you received when you moved into your first apartment.

If you have so many pans stored in the bottom of your stove that it takes several minutes to find the right one, you have too many down there. If getting a pot out of an overhead cabinet starts a shower of pots, pans, lids, dishes, and Tupperware, you have too many things stored in the overhead cabinet.

Here are ideas for working out storage problems in your kitchen cupboards and shelves.

Use it or lose it

If you have sets of crystal, china, or serving platters that are seldom used, move these items to other storage areas to free up cupboard and shelf space for more commonly used items. Here's a good rule of thumb: If an item in your kitchen doesn't get used at least once a month, find a new home for it.

Toss out the old, bring in the new

When you buy new pots, pans, or cookie sheets, let go of the old ones. Give up any strange attachment you may have to a five-year-old cookie sheet that is so stained that the dog would be scared to eat off it. When you do buy new pots and pans, give the old ones to friends or relatives who may be starting out and can use them. Invest in quality cookware so you don't have to replace items as often.

Discourage dumping

Don't let your kitchen be a dumping ground. Often, you, your spouse, or your kids will use the kitchen as a place to plunk down books, toys, and other supplies. Make every effort to put things in their proper places after they're used, or you're going to run out of work space fast. Then you'll be forced to pick up or rearrange all of the stuff that has accumulated in your kitchen, which wastes your time. If there isn't enough free space in your child's room to store toys and school supplies, then buy him a desk or storage cabinet.

Get the hang of it

Next time your can opener, toaster oven, or hand mixer wears out, consider buying a model that can hang from the bottom of your cupboard. These are great space savers. (Hang them up securely so they don't fall.) Also, avoid hanging particularly heavy appliances underneath cabinets—you don't want to overtax the structure of the cabinets.

Steel Yourself

Buying a set of pots and pans can be confusing. Some are relatively inexpensive, while others cost hundreds of dollars. On top of that, they're made of a variety of materials with different finishes. Which type is the simplest to use and maintain?

For most people, the answer is stainless steel. Stainless steel pots and pans are durable and hold up well to repeated cycles in the dishwasher.

Aluminum pots and pans are quite common, and most are inexpensive, but they're susceptible to staining and denting. They're harder to keep clean, and you'll have to replace them more often. Copper pots conduct heat well and do a good job if temperature control is important, but they're a lot of trouble to keep polished. Cast iron is a favorite among many seniors, but they're very heavy, which can be dangerous—especially if small children are around.

Count your pots

If you have many more pots in your cupboard than burners on your stove, get rid of some pots. However, be careful to keep at least one pot of each common size near the stove in case you have to cook for a larger crowd. Store your lids together in an area separate from your pots. Your pots will stack easier without them. Some discount stores sell round plastic containers that are specially designed for storing lids. They can be attached to the inside of cabinet doors.

Slide into simple storage

Imagine this scenario. Your mother-in-law is pulling up in the driveway for Sunday dinner. Recently, she gave you a tacky serving bowl that you stowed away under the sink. Realizing that she expects to see the bowl with a pile of food in it, you dig and dig under the sink looking for the dang bowl and strain your back in the process.

The solution? Don't get married. Just kidding. Actually, here's a practical way to keep items tucked away in your kitchen yet easy to retrieve: Go to a discount store and pick up a set of plastic shelves with slide-out drawers. Install these under your sink, and you'll have handy access to all of those items that were once piled in a jumble—not only your mother-in-law's bowl but also dish detergent, cans of cat food, sponges, rubber gloves, and more.

Try some cold storage

Oversized, display-worthy pots take up an enormous amount of space. Stacking these pots can scratch the coating or chip the porcelain. If your refrigerator is not enclosed in the wall, store some of these pots above it. This provides a nice decorative touch to your kitchen and keeps the pots out of the way but within arm's reach.

Simply Stated

If I am incapable of washing dishes joyfully, if I want to finish them quickly so I can go and have dessert, I will be equally incapable of enjoying my dessert. With the fork in my hand, I will be thinking about what to do next, and the texture and flavor of the dessert, together with the pleasure of eating it, will be lost. I will always be dragged into the future, never able to live in the present moment.

**—Thick Nhat Hanh,
Buddhist monk and philosopher**

Under the Sink Lie Hidden Treasures

The space underneath your kitchen sink can be a valuable hiding spot for kitchen necessities you don't use often. Typically, household cleaners are stored underneath the sink (we will revisit this habit momentarily) along with drip pans for leaky pipes, insect repellents, and other potentially toxic substances. There are better and safer ways to use this space, especially if you have small children in your home.

Put poison in its place

Few among us have chemistry degrees, and many people don't realize how hazardous storing certain household cleaners together can be. For example, people will store lime deposit removers containing phosphoric acid next to drain cleaners that contain potassium hydroxide. These two chemicals react violently when mixed and are corrosive. There is always the potential for a spill, and the kitchen is the last place this spill should occur, because some chemicals are tasteless and colorless and can contaminate food without your noticing.

Put household cleaners in a laundry room or on a high shelf far away from the kitchen. If you have a special cleaner that is used only in the kitchen, put it on a kitchen shelf or in some other place that is well out of a child's reach. If you're wondering what this has to do with simplifying your life, consider the stress and hassle that an accidental poisoning would create.

With water filters, don't go overboard

If you live in an area where tap water is odorous or full of minerals, water softening systems and carbon filters

can help. If you are only having problems with, say, lead (which is hazardous to your health and especially dangerous to small children) or some other specific mineral, there's no need to buy a complex, expensive system that takes care of everything. Fortunately, there are good, inexpensive systems that take care of only your specific needs. If you have fresh water, consider yourself privileged.

Stage a Counter Revolution

Whether you have a small amount of counter space or counters from one end of your kitchen to the other,

leaving them with less mess is a good way to increase productivity and decrease aggravation when you're baking or cleaning.

Tap into triangles

If your kitchen is laid out well, you'll spend less time preparing meals and cleaning. The best strategy is to have your appliances arranged so you have as many items as possible within arm's reach. Sure, you may not have the option of changing the layout of your kitchen, but you can be aware of efficient designs in case you are in a position to remodel.

What is the most efficient layout for your kitchen? Consider what you use most: the stove, the refrigerator, and the sink. Therefore, it's necessary to minimize the distances between these three stations without crowding yourself (which would just make it more difficult to work efficiently). Positioning the refrigerator, stove, and sink in a close triangle will save you a lot of footwork when you're preparing meals.

Be sure to store all of the most commonly used kitchen utensils and appliances within easy reach of this triangular area. You'll save yourself a lot of walking, and you'll be able to prepare meals more quickly.

Take a stand with microwaves

If you have a standard, freestanding, countertop microwave, try to avoid positioning it beside the stove. You need this area for food preparation. Place your microwave closer to the refrigerator if possible. If counter space is limited, put the microwave on a cart. If you do keep it on the counter, experiment by

moving it left, right, backward, and forward to see what you gain or lose in terms of counter space and ease of use and cleanup.

Seek new heights

It's not often that you get to install new countertops, but if you do get such an opportunity, choose an easy-to-clean surface such as Formica. It's durable and comes in a variety of colors and textures. While you're at it, adjust the height of the counters and cabinets to the comfortable working height of the kitchen's primary user. That way, your family's favorite cook will feel better and work more efficiently day in and day out for as long as you live in your current home.

Keep two yards clear

In most households, blenders and mixers are stored on the counter in the kitchen. Unless you cook more cakes and pies than Martha Stewart each day, it's not necessary to store these appliances on your counter. In fact, researchers at the University of Illinois at Urbana–Champaign concluded that the ideal stretch of counter space for preparing meals measures no fewer than 72 inches. So if your small appliances are taking up your elbow room, stash them in a cabinet out of the way.

Think like Smokey Bear

Making fire safety simple and easy in your home could save lives. So have a fully functional fire extinguisher handy in case a small fire breaks out in your kitchen. You can purchase smaller models that sit on the countertop near the stove. Contact your local fire department to find out where you can have your fire extinguisher recharged. Make sure it's recharged after every use.

Dispense with can clutter

If members of your family are fans of canned soft drinks, pick up a soda dispenser. They are lightweight, inexpensive, and attach underneath a shelf in your refrigerator. Most are gravity-fed, meaning that when you remove one can of soda, another rolls down to take its place until the dispenser is empty. It sure beats having cans scattered willy-nilly about the icebox. Such dispensers are popular now that soda is available in cases of 12 and 24 cans.

Pull the plug on unnecessary appliances

In the eternal quest to make your life simpler, product manufacturers are always developing novel kitchen appliances. Before you buy the brand-new muffin maker, think about whether you need one taking up more space in your kitchen. Don't you have a muffin pan and an oven that do the same thing? Are you making that many muffins? (And if so, why?) Save your money.

Catch the splash

You may not think of yourself as a wild cook, but the evidence inevitably appears on the wall above your stove in the forms of flecks of tomato sauce or splatters of bacon grease. Installing a good backsplash will save you loads of cleanup time. Use an easy-wipe surface like plastic laminate. Make sure it covers the back wall from the top of the stove all the way up to the cabinet or ceiling above.

How Complex Can It Get?

Makes You Thirsty, Doesn't It? There is no more fresh water on the planet today than there was 2,000 years ago. Yet, Earth's population has grown by nearly seven billion people. Chronic fresh water shortages are predictable in Africa, the Middle East, Northern China, parts of India, Mexico, Brazil, several former Soviet republics, and the western United States.

Mastering Space Technology

If you've weeded out the things you don't use in your kitchen and have moved seldom-used items out of the way, you have accomplished something that few others have. Give yourself a pat on the back, and prepare to go to the next level. Now that you have more space, it's time to make the best use of that space. No area will be left unexploited, from the stovetop to the floor, from the refrigerator to the cupboard doors.

Convenience Is Key

Here are ways to save time in the kitchen and use its space as efficiently as possible.

Keep your top tools handy

If you make an average of two meals a day, you can travel 120 miles a year in the process, according to Sir Terence Conran, author of *Living in Small Spaces*. Make a quick inventory of your kitchen tools, and decide which ones you use the most often. Make sure each of them is easy to grab when it's needed. If you have a favorite frying pan, keep it close to the stove. Keep large spoons and cutlery near the stove for stirring and turning foods over when you're cooking.

Save your back

Most stoves have a storage area at the bottom. This is a convenient place for you to put pots and pans. But if you have back trouble or if bending is just not your favorite activity, put your commonly used pots and pans in cupboards close to the stove. Then use that under-the-stove space for seldom-used objects.

Don't sell yourself short

If you're short in height, don't waste time putting items on high shelves. It's potentially hazardous, and there may not always be a tall person around to reach things for you. Put the items you use less frequently—or items used frequently by taller people—on the higher shelves.

Get the hang of mug storage

If you happen to have cupboards or shelves that are sufficiently high, install cup holders underneath your cupboard. This is convenient if you have a lot of coffee mugs and teacups taking up space in your cupboard.

Stack bakeware by usage

If you have a specific area where you store bakeware, stack the least-used items on the bottom and the items that are used more frequently on top. You'll save time and effort by having common pans nearby when you need them.

How Complex Can It Get?

Better Get Cooking: If you have, say, eight recipe books in your household, each offering 250 to 650 recipes, they can add up to as many as 5,200 recipes. If you tried one new recipe each week, it would take 100 years to prepare them all.

Repackage those dry foods

This is an especially good tip if you don't have a pantry: Store your dry foods, such as oatmeal, spaghetti, cereal, flour, mashed potato flakes, and such, in stackable plastic containers. This makes the most efficient use of your space and also keeps food fresh. There is less mess, and you'll keep bugs, contaminants, and other uninvited guests from getting in your food.

Tape up those favorites

If you have one or two favorite recipes that you or your family enjoy, tape the recipes to the inside of your cupboard door. This way you won't waste time looking through a bunch of loose recipes or trying to remember in which cookbook a particular recipe is. Be careful—no need to turn your cupboard door into a bulletin board. A few recipes may be all you need and all you ever use.

Every Drawer Is an Organized Hiding Spot

If you have a small kitchen, a well-organized drawer can provide you with more helpful space. The key is getting organized, which, knowing what you're up against, may take a while.

Look in all of your kitchen drawers. Which one is the monster drawer? You know—the drawer that you have to spend ten minutes sorting through to find the ice cream scoop. The drawer that has every utensil imaginable. Is all this necessary? You probably don't need enough cooking utensils to serve a small army. Here's how to organize your small and large utensils so you don't have to look for them.

Organize your stainless steel jungle

Many discount retail stores sell low-cost cutlery trays. If you don't have one, get one. Most of them are simple and have spaces for forks, knives, and spoons, with a few other compartments. If you want something fancier, you can probably find what you're looking for at larger department stores. But why bother? Few houseguests will ever have occasion to open your utensils drawer. And those who do are not likely to draw any conclusions about your worthiness as a human being—or your net worth, for that matter—upon finding a common cutlery tray.

The Simpler Route to a New Look

Maybe you have the redecorating bug. Before you rip all of those cabinets, countertops, and appliances out of your kitchen, consider some alternatives. You can achieve a new look without all of the expense and hassle. For instance, painting your storage areas a brighter color or staining them will produce a welcomed change. Or to freshen up your cabinets, install new doors on them to create the illusion of something brand new. New moldings will also liven up a dated kitchen.

Obey the three-knife rule

For some reason, people hate to throw out knives. Nevertheless, "all you really need to get by are three knives: a paring knife, an 8-inch chef's knife, and a 10-inch serrated-edged slicing knife," according to *Prevention* magazine's former food editor, Tom Ney. "Since you're going to be using only three, buy top-quality brands. They'll stay sharper and last longer."

Use drawer dividers

Kitchen drawers are not only a refuge for forks, knives, and spoons. Corkscrews, mixing spoons, spatulas, and ice cream scoops are all thrown into utensil drawers. As with the plastic cutlery trays, drawer dividers work well in organizing these odd utensils to save you some time. They're available at most discount retail stores. Think of it this way: Every time you open the utensil drawer and you don't have to hunt around for what you want, you experience simplicity.

Let them dangle

Dealing with too many utensils? One kitchen designer suggests mounting a pegboard on the back of your pantry or cupboard door and hanging some of your larger

utensils there. Utensils such as large wire whisks, ladles, spoons, and forks work well in this situation and save you some drawer space.

More Top-Drawer Advice

There's more to a kitchen, of course, than flatware and cooking utensils. Some kitchen items that are stored on counters and other areas can be moved to drawers with little modification. A little drawer re-engineering goes a long way.

Move tools to the toolbox

Kitchen drawers are not the place for a bunch of tools. Sure, a few tools are handy in the kitchen—a screwdriver and hammer, perhaps. But find another home for the socket set.

Use a drawer divider so your tools don't scratch the wood. You may also keep small amounts of nails, screws, or washers in small cups or small sections of the drawer divider. This is an easy way to make sure you have a nail available whenever you want to hang a picture or move decorations.

Have the wraps handy

Instead of keeping your plastic wrap, aluminum foil, wax paper, and plastic bags in your cupboard or pantry, put these in a drawer under your countertop so they will be accessible when you need them. These items are commonly used in the kitchen, and you shouldn't have to stop what you're doing and walk over to the pantry to get one of them.

Keep your coupons close

Instead of putting your coupons in a drawer in no particular order, purchase a coupon organizer or, better yet, make one yourself. Section off a folder into categories, such as meats, drinks, frozen items, pet foods, and dairy items. When you clip your coupons, put them in the appropriate categories in your organizer. This will save time when you're looking for a coupon.

Store pot holders close to the action

If there is a drawer close to the stove, put your pot holders there so they will be convenient when your favorite concoction starts boiling over. Also, place your dry washcloths or sponges and dish towels in a drawer near the sink so they are accessible when you wash dishes.

Relocate your recipe books

Deep drawers can be used to house recipe books, loose recipes (in a folder, please), instruction manuals, and warranty information on appliances or electronic equipment. This way, you don't have to fill your personal files with warranty information you may never need. It's a good place to keep a book of quick recipes so you're not in the kitchen all day long.

Junk Drawers and Other Unnecessary Items

There is no need for a junk drawer in your kitchen, because there is no need for junk in your kitchen.

Have you ever been cleaning out a closet or drawer only to find something you needed last week or something you forgot you had? And still worse, did you make the mistake of buying a brand-new item, only to find the missing original stuck in the back of the drawer? No need for alarm, just disarm.

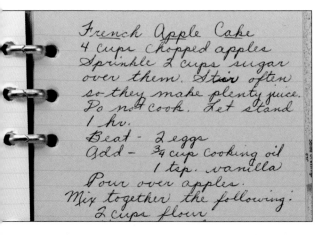

French Apple Cake
4 cups chopped apples
Sprinkle 2 cups sugar
over them. Stir often
so they make plenty juice.
Do not cook. Let stand
1 hr.
Beat - 2 eggs
Add - 3/4 cup cooking oil
        1 tsp. vanilla
Pour over apples.
Mix together the following:
        2 cups flour

Avoid the problem altogether by resisting the urge to be a junk-drawer junkie. Typically, junk drawers are created when seemingly there is no other place to put items. Buttons, paper clips, nails, screws, and pennies are among the things carelessly thrown in junk drawers. Instead of taking the time to properly store items, it's tempting to throw them in a drawer to hide them.

If you have many drawers, you may find yourself storing even nonjunk items in drawers where they don't belong. If it happens to be a precious memento or some remarkable piece of art your kid made at camp (remember the ever-popular clay ashtray?), put the item in a special place, not in the junk drawer.

Evict your tablecloths from your drawers

Instead of stacking (and potentially mashing) your tablecloths into a kitchen drawer, consider storing them elsewhere, such as in a linen closet. You probably don't use tablecloths on a daily basis, so get them out of your way. Storing them in a drawer makes it difficult to look for a specific tablecloth and takes up valuable drawer space. And, of course, as soon as you pull a tablecloth out, everything else in the drawer falls out as well.

Create a pay-the-piper drawer

If you spread your bills on the kitchen table once a month when you pay them, consider keeping all of your incoming bills and a calculator in a drawer near the kitchen table. You won't have to go all over the house searching for your light bill, and you won't have to carry things far when it's time to give all your money away.

Managing Your Food Storage

The pantry has to be one of the kitchen god's greatest inventions, along with sliced bread, microwaves, and indoor plumbing. Unfortunately, some people have to use cupboards for food storage, but for those lucky enough to have pantries, a whole new opportunity for storage awaits.

Use Every Inch Wisely

The first time you looked in your pantry when you moved into your house, you may have thought, "I'll never fill up all of those shelves." Wrong. It doesn't take long to fill an empty space, but there are constructive ways of doing it.

Make the door do double duty

If your pantry only has a few shelves, add some plastic-covered wire shelves to the back of the door. These shelves are usually only wide and deep enough for canned goods, although there are some wider shelves to hold boxes of pasta and such. This is an easy way to add a lot of extra storage space.

Trash it in your pantry

If you have room in the bottom of your pantry, put your kitchen trash can there. It keeps an unsightly trash can out of your kitchen and out of your way. Be forewarned, though: Out of sight doesn't mean out of mind. Use bag liners and keep a top on your trash can. Or pour some baking soda in the bottom of the trash can or bag to absorb odors. Empty your trash can frequently so your pantry doesn't start to smell.

Keep the trash bags handy

Equip the inside of your pantry or cupboard door with lightweight shelves or dividers deep enough to hold your boxes of kitchen trash bags. You can also store other infrequently-used items such as paper and plastic grocery bags.

Store the old with the new

The pantry is also a good place to store recyclables. Store containers for plastic bottles and aluminum cans in the bottom of your pantry if the pantry is deep enough and space allows. Avoid overcrowding the pantry, however. If the containers are a tight squeeze, put them in the garage or some other convenient spot.

Group like items

You're probably in a hurry to unload your groceries, but instead of putting items wherever there are empty spots, put similar items together. That is, put the canned foods like soup together, put the cereals together, put the pastas together, and so on. A little organization in stocking your shelves will save you from having to search for that can of pork and beans you know you bought during your last grocery trip.

Don't Overload Your Pantry

It's tempting to stick things in the pantry, especially if you know you're going to be needing them later—perhaps a pair of gloves, batteries, a flashlight, coupons, or a pair of sunglasses. Avoid stocking your pantry with items that don't really belong there. If possible, designate your pantry for food only. If it takes more than five to ten seconds to get an item out of the pantry, here is some sobering news: your pantry is overstocked.

Trim down on bulk buys

Unless you have a large family, you don't need to buy in bulk. Remember: when you get home, that 50-pound box of cereal has to go somewhere. Do you want to have 50 pounds of powdered milk sitting in your pantry for half the time you reside in your home? Although there are cost savings on certain products, don't buy it if you don't need it.

Prune your pantry of pots

If space is limited in your pantry, avoid putting pots and pans there. One good trip to the grocery store will stock up an average-size pantry. Once you start putting pots and pans in the pantry, too, there will be no room for your soup, crackers, macaroni and cheese, cereal, and snacks. You don't really need an extra headache every time you return from the supermarket.

Use it or move it

Occasionally, the grocery store runs a good sale on items you and your family consume regularly. In this instance, purchase the items and place them in the back of the pantry so they will be out of the way. If necessary, prepare a backup pantry in the basement or garage for items that you don't use often.

On the other hand, if your kids go through potato chips quicker than bees make honey, keep the potato chips in a handy location. This way, those hungry kids won't knock over everything in sight to get to the chips.

Assign everybody shelf space

If your family is small or if you have many pantry shelves, consider allocating one shelf per person. This is an especially good strategy for roommates. With two to four people who seldom cook, an unorganized pantry can be a nightmare. With separate shelves for each roommate, there will be less confusion and fewer arguments over who ate all the peanut butter. Also, consider each person's height. Give the tall people the highest shelves. It will make life simpler for everybody.

Corral the coriander

Buy a spice rack to organize your spices. With the thousands of low-fat recipes available, spices are being used

more than ever. Instead of searching your pantry for spices, keep them all in one place, and your cooking will go smoothly.

Be wary of expired beans

Use the oldest canned food items first. If you're dying to try the new brand of spaghetti sauce you just bought, resist using it before the older jar of sauce that has been stored in your pantry for a month and a half. Although you store mostly dry goods in your pantry, some of them do have expiration dates. To avoid this problem, put newly purchased items behind the older ones on the shelf.

An Orderly Refrigerator Is a Happy Refrigerator

Refrigerators have come a long way, baby. New refrigerators are 200 percent more efficient than models manufactured earlier than 1993, reports the Maytag Corporation. Whether you're a perpetual bachelor or bachelorette or part of a big family, your refrigerator is very likely to need serious attention. At any given time, it's likely that one cooked item at least a month old sits somewhere in your refrigerator. Are you among those who marvel at the new bacterial creations produced right in the coziness of your own home? Your mother might never have let this happen, but she's the only person you know who wouldn't.

Aside from the scientific fascination, there is little point in letting food stay in the fridge that long. It's wasteful and unsanitary. Besides, unusable leftovers take up space and, eventually, all of the bowls in the house. If you doubt this, try to find an unused bowl right now—bet you can't. To avoid spending half of your weekend cleaning out the fridge and then washing four sinks' worth of dishes, keep daily track of what's in your refrigerator. Here are some suggestions to make that easy.

Toss it before it walks away

Adopt a seven-day limit on leftovers: If something has been around longer than a week, throw it away. Sure, many leftovers will keep longer. However, if your leftovers haven't been eaten after a few days, the odds of their being eaten at all diminish drastically. This is especially a problem for singles who may have the habit of fixing too much food for themselves.

If you know that you or your significant others are not going to eat the food, give it to the dog, the neighbors, or the poor unsuspecting bachelor or bachelorette down the street while it's still good.

Make a little, hold the rest

Get in the habit of cooking only what you need for one meal. You may sometimes think, "I'll fix enough to take for lunch this week." But be honest with yourself: After two helpings, don't you want something else to take for lunch? This can be a huge waste of money.

Temper your take-out habit

If you're ordering take-out food, don't order too much. Take-out food generally is more expensive than food you prepare yourself. That means that leftovers can quickly turn into a waste of money. So let your brain do the ordering, not your stomach.

Remember the first in, first out rule

Put your newest refrigerated items behind the older ones. When someone opens a new gallon of milk before the old one was empty, for instance, there's sure to be a lot of waste.

Attack those odors

If your refrigerator smells like the onions you threw out two weeks ago, don't feel badly. It happens to all of us. Just when you think it's safe to open the refrigerator door, whoa, the stench slaps you in the face. The easiest way to prevent this and provide you and your family with more storage space is to totally clean out your refrigerator every once in a while. First, remove every item. Then mix a tablespoon of baking soda into a quart of warm water and wipe down all the interior walls, shelves, and compartments. When you restock the fridge, add a fresh, open box of baking soda to keep future odors to a minimum.

Keep a lid on it

Refrigerate your leftovers in glass or non-degrading plastic containers with tight-fitting lids. Avoid storing leftovers in metal or enamel containers and cookware. In time, the salts and acids in the food can damage the container's surface. Worse yet, metal containers can cause food to spoil quickly and possibly lead to health problems for you and your family.

Make Your Refrigerator Work for You

The refrigerator is the most-often-used appliance in your home. Many people think their refrigerators are indestructible: Someone delivers it, you plug it in, fill it up, and that's all there is to it.

Although some refrigerators can last 10 to 20 years, a bit of preventive maintenance and good sense can make your refrigerator as well as your food last longer. And if you've ever bought a refrigerator, you know that delaying the need for such a task is definitely the simpler path to take. One way to make your refrigerator last a long time is to avoid changing the temperature dial in your refrigerator often. This leads to extra work for the compressor and will shorten its life. Decide on the best temperature setting for your food and leave it there.

Here are some other cool ideas.

Clear the air

A 15°F rise in temperature in your kitchen will double the amount of energy that your refrigerator consumes. So keep your kitchen well-ventilated and make sure that your appliance's motor has room to breathe. Periodically, vacuum the grilles below and behind the fridge. Also, keep your refrigerator away from heat sources, like direct sunlight, the stove and oven, and the dishwasher.

Handle the eggs with care

Store your eggs on a shelf in the refrigerator rather than in that little bin that's built into the door. Your eggs will keep longer when they're not jostled and subjected to temperature changes, according to *Consumer Reports* magazine.

Make every shelf serve a purpose

By grouping similar items like milk and juice together, your refrigerator can serve you better. Keep like items together so you don't have to launch a major hunt every time you open the icebox. Put condiments in the side

---

How Complex Can It Get?

All in a Day's Work: The typical American generates 3.5 pounds of garbage daily, equal to more than a half-ton annually and 37 tons in a lifetime. This accumulation is equal to the weight of 18 midsize cars.

compartments together with salad dressing. Give milk, juices, and soft drinks their own shelf, located farther back in the refrigerator (for better cooling), and place cheese and lunchmeat in a separate drawer.

Keep cool when the power goes out

If the power goes out, it may be tempting to check whether your ice cream has melted. But keep the cool in by keeping the doors closed as much as you can. The longer you can keep food cool, the less likely you'll have to pack items in ice before the power is restored. A full freezer will remain frozen for about 48 hours, according to the Maytag Corporation, while items in the refrigerator will keep for four to six hours.

Your Refrigerator Door Is Not a Bulletin Board

Have you ever walked into someone's kitchen and been unable to find the refrigerator because it was covered with magnets, memos, reminders, message boards, and every picture the resident kids had drawn since they

---

Caution: Kitchen Traps to Avoid

Put your kitchen and its contents to work for you, not the other way around. If you're feeling overwhelmed by the task of simplifying your kitchen, here are some ideas:

- Clean up the kitchen as soon as you finish eating each meal, while you still have the energy. Once you begin digesting the food, you may be too sluggish.
- Put each new kitchen item where it belongs so you can find it two months from now.
- With a marker, label and date all foods you put in your freezer so you don't have to guess if they're two days old or two months old.
- For foods that are labeled "Refrigerate after opening," write the date the food was first used on the label and throw out anything you consider too old.
- When cleaning your kitchen, disinfect all surfaces that food has touched. Don't just wipe the surface—clean everything with a disinfectant.
- Don't mix household cleaners when cleaning your kitchen. Just because you can buy it in the store doesn't mean it can't be harmful to you or your family.
- If you have small children, consider buying food containers and cups. Minimize the chance of breaking anything.

---

were five? Oh, it's a nice gesture for parents to hang children's artwork where everyone in the family can see it. But turning your refrigerator door into a bulletin board is, at best, a tenuous way to stay organized. Besides, if you're trying to control your eating, you don't want to be drawn to the fridge any more than necessary. Here are some better ideas.

Make a record of your dates

You can put an appointment reminder on the refrigerator door, and days later it will be totally forgotten. Instead of hanging doctor or dentist appointment reminder cards on the refrigerator, write down the appointment on a calendar or date book in your office or at home.

Read the writing on the fridge

If you insist on using the refrigerator as a message center, use a small message board. If it's used correctly, this is a convenient way to convey messages to other family members. Make sure to erase each message after you read it. If the message board is never erased, then no one will notice the new messages.

Tickle yourself

If date books are not your thing or if you have many items to keep track of, consider creating a tickler file for every week or month. Place letters, business correspondence, and appointment reminders in the appropriate file. Refer to these files often so you don't forget important dates.

Deck the halls

Around the holidays or on birthdays, people often hang cards or decorations on refrigerators using magnets. Unless your magnet has the magnetic force of a small planet, avoid this habit. If the decoration is heavy, it's probably going to fall down the first time you open the door.

Don't Buy on the Fly

How many times a week do you go to the grocery store? Once, twice, three times a week? You probably don't need to be going as often as you do. Consider how much time you spend in your commute to and from the grocery store. This is valuable time you could spend doing something else. Also, consider wear and tear on your car and the added gasoline expense.

With all of that time and money wasted, why make extra shopping trips? Could it be the joy of fighting for a parking space after you and everyone else in town get off from work? The cute cashiers and baggers? Or growing old as you stand in the deli line? Here are some ways to avoid frequent shopping trips and save your nerves some stress.

Make a list, check it twice

When you go to the grocery store without a list, you're tempted to buy items you don't need. Before you leave for the store, take a few minutes to look through your shelves or pantry to see what you need from the store. Then add a few items that you and your family want. Next, go through any coupons you've diligently cut from the newspaper or downloaded. It's a pity to buy an item at the full price because you've left the coupon at home.

Take advantage of a bargain

Sure, once in a while you'll run across a fabulous bargain at the grocery store. It may not be on your list, but you sorely want to drop it into your cart. That's okay, but before you commit to the purchase, ask yourself whether you'll use the item within the next few weeks. Ask if you have room to store it. Ask whether this is truly a money-saving purchase. Give in to temptation only if you can answer yes to these questions.

Feed your face

Going to a supermarket when you're hungry is a bad idea. You're sure to pick up three extra boxes of cookies, wasting money on items you don't need and taking up too much precious space in the pantry.

Shop for the immediate future

If you're cooking for the holidays, stock up on as much as you can ahead of time. You can never find a bag of ice on the Fourth of July, the good candy is all gone by Halloween, and you can barely find a can of cranberry sauce the day before Thanksgiving. These are cold, hard facts of life. Also, stores have the funny habit of jacking up the prices of these high-demand products closer to the holidays. Buyer beware.

Keep your eye on the skies

Take advantage of five-day forecasts. What does this have to do with grocery shopping? If it looks like bad weather may be approaching, stock up on needed items. Don't wait until it starts sleeting and snowing to go buy a gallon of milk—the store is likely to be out. Besides, you'll want to avoid the masses who waited until the last minute. Wise shopper that you are, you'll be sitting by a fire eating soup.

The Wonders of Baking Soda

Baking soda is a miracle worker around the house. It's so handy, versatile, and inexpensive that it easily substitutes for any number of household products. Let us count some of the ways in which it can be used.

- As a refrigerator deodorizer. Simply keep a half-open box in the back.
- As a fabric stain remover, particularly in treating perspiration stains. Moisten and brush a little right into the stain before putting the garment in the wash.
- As a paste made by mixing with water, to take the bite out of bee stings, bug bites, and burns.
- As a toothpaste and gum freshener. Make a light paste with a small amount of hydrogen peroxide. Gently brush all areas of your gums. Your mouth will be cleaner than ever.
- To clean carpeting beset with wine or grease stains. Put a little on a damp cloth, then blot the stain. You can apply more pressure if you need to, but be careful not to rub too hard.
- To snuff out grease and electrical fires. Quickly sprinkle it on the flames.
- To clean enamelware. If food sticks to the bottom of a pan, add three tablespoons of baking soda to enough boiling water to cover the bottom of the pan. Let it soak for an hour.
- To keep your car spiffy. Make a light paste with water. Using a rag, apply the paste to bug stains and bird droppings. Let it set for about five minutes, then wipe clean. Also use it on bumpers, hubcaps, and chrome trim.

Some Clean and Simple Wisdom

There are few things more frustratingly complex than cleaning. Gosh, you cook a nice meal for your family, and there are splatters and spills to mop up. Plus the messy pots and utensils. And, of course, a table load of dishes. By the time you're done, it seems, you have to plunge into the next meal. On top of that, virtually every kind of item in your kitchen has different requirements for cleaning. And the grocery aisles offer scores of different cleansers and tools to do it with.

Let's look at some strategies for simplifying kitchen cleanup.

Secret Helpers in Your Cupboard

Don't spend too much on cleaning products the next time you visit the supermarket. To save money, follow some of these tips that use materials you probably already have in your kitchen.

Take these counter measures

For grease stains on your countertops, use rubbing alcohol to clean the stain instead of paying $2.89 for the fancy kitchen cleaner. Just pour a small amount of alcohol on a sponge or rag and rub the stain until it's gone. The rubbing alcohol disinfects the countertops at the same time.

Food Storage Checklist

Here are some general rules for how long common foods can be stored in the freezer safely. These times will vary, depending on how well you wrap your food, the temperature in your freezer, and the state of the food upon storage.

Food	Freezer
Bacon	1 month
Frankfurters	1–2 months
Ground beef	3–4 months
Ham, smoked	1–2 months
Lunch meat	1–2 months
Sausage	1–2 months
Steak	6–12 months

Remove dyes decisively

One of the easiest ways to remove Easter egg dye from a countertop is to clean the stain with fingernail polish remover as soon as possible. But be careful: Polish remover can damage some special finishes, so test it on an inconspicuous part of the counter first.

Give crumbs no quarter

Ever notice how a broom leaves behind the finest crumbs and small particles on the kitchen floor? Here's the easiest way to clean them up: Wrap an old pillowcase or towel around the bristles of your broom, secure it with a rubber band, and then sweep.

Don't skip the drip pans

Dirty drip pans under your stove burners are a fire hazard. But taking care of them is a snap. Most manufacturers recommend simply washing drip pans on the top rack of the dishwasher. Don't scrub them with abrasives or scouring pads. That can damage the coating.

An Easy Route to Clean Machines

There's no need to spend a ton of money when cleaning your kitchen appliances and utensils. In fact, some appliances clean themselves. You do need to be careful, however, because the interiors of some small appliances are delicate and can be scratched or corroded if an abrasive cleanser is used. Instead of using strong cleansers, use some of nature's remedies for cleaning your kitchen equipment.

Dish up some vinegar

The Vinegar Institute in Atlanta recommends cleaning the dishwasher once a week with vinegar to remove the hard-water stains and film. To do this, put one cup of vinegar in the bottom of the dishwasher and run it through one cycle. It's okay to put some glassware in at the same time. Your dishwasher will be renewed, and your glassware will come out bright and shiny.

Don't Buy Into Complexity

Avoid installing more than you want or need in your kitchen. Here's how to make sure you aren't buying into a more complex lifestyle.

- Don't get caught up in the high-tech trap. Even though the brochure for the shiny new refrigerator makes it sound like you can't function without the high-tech model, take a good look at what you need. If the standard model serves the purpose, don't waste the extra money on a higher-priced model. More new gadgets mean more opportunities for breakdowns.
- When purchasing major appliances, not signing service contracts can sometimes save you considerable sums. If you did sign a service contract, think hard before renewing it next year. If you're going to have a major problem with your appliance, chances are it will come in the first year while the appliance is still under warranty. Over time, renewing service contracts can cost you almost as much as the appliance did originally.
- If you're moving soon, it may seem like your problems will vanish with a bigger kitchen. But don't buy more kitchen than you need. It's just an excuse to buy more stuff to fill it.

Turn up the heat

You probably have one of the easiest cleaning aids in your kitchen already. Self-cleaning ovens are commonplace now, but some people are leery of the high temperatures required. No worries, mate. If your stove couldn't handle it, it wouldn't be designed to be self-cleaning in the first place. But avoid using oven cleaners in a continuous- or self-cleaning oven. They can damage the interior finish so it won't self-clean anymore.

Clean up that mesh

If you have a ventilation hood over your stove, check the aluminum mesh screen that traps grease. Stick it in your dishwasher now and then for a good cleaning. Just remember to replace it before you cook again.

If life give you lemons, use them

If you have an old lemon, cut in into small pieces and run it through the garbage disposal to freshen your drain. Also, if you're going on vacation, cut a lemon in half and leave half sitting out on a saucer in your kitchen to prevent the house from developing that shut-up odor. Place the other half in a room at the opposite end of the house.

Give your microwave a steam bath

An often-used microwave oven can be one of the dirtiest appliances in the kitchen. When food has splattered on the sides and cooked there for a few minutes, cleaning it off can be a major chore. To clean and sanitize your microwave, pour one cup of water into a microwave-safe bowl and boil it in the microwave on high for two or three minutes. Carefully remove the bowl after it has cooled and wipe the microwave walls clean. Your microwave will thank you.

Simply Stated

Never eat more than you can lift.

—**Miss Piggy**

Coming Clean with Glassware, Silver, and More

Along with appliances and kitchen surfaces, kitchen utensils and glassware also need to be cleaned and disinfected. Most people keep silver items in a safe place and only bring them out occasionally. Unfortunately, they usually need some polishing before they can be used. Since cleaning polishes are expensive, try using some preventive maintenance with your kitchen items.

Let your silver shine

Tarnishing is the result of a natural chemical reaction between silver and sulfur dioxide in the air, so it can't be eliminated entirely. But there are factors you can control. To keep your silver shiny, don't let salt or foods like eggs or mayonnaise stay in contact with the silver for long. Salt will corrode silver, while eggs and mayonnaise can cause tarnishing, according to the Soap and Detergent Association.

Have some more vinegar

If you have glassware or crystal vases that have hard-water stains (lime deposits) in the bottom, rinse the glassware with vinegar, then promptly rinse with water

Protect Those Cookies

It's natural to want to protect your cookies—who could possibly want the little darlings to get scorched in the oven? But you don't have to buy an insulated cookie sheet to protect your goodies. Take an old cookie sheet, turn it upside down, and place it on the oven rack. Then place the cookie sheet with the cookie dough on top of that. This prevents the cookies from being burnt on the bottom, and it works even better than an insulated sheet.

---

and wipe dry. Don't let vinegar dry on fine glassware, however. It may etch the glass, especially in carved patterns and crevices.

Shake your rice

If there are stains in the bottom of some of your small jars or bottles, pour a handful of rice in the jars, add some warm water and detergent, and shake. The rice does a good job of cleaning. Make sure you wash the jar thoroughly afterward. The rice has starch in it, which will leave a ring around some jars. (Beach sand works well for this cleaning technique, too. So, the next time you're at your vacation home. . . .)

Safeguard your sponge

Bacteria love to grow on sponges. This is hazardous, especially after prolonged use. The bacteria present in meat, for example, can contaminate any surface the meat touches and take up residence in your sponge after you've given your counter a well-intended wipe down. To disinfect a sponge, attach it to the top shelf of the dishwasher and run the dishwasher on the hottest setting. And there's an even simpler alternative: throw away the old sponge and use a new one.

How COMPLEX Can It Get?

Now You See Them, Now You Don't: In 1978, the typical supermarket carried 11,767 items—food and nonfood merchandise, including cleaning supplies, reports Gorman's New Product News. By 1987, that figure had risen to an astounding 24,531 items—rising to an incredible 46,852 items by 2008. Over that same 30-year period, 185,000 new items were introduced, and most failed. Only a fraction of the products available at any given time are still available 10 years later.

The Simplest of the Simple

Here is the essence of the preceding chapter, the simplest of the simple ideas for managing your kitchen:

- Store frequently used cookware and ingredients so that they're close at hand.
- Invest in high-quality cookware. It will last longer, save you money in the long run, and chances are, cook more evenly.
- Since pots and lids don't stack well, separate and store all of your lids together.

- Be selfish. If you spend more time in the kitchen than anyone else, arrange everything the way you think is the most logical and convenient.
- Arrange appliances in a triangle for maximum efficiency when preparing meals.
- Throw out leftovers after seven days.

The Ins and Outs of Pots and Pans

Undoubtedly, you have several types of pots and pans in your home. Many of them come clean with standard dishwashing, others are a perpetual chore to clean, and still others seem permanently battle-scarred with stains. Don't scour them to death. Here are hints for bringing pots and pans back to their original glory.

Aluminum. Here's how to fix discolored aluminum pots: In the pot, mix 1 or 2 tablespoons cream of tartar or lemon juice into each quart of water you use, and boil for 10 minutes. To remove mineral deposits from a teakettle, mix a one-to-one solution of water and vinegar in the kettle, and bring it to a boil. Turn off the heat, and leave the mixture in the kettle for several hours. Follow up by rubbing with steel wool.

Copper. To remove tarnish, sprinkle on some salt plus a little vinegar or lemon juice, then rub and rinse. An alternative for small stains: put some toothpaste on a damp sponge or soft cloth and rub vigorously.

Iron. To remove cooked-on food from an iron skillet, mix 2 teaspoons baking soda per 1 quart water in the skillet, and bring to a boil.

Nonstick. For baked-on food, mix 3 tablespoons oxygen bleach (also called all-fabric bleach) and 1 cup water in the pan, and simmer for 15 to 20 minutes. Then wash thoroughly and rinse. Avoid abrasive cleaners, which will ruin the nonstick quality of your pan.

Pyrex. For baked-on food in bakeware, soak in a solution of liquid dishwashing detergent and water. For burned-on sugar or starches, add baking soda to the presoak solution. After soaking, the food should scrub away easily. Avoid metal scouring pads, which can scratch the material.

Stainless steel. Pour white vinegar on the stain. Scrub it with a stainless steel pad.

Chapter 5

Living Rooms and Dining Rooms

Make These Living Areas
Worry-Free, Relaxing Refuges

The living room and dining room areas assume different roles for different families. From the kids' video games to the old recliner that everyone races to first, the living room represents your family and its collective habits. The key to keeping your living area clean, neat, and simple is to determine which style fits you and your family.

Are you a den person or a living room person? What's the difference? The den is a more informal living area—your family's stretch-out-and-relax room. The living room–dining room is a more formal area you use for dinner parties or other activities where etiquette is either necessary or desired. Some homes have one room for family entertaining, while others have two rooms. If you have one room that serves both purposes, use ideas from both the den and the living room sections.

This chapter will also examine areas of your home that are adjacent to your living room and dining room. If the front door opens into your living room or foyer, for instance, you'll find useful tips for making that area more functional. There are also some ideas on simplifying window treatments, decorating around your fireplace, protecting and cleaning carpets and upholstery, making your home secure, and more.

A Den of Simplicity

In many families, the den provides a more comfortable environment than does the traditional living room. Because this area is generally more relaxing for your family, it tends to become a popular dumping ground for things that are used and then not put back in their proper places. Therefore, your den can get disorganized quickly. You may find yourself cleaning and searching for lost items more often than necessary.

Clobber That Clutter

Less mess means less stress. Here are some tips on simplifying your den, whether you live alone or are the parent of five.

Clean as you go

Avoid leaving things lying around your den that don't belong there. If you decide to write a hand-written letter to a friend while watching television in the den, make sure you put away the stationery when you finish. Get all of your family members involved in this. Don't let kids leave their toys or homework lying around when other places are designated for these things.

Limit the furniture

Comfortable sofas and chairs work well if you or your family members stretch out when watching television, listening to music, or reading books. Yet if you have more furniture in the den than your family ever needs, you're creating a cleaning headache for yourself. Over the course of a year, a five-person household will accumulate 40 pounds of dust, according to one estimate. If you need more chairs for visitors, you can borrow some from another room in your home.

Stash your books

Some people have walls of bookshelves in their dens or living rooms and thus have homes for their voluminous collections. If you don't have enough books to fill a library or if the idea of wall-to-wall shelving doesn't appeal to you, consider a corner bookcase. It provides a storage area for many books, looks attractive, and doesn't crowd your room. These units may be hard to find, so you may have to find someone to build a simple connecting bookcase.

Drop the leaf

Drop-leaf tables are versatile items in the den because they can instantly expand your table surface area. Many times, drop-leaf tables are placed behind sofas. There's no problem with this as long as you can easily walk around the table, observes author Sir Terence Conran in his book, *Living in Small Spaces*. Drop-leaf tables can be used to display decorative items or pictures and can be folded up as a desk or play area to hold board games or

art supplies. Some drop-leaf tables have drawers where you can put your television schedule or warranty information for the television, DVD player, or other equipment housed in the den.

Frame your family

You may want to put a few pictures of your family in your den or keep your child's soccer trophy in there. Nothing says "I belong here" better than tangible evidence. Pictures convey pride and can help promote closeness in the family.

A good place to display pictures is on top of an entertainment center. Most of the time, an entertainment center houses the television, which obviously makes it a focal point in your den. Your family's pictures will always be in full view, and you won't be cluttering up the other flat surfaces that see constant action in the room. Another prominent area to display pictures is the mantle.

Let up on your walls

You may want a few decorations on the wall—there's no problem with that. Be careful, however, not to clutter up your walls. Your room doesn't need two or three pictures, plaques, or posters on every wall. Overcrowding your walls makes your den look smaller and more cramped. Also, an excess of pictures can make it difficult to stay with one color scheme in your den. If you're lucky enough to find appropriate pictures that match your den's color scheme, use only a few.

Built-Ins Are Shoo-Ins

If you're reconsidering the layout or furnishings in your living room or den, here's a simple strategy that will save you loads of time and effort: built-in furniture. Built-ins won't tip over, and they protect electronic equipment better than freestanding furniture. They also save space, and dust doesn't collect underneath them.

Give your kids space

If you have children, devote a basket, shelf, or chest in your den to their board games and toys. This way, you and your kids won't have to lug toys all over the house at cleanup time. And if visitors drop by, you'll have readily available places to stash things quickly.

Raid your parents' house

Your relatives may have older furniture that they no longer use. If you have the space, volunteer to take it off their hands. You can save hundreds of dollars by refinishing an old table or re-upholstering a sofa or stuffed chair. Sometimes yard sales are good opportunities to buy inexpensive furniture that needs just a little work. Carefully inspect items before you buy them. Poor-quality furniture will only cost you more money and aggravation in the long run because you'll be buying replacement furniture in short order.

Illuminate inexpensively

Avoid expensive light fixtures in the den, where the rough-and-tumble gang hangs out after school. In addition, sentimental items like antique lamps that have been passed down through your family belong in an area where there is less chance of breakage. If you're fortunate enough to have a den with overhead lights, don't waste your money on stand-up light fixtures that may get broken or need special cleaning or maintenance.

Sound Advice on Audio and Video

Your entertainment center probably has a variety of electronic equipment. In a typical home today, a television,

DVD player, cable or satellite box, sound system, and video games can all be stored together in one place. Some entertainment centers have enough shelves to hold each piece of equipment, while others come up short. Some centers have small cabinets where you can store a few of your DVDs.

Nevertheless, you may need extra room for your entertainment center. And you may want to dress up such a cold and electronic feature of your home. The following tips should help you determine the easiest way to maximize your entertainment space.

Unpile your pile

Even if you're short on room, don't stack your equipment or pile other objects like CDs, DVDs, books, and TV schedules on top. Your entertainment equipment wasn't made to carry heavy loads. You might get away with putting the cable box or DVD player on top of the television, but stop there. Electronic equipment accumulates heat, and keeping the surrounding space open helps to dissipate that heat.

Remove the remotes from solitary confinement

If you have three or four remotes in your den—you know, one for the television, another for the CD player, and another to operate the DVD player—keep them together. They can be stored on a coffee table, entertainment center, end table, or wherever they are most convenient for you. Or get a universal remote that replaces all of your others. Operating one takes time to learn, but the convenience of having all the controls in one remote makes it all worthwhile.

Toss Out the Magazine Rack

If you have enough magazines in your house to start a periodical section in the library, it's time to discard some or even pitch the magazine rack. Unless you take a clear-them-out-as-you-go approach, the contents of your magazine rack will be spilling out onto the floor. When cleaning time comes around, you'll have so many outdated magazines that you'll need a bulldozer to clear a path through the pile.

Read, reap, and recycle

If you've already looked through a magazine and found nothing of interest, dispose of it. Either throw it away, put it with the recyclables, or give it to a friend. If you stick to this habit, you won't have to sort through mountains of magazines to figure out why you kept them and if you still need them.

Use those scissors

If you've found an article in a magazine that you want to keep, cut it out and dispose of the rest of the magazine. Allocate all of these articles to their final destination as soon as you comfortably can. If it's a recipe, put it in your recipe file or cookbook. If it's an article for your child, give it to him. Keep your own articles in an organized folder in a desk drawer or save them on your hard drive. If you clip many articles, go through your file once a month and discard articles that no longer are relevant. This a simple way to avoid a buildup of publications and clippings.

Collect cautiously

If you're collecting issues of a certain magazine, keep these issues where they will be safe. You may wish to store them in a fireproof box in the closet or elsewhere in your home. But keeping them in the magazine rack only clutters your living room, risks damaging them, and increases the risk that someone else will toss them out.

Sack your subscription

If you're drowning in clutter, check online orwith your local library to see if it carries the magazines you subscribe to. If so, cancel some of your common hard-copy magazine subscriptions. Plan a reading day for you and your kids to go to the library to read magazines or books. Concurrently, you will win back your living room or den.

Prune your name from lists

Here's guessing that some of the items in your magazine rack are catalogs. To prevent these from being sent, call the vendor's customer service department (most have toll-free numbers) and ask that your name be removed from the mailing list. Also visit www.the-dma.org and register with Direct Marketing Association to receive less junk mail.

Are You Slowly Killing Your Coffee Table?

Your coffee table takes a beating. Your kids may sneak in and use it as a footrest, or it may get constantly bumped when people walk around it. Here's how to give your coffee table long life in the living room:

- Using coasters under your drinks will keep your tabletop looking new. Napkins aren't a good substitute. Even if your coffee table has a protective finish on it, it may not be protected from excess wetness.
- Allow enough leg room between the table and the sofa so that people can walk around it without smacking into it. Designers recommend at least a foot of space—more if you have tall people in your family. Your son "Stretch" will thank you.
- Consider using end tables instead of a coffee table. End tables are usually placed closer to the sofa or chair, which will protect them from damage.
- If you have a coffee table that's wobbling because one leg is shorter than the others, here are easy ways to remedy the situation. Put some plastic wood or wood putty on wax paper. Then put the short leg of the table on top of that. After

the plastic wood or wood putty has dried, smooth it down with sandpaper until the leg's length matches the others. An alternative: cover the short leg with a rubber cap (if you don't mind the one leg looking different). Or glue a button or rubber washer to the bottom of the troublesome table leg.

Take Back Your Living Room

Because your living room is a more formal area, it conveys a more refined atmosphere. This is the room where you may wish to display your special and more cherished items. Many people consider this room their show-off room. This doesn't mean the room should be ostentatious, but a lovely living room will provide you with a certain sense of pride. Even if the room is seldom used, it's a good idea to keep it simple and organized so the next time you do use it, you won't have to spend a lot of time cleaning and arranging.

Simplicity by Design

Here are tips for making your living room worry-free.

Get stylish in the living room

Typically, living room furniture is more stylish and more refined than den furniture. This makes the living room ideal for more lavish furnishings. You're not going to be sleeping or spending a lot of time in there. Hence, this is one room where you can decorate with somewhat less concern about simplicity. Pick the most stylish furniture you can reasonably purchase within your budget.

Sofas and chairs should be positioned so that they have at least 1½ feet of leg room in front and 2 feet of clearance in back. This creates a walkway so people can easily travel around the furniture. Traffic that can't pass is complexity.

Comfort your guests

Make it simple for your guests to interact by arranging your furniture based on the way people talk to one another. Chairs or sofas that are directly opposite each other are confrontational. "Go for an L-shaped seating arrangement with two couches or a couch and love seat forming a right angle," recommends Carol Venolia, author of *Healing Environments: Your Guide to Indoor Well-Being.* "The worst conversation-killing arrangement is to have chairs or couches directly across from each other. It's just too formal."

Shade your shades

Plastic lamp shade covers will prevent your shades from getting too dusty, eliminating one of your cleaning chores. Make sure you remove the covers before company comes over. You don't want your guests' first impression to be, "Tacky, tacky, tacky. . . ."

Position your piano

If you have a piano in your home, ponder where you're going to place it. (You don't want to move it every other week, do you?) Unless you're staging an Alicia Keys mini-concert, you probably don't need to have the piano sitting in the middle of the floor. Move it closer to a corner—but not completely in the corner. If you play the piano when you have guests, for instance, people will be drawn to the music. If the piano is too close to the corner or wall, you'll quickly have a case of overcrowding because there will be no room to walk around the person playing.

Say no to noise

With a little strategic decorating, you can turn down the volume on everyday noise. "Anything with texture absorbs sound and quiets a room. Try hanging tapestries on walls and putting rugs on bare floors," suggests Sarah Little Turnbull, PhD, of the Stanford University Graduate School of Business.

Evict the electronics

For a formal living room, less is more, especially when it comes to electronic equipment. Excess electronic equipment diminishes the formality of a living room. So save yourself the expense of an extra television for this room. Yes, you might want a sound sytem in the room, but many folks do just fine without that, too. When you're entertaining, let your guests be the focus of attention, not the big screen or the music.

Get a Handle on Your Front Door Area

The front door of most homes opens into the living room or a foyer. Use this area to help organize your day's activities. This may save time when you're late for work and help keep your kids organized for school. If you and your family use your back door more often, the ideas in this section can apply to the area around that door, also. At all times, cut through clutter like a hot knife through butter. This section focuses on keeping things where you need them, when you need them.

Assemble an out-table

Imagine waking up in the morning to find that you're late for work. You rush around and start to panic when you can't find your car keys. On top of that, your child can't find his spelling book.

One way to avoid this is to keep an out-table beside your front door. This table is only for items going out, not for things coming in. Before you go to bed at night, put your car keys, umbrella, grocery list, kids' books, or whatever else you'll need the next day on the out-table. When you are ready to leave the next morning, given there are no goblins in your house, everything will be waiting for you. Make sure that you clear the table each day so it doesn't turn into semi-permanent storage for items that are not headed out the door anytime soon.

Stash your gloves

If you have a drawer under your out-table, store gloves and scarves there when the weather gets cooler. Keeping them in a drawer in your out-table will keep them accessible. If the out-table does not have a drawer, store them in a cabinet or closet near the front door. Don't leave them on top of the out-table, unless it is particularly roomy. Otherwise, you diminish the effectiveness of using an out-table in the first place.

Get a rack on back

Consider hanging a coat rack on the back of your door. Everyone's coats will be accessible, and you won't have to run to some other part of the house to find them. Also, this will prevent lightweight jackets from getting wrinkled, which easily happens when they're stuffed into a crowded closet. If the appearance of a bunch of coats on the back of the door does not appeal to you, use a stand-up coat rack behind the door or in the foyer.

Cover yourself

You know your day is starting out badly when it's pouring outside and your umbrella is in the car, guaranteeing a sopping walk across the driveway. Keep a container or umbrella organizer near the door of your house so you have a convenient place to keep umbrellas when they're needed. This is also a convenient place to put a wet umbrella when you enter the house, so you don't drip water all over the floor.

Damage Control for Your Living Room

As much as you take care of your living room furnishings, something can always happen to mess them up. Murphy, of the famous law, seemingly is alive and well, and in your living room. Here are some suggestions to help you find a loophole in the law.

Clear the air

The American Cancer Society reports that smoking . . . aw, you already know about the dangers of smoking. And if you've had a party at which you allowed smoking, you already know that it's hard to get rid of the smell after the party is over. If it's the dead of winter, you won't want to open the windows, so put a few fabric softener sheets in your living room. The smoke smell will probably be gone in a day or two. If this doesn't help, you will probably be forced to air the room out for a few hours.

Soak up the water marks

Try not to get upset, at least in front of others, if someone places a drink on your coffee table and the glass leaves water marks. Instead, place several blotters or tissues over the mark. Then press it with a warm iron. If the mark remains, buy some camphorated oil and, using lint-free cloth, rub the mark in the direction of the wood grain until the mark is dry. Sop up any remaining oil on the table so you don't damage your table's finish in yet another way.

Polish your nails—not your table

You or your significant other was in a hurry and knocked over a bottle of nail polish. In case you're wondering, bright red nail polish doesn't go well with wood furniture. Ironically, while polish won't stay on your nails longer than two days without some chipping, it will stay on your furniture indefinitely. If this scenario sounds familiar to you, mop up the nail polish, then rub whatever remains of the accident with a nylon brush that has been dipped in furniture wax. Don't use nail polish remover—it will damage the furniture's finish.

Pamper your paneling

If you have real wood paneling, simple dusting will suffice for most situations. If it needs more cleaning, try a spray polish or a neutral cleaner (meaning non-acidic and non-alkaline) like Murphy's Oil Soap. Avoid using water on real wood.

To clean hardboard paneling—the stuff with the faux wood finish—squirt some dishwashing liquid into a bucket of warm water, and wipe the paneling down with a sponge or cloth. Then toss out the soapy water and wipe the paneling down again with fresh water.

Relieve your TV of static

Television screens get dusty in hurry. But using a cloth dampened with water or other liquids and oils can damage a TV screen. Instead, clean the screen with window cleaner applied to a fabric dryer sheet. This will both remove the dust and help repel dust in the future.

Neutralize shocking video games

Heaven forbid you should have to remove your child from his video game long enough to clean it. But paper towels or small cloths can be used to clean the video game cartridges. If you don't clean them, in time, static electricity can build up on the element and shock someone. Spray a light layer of a static-control product like Static Guard on a cloth and let it air-dry until it's slightly damp. Rub the cloth over any metal surface on the video game.

Dining Rooms Made Easy

"It must be great to be rich and let the other fellow keep up appearances," goes an old saying. If you rarely use your dining room, you may consider it wasted space. Many people don't have a dining room, yet they seem to function quite nicely. Conversely, some people use their dining rooms frequently, either for entertaining or for dinner with the family.

If you have a dining room, how do you use the space? Are you a frequent entertainer, or are you thinking of using the space for another purpose? Here are some tips that may help you make better use of the space and thus make your life easier.

Think adjustable

If you use your dining room quite a bit, make your next table an expandable one. By adding table leaves, you can seat as many people as necessary. Allow a minimum of 32 inches between the edge of your dining room table and the nearest wall or piece of furniture. This gives enough room for your guests to move their chairs back. Later, you can shorten the table to increase the space in your dining room. This will make it easier to walk around your dining room table.

Shelter your goods

Dining room tables and chairs are expensive purchases, but when taken care of appropriately, they can stay in good condition for years. A good way to protect your table surface from scratches is to use a table cover or tablecloth. Avoid placing vases or other decorative items on an unprotected table. They may leave marks or scratches.

Check your coverage

If you plan on placing a rug underneath your dining room table, buy one large enough so that when your guests move their chairs back, the chairs are still on the rug. A rug that is too small may catch your guests' chairs, cause them to trip, or cause them to spill food or drink. Also, sliding the chairs can scratch hardwood floors.

Using Your Dining Room Accents

You may only need a few simple accessories in your dining room to achieve the utility and style you want. Sometimes the difficult part is not what to put in the

---

Media Madness

The average American household of four people spends anywhere from $2,400 to $4,500 annually on televisions, radios, recorded music, DVDs, and movies as well as newspapers, magazines, and books. Even if one purchase was for, say, a $400 television set, that still leaves $2,800 or so, which could add up to 100 $9 movie tickets, a $50 radio, 15 $10 CDs, 40 rented DVDs, dozens of magazines, a daily newspaper, several paperback books and money to spare!

dining room but how to arrange it and take care of it. Here are some easy ways to accentuate and take care of the accents in this area.

Display china proudly

It's a shame to hide your fine china in an opaque cabinet or cupboard. Fine china is considerably more costly than everyday china or kitchenware, so show it off. China can be displayed in a windowed china cabinet as a decorative showpiece. Many windowed china cabinets also have drawers or cupboards for extra storage of additional place settings.

Drawers can be used to house flatware, place mats, or tablecloths. Also, candles can be stored in a drawer divider in your china cabinet. Use a drawer divider so wax doesn't damage the inside of your drawers.

Choose the right place setting

If you prefer not to use a tablecloth in your dining room, consider place mats. These are generally less expensive

than a traditional tablecloth, but they still provide the protection you need for your table. You can change your decorative theme by changing place mats. Choose place mats that pick up colors in your curtains or your dining room chairs (if they're upholstered). If you prefer, you can always use white, but keep in mind that white will be more difficult to clean.

Add a subtle glow

Candles are a quick and easy way to provide a warm ambiance to your dining room. Whether you're using a candelabra or candlesticks, use disposable protective coasters to keep wax from dripping on your furniture.

Get dimmer

If you don't have a candelabra, install a dimmer switch in the dining room. Very bright light in the dining room may make guests uncomfortable. With a dimmer, you can control the lighting for each occasion with a quick turn of a knob.

Buy quality neutrals

Chances are you won't use your dining room for entertaining many times during the year, so decorate smartly. Buy good-quality curtains in a neutral color that will match any color in your rug, upholstery, or carpet and will last until you're ready to redecorate.

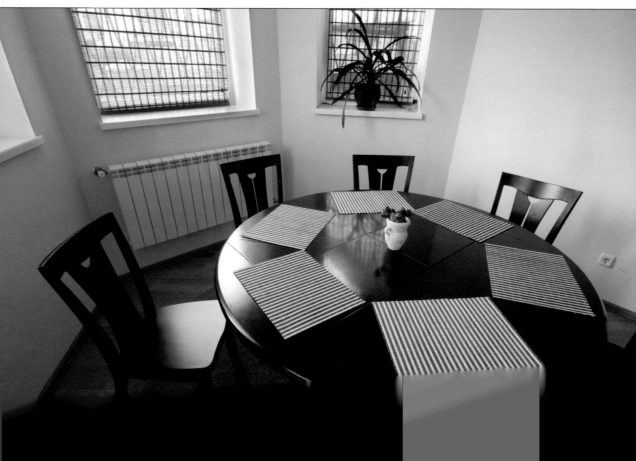

Save space with sideboards

Space—the final frontier. If you still need more storage room for holiday dinnerware or other serving utensils, consider a corner cupboard or sideboard. Corner cupboards provide good storage space without taking up too much floor space. If you already have a china cabinet in your dining room, this may be your best alternative when looking for more storage space.

The Performing Arts Are Jumping through Hoops

The quest for simplicity is putting a lot of pressure on the businesses that stage live performances.

"The performing arts are suffering in every city across America, but not because people aren't interested in the arts," observed the late Tom Havrilesky, PhD, an economics instructor at Duke University in Durham, North Carolina during the 1990s. "People don't want to invest in getting dressed, making the commute, finding parking, standing in line, making the way to their seats, enjoying what may or may not be a fine performance, and then turning around and doing the whole thing again to get back home. Many events are often held on weekdays, meaning that would-be patrons have to get up the next morning and go to work."

In the future, expect to see event sponsors—those who want to thrive, anyway—finding ways to collect their patrons, whisk them quickly into town and into their seats, and then whisk them quickly home afterward. They'll also have to rearrange times to accommodate people who want to leave directly from work.

"We'll see the death of the 8 PM or 8:30 PM performance, in favor of the 6:30 and 7 show," Dr. Havrilesky said.

Make Your Dining Room a Convert

If you don't use the dining room, consider converting it into something you will put to use. Perhaps you've been wanting a home office or library. Your dining room may be the right size for this. Maybe you've always wanted a sewing room or a playroom for the kids. Why not convert the room now and actually use it, instead of merely having it take up space? As French poet Charles Pierre Baudelaire once said, "In putting off what one has to do, one runs the risk of never being able to do it."

Rally Round the Fireplace

People are drawn to a fireplace because of the warmth and feeling of relaxation it provides. It's a practical feature of your home, too: If your power goes off during a winter storm, you'll still have a source of heat and a place to improvise some cooking. But fireplaces present potential complications in your life, too—the lingering ashes and soot, tricky cleanup problems, and safety concerns, for instance.

Keep Those Flames in Their Place

Remember, fire is a powerful force. One minute you could be relaxing in front of the fire, and the next minute your home could be in flames. You face potential harm each time you start a fire in your home, and forestalling such disasters is definitely a component of leading the simple life. So to increase your peace of mind, make sure your fireplace is properly maintained.

Clear the creosote

Creosote is a gummy, flammable substance that looks like tar. It can build up in your fireplace and flue after continual use, particularly when you burn paper products, burn wood slowly, and burn green wood. If you have creosote, don't attempt to remove it yourself; the stuff is sticky and entirely crummy to deal with, and you probably won't get it all. For simplicity's sake, hire a professional to do this.

Get diligent about danger

Ninety-six percent of all homes have smoke detectors. Unfortunately, some of these homes don't have as many as they need for optimum protection. So, give yourself some peace of mind—install smoke detectors in all of your hallways and on all floors of your home. If you have a fireplace, buy a carbon monoxide detector as well. These are sold at the same stores that sell smoke detectors. Faulty heating devices such as clogged fireplaces can emit this colorless and odorless gas into your home. As with the smoke detectors, put carbon monoxide detectors on every floor in your home and near the bedrooms.

Keep fire extinguishers handy

Putting out a fire in your home is definitely something that you want to be quick, simple, and easy. So keep a fully functional fire extinguisher on each floor in your home, in the kitchen, and near the fireplace. Remember, a single spark can ignite any

Put it under glass

If you install glass doors across your fireplace, you'll reap a lot of rewards. For one thing, they provide a natural, unobstructed view of the fire. Also, the doors prevent the heat inside your house from being drawn up the chimney. And they're a safety feature, allowing you to close off the fire before you go to bed.

Add up the figures

Before you start depending on your fireplace as a source of heat, weigh the costs—both financial and in terms of effort and upkeep. Consider where you are getting the wood to build the fire. Is it from your land or do you have to buy it? If you are cutting the wood, review the theoretical cost of your time. In the end, you may conclude that a conventional furnace is more economical and less trouble.

Check your chimney

Have your chimney checked annually before you begin using your fireplace. Also, make sure the firebox has no cracks. If you're not absolutely sure of what you're doing, have a professional inspect for ashes, corrosion, and other items (such as birds' nests) that don't belong there. Spending the money on a professional who knows what to look for can save you loads of messy trouble in the future—and might even save your life.

Easy Steps to a Perfect Fire

You don't have to be a dyed-in-the-wool woodsman to build a good, long-lasting fire. Your embarrassing days of smoke-filled living rooms are over. These simple tips will help you build a fire that doesn't go out until you want it to.

1. Always give your fire plenty of air. Make sure the flue is open all the way.
2. Crumple up three pieces of newspaper. Put two under the grate in your fireplace and one on top. The grate will keep air circulating under your logs.
3. Build a tiny teepee out of twigs or hardwood kindling, stacked against the paper. The kindling should be no more than ¾-inch wide, ¼-inch thick, and 10 inches long. Don't pack it so tightly that air can't circulate.
4. Position two split logs, at least 4 inches apart, on top of the kindling and paper. Put a third log diagonally across the first two.
5. Hold another wad of newspaper near the top of the fireplace and light it to get an updraft going in the flue.
6. Light the newspaper under your kindling in three places.
7. As the original logs turn into hot coals, add more logs—but not so many that you smother the fire. Once in a while, prod and roll the logs over with a poker.

combustible material. Make sure the extinguisher is recharged after every use. Contact your local fire department for information on recharging your fire extinguisher.

Hot Decorating Ideas for Hearth and Home

The fireplace is a focal point in your living area. Even if you don't use your fireplace for heating, it's a designer's dream. It provides a versatile backdrop to different types of accents and decorations. From the fancy formality of the living room to the casual atmosphere of the den, the fireplace can be used to accent virtually any decor. However you decide to decorate around the fireplace, don't let the task complicate your life unnecessarily. Here's how to keep your decorating simple.

Mount a mantle

If you don't already have a mantle above your fireplace, consider installing one. It is a simple way to add shape and character to your fireplace and provide you with a space to display pictures, clocks, candlesticks, vases, and other decorative items. And where else are you supposed to hang your Christmas stockings?

Feel empowered, not overpowered

If you have a small living room, an overdecorated fireplace can overwhelm the room. In this case, a few simple items or a clock on the mantle will suffice. You don't need to hang pictures and portraits from mantle to ceiling. That will tend to make the room seem off-balance, which may provoke you to add more pictures on opposite walls. This compounds the problem and overcrowds your living room. Remember, the idea we're striving for is simplicity.

Change with the seasons

If you're at a loss as to what to do with your fireplace in the spring and summer, try filling it with pottery, baskets, or other decorative items that you may have lying around your house.

Windows, Floors, and More

Windows, doors, carpeting, hardwood floors—they're all immobile and permanent aspects of your house. So what possible influence could they have on the simplicity or complexity of your life? Actually, the choices you make in materials and design will directly affect your household for years to come. A cream-colored carpet could have you vacuuming every other day, for instance, and make you perpetually anxious about the possibility of spills. So let's take a look at how these aspects of your home can make your living space a place where you can truly kick back and relax. Note that while a chapter on living rooms and dining rooms is the natural place to discuss these features of your home, much of the following advice will serve you well all over the house.

Make More of Your Window Treatments with Less

Curtains and window coverings today are often designed for style and ease of hanging. Many different types of window treatments are on the market and cover all of the possibilities between casual and elegant. Even if you don't have a large living area, you easily can create the illusion of more space by using windows and window treatments. These ideas will take some of the angst, fretting, and hassle out of decorating your windows.

Sprinkle baking soda on carpets before vacuuming to give them a fresh and clean smell.

Choose an easy look

To furnish your living area simply, buy what you like and what looks good in your home. You can't go wrong with curtains, but there are other simple decorative options. Valances can be used alone, with curtains, or to accent shades or blinds. Valances are popular because of this versatility and because they're less expensive than curtains. Also, it's easy enough to replace valances whenever the mood suits you.

Settle in with shades

Are you tired of dusting miniblinds every other week and having the strings break when you raise and lower the blinds? Shades are a simple alternative. Shades are making a comeback in some circles, and for good reason—they keep the light out in varying degrees. You get to choose from little coverage to total blackout. Aside from that good old standby, the white plastic shade, solid and printed decorative fabric shades are available in hundreds of patterns and designs. These shades are easy to hang and most can be dry-cleaned.

Hang 'em high

Traditionally, when you bought curtains, hanging them was always a pain. New designs, such as tabbed curtains, are now available. The loop-shaped tab slips over the curtain rod, and that's it. Your curtains are up in a flash. When hanging traditional curtains, you have to be careful to gauge the distance between clips so your curtains hang correctly—a much more difficult task.

Give those sheers a spin

Hanging sheers under regular curtains is a great idea because they shield the curtains from sun damage. If they start to look a tad dingy, you'll be tempted to wash them, but a couple of simpler techniques might take care of the problem. Vacuuming will remove much of the dust that accumulates. Use a low-suction setting (many vacuums have a device on the handle that lets extra air into the hose, reducing the force of the suction). Or just toss them into your clothes dryer on a no-heat setting.

Keep Your Carpet in Top Condition

The American colonists cried out to the British, "Don't tread on me." Your carpet has no say, yet it handles all of your living room, den, or dining area foot traffic. Regardless of whether you have old or new carpet, it takes a lot of abuse from you and your family.

When guests walk into your room, the carpet will be one of the first things that catches their eye. You don't want their first impression to be, "Don't they ever clean the carpet around here?" Keep your carpet in shape, and you won't have to replace it until you're ready for a decorating change. Here are simple ways to do that.

Invest in the best

When you buy carpet, buy the good stuff. Sure, your carpeted areas are lived in, traveled through, and played in quite a bit. But a lower-grade carpet will not hold up and will cost you more money in the long run. (More money means more work and, hence, less simplicity.) Avoid putting wool carpet in highly traveled areas. The first time something is spilled on it, you will have a chore cleaning it.

Make light of light colors

Sure, light-colored carpets look fantastic in the carpet emporium showroom. But when you get home, you'll be hounded by the reality that light carpeting shows dirt much more than darker colors. If you prefer a lighter color because of the color scheme in your living area, try a tan or beige that will hide the dirt and stains better. Avoid white or cream carpets. Even if you and your family are ultra-careful, these colors will get too dirty too fast. Do you want to be the primary supporter of Joe's Hug-a-Rug Cleaning Service? The extra cleanings necessary for a white carpet waste your time and cost you money.

Kick off your shoes

"Nothing is so fatiguing as the eternal hanging on of an uncompleted task," said the psychologist-philosopher William James. And nothing will feel more like an uncompleted task than cleaning the carpet after people track dirt, mud, and other unmentionable things through your house. Persuade your family members to remove their shoes when they enter the house. Doormats don't catch everything, and dirt and mud are your carpet's worst enemies. The more that's tracked in, the dingier your carpet gets, and the faster it wears out—which means more time and money wasted.

Refrain from Using Stain Repellants

The chemical companies probably would prefer you didn't know this, but you may be doing more harm than good by spending money on stain-repellant finishes for your furniture. There is no finish that will repel every stain.

Stain repellant finishes form a barrier between your stain and the upholstery, which means that you have to clean the stain quickly when an accident occurs. If the stain is left to dry, you will have difficulty removing it because the finish will actually bind to it. This same principle applies to carpet stains.

Change the layout

Carpet in high-traffic areas—around doors, couches, and favorite chairs, for instance—tends to get crushed quickly. To prevent this, rearrange the furniture in your living room or den a couple of times a year to alter the traffic pattern. Also, put sturdy foam pads under heavy furniture to prevent crushing.

How Complex Can It Get?

Pity the Poor Postman: The Harvard University library annually subscribes to a staggering 160,000 journals and periodicals. If pressed, could you guess the names of even a hundred of them? Ready, get set, go. . . .

Sell yourself short

Don't put down a high-pile carpet in your living room. "Rather than standing straight up, long pile tends to lie over, providing a smoother surface that's easier to slip on," says Lori Tietz, formerly of the National Safety Council in Washington, D.C. "It's easier to get high heels tangled in the longer pile." The last thing you want during a dinner party is for someone to slip and spill a drink or get hurt.

Coddle Your Hardwoods Easily

Hardwood floors are durable but, like carpets, also need some tender loving care. Hardwood floors serve well in areas of heavy traffic, such as your foyer and eating areas. Keeping wood floors in good condition can be a gargantuan task, though. And you weren't looking for more work to do, were you? Fortunately, taking small steps to protect the floors goes a long way. One of the easiest and most effective ways to protect your hardwoods is to partially cover them with decorative rugs. Here are some other tips to keep your floors looking fabulous.

Heed your mood

If you were born to redecorate, area rugs may be your least expensive alternative for protecting your wood floors. Larger rugs can be costly, so stick with smaller throw rugs and area rugs in places where you'll want to make frequent changes. Use different rugs every season to give your room a new look and a festive atmosphere around the holidays.

Watch your footing

An unsecured rug can be an invitation to a fall. Many discount and hardware stores sell adhesive strips that you can stick or glue on the back of your rugs so they

New Uses for Old Magazines

So you've decided to part with all of your old magazines. Seems like such a waste to throw all that reading material away. Here are useful and creative ways to part with the old standbys:

- Give old copies of magazines to your local library. If you live in a small town, the library may not have adequate resources and can use the extra reading materials.
- Give copies to the neighbors. If you have a neighbor with a special hobby, give him some magazines that apply to that interest.
- Pass some copies to people who are sick or shut-in. It gets boring watching television or surfing the Web all the time. People who are incapacitated for some reason might appreciate the variety.
- Decorate your room. Use magazine covers related to your special interests as artwork in your home. This takes a little bit of work, but it's definitely a conversation piece.
- Establish a freebie table at work, where anyone may drop off magazines they're done with and pick up new ones.
- At the least, take all the old copies to a recycling center so more trees won't have to die to inform people of the latest gossip.

will stay in place. Make sure none of the glue seeps out, and turn the rug upside down until the glue dries completely.

Go east, young rug-buyer

If you need a larger rug or if you're looking for something ornate, consider an Oriental rug. You can find simple or elaborate designs that can hide dirt better than light carpet and give your room a stylish look. To protect them from drink spills and other accidents, consider confining expensive Oriental rugs to rooms that aren't used as much. Dining rooms are often a good bet. Oriental rugs are expensive to clean because most of them are made of wool.

Master casters

If you choose to leave the natural beauty of your wood flooring exposed, use casters or felt underneath furniture legs. If you don't resort to such protection, wood flooring can be damaged or, at the least, be scuffed when your chairs slide back and forth. Beat-up, scuffed-up floors require more maintenance and hence less simplicity.

Also, try to avoid subjecting your hardwood floors to high-heeled shoes. The pressure of the heels can make indentations in the finish.

Protect it with poly

When you carry hot items from the kitchen to the dining room, spills can damage unprotected wood. Polyurethane finishes provide good protection and can withstand higher temperatures.

Under Your Feet, Under Your Seat: Carpet and Upholstery

Taking care of your carpet and upholstery may be trickier than you think. There are so many natural and synthetic fibers on the market now that it can be difficult to determine what you have and how to clean it. Here are some suggestions to make it easier.

Name that carpet fiber

Wool and polyester carpets require different cleaning agents. If you're not sure what type your carpet is, try cleaning the stain with water first. If this doesn't work, look for carpet cleaners at the store that are safe for any carpet type.

Let Fido lie low

If your dog or cat has an occasional accident on the carpet, clean it up as soon as possible. If you smell the accident but can't find where it happened even after doing your best Sherlock Holmes impersonation, take heart. Most pet stores carry enzymatic carpet cleaners that chemically break down the stain and eliminate odors. Test the cleaner on a hidden area of your carpet, like the back of a closet, before you apply it to the whole carpet. You want to make sure that the cleaner won't discolor the carpet.

Head for cover

For sofas and chairs, darker upholstery and tighter weaves hide dirt and spills. Tighter weaves, however, are generally not as comfortable as looser fabrics, so consider using slipcovers on your sofas and chairs. This is an inexpensive way to redecorate, and if you spill dark-purple, quick-spreading, indelible grape juice, you've only ruined a slipcover, not a couch. Slipcovers can be changed every season to give your living room a completely different look.

Recruit a pro

It's tempting to try to save money by cleaning your upholstery yourself—tempting, but not simple. The problem is that it's hard to remove all of the cleaner from the upholstery once you start cleaning. If it's left on the upholstery, the fabric will get dirty again more quickly because the soap will trap the new dirt. Hence, you'll end up spending more in the long run on extra cleanings. Professionals have equipment to remove all of the soap.

Security Means Peace of Mind

Having peace of mind is simpler than worrying, especially when it comes to the safety of your home. The Department of Justice reports that there is a burglary somewhere in the United States every 15 seconds. With 120 million homes in America, yours might not be next in line.

Imagine You're a Burglar

If you were staking out your own place, how easy would it be to get in? If you're objective about it, your answer most likely would be, "Piece of cake."

Approach the issue of safeguarding your home a second way: Have you ever locked yourself out of the house? If so, how did you get back in? Did you call someone who had a key, or did you break in? If you had to break in, you may have been amazed at how easy it was. Don't make it that easy for a real thief.

Lock it up

If you occasionally leave your patio door or screen door unlocked when you're home alone, stop this habit. Invest in dead bolts or chain locks, and keep your doors and windows locked at all times. If you have sliding doors, purchase wooden dowels or rods to go in the track along the floor so that the doors cannot be opened if the lock is removed or destroyed.

Throw strikes over the plate

The strike plate is the part of the lock attached to your wall that the dead bolt slides into. If the strike plate isn't securely anchored to the wall, a criminal can easily kick the door in, even if you have multiple locks. So buy reinforced strike plates for your doors and install them yourself—or, if you're not handy with tools, hire a locksmith to do it. Also, make sure to replace rotting wood around your door.

Shield your stuff

Keep your blinds or curtains closed. When burglars plan an attack, often they will first "case the joint," meaning that they decide in advance what they want to take based on what they can see before breaking in. If there's no way to see in, the burglar may decide to move on to another home.

Declare your possessions

Keep a household inventory of everything you own. "If you are robbed, it may be difficult to prove what belongs to

---

How Complex Can It Get?

Pity the Poor Postman, Part 2: Despite the prevalence of the Internet the typical family of four in America annually receives more than 100 catalogs, with a third or more arriving between October 1 and December 25. Most catalogs contain 40 to 140 pages. In some households, catalogs represent more than 50 percent of the mail received annually.

---

you in the event your stolen items are found. You will need sales receipts, photographs, or appraisals to prove what belongs to you," warns *USAA Life Insurance Magazine*. Contact your insurance agent or local police department to learn in advance what information they need in case you are burglarized. As the Boy Scouts say, "Be prepared."

Protect the Perimeter

Often, the simplest measures for protecting your home from intruders can be applied outdoors. Most active thieves are pretty good at assessing risk. (The ones who aren't are more likely to be in jail.) A thief will examine the security of your surroundings first before ever considering your inside possessions. If approaching your house is very difficult—because your house is illuminated by bright lights, for example—then the burglar may choose an easier target.

Buy a big dog dish

"Dogs not only seem to hear a footstep on the front porch long before you do, but usually make a lot of noise when they hear it," according to Detective J. J. Bittenbinder of the Cook County (Illinois) Sheriff's Office. "This makes even a small dog an excellent deterrent since an intruder doesn't know the dog's size . . . or, more important, its temperament."

If getting a dog isn't in your plans, Bittenbinder recommends at least buying a bowl. "Make it a big one, and leave it outside where a potential burglar can see it. The trick here is to put a doubt into the intruder's mind," he says.

Install an arf machine

Several retail electronics stores and Web sites sell a small device to hang on a doorknob inside your house. If someone attempts to turn the doorknob of your house at 3 AM, the intruder hears a recording of a dog barking furiously.

Stop the paper delivery

If you're going on vacation for a few days, suspend your mail and any newspaper subscriptions. Nothing says "nobody's home" better than five newspapers at the end of the driveway. Also, don't tell everyone that you're leaving. Selectively tell only people at work, in

---

A Nation without TV?

On average, between 103 and 108 million Americans are tuned to their television sets during prime-time hours on weekday evenings. These figures are for total viewership, including network, cable, satellite, and other television broadcast sources.

Imagine that for one hour on Monday evening and one hour on Tuesday evening, 103 million people decided to skip regular television viewing and devote that time to cleaning up sidewalks, vacant lots, and pathways in their neighborhoods, or to cleaning up their own homes. That would instantly produce 206 million work hours in just a two-day period. If these same people simply took one hour off from viewing on a Monday and Tuesday once every five weeks, that would produce 2 billion hours in a single year. At that pace, the appearance and very nature of our society would be transformed.

the neighborhood, and in your family that need to know. There's no need to let the whole town know you're not going to be home.

Put on a light show

Use as much outdoor lighting as you and your neighbors can stand. This is especially important for areas in your yard that are not well-lit from the street. Make sure that if you have a wooden fence surrounding your home, there is enough light to make the area visible from all angles.

Make commotion with a motion light

Many models of powerful, sensitive motion lights are available that will automatically light the path and grounds when anyone—friend or foe—approaches your home. Honest visitors won't be put off by this and indeed may appreciate it. Ne'er-do-wells will rapidly retreat.

Consider a home security system

If your budget allows, you may want to consider using a security system to help protect your home. Companies such as ADT, on the Web at www.homealert.com, and Honeywell, at www.firstalertprofessional.com, among others offer complete security packages, including off-site monitering.

If you can't afford a security system, a simple alternative is to install authentic-looking security system warning signs or stickers around your house. Even if you don't have a system, the thief may not make the effort to find out for sure, especially when there are less risky targets to consider.

> ### Simply Stated
>
> *Simplicity of life, even the barest, is not a misery, but the very foundation of refinement.*
>
> **—William Morris,
> English writer and artist**

The Simplest of the Simple

An easy way to keep things simple is to try a new tip each day. Here are some easy ones to start with, culled from this chapter.

- Instead of using a separate remote control for every electronic device in your home, buy a universal remote.
- After you read a magazine, throw it away or put it in the recycling bin.
- Keep an out-table beside the door for things going out the next day. Make sure the table is cleared each day.
- Make sure family and guests use coasters when placing drinks on coffee tables or furniture.
- Instead of using elaborate curtains, try decorative blinds or shades.
- Use darker fabrics and carpet in your living room and den. These hide stains and dirt.
- Try to have everyone in your family take their shoes off when they come in the house. Your carpet will live longer.
- Always keep your doors locked, even when you're at home.

A big dog makes for a great burglar alarm.

Chapter 6

Washroom Wizardry

*With These Storage, Decorating,
and Cleaning Secrets, Things Will Bubble Along*

In the 1980s, huge designer bathrooms containing everything from saunas to whirlpools were all the rage among the livin' large crowd. Now flash forward to the present, to your life, your home, and your bathroom. It's not that large, but it contains the necessities. Curiously, even though it's modest in size compared to that overblown 1980s ideal, it seems to get out of order in a hurry. Whether you have one bathroom or more, how do you simplify the bathroom and make it less cluttered and more efficient?

You may want to approach your bathroom by sections and see if each section is organized in the most constructive way possible. Can you and your family reach every item you need? Do you have to look all over the place to find what you need? Do you spend 10 minutes looking through cabinets or the medicine chest searching for an item you know you put in there a week ago? Do you have enough space in your bathroom? If not, is it possible to store some items in a closet near the bathroom?

Is your sink area cluttered with items that aren't used often by your family? What about the cabinet under the sink? Do items fall out when you open the door? Does your shower or bathtub look like the shampoo aisle in the grocery store? Perhaps it's time to reorganize.

Have you ever gotten in the shower only to have one of the 10-ounce bottles of shampoo tumble down onto your toes? Ouch! This is not the kind of wake-up you were hoping for at 6 AM.

Does cleaning the bathroom give you the creeps, not because it's so dirty, but because you have to rearrange everything in sight just to clean the countertop?

Let's examine ways to make this most personal of rooms a hassle-free haven.

About That Army of Toothpaste Tubes . . .

Your bathroom needs to be a functional refuge. It's an area where you and your family can replenish yourselves. Ideally, it should be one of the least cluttered rooms in your home. A little sorting, cleaning, and moving should do the trick and leave your bathroom in meticulous order.

Saving Space above the Sink and Beyond

If you have shelves or cabinets in your bathroom, you may think they are opportune places to store items you don't need often—or don't need at all. Space is at a premium in bathrooms, however, so reserve it for frequently used essentials only.

If you only have one bathroom, it becomes even more complicated when you have to share your space with other people. A husband may ask his wife, "Do you really need all that makeup?" A wife may ask, "Does all your shaving equipment have to stay out all day?" Then there's the all-time gender-neutral inquiry, "Do you think you could clean the mirror after you floss?"

When you're getting ready in the morning, you need space to maneuver. If there are too many things in the way, there's a greater chance you'll knock over or break things, which means you'll spend valuable time cleaning up instead of getting ready for the day. Your mission: Arrange items so that both of you have enough space and storage for the things you need.

Be a basket case

If you have no shelf space in your bathroom, you probably keep some items on or around the sink. If so, move these items to organized baskets that hang from the wall or ceiling. A small basket can be used to hold makeup, shaving cream, hair spray, and such. If you still have extra items, put another small storage basket on top of the toilet tank. In addition to saving space, these baskets add a decorative touch to your bathroom.

Hide from your guests

Hang a small cabinet over the toilet and use it to store items that you don't want visitors to see—stuff like extra rolls of toilet paper and personal hygiene products. This isn't the place for heavy items, however—they go in the cabinet under the sink.

If you don't want to hang a cabinet, pick up a tall shelving accessory that's made to fit over a toilet. It rests on the floor but reaches up to several feet over the toilet tank. Many include a small cabinet area and

one or two shelves. A great variety are available at discount stores. Again, be careful about what you store way up high: If you wouldn't want it dropping on your head from several feet up, don't store it up there in the first place.

A third alternative is to install permanent shelves over your commode. These shelves may look more stylish and take up less space than a stand-up unit. Since shelves are visible to everyone, don't overcrowd them. This is a good place to store and display colorful accessories such as plants or bubble bath gel.

Divide and conquer

Bathroom drawers get almost as messy and cluttered as kitchen drawers. Drawer dividers come in a variety of sizes, so pick up some at a discount store. Use drawer dividers to consolidate bathroom items like brushes, makeup, razors, and nail files. This is also a good place to store nail polish bottles together so they won't get knocked over.

Save Space in Strange Places

If you've taken up all of your traditional storage areas, what else can you do to save some space and make your bathroom easy to use? After all, when you're in a hurry, you want things to be at your fingertips. You don't want to paw through clutter or waste time cleaning up. So here are strategies for keeping frequently used items close at hand instead of storing them in a cabinet. That way, you'll get in and out of the bathroom in no time.

Get off on the right foot

Hang a shoe bag on the back of your bathroom door—you know, the kind that has compartments for many pairs of shoes. These bags are generally made of a mesh material that you can see through, which makes it easier to find what you're seeking. The compartments are big enough to hold soap, cotton balls, disposable razors, and such. This saves space in your cabinets and makes finding items more convenient.

> **How Complex Can It Get?**
>
> **Lip Service:** Hundreds of colors of lipstick and far more colors of fingernail polish are on the market today.

Mount an offense

Instead of keeping your hair dryer or curling iron in a cabinet, mount it on the wall. Some of these appliances come with wall mounts in the packaging. If yours did not, many hardware stores carry the appropriate equipment and some even carry wall-mountable caddies for a hair dryer, curling iron, flat iron and hot rollers. Be careful not to mount these items too close to the sink.

Socket to me

If you don't have the room to mount bathroom appliances on the wall, have an electrician install an extra bathroom-safe electrical outlet under the sink. Leave your hair dryer plugged in and stored under the sink. That way it'll always be ready for duty, and you won't have to fumble around groping for a power source. Let it cool down completely before putting it back in the cabinet.

Hook up your robe

You never know when company will drop by or when a family member is going to bring someone into the house without your knowledge. So it's wise to have a bathrobe with you in the bathroom. Purchase some plastic hooks to install on the back of the bathroom door or by the shower, and hang your robe there full-time in case you need to go undercover in a hurry.

Rack 'em up again

Most likely, when you moved into your home, there was a towel rack hanging in each of your bathrooms.

Consider adding a smaller rack above or below the existing rack. A two-tiered towel rack will allow you to hang double the amount of towels in virtually the same space. Convert all of your towel racks to the two-tiered system and you'll maximize this space in your bathroom.

Give them a yard

Designers recommend that your bathroom have 36 inches of towel rack for every family member who uses the room. That will accommodate bath towels, hand towels, and washcloths. Have a big family? Install a towel bar the entire length of one of your walls. If you have kids, make sure the towel bar has rounded edges.

Stay stocked

It's darned inconvenient if you run out of toilet paper at an inopportune moment, and it's a dreadful social gaffe if you let it happen to a guest in your home. To avoid this embarrassment, always store a second roll within easy reach in a decorative container. Keep plenty of extras in a nearby storage room or linen closet.

Keep a spoon handy

Use an extra slot in the toothbrush holder to keep a medicine spoon handy.

A Prescription for Your Medicine Chest

The medicine chest is one of the most dangerous storage areas in your home. Most contain medicines that, taken in improper dosages, can harm any family member, especially children. Often, the medicine chest also becomes a repository for out-of-date medications. That's dangerous because, over time, medicines can break down into substances that are completely different from the original drugs.

Unsure? Toss it

Author Edwin Bliss coined the popular phrase, "When in doubt, throw it out." Although he was discussing files and paperwork, the advice is no less valid when it comes to your medicine chest. If you have a prescription for a forgotten illness you had last winter, chuck the leftover pills.

Many people keep medicines on hand, reasoning that the drugs might be useful if another family member gets sick. Don't do this. It's dangerous to take medicine that was prescribed for another person or to give your medicine to someone else.

Old medicines should be disposed of as if they were toxic wastes. Keep old medicines in their child-proof containers and put them in the trash just before they are taken out for disposal. If the medicines or cosmetics are liquids put something absorbent, like kitty litter or cotton balls in the bottle so that, if the bottle breaks in the landfill, there won't be any fluids to seep into our groundwater.

Lock up the tasty stuff

Many kids' medicines taste better than they did a couple decades ago. Having children want to take their medicine, however, has an unfortunate, dangerous side effect: Children may want to check out everything in your medicine chest, especially the liquids.

To prevent them from doing this, make sure there is a childproof lock on the medicine chest. You don't want to have to take your kid to the doctor because he overdosed on cherry-flavored cold medicine.

Keep dry and cool

The heat and dampness of the bathroom can make medicines age faster. Consider storing medicines someplace else, like on a high shelf in your kitchen. If you do keep medicines in the bathroom, keep the bathroom door open, if possible, when taking hot baths or showers.

Watch What You Ingest

People between the ages of 20 and 49 are far more likely to die from poisoning than from accidents involving firearms, drowning, or suffocation, according to the National Safety Council in Washington, D.C. In fact, the average adult is six times more likely to die from accidental poisoning than from firearms. In any given year, nearly one person in 100 accidentally ingests a toxic substance.

Manage your medicinal mess

Medicine chests often hold a plethora of things, so a little organization is needed. First, don't stack things on top of each other. There's a natural law that states they're going to fall over—and into the sink—as soon as you open the door. Second, keep similar items together. Store all of your bandages together and all of your cold medicines together.

Dealing Down Under (the Sink)

If you have a cabinet of shelves under your sink, you have a built-in storage space. If you have a stand-up or wall-mounted sink with no shelves or cabinets underneath, making use of this space may require a little creativity. In either case, keeping the area under your sink organized will save you time. If you lack a cabinet or shelves under your sink, keeping this area organized will save you time.

Purchase ready-made storage

If you have a wall-mounted sink with no storage underneath, you can buy a ready-made storage system, a mini-cabinet, or a mini-set of drawers that sits on the floor and fits under the sink plumbing. Some of these systems have fold-out doors with small divided shelves to hold extra toiletries.

An alternative: Buy a set of open mini-shelving units that sits on the floor and still fits under your sink.

Store Susan below

Consider installing a Lazy Susan in the cabinet under your sink. Lazy Susans revolve 360 degrees, so you can keep your bathroom items on one and simply give it a spin to quickly reach any item. Lazy Susans are available in the kitchenware section of department stores. (No need to confess it's really for the bathroom.)

Avoid using a wooden Lazy Susan. Plastic works best in the bathroom. If shampoo, rubbing alcohol, or another product spills, the plastic will be a snap to clean.

Reserve the front row

If a shelf or a Lazy Susan is not practical for you, try this simple trick. Put the items that you use on a daily basis in the front of the under-the-sink cabinet. Keep those that you need only once or twice a week farther to the back. If you also keep towels and washcloths in your cabinet, install a divider between the towels and other items. You don't want the towels to tip over and knock everything down.

Stow supersize stuff

If there is a vanity in your bathroom, put only large items in the cabinet under the sink. Big items such as hair dryers, personal hygiene products, and toilet paper will be

easier to find, and you won't have to worry about knocking over smaller items. Keep the smaller items such as makeup in a vanity drawer.

Get wired

Buy a set of small plastic-covered wire racks for the back of the cabinet door. Store small items such as soap, razors, brushes, and other necessities there. Avoid putting heavy items in this wire rack, so you don't damage your cabinet door. Shaving cream, shampoo, and other liquid products belong in a sturdy cabinet.

Park your caddie

If you have cleaning materials that you use in the bathroom, store them there so they'll be handy. Keep them in a plastic caddie, available at discount stores, so you can move them around.

Caution: If you have children around, under-sink storage is not a good idea for your cleansers.

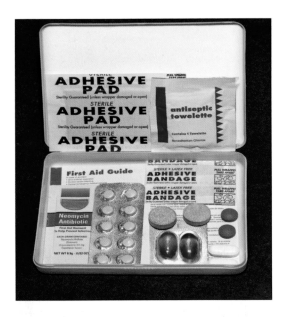

Keep first-aid first

Place a first-aid kit in a cabinet under your sink. Such a kit, available in any drugstore, is vital because most accidents occur at home. A complete first-aid kit will have everything organized and in one place. Naturally, you want to restock items as they are depleted. If you have small kids, lock the kit. If you have older children—say, eight and up—coach them on the proper use of every item in the kit.

Brush Up on Shower Power

Have you ever noticed that shampoo bottles breed? If you have a large family, you probably have observed

---

Tool Kit in a Tube

You thought it was just for brushing up your pearly whites, but here are some other ways toothpaste can help you out around the house:

- Rub a little on food stains to remove them from garments.
- Rub it on your watch crystal to reduce the visible scratches.
- Temporarily fill nail holes in dry wall.
- Use the tube as a makeshift doorstop.

---

that the bathtub and shower get cluttered posthaste. Life would be so much simpler if everyone used the same shampoos and other products. That may be hard to accomplish, but here are some other tub tactics that will bring you order and elbow room.

Collect caddies

It's likely that every member of your family has a different set of items to use in the shower. So give each person his or her own portable shower caddie to take in there at bath time. This way, three different shampoos and conditioners, two different soaps, and three different types of razors won't be spilling off the minimal shelf space. This is an especially good strategy for roommates.

Hang your sundries

If you have a small family or you live alone, a small caddie that hangs over the shower head may suffice. These devices are generally large enough to hold shampoo, conditioner, shaving cream, soap, and a razor. If you choose a hanging caddie, make sure you purchase one that fits tightly on the shower head. One that slips off easily will surprise you with an avalanche of bottles and gear.

Create tension in your bath

If you have a bathtub-shower combination, install a tension-mounted vertical storage bar. These generally have three shelves where you can store your bathroom necessities and an attachable mirror for shaving your beard in the shower. Give each family member a shelf (the top shelf going to the tallest person, naturally).

Have a bag handy to store your childrens' bath toys so they don't collect at the bottom of the tub.

Try tray chic

If you prefer soaking in the tub to taking a shower, try a bathtub tray for holding soap, razors, loofah sponges, and other lightweight items. The tray fits across the tub, with the ends of the tray resting on each side. You merely bring your bath tray along with you, get in the tub, and then place all of your bath items together on the tray. For advanced bath-tray users only: Some bath trays come equipped with reading racks that hold your books or magazines while you relax in the water.

Bag your children's toys

If bath time for your small children turns into a free-for-all with toys scattered from one end of the bathroom to another, put all the toys in a mesh bag and hang them from the bathtub faucet. There, the toys can drip dry and stay in one place. If you don't have a mesh bag, use a nylon bag that formerly held onions or potatoes.

Lay down the lids

Save your plastic lids from Pringles potato chips containers or any other plastic lid of roughly the same

dimensions. Fit one of these lids over the bottom of your shaving cream can so rust won't get on your tub or countertop.

Hit a hole in one

So your golf game is not what it used to be, or maybe it never was much to begin with? Before you get aggravated and throw away all your golf balls, Dale Burg, co-author of *Mary Ellen's Clean House*, suggests using a golf ball as a replacement for a bathtub drain plug. Since it's under the faucet, you're not likely to step on it. And, if it is dislodged, it will roll back to the drain.

> ## Make Your Bathtub a Haven
>
> Once you've stored items efficiently, cleaned, decorated, and possibly remodeled your bathroom, you deserve a real break. A good place to relax and enjoy the progress you've made in the bathroom is the bathtub. Pick a time when absolutely no one can bother you. Pack the children off to the grandparents and spend some time pampering yourself. Turning your bathtub into a totally relaxing environment is easy when you have the right equipment.
>
> **Create a whirlpool sensation.** Having your own whirlpool is easier than you might think. Catalogs and online vendors offer whirlpool units for around $200. These units attach to the side of your bathtub.
>
> Once you climb into the tub, be careful not to get so relaxed that you fall asleep. When you sit in hot water for extended periods of time, your body pumps more blood to your skin to dissipate the heat. This means that as soon as you stand up, you may get dizzy because there is less blood being pumped to your head.
>
> **Accent the aroma.** Make a relaxing atmosphere for your bath. Scented bath oils and bubble bath are a good start. Turn off the lights and fire up some candles. Take some light reading into the tub. Soft music in the background will take you away from your hectic everyday schedule.
>
> **Bubble troubles away.** Bubble baths are not only relaxing, but they simplify your life by helping to remove the soap ring around the tub. Be stingy with the amount of bubble bath you pour in the tub—the stuff from department and specialty stores can be high-priced. Try generic children's shampoo instead.
>
> **Uncoil in oil.** Always wait until the tub is full of water before adding any scented oil. The scent will evaporate more quickly if you add the oil to the bath when the water is running. Instead of spending money on expensive oils, try good old-fashioned baby oil.

Safety: The Bathroom Basics

More than 200,000 people are treated every year for bathroom-related injuries, according to homecare supplier Aurora, located in North Ridgeville, Ohio. This is not surprising when you consider all of the potential safety hazards in your bathroom. From razor blades to wet floors, the bathroom could be the most dangerous room in your home. To safeguard yourself and your family, prepare to make some changes in the bathroom. Remember, accidents are the worst kind of complexity; preventing them is a fundamental move toward simplicity.

This Is Not a Place for Slipups

Even if no one has ever been injured in your bathroom, don't take anything for granted. John Glenn was one of the original Apollo astronauts in the early '60s and the first man to orbit Earth. But his initial run for the U.S. Senate was postponed for several years after he fell in his bathtub and was injured. Anyone can slip, fall, and hurt himself in the bathroom, especially in the tub.

Foil falls

Nearly everyone has slipped in the bathtub at some point. To prevent this from happening again, install

nonslip flooring. If you have a new tub, it probably came with nonslip flooring. If not, you can purchase mats or floor decals to make the bottom of your tub less slippery.

Trade in the towel

Maybe you spread a towel on the bathroom floor to step on when you get out of the tub. Do your bones a favor: use a bath mat with nonslip backing instead. When you step on it, it won't zip out from under you like a towel may. Bath mats are inexpensive and can be tossed into the washing machine when dirty.

Head for the bar

Any hotel worth its salt contains a grab bar on the wall over the bathtub's soap dish. In homes, grab bars are usually installed only for older people. But bathtub slips and falls are an equal-opportunity disaster waiting to happen. So no matter the age of your family members, install a grab bar. It will help you pull yourself up from the bathtub, pull yourself up if you fall, or steady yourself if you're about to fall. For even more help and protection, install a grab bar outside of your tub or shower.

Get a handle on temperature control

Check the positioning of your shower faucet controls. If you have to lean into the spraying water to adjust the temperature, then sooner or later you're going to be shocked by a splash of scalding or freezing water. You could easily hurt yourself trying to get out of the way.

Shower controls should be installed close enough to the door so that you can adjust the water temperature without getting wet, recommends the National Kitchen and Bath Association, based in Hackettstown, New Jersey.

The association also recommends installing a single-handed control that adjusts both cold and hot water. Talk to a plumber or pick one up at your local hardware store.

Kids Present a Special Challenge

A tropical island may be your idea of an enticing playland. To a child, playland is the bathroom, with all of those cabinets to open, faucets to turn, and water to splash in. If you have small children or if children visit your home occasionally, then you have two choices: either supervise the kids for every moment they're in the bathroom (which would be tedious, at best, if you could manage it at all), or make your life easier by following these tips.

Turn down the heat

Turn your water heater down to no more than 115°F. This will prevent scalding should some little tyke turn on the hot water full blast. Or install temperature-limit or pressure-balanced faucets, which automatically safeguard against high temperatures.

Lock up your lavatory

If you have small kids, it's locks galore for the bathroom. On the outside of the door, install a latch that's out of reach of little hands. Inside the bathroom, locks

Have a step stool handy in the bathroom for younger children to reach the sink.

on the medicine chest, cabinets, and even the toilet will forestall dozens of potential disasters. Drop by a home improvement store to check out all of the hardware options.

Soften the edges

If anything in your bathroom has sharp corners—towel racks or counters, for instance—get busy. Sharp corners are a hazard not only for children but also for anyone else who slips and falls. You can buy towel rings that are double-tiered to replace your towel racks, and rubber molding to put around the sharp edges of a bathroom counter.

Let them see red

Paint the lids of all potentially dangerous substances bright red so children can learn to avoid those substances by the color. Stickers from poison control centers and civic organizations also warn children.

Keep a lid on it

Insist that all drugs come with childproof lids or other packaging that is difficult for children to open.

Give them a boost

Provide a sturdy step stool to safely raise your child high enough to easily reach faucets and countertops.

A Simpler Path to a Spotless Bathroom

Bathrooms are dirt magnets, regardless of how diligent you are about cleaning. Some people think that the toilet bowl is the worst thing in the home to clean. The cemented layer of dried hair spray that has settled on every bathroom surface, however, is no picnic to clean, either. Neither are the hair all over the floor and the hard-water stains in the tub. The cleaning cycle may be endless, but here are ways to make it go more smoothly.

Cleaning Tools, Straight from the Pantry

Here's a set of cleaning techniques that rely heavily on common household materials in lieu of expensive cleaning products.

Bunch up backup bags

Plastic grocery bags are about the right size to use as liners for the small wastebaskets often used in bathrooms. Simply crunch up several into a tiny ball and store them in the corner of a bathroom drawer. That way, you avoid

having to trudge back and forth to the pantry every time the basket gets full. With a fresh trash liner on hand, perhaps you'll get the chore done a little easier and a little more often.

Bleach your bathroom

One of the least expensive cleaners you can buy is nonchlorine bleach. Nonchlorine bleach whitens stains and kills bacteria. For less than $2 per half-gallon, it's tough to beat. It also kills bacteria and germs in the toilet bowl and works well when used as a mopping solution for dirty linoleum floors. (Mix ¾ cup of bleach in a gallon of water.) Avoid contact with any colored clothing, unless you want it decorated with peculiar white spots.

Arrest the rust

Here's how to remove rust stains from your tub and sink. First, rub down the stains with a sponge and a splash of lemon juice or white vinegar, then rinse. Still have a stain? As a second step, rub it with a cloth and a dab of kerosene, then rinse with soap and water.

Polish the chrome

Chrome fixtures in the bathroom can be aggravating to clean with traditional household cleaners. There always seems to be a film left after cleaning, which means you have to go back and polish the fixtures. The easiest way

to clean chrome is with isopropyl alcohol or window cleaner (which are also great for cleaning mirrors). The alcohol evaporates so you don't have to do a wipe down.

Mop your shower into submission

There's no reason to have a backache after cleaning your bathtub or shower. Use a mop to clean the floor and walls. This eliminates reaching and covers a larger area at a time. If you have stubborn stains that you need to scrub, apply this same principle but with a clean toilet bowl brush. You'll need to reach a little more, but it's better than scrubbing with a hand brush. Come to think of it, anything is better than scrubbing by hand.

Filter out the foul

Hard water comes from an excess of calcium and magnesium in the water. This leads to a variety of cleaning problems in your home, especially in your bathroom. Soap won't lather or clean as well, and the ring around the tub is more prevalent. Installing a water-softening filter will control this problem. Attach the filter directly to the plumbing underneath the sink or to the main line supplying water to your house.

Remove true grit

If you have an aluminum soap dish, you're familiar with the chalky, gritty substance that forms after the

soap has been in the dish for a while. That's corrosion caused by alkaline soap, according to the Aluminum Association, based in Washington, D.C. To prevent it, cut up a kitchen sponge to a size that will fit into the soap tray, and then lay the soap on top of that. A soapy sponge is a trillion times easier to clean than a corroding soap dish. Just make sure you replace the sponge frequently—the excess wetness can allow bacteria to build up.

Wax your shower

To prevent hard-water stains and soap scum from reforming, literally wax your shower walls. First, of course, you'll need to get the walls clean. Then, let the

walls dry completely. Apply a thin layer of any inexpensive wax to the walls, just as if you were waxing the kitchen floor. Buff the area and let it dry. The next time you shower, the water won't cling to the walls long enough to leave a deposit.

> ### The Secret Life of Petroleum Jelly
>
> Like baking soda, petroleum jelly is a product with endless uses, among them:
> - Lubricating the working elements of your toilet tank
> - Substituting for lip balm
> - Preventing rust on cooking utensils
> - Preventing rust on shovels, skate blades, skis, and the exterior trim on boats, cars, bikes, and motorcycles
> - Protecting windows when painting window frames

Have a good rubdown

Wear rubber gloves when you use any type of cleaning product. If you don't have any, however, rub your hands and arms with petroleum jelly for protection. Petroleum jelly or a heavy lotion such as udder ointment will repel the water and shield your arms and hands (unless the cleaner is especially strong). An added perk is that after you're done cleaning, your hands and arms will be silky soft.

Spread it around

Take just a few minutes out of the middle of your week to clean your sink. The next day, give the toilet a once-over. Your bathroom will look nice throughout the week, and there will be less grit and grime to deal with when it is time for your weekend cleaning.

Be Victorious with Vinegar

Versatile vinegar is used for so many tasks around the home that it's surprising it doesn't have its own appointment secretary. Vinegar is an inexpensive weak acid that not only wakes up a salad but also is particularly handy for cleaning in bathrooms and kitchens. When you can use one common substance in lieu of a dozen expensive commercial products, well, that's simplicity indeed. Here's how to perform miracles with vinegar in your home.

Free your showerhead

If you have hard water, minerals can build up in your showerhead and clog the holes. Remove the showerhead and soak it overnight in a container of vinegar. If you have particularly hard water or if it's been a while since you've cleaned the head, you'll probably need to repeat the procedure.

Take your vinegar straight up

To remove soap scum from a shower door or wall, apply straight vinegar to the surface and then wipe it down.

Clean your tile every blue moon

Ceramic tile is versatile and durable for the bathroom. You don't have to clean it much, and when you do, all you need is bleach and vinegar. Clean the grout first. Scrub the grout with bleach (mix ¾ cup of bleach in a gallon of water) and rinse well. Next, use undiluted vinegar to clean your tile. Then rinse the tile and dry. If there is streaking, you may have to buff the tile. Remember to wear gloves.

Make your washer do the scrubbing

If your shower curtain has layers of soap scum built up on it, don't throw it out. Toss it into the washing machine along with some towels to provide scrubbing action. Wash this load with your regular detergent, plus a half-cup of baking soda. At the start of the rinse cycle, add a cup of vinegar. Stop your washer after the rinse cycle and hang the curtain up on its rod to dry.

Simply Stated

If you want a golden rule that will fit everybody, this is it: Have nothing in your houses that you do not know to be useful or believe to be beautiful.

**—William Morris,
English artist and writer**

Simple Solutions for Bathroom Decor

You probably spend 30 minutes or more in your bathroom each day. So it's worth it to make your bathroom a pleasant, attractive, inspiring, and supportive environment. Even though your bathroom is probably one of the smallest rooms in your home, it can be one of the most challenging to decorate.

In Search of a Soft Touch

Now that you're a master at saving space, you'll probably have a little more room to work with. Your bathroom may appear hard, glossy, and unworkable. Wallpaper may jump to mind, but you can soften the look with less effort, too. How? My dear Watson, simply accentuate what you have.

Reflect on yourself

Mirror, mirror, on the wall, how can this room appear less small? Install another mirror and your small bathroom will instantly look larger. The smaller your bathroom, the more difficult it is for two people to maneuver in it, and that's exactly what they'll have to do in a one-bathroom household. Another mirror will give two people more room to get ready. Mirrors are relatively inexpensive as long as you stay with one that's not fancy.

Create a mini-jungle

Most plants will flourish in the humidity of the bathroom. You can arrange your plants near a window, on a high shelf where they won't be in your way, or hanging from a

Storing items in a shelf over the toilet frees up valuable space in your cabinets.

ceiling hook. Plants are an inexpensive way to decorate, but don't pack the potting soil all the way up to the top of the pot. Fill the pot only to about an inch from the top so soil doesn't sprinkle out when you move or water the plant. You don't want to have something else to clean up.

See the light

You may have already discovered that a single overhead light fixture is not the best source of illumination for putting on makeup or for shaving, because it can cast shadows on the face. For the best lighting, install incandescent light fixtures on the same wall as the mirror you're using. That way, the light comes more directly toward you and shadows are eliminated.

Ditch the decorative soap

Avoid putting fancy soaps out in the bathroom for decoration. Usually they serve no purpose and sit around collecting dust. The most popular ones seem to be the seashell-shape soaps. If you want seashells in your bathroom, go to the beach and bring some back to put in your bathroom.

Close the library

Magazines and other reading material in your bathroom take up valuable space that you may need for storing necessities. Moreover, reading while attempting to take care of personal business is not a desirable combination. Doctors routinely advise not prolonging your stay on the toilet seat unless, of course, you're a major shareholder in the company that produces Preparation H.

If you insist on reading while you're in the bathroom, take the reading materials in with you and bring them out with you.

Make it final with vinyl

If you have wallpaper in your bathroom, you may have noticed that it's curling at the edges or developing a bad case of mildew. Vinyl is a viable alternative. Vinyl wall covering looks the same as wallpaper, but it's sturdier and easier to clean.

Hang vinyl wallpaper in your bathroom for easy cleaning and upkeep.

How Complex Can It Get?

Decisions, Decisions . . . More than 1,400 varieties of shampoo and more than 2,000 skin care products are currently on the market. Sometimes it seems like every one of them is jammed into your bathtub area.

Powder Room Powerhouses

You don't replace water fixtures or remodel the entire bathroom every day, so when you do make changes, the potential for making expensive mistakes is enormous. To take the worry and waste out of any bathroom project, contact these helpful organizations.

- The National Association of the Remodeling Industry, www.Nari.org
- The National Kitchen and Bath Association, www.nkba.org
- The Tile Council of America, www.tilesusa.com
- American Home Lighting Institute, www.americanlightingassociation.com
- Kohler Company, www.kohler.com

When It's Time to Make Big Changes

Do you have gobs of money? Can you afford to install a whirlpool tub large enough to hold all the neighbors? If not, then the next time you remodel your bathroom, you'll want to keep to a tight budget and make your new bathroom as efficient and ergonomic as possible. These tips will help you achieve lasting durability, economy, and easy cleaning.

Tile with style

Ceramic tile is durable, easy to clean, and comes in a variety of textures and colors. To make your bathroom appear bigger, use larger tiles on the walls and floors. (Psst! This will also save you a lot of cleaning time since there will be less grout to clean.)

Single out your sink

A double sink sounds enticing but ultimately takes up too much space in your bathroom. If you have any say in the design of your bathroom, stay with a single sink. There won't be too many times when two people will need the sink at the same time. Besides, two sinks crowd your bathroom and present you with more to clean.

Go with adequate flow

Is your bathroom ventilation fan tough enough for the job? Your ventilation fan should be able to change over the air

in your bathroom at least eight times in an hour, according to the Home Ventilating Institute. If your ventilation fan falls short, you'll have more of a mildew problem.

And speaking of ventilation fans, did you know they are rated for the noise they produce? Strike a blow for peace and quiet by picking a fan with a low noise rating.

Deter the mildew

Even with a ventilation fan, your bathroom can be a damp place. So choose wall coverings that will deter mildew formation. Oil-based paints are traditionally used because of their durability and ease in cleanup. However, mildew-resistant latex-based paints are widely available, and some are as durable as oil-based paints.

Privatize your panes

Avoid using nice fabric curtains or shades in the bathroom. They're too likely to stay wet and grow mildew. Instead, install plastic mini blinds or shades. They're easy to wipe clean and are more durable. Buy

a kind that creates the most thorough visual barrier possible—no need to unknowingly put on a show for the neighbors.

Make a Splash with Conservation

We all need to do more to protect Earth's resources for future generations. Most newer bathroom fixtures and equipment are made with water conservation in mind. Not only will this help the planet but it will also help you save money on your water and electric bills. In some areas of the country, you can get an additional credit from your electric company for using water-conserving devices.

Here are simple and easy ways to conserve water.

Let the force be with you

Traditional toilets can use up to five gallons of water per flush. That's a lot of wasted water down the drain. So the next time you remodel, buy an ultra-low-flush toilet—they use approximately 1½ gallons per flush. These toilets offset the lack of water by generating greater water velocity. Such water-saving devices can also be installed on older toilets.

Spread the spray

If you have an old showerhead, pick up one of the newer water-conserving models. A federal law years back reduced the maximum flow rate of a shower faucet from 3.4 gallons per minute to 2.5 gallons per minute. The problem, of course, is to reduce the flow of water without noticeably lowering the water pressure when you take a shower. This is partly accomplished through the use of fine mesh wires and aerators that spread the water droplets over a larger distance. Be careful when purchasing showerheads, though. A larger showerhead doesn't necessarily mean more water pressure.

Some Squeaky-Clean Advice

For decades, soap advertisers have targeted people with dry skin, oily skin, sensitive skin, and, of course, the few who have "normal" skin. Is all this necessary? There are many different types of soap on the market, but they all share a common purpose—to clean your skin. Here are a few easy ways to select the right soap:

Go solo on the soap. Unless you have extremely sensitive skin on your face, you can use the same soap for your face as you do for the rest of your body. Face soaps are marketed as having more moisturizing ability than other soaps, and this may be true. Many women, however, put moisturizers on their faces after showering, anyway. Hence, a different type of soap isn't necessary. Buying extra soap wastes your money and takes up space in the shower.

Use soap with additives. If you have sensitive skin, stay away from pure soaps. These soaps are so pure they have no glycerin additives to keep moisture in your skin, which can lead to irritation. The more additives a soap has, however, the less effective the soap is at cleaning. For normal skin, stay with fragrance-free soap to maximize cleaning.

Beat down bacteria. Many people prefer deodorant and anti-bacterial soaps. This can be a problem for sensitive skin because both types of soap tend to dry out the skin. Deodorants mask odor with fragrance. Anti-bacterial soap eliminates the bacteria that causes the odor. So if you work out heavily, an anti-bacterial soap may your ticket—followed by some moisturizing lotion.

Find a good bar. Save your money and buy bar soaps. Liquid soaps are more expensive than bar soaps and don't last as long. Although there is an advantage with liquids—there is no mess in the soap dish to clean—you're wasting too much money on a product that is mostly water.

Winnin' with Linen

If you've optimized your bathroom storage space and you still have some essential items without a home, what do you do with them? Perhaps you have an adjacent or nearby linen closet. If your linen closet looks more like a stuffing ground for every towel, washcloth, set of sheets, and bathroom item you've had since yesteryear, you need to roll up your sleeves and start cleaning out.

Terrific Towel Tactics

Generally, avoid putting anything in your linen closet other than towels, linens, and extra bathroom items. The linen closet has a specific function, which doesn't include serving as the household catchall. The linen closet's function is to store your linens and bathroom accessories in an organized manner so all you need to do is open the door, and behold, everything you need is at your fingertips. A secondary function is to house any essential bathroom items that can't comfortably be contained in your bathroom. Since the bathroom organizing fairy will not be stopping at your house, it's up to you to make sure that your linen closet is in order.

Put each in reach

Avoid stowing towels or other frequently used items on high shelves. Short people and smaller children will have trouble reaching them. It also makes it difficult to return laundered towels to the closet if you have to stretch and strain to reach the right shelf. If people are going to retrieve towels and washcloths from the linen closet every other day or so, it makes sense to have them be accessible to everyone who needs them.

Roll your own

Store all towels of the same size together, and instead of folding them and stacking towels on top of each other, roll your towels in jelly-roll fashion. Folding and stacking towels is slow and takes up too much space. High piles always tip over, which leaves you with a refolding job. Rolling your towels is fast, prevents them from tipping over, and actually saves space. You can store many more rolled towels in a given space than you can folded towels.

Thereafter, carry the dirty clothes to the laundry room often. You don't want your clean towels to smell like dirty clothes.

A Quick Linen System That Works

Getting housework done as quickly as possible will free you up to do other things that you enjoy, like working on hobbies or spending more time with your family or friends. One place to save oodles of time is your linen system. Here's how to get washed linens and towels put away pronto.

Signify one storage space

Set aside a specific area for each type of item in your linen closet. One shelf could be allotted for sheet sets, one shelf for large bath towels, and so on. Avoid placing things "anywhere." If you keep the same spots designated for certain items, finding these items will be easier and putting away clean linens will take less time.

Tuck in your sheets

If you want your sheets to stay together, you should make sure they lay together. That is, group your sheets according to which room they're used in. In addition, keep the pillowcases and flat sheet tucked inside the fitted sheet. That way, you won't have to grope around looking for the parts of a set.

Become more well-rounded

When storing your sheet sets, store them with the spine of the fold facing out. In other words, you want the rounded middle part facing you instead of the edges. If the edges are facing you, it's hard—maddening, actually—to figure out how many sheet sets you're taking.

Send your sheets to bed

On wash day, strip your bed, wash and dry the sheets, and return them directly to the same bed. Bypass the linen closet altogether. This way, you'll save time by not having to get a clean pair of sheets out of the closet and not having to put the set that you recently washed back into the closet. The newly laundered set will go straight to the bed.

Simplest of the Simple

Here are the simplest of this chapter's simple ideas for saving time, money, and energy while managing your bathroom:

- Use drawer dividers in your bathroom to organize your sundries.

Get high with extras

Ideally, all of your bathroom supplies will be kept in the bathroom. Sometimes, however, extra items have to go in other places. Keep extras on a higher shelf, since you won't be reaching for those every day. The highest shelf of your linen closet, for instance, is a good place to store extra rolls of toilet paper and tissues.

Encourage others to strip

Place a laundry basket in the bottom of your linen closet. This is a good way to keep dirty clothes where they're supposed to be instead of on the floor. Your family won't have to go far with their dirty clothes when they shower.

How Complex Can It Get?

Not a Drop to Drink: In early 2010, 1.2 billion of the 6.9 billion people on the planet had no access to drinking water that would be considered clean by U.S. standards. Also, one person in 15 lived in an area defined as water-stressed or water-scarce, although the water that was available was clean. By 2025, this number could rise to one in three people.

- Mount a hook on the back of the bathroom door or near the shower to hang your bathrobe.
- Treat old medicines as if they were toxic waste.
- Hang a shower caddie.
- Install nonslip flooring in your bathtub and shower.
- Keep bleach and vinegar on hand for inexpensive bathroom cleaning.
- Don rubber gloves when you clean, or apply petroleum jelly to your hands and arms.
- Wash with bar soap instead of liquid soap. (It's less expensive.)
- Decorate your bathroom with plants.
- Use generic children's shampoo instead of expensive bubble bath.
- On wash day, bypass the linen closet altogether. Strip your bed, wash and dry the sheets, and return them directly to the same bed.

Chapter 7

Bedroom Basics

Smart Strategies to Create
the Perfect Setting for Slumber

Bedrooms apparently aren't just for sleeping anymore. These days, they serve as entertainment centers, studies, storage areas, and dressing rooms. Yours may even double as an office, especially if you have a small home.

The more elements of life you incorporate into your bedroom, the more complicated your bedroom becomes. You have more items to keep track of and to clean. If you use your bedroom as a study or an office, you may not be able to relax because you're constantly exposed to your work area and all of the unfinished business stacked up there.

More than any of the other rooms in your home, your bedroom needs to be a sanctuary. You need to take steps to protect this sacred turf—to preserve it as your space for relaxation and slumber (and, of course, the occasional romantic interlude). If you have a family, your bedroom may well be the only room that is uniquely yours. Do with it what makes you happy.

If your bedroom is disheveled and in disarray, with clothes lying in every corner and stuff stacked on every available surface, you need to engineer a complete overhaul. Simplifying your room may mean doing away with some of the extraneous objects you keep there. Remember, this is the room you want and need to relax in.

By using the tips in this chapter, you can simplify your bedroom and turn it into a haven of respite and rejuvenation. Think of it as your own in-home hideaway.

Soothing by Design

The golden rule of bedroom decor is this: If some identifiable item causes you worry or stress, remove it. If some identifiable item comforts you, leave it.

For instance, keeping your paperwork in your bedroom for convenience can become a complication if looking at it makes you uneasy. Transferring your work to a spare room (if you have one) can enhance your peace of mind and make you feel less stressed.

On the other hand, if reading helps you to relax before you go to sleep, then keeping a selection of books and magazines in your bedroom makes sense. In this case, convenience works to your advantage.

An Enticing Atmosphere

The next time you walk into your bedroom, imagine that you're a guest who has never seen the room before. Would you arrange the furniture the way you have it? Do you find the decorations inviting and comforting?

If you think your bedroom is suitable as is, congratulations—you're one of the lucky few. If not, use the following tips to create a more enticing sleep space.

Become a trailblazer

Walking around furniture to get from one part of the bedroom to another is time-consuming and difficult. Rearrange the furniture in a way that saves you time and energy. Establish a clear, unobstructed path from the entrance of your bedroom to the closet or bathroom (if you have one in your bedroom), says Dale Burg, coauthor of *Mary Ellen's Clean House*. Avoid positioning the bed in a way that causes you to have to circumnavigate it to get to your closet or bathroom. The same rule applies to your dresser or chest of drawers.

Let there be light

Good overhead lighting is essential in the bedroom, especially if you get dressed there. You have to see what you're doing. Otherwise, you won't know until you get to work that you're wearing one black sock and one blue one.

You should have access to sufficient lighting with the flick of a wall switch. You don't want to walk over to your nightstand to turn on a lamp every time you enter your bedroom. If you prefer, you can install a dimmer switch, which will enable you to adjust the amount of light in the room to suit any purpose or mood.

Make yourself at home

For your walls and furnishings, choose colors and patterns that feel warm and welcoming. Something as simple as a fresh coat of paint or a wallpaper border can alter the entire ambiance of your bedroom. Blues, greens, and other hues drawn from nature seem especially relaxing to many people.

While you are at it, consider investing in replacements for dated or worn-out furnishings such as bedspreads and decorative pillows. Even minor changes like these can transform your bedroom into a place where you want to spend more time.

Windows: An Open and Shut Case

During the day, if you're stuck indoors, a window can provide a feeling of freedom and space. At night, when you want to sleep, a window can be a hindrance of sorts. It lets in light, though most people tend to sleep best in dark rooms.

The following strategies can help you outfit your bedroom windows in a way that's flattering yet functional.

Hanging shelves give extra storage and display space while ceiling fans help with air circulation.

Seek shade

Whether you sleep during the day or at night, light can penetrate your windows, even with the curtains drawn. A full moon or a neighbor's backyard light can make falling asleep nearly impossible. Hang blackout shades, either by themselves or underneath drapes. They come in a variety of colors and styles and are easy to clean. They'll keep almost all of the light out of your bedroom.

Play matchmaker

Pair your shades or blinds with valances instead of curtains. At discount stores, this ensemble will cost you less than $15. Most valances are machine-washable, so they're easy to maintain.

Decorating Made Easy

The following items make indispensable, functional additions to your bedroom furnishings:

- Plastic shades are inexpensive alternatives to fabric shades. When they get dirty, you can take them down and hose them off outside, unlike fabric shades, which have to be dry-cleaned.
- An out-table in the bedroom serves the same function as an out-table near the front door. Keep everything you need for the next day on the table so you don't forget clothing that needs to be dry-cleaned, the library books that need to be returned, and so on.
- A freestanding makeup mirror on the dresser serves the same purpose as a vanity. Plus, it's cheaper, and it takes up less space than having both a dresser and a vanity.

Essential Equipment

Simplifying your bedroom involves arranging the room so that it's easy for you to live there. Use this as your gauge when deciding what stays and what goes (to another room or out in the garbage). Here are a few essentials that no bedroom should be without.

Unplug your alarm

An electric alarm clock can fail in the middle of the night for a variety of reasons, ranging from a power surge to a power outage. A small battery-powered timepiece may run for as long as a year before the battery needs replacement. Wake up on time. Don't miss that important appointment.

See yourself as you are

Even if you have a mirror attached to your dresser, chances are that it doesn't give you a head-to-toe view. Hang a stylish full-length mirror on your closet door. That way, you can give yourself a quick once-over after you've dressed. A mirror makes your bedroom appear larger, too.

Set up a screen

A large decorative screen, set across one corner of your bedroom, adds flair while serving a function. You can stand behind the screen to get dressed rather than risk someone walking in on you and catching you in your skivvies. Also, you can hang your outfit for the next day on the back of the screen, where it's hidden but easily accessible.

Allergy-Proofing Your Bedroom

If you have allergies, your bedroom is the one room that can seriously aggravate them. And because you sleep there,

you are probably spending more time in your bedroom than anywhere else in your home. By keeping your windows closed all the time and following these few helpful hints, you can allergy-proof your bedroom and sleep easier.

Eliminate dust-catchers

Your bedroom houses some of the most effective dust-catchers in your home. A canopy over your bed

Wash all bed linens, including mattress pads, to keep your bedroom clean and fresh.

attracts dust, and the dust tends to stay there because a canopy isn't often cleaned. Your mattress and box spring also act as dust magnets. Avoid using a canopy in your bedroom, and frequently vacuum your mattress and box spring. Consider a mattress cover and pillowcases that block dust mites. Some companies make these out of tightly woven organic cotton that is free of chemicals.

Pick the right pillow

Foam pillows have become all the rage for people who are allergic to down-filled types. You may need to go one step further than that and invest in Dacron polyester–filled pillows. They are more durable than traditional foam and won't get moldy, as some foam pillows can when exposed to dampness.

Vacuum with a vengeance

If you vacuum your home just once a week, consider adding a session or two just for your bedroom—and especially under your bed. Make sure your vacuum cleaner is in good condition so dirty air won't pollute your bedroom and do more harm than good. If your allergies are especially severe, outfit your vacuum cleaner with a HEPA (high-efficiency particulate air) filter, which traps even the smallest of irritants. A HEPA filter costs more than a regular filter, but it will pay for itself in the long run.

Close the door on kitty

Cats and dogs have dander—small pieces of dead skin, similar to human dandruff. Cat dander, in particular, can trigger allergies in some people. If you have a cat or a dog that lives indoors, brush and bathe it frequently and keep it out of your bedroom. Bathing won't catch all of the dander and certainly won't get rid of all the shedded hair.

After you've cleaned your bedroom, close the door immediately. That way, there's less chance of a pet running in and contaminating the air.

Add a strip of security

Along with keeping your bedroom door closed, consider installing weather stripping on it. This will prevent bugs and most dust mites from floating into your bedroom. It will also keep cigarette smoke and other irritants out of the room.

Preparing for Guest Appearances

When you have houseguests, you want to make them feel as comfortable as possible. This means providing them with a clean and cozy place to call home—at least for a few days. You can do so simply, without a lot of fuss and expense. Here's how.

> **Simply Stated**
>
> *He who sleeps in continual noise is awakened by silence.*
> —**William Dean Howells, American author**

Give them your old bed

If you're planning to replace your mattress and box spring, don't give away the old set if it's in suitable condition. Put it in your guest room instead. It's certainly adequate for use on a few occasions each year.

If you don't have a bed to put in your guest room, ask family members and friends if they have one that you could take off their hands.

Make a blanket statement

The guest bedroom is the perfect place to store extra blankets and pillows. Your guests will need them anyway, so keeping them where they're convenient makes sense. Plus, these items won't take up space in your own bedroom closet.

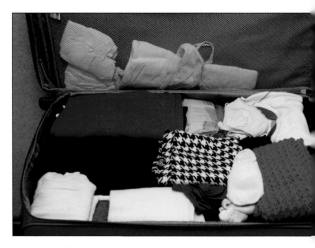

If you travel often, having a spare set of clothes makes packing a breeze.

Equip the closet

Although your guests probably won't stay long enough to hang too many clothes in the closet, make sure that they have plenty of hangers to use. In fact, the guest room closet is a good place to store your extra hangers so they won't clutter your own closet.

Let them reflect upon themselves

Install a mirror in the guest bedroom to prevent your guests from traveling to your room to use your mirror after they've dressed. This allows you and your guests to maintain some privacy.

Move in the heavy equipment

If you have a treadmill or a small weight machine, you may want to store it in the guest bedroom. It gives your guests something to do during their visit, and it gets the equipment out of your bedroom, where it's probably in the way. Make sure the machine is located appropriately and is in good condition so your guests won't hurt themselves.

Cut back on cleaning

When your guest room is not in use, save yourself time and effort by not cleaning it as often as you do the rest of the house. That's not to say you should ignore it. But since you probably don't have as much furniture or as many accessories in that room, it won't catch as much dust. Clean your guest bedroom once a month and, of course, right before guests arrive.

A Place for Everything

The American humorist Will Rogers reportedly once said, "Buy land. They ain't makin' any more of this stuff." In your bedroom, the following corollary applies: conserve space, especially when you can't make any more of it.

Stand by Your Bed

A nightstand is almost a necessity in the bedroom. Where else are you going to put personal items that you may need throughout the night, such as tissues or cough medicine? Also, if you need an alarm clock to wake you in the morning, a nightstand is the most convenient place for it. (If the alarm doesn't rouse you, it may rouse your mate. If it's on the nightstand, then at least your spouse won't have to crawl out of bed to shut it off while you're sleeping soundly.)

So what makes the ideal nightstand? Here's what to look for.

Take it lying down

Ideally, a nightstand should be no taller than the top of your mattress. This gives you a clear line of vision while you're lying down, in case you want to look at your clock or reach for a tissue. In fact, for this reason, you may want a nightstand that's a few inches lower than the top of your mattress.

Don't go drawerless

Make sure the nightstand beside your bed has at least one drawer. You'll need it for personal items that you may use in the middle of the night or for items that you don't want other members of your family to see. A drawer is a good place to stash a book or magazine so you can read before dozing off.

Use a stand-in

Instead of a traditional nightstand, you may want to place a small wicker chest or cedar chest beside your bed. It can be used to store items such as a book, tissues, and perhaps an extra set of sheets for your bed. If you don't have a chest of drawers or a dresser in your bedroom, you can use the chest for storing underwear and other small clothing items.

Lose the lamps

If you want extra lighting by your bed, install track lighting or wall-mounted lights that you can aim wherever you want. These fixtures provide directed light, so you won't bother your sleeping mate if you are reading. Doing away with traditional bedside lamps also means having one fewer accessory to move when you're dusting.

Drawer-ing the Line

If you haven't cleaned out your drawers lately, there's no telling what you may find. In fact, you may have reached the point where you can't find anything, so you just buy more stuff to replace the stuff you already own. If you have to share drawer space with your significant other, your clothing undoubtedly intermingles. You end up wearing each other's shirts, T-shirts, and socks.

On the other hand, if your drawers are in tiptop shape, you can save time getting dressed in the morning. Get organized with these strategies.

Give them the old heave-ho

Go through your drawers and remove all of the clothes that you don't wear. Then put these items in a box and give them to a family member, a friend, or a charity. If you find socks that have holes in them, throw them out or use them as dust rags. Whatever you do, remove them from your drawers.

Set boundaries

Designate the chest of drawers as yours and the dresser as your partner's (or vice versa). If this isn't practical because one of you needs more drawer space than the other, or if you have only one piece of furniture, designate specific drawers for each person. Stick with this arrangement so that your clothes don't get mixed up.

Group like items

Put all of your underwear in one drawer, all of your casual clothes in another, and so on. If you have some items that you wear more often than others, keep these near the top of their respective piles. You can quickly grab them when you open your drawers.

While My Pretty One Sleeps

Your body temperature is not a constant 98.6 °F. Over the course of 24 hours, it varies by about 1.8 °F in a predictable pattern that is controlled by your body's internal pacemaker, its biological clock.

Changes in body temperature correspond most closely to the peaks and valleys of performance. "When your temperature is lowest, performance is also lowest," says Phyllis Zee, MD, PhD, a neurologist who directs the sleep disorders program at Northwestern University Medical School in Chicago. You'll notice dips in overall alertness, memory, and problem-solving ability as well as in physical coordination. Becoming attuned to your body's clock can help you make the most of every moment of the day.

7 AM Sexual power is at its peak. Despite the age-old tradition of sex just before sleep, you're probably more sexually aroused in the early morning.

8 AM You're feeling no pain. People tend to tolerate pain best between 8 PM and 8 AM. So you might want to schedule that dentist appointment for early morning, when your pain threshold is highest.

10 AM Mental skills begin to rise. Between now and noon is the best time to attack a challenging project or to make that pitch for a raise.

12 PM Brain power takes a nosedive. Contrary to popular belief, this postlunch slump probably can't be blamed on your midday meal. Scientists aren't sure what prompts it. The dip comes on even though temperature is curving upward.

3 PM Alertness returns as the post-lunch slump finally begins to loosen its grip.

4 to 5 PM The best time for exercise. Muscle tone is at its peak at this time of the day.

6 PM Pain sensitivity increases.

7 PM Allergy problems are at their most severe. Twelve hours later, at 7 AM, the same dose of the same allergy-relief medicine works twice as long.

8 PM Last call for alcohol. Now is the time to stop drinking booze if you want to sleep soundly during the night.

Go on a roll

You can store many more articles of clothing in your dresser or chest of drawers by rolling them instead of folding them. Rolling works best with T-shirts and knit items. Fold the sleeves of your T-shirts in, then roll from the bottom. Besides freeing up more drawer space, rolling minimizes wrinkling. This technique also works well with bulky sweat suits.

Take a lot off the top

If you have a chest of drawers or a dresser/mirror combination in your bedroom, clear off the top surface. Photos, jewelry, knickknacks, or—let's call it what it is—outright junk may eat up usable surface space. What's more, these items collect dust, and they create more work when you clean, because you have to move them around.

If you keep piling things on your dresser, they'll eventually reach a point where they're obscuring the mirror. You'll have to go in the bathroom or to another room to get a good look at yourself.

Add an armoire

The versatile armoire—basically, a freestanding closet—can serve a variety of purposes in your bedroom. Some have rods for hanging your clothes, with drawers underneath for foldable items such as underwear, T-shirts, and sweaters. Others are designed as entertainment centers.

If you must have a television in your bedroom, an armoire is a perfect place for it. You can close the door so the set doesn't become dusty and dirty.

When brand-new, an armoire can set you back hundreds or even thousands of dollars. You may be able to purchase an unfinished one relatively inexpensively at a flea market or an auction.

Invest in a chest

If you have room, consider putting a cedar chest at the end of your bed to store clothing that you seldom wear or that is out of season. This frees up space in your drawers and closets and saves you from having to pack your clothes in boxes stashed around your home. The chest also adds a nice decorative touch to your bedroom. If you prefer, you can use it to store items besides clothing.

Simply Stated

Time is a circus always packing up and moving away.
—Ben Hecht, American journalist and screenwriter

How Complex Can It Get?

Where Does All this Stuff Come From? In the United States, the typical bedroom prior to the 1940s was threadbare compared with the typical bedroom of today. Back then, people hadn't yet heard of television sets, let alone stereos and CD players. Most folks had fewer than half the articles of clothing that most of us have today, and they each had a few pairs of shoes at best. Bedrooms of 1840 and, indeed, 1740, contained a fraction of the items found in the modern bedroom.

Go Ahead—Be Shelve-ish

Sometimes the bedroom becomes a dumping ground for trinkets that have no other place in the home. In the bedroom, they're hidden from guests and out of the reach of children.

To simplify your bedroom, most tchotchkes should be tossed . . . chucked . . . deep-sixed. As for those you can't bear to part with, keep them from cluttering your space with these strategies.

Set them on shelves

If you have photos or other items that you want to display in your bedroom, consider mounting a few shelves on your walls for this purpose. The items will be visible but out of your way. Just remember: The more you have on display, the more you have to dust. So don't overload your shelves with too much.

Establish a personal library

If you do most of your reading in bed and if you have the space, build or purchase a bookcase for your bedroom. By keeping your reading materials close by, you'll save time and energy by not having to search the entire house at bedtime for a particular book or magazine.

Make Your List and Check It Twice

If you're moving into a new home or if you simply want to rearrange your current home, consider these issues before deciding which bedroom to designate as your own:

- Is the room for one person or to be shared?
- How close is it to the bathroom/toilet?
- Is the room to have a second purpose?
- How much storage space do you need?
- Do you want built-in or freestanding storage?
- Do you want a separate dressing room?
- Does the room catch the sun in the morning or evening? Or does it get no sunlight at all?
- Do you prefer to awaken in a dark or bright room?
- Is the room quiet, or will you need heavy curtains and carpet to reduce noise?
- What kind of flooring do you want?
- Are there enough electrical outlets near the bed?
- Is there a switch near the bed to control all of the lighting?

Closet Cleanup

You know this sitcom gag: Some hapless Harry opens a closet door and instantaneously finds himself buried under a big pile of stuff. Canned laughter ensues.

In real life, of course, we're not nearly as amused when we find ourselves standing knee-deep in sweaters or shoeboxes that have tumbled from a closet shelf. Even worse than having things fall at our feet is not being able to find what we're looking for.

Assembling Accessories

Organizing your closet takes some effort. But once you're done, your closet space will be infinitely easier to navigate. You'll save several minutes just selecting your outfit each day.

One of the first steps you can take to simplify your closet is to gather up all the non-clothing items: ties, belts, shoes, and anything else that may be hung up haphazardly or parked on the floor. What do you do with them? The following tips should provide some answers.

Get hooked up

Instead of throwing your belts on the closet floor or stashing your ties in a drawer, screw a few C-hooks into the closet wall. (These hooks actually look like Cs or cup

handles.) Hang your belts and ties on the hooks, and you won't have to search through a tangle of belts for the right one or iron the tie that was smashed between the 10 you never wear.

Put your footwear in its place

Ready-made shoe caddies or shoe bags are available in most discount stores. You can hang the shoe bag on the closet wall or on the back of the closet door. If you use a shoe bag made of a mesh material, you can see which shoes are in which compartment, so they're easier to find.

Replace the chardonnay with sandals

A wine rack is perfect for stowing away shoes. It's certainly better than a closet floor that looks like a shrine to Imelda Marcos.

> ### Simply Stated
>
> *To every thing there is a season, and a time to every purpose under the heaven.*
> **—Ecclesiastes 3:1**

Use a wine rack to store your shoes in your closet.

What the Fashionable Closet Wears

Once you've taken care of the miscellaneous items, you're ready to tackle your clothes. Lots of nifty gadgets can help you get your wardrobe in order, even if you have precious little closet space.

Give yourself more room

A closet organizer can make the most of minimal space. One with wire shelves is best because it allows air to circulate between all of your garments. Buy only the smallest one that you need. Any extra shelves are bound to quickly fill up with junk. You can find closet organizers in most discount stores.

Make your clothes go round

If you and your partner share a closet, an electric (or manual) carousel can make finding clothes easy—provided the closet has enough room to accommodate one. Just flip a switch, and your wardrobe appears right before you. Flip the switch again, and your partner's wardrobe moves to the front. No more digging through racks and piles of clothes to find just the item you're looking for. You can buy clothing carousels in home furnishing stores and some home improvement stores.

> ### Walls with Verve
>
> If the ambiance in your bedroom leaves you uninspired, a little redecorating may do the trick. One of the easiest ways to significantly alter the look of any room without spending a lot of money is to use a painting technique that gives the walls texture. Here are a few to try.
>
> *Rag-rolling:* Bunch and press a rag in different directions over wet base paint. You achieve a soft and mottled texture—the appearance of crushed velvet.
>
> *Sponging:* Choose any size sea sponge and soak it with paint. Dab a new color over your wall's base paint in any pattern you prefer.
>
> *Stippling:* Press a small, hard-bristled stippling brush into wet glaze. When you lift the brush, it removes particles of the glaze. This creates the effect of tiny, delicate freckles over an even base.

Procure poles

Install an extra rod or dowel on which to hang clothes. You can position the rod side by side with the original one or hang one from the other. They'll keep your and your partner's wardrobes separate so you're not looking through your mate's clothes for a shirt you know you

You probably have your fair share of clothes that no longer fit or that have gone out of style (and have no chance of making a comeback). The following guidelines can help you decide what goes and what stays—and can create a more user-friendly closet in the process.

Discard the duds

Worn or outdated clothes simply take up space in your closet. If you're enterprising, have a yard sale and try to make a few bucks off your castaways. Or you can donate them to an organization that collects clothes for the needy, such as Goodwill.

Identify the misfits

An unhealthy attachment to an old prom dress is suspect. So is holding on to a pair of jeans that is two sizes too small. Even though you probably don't need to keep these things, if you can't bear to throw them away, don't. Instead, pack these clothes in a box and store them someplace in your home where space isn't at a premium.

Get your shirts together

Once you've weeded out the clothes that you no longer need or want, rearrange what's left so that like items hang together. In other words, group your blouses or dress shirts, your dress pants, your jeans, and so on. By hanging similar items near each other, you don't have to hunt for something when you're in a hurry. Do the same with your mate's clothes, and neither of you should have problems finding just what you're looking for.

Flock birds of a feather together

You can create entire outfits by grouping complementary items. This probably works better for men than for

hung up last Thursday. You can buy extra rods in home improvement stores and some department stores.

Have a hang-up

If you don't have space in your bedroom for a folding screen on which to hang your next day's wardrobe, you can probably make do with a wall hook on the back of your closet door. Certainly a hook costs less and you can still put your next day's outfit at your fingertips, which will save time if you're in a hurry.

A New View of Your Wardrobe

Perhaps the most obvious step you can take to organize your closet is to clear out and pare down your wardrobe.

Simply Stated

The difficulty in life is in the choice.
—George Moore, Irish author

---

women since men generally don't have as many suits or complete outfits. If you're a woman who tends to coordinate a piece from one suit with a piece from another, you may find this arrangement more time-consuming when trying to assemble an outfit. You'll have to remember where you put the peach turtleneck so you can wear it with the new pants you just bought.

Make seasonal adjustments

If you're blessed with many outfits that you actually wear, divide them into summer and winter wardrobes.

Pack away the out-of-season clothes in a cedar chest or a box (store the box in an area that isn't damp). You'll have tons more room in your closet, and your clothes won't wrinkle as much because they won't be smashed together. Your mate, who is probably sharing the closet with you, will be oh-so-grateful.

By All Means, Keep It Clean

By arranging your closet for maximum space and accessibility, you'll cut down on the amount of time you spend hunting for clothes and getting dressed. You'll have more time—even if it's just a few minutes—to spend on other aspects of your daily routine . . . or on yourself.

The following strategies can reinforce your efforts to steer clear of clothing clutter.

Put an end to piles

This tip won't cost you a Roosevelt dime, but it will pay off big in terms of the time you save. Instead of throwing your clothes on the bed, a chair, or the closet floor after you've worn them, put them in their proper places. If an item is dirty, throw it in the hamper. If it can be worn again without laundering, hang it up pronto. Strongly encourage your mate to do the same—for simplicity's sake.

Stow away your shoes

If the first thing you do when you walk into your bedroom is take off your shoes, make sure you put them in the closet or in their proper place. If you're in a hurry or not paying attention, you may trip over your shoes and fall. This rule also applies to other clothes as well as to any other item that may lie on the floor and block your path.

Take a whiff

It should go without saying. But hey, just to be thorough: To quickly determine if an article of clothing can be worn again without washing, smell it.

Separate for simplicity

Keep separate hampers for clothes that can be washed and clothes that have to be dry-cleaned. You won't make a mistake and ruin an item that wasn't supposed to be washed. Plus, you can quickly pick up items that need to go to the dry cleaner without having to sort though a pile of dirty clothes.

Put a hamper in every room

If you have children or if guests are staying with you, keep an extra hamper or a small laundry basket in each bedroom to collect their dirty clothes. Have your kids take all of their clothes to the laundry room on wash day so you don't have to pick up clothes from each bedroom. If the laundry doesn't get delivered to the laundry room, it shouldn't get washed.

Plan ahead

Always get your clothes for the next day ready the night before—you know, like you had to do when you were five years old. If you have to ask why, think back to a time when you woke up late for work and had about two seconds to pick out an outfit. You had no choice but to go to work in clothes with so many wrinkles that you looked like a walking prune. On top of that, a strategically placed button was missing. If you had set your clothes out the night before, you could've ironed what needed ironing and sewn what needed sewing.

Your Best Bed

No bedroom would be complete without . . . well, a bed. This one piece of furniture can make or break a good night's sleep. In fact, none of the previous bedroom-simplifying strategies will make much of a difference if you have a bed that denies you an evening of relaxing, restorative slumber.

To Sleep, Perchance to . . . Save?

If you sleep in your bed every night, you should replace your mattress and box spring every 10 years, recommends the Serta mattress company. If you often sleep away from home or you frequent the sofa, your mattress and box spring may last even longer.

Assuming that you have no other back ailments, waking up every morning with a sore back is a sure sign that you're in need of a new mattress. So is feeling more exhausted in the morning than you did the night before.

Of course, buying a bed can in itself be an exhausting experience. Mattresses are expensive, and you're never quite sure that you're getting the right one. You can save yourself money and hassle just by knowing a little bit about how bed sets are marketed.

Pick the tacky ticking

Ask anyone who works for a mattress manufacturer: The reason the ticking (a mattress's fabric covering) comes

in so many different styles and colors is that women buy the majority of mattresses. Would you rather buy a pretty mattress or an ugly one? If you're like most people, you'd opt for a pretty one. Yet the ticking—not the back support—accounts for more than half the cost of the mattress. And it gets covered with a sheet anyway. Choose support over style the next time you buy.

Splurge on size

Be willing to pay a little extra for a bed that is the right size for you and your mate. Being cramped into a too-small bed can make you both feel miserable. The more room you have to move around, the more comfortable you'll both be.

Don't forget about the length of your bed. If you or your mate is tall, purchase an extra-long mattress and box spring.

Do whatever you must to make your bed as relaxing as possible. After all, you have to sleep in it thousands of times.

Skip the box spring

Consider sleeping on only a mattress. Unless you have back problems or simply prefer the firmer feel of a mattress and box spring, purchasing only a mattress can save you money. This is an especially good idea for a child's room, since you may have to purchase another bed within a few years because your kid is growing into a six-foot-plus future basketball star.

Dream of a daybed

Daybeds have always been popular in college dorms. Now they're going mainstream. Instead of shelling out a bundle of money for an expensive model, buy a twin-bed set (frame, mattress, and box spring) and set it up against the bedroom wall. Then decorate with large mix-and-match pillows along the length of the bed. Voilà! You have an instant daybed at about half the cost.

Frame your bed

Many bedroom furniture suites are beautiful and extravagant, with equally high price tags. Instead of spending hundreds of dollars on a headboard, purchase only the frame. It's considerably cheaper. You can hide the fact that you don't have a headboard by placing large decorative pillows at the head of your bed. With no headboard in the way, you'll also have an easier time making the bed.

Stay with the standard

Some bed frames come equipped with drawers underneath the mattress or box spring. This is a good idea but also an expensive one. You can skip the high price by purchasing a standard bed frame and creating your own storage areas. Use long boxes of just the right depth to fit underneath the frame. Or buy vinyl-covered storage boxes from your local discount store.

Care Tactics

For you to get a good night's sleep, your bed has to be in tip-top condition. A mattress and box spring can last for many years, provided you take care of them properly.

Dust, dampness, rowdy kids, and cats with sharp claws can take a toll on a mattress and box spring and cause them to wear out prematurely, forcing you to spend money on replacements. To extend the life of your bed set, heed this advice.

Flip over your bed

Flip your mattress every six months or so. That way, it won't sag on one side or in the middle. Unless you're particularly strong, don't try to do this alone. A mattress—especially a king-size model—can be heavy, putting you at risk of hurting your back. After you have removed the mattress in order to flip it, vacuum the box spring to remove any dust and dirt that may have settled there.

Seek cover

You may wonder why you should use a mattress cover to protect the ticking when you're going to be putting a sheet over it anyway. The answer is that even with a fitted sheet on your bed, your mattress can get dusty and dirty. A mattress cover can help lengthen the life of a mattress by protecting the ticking from spills, bed-wetting accidents, and a buildup of dust. You may also put one over your box spring to keep it from getting so dusty.

Banish jumpers

If you have kids or grandkids, you know how much they love to jump on their beds—or, better yet, on your bed. Turning a bed into a mini-trampoline is fun but costly: You'll have to replace the mattress and box spring sooner than you expect.

Put pets in their places

Dogs and cats take their toll on a bed. Just because your 80-pound German shepherd believes that your bed belongs to him doesn't mean that you should allow him to lie down on it every day. Likewise, your cat may love to use your mattress ticking or, better yet, the box spring, as a scratching post. Placing a mattress cover or fitted sheet over the box spring discourages scratching—but keeping kitty out of the bedroom will solve the problem altogether.

Buying Bedclothes

Selecting accessories for your bed can seem daunting at first. Bedspreads, comforters, and quilts come in literally thousands of styles and colors. Then there are all those pillows: fiber-filled, foam, polyester. How do you know what kind to choose?

Consider your and your mate's sleeping habits and personal preferences. These should help determine which accessories you buy.

Weigh form and function

Both bedspreads and comforters come in a variety of styles and provide different degrees of warmth. With a bedspread, you need only one piece to cover everything, including your pillows. With a comforter, you need pillow shams and a dust ruffle to complete the ensemble. Although making a bed with a comforter takes longer because you have to tuck the pillows in the shams, the dust ruffle hides anything you may have stored underneath your bed.

Unplug your blanket

Most of the small appliances in your home, including electric blankets, emit low-frequency electromagnetic fields that radiate a few feet away. Extended exposure to these low-frequency fields may be linked to cancer. To protect yourself, avoid using an electric blanket. Use extra quilts or blankets instead.

Simple Ways to Sleep More Soundly

The best ways to guarantee a good night's sleep don't cost a thing. With a bit of cooperation from your mate (and perhaps your neighbors), you should snooze with ease.

Beg your mate for a massage. Well, hopefully you won't have to beg. A gentle back and neck rub relaxes tense muscles so you zonk out more quickly.

Leave the ceiling fan on low. If your body's thermostat is set on hot, a ceiling fan can provide enough air circulation without putting your mate in a deep freeze.

Keep pets out of the bedroom. Rover may decide he wants food at 3 AM. Or Fluffy may claim your side of the bed as her own. Whatever the reason, your pet can wake you and prevent you from getting back to sleep.

Ban barking. If your neighbor has a dog that barks through the night, request that the dog be kept indoors. If your neighbor says no, you may need to go a step further and report him to the police.

Cushion your cranium

The type of pillow that you should choose depends on how you position yourself to sleep. If you lie on your stomach, select a soft pillow so you won't strain your neck. If you lie on your back, opt for a medium pillow so you hold your head as though you were standing upright. If you lie on your side, use a firm pillow so you can breathe easier. If you roll around a lot and don't stay in one position, go with the medium pillow. You may need to have two different types of pillows on your bed if your mate has a different sleeping position than yours.

Bypass body pillows

Unless your doctor recommends a full-length body pillow for you, save your money. Like so many other products marketed as sleep aids, these pillows do little to improve the quantity and quality of your slumber. They'll help only if they're specially designed for a specific medical condition that you may have.

Prevent the flames from breaking out

A representative of one of the country's leading fabric manufacturers recommends using only flame-retardant pillows and coverings for your bed. The bedclothes that you buy in department stores are required by federal law to be treated with a flame-retardant chemical that passes horizontal and vertical flame tests. Mattress ticking has to pass this test as well.

If you've purchased your bed coverings from a flea market or antique shop, because of their age they probably don't have this flame-retardant finish. You can buy the chemical and apply it yourself, but some products can yellow fabric or otherwise change its color.

Getting a Great Night's Sleep

The softest sheets, the perfect pillow, the coziest comforter—all help create just the right atmosphere for sound, restorative slumber. Yet you can do even more to guarantee your ticket to dreamland.

Perfect Conditions

To get a good night's rest, you need to feel comfortable in your bedroom. Everything from temperature to light and sound can affect not only how quickly you fall asleep but also whether you stay asleep. If you're uncomfortable, you're more likely to toss and turn and to wake up in the middle of the night. And if you wake up, your mate likely will too.

The following tips can increase the chances that you (and your mate) sleep like a lion after a feast and feel refreshed the next morning.

Control the bedroom climate

Whether it's the dead of winter or the middle of a hot, sultry summer, keeping your bedroom slightly cool can help you sleep better. Of course, what constitutes cool varies from one person to the next. You may feel hot while your partner feels cold—or vice versa—even though you're both in the same room. If this happens, compromise: adjust the thermostat so that the hot person is comfortable, then bring out the extra blankets for the cold person.

Sock it to your feet

As unromantic as it may seem, your mate would probably prefer that you wear socks to bed instead of putting your cold feet on him. According to Thomas Smith, PhD, a researcher at Bowman Gray School of Medicine of Wake Forest University in Winston-Salem, North Carolina in the early 1990s, women are five times more likely than men to experience constriction of the blood vessels in their hands and feet when they're exposed to cold. This constriction, in turn, causes the hands and feet to become frigid. If you don't want to wear socks, then at least wrap your feet in a blanket.

Pull the plug on the phone

Don't be jostled out of a deep sleep by a ringing telephone. Whether it's an important call, a wrong number, or a prank, it disrupts your sleep pattern for the night. And when that happens, you may not experience the full restorative benefits of sleep.

Turn off the ringer before you go to bed. Or have your calls rerouted to an answering machine or answering service. This goes for cell phones, too.

Kill the noise

If you have trouble sleeping, do what you can to minimize distractions in your bedroom. This means no listening to your iPod and—read this carefully—no watching television. You may be more comfortable falling asleep with the television on, especially if you live by yourself. But most likely, the television will wake you up in the middle of the night with the volume seemingly a lot louder than when you went to sleep. Even if you have a television that turns off automatically, the extra time you spend in bed watching will have a cumulative de-energizing effect.

Arise at the first alarm

If you need an alarm clock to wake you up in the morning, make sure you get up the first time it goes off. If you hit the snooze button and fall back to sleep, you're doing yourself more harm than good. You'll have just fallen back to sleep when the alarm goes off again, disrupting your sleep and leaving you feeling even worse than if you had just gotten up to begin with.

Sync and Swim

Spending quality time with your mate is difficult enough if you both work the same hours. If you work different hours, it can seem next to impossible. Moreover, it can turn your entire household schedule upside down. The complications generally start in the bedroom. If you're getting out of bed at 7 AM and your mate is just turning in, you have precious little private time for the two of you.

Here's what you can do to ensure that both of you get the sleep you need and keep your lines of communication open.

Put time on your mate's side

Perhaps you wake up at the same time every morning without an alarm clock, but your mate wouldn't rouse during an earthquake. In this case, make sure there is an alarm clock on your spouse's nightstand, where it's accessible. If you don't need one, then don't clutter your own nightstand with one.

Leave the light outside

If your mate sleeps during the daytime, blackout shades (which I mentioned earlier) are a must. They may let in some light around the edges and at the corners. If this happens, drape a blanket over the window to keep out all the light.

Since you're nice enough to hang the blanket, ask your significant other to remove it when making the bed. That way, you won't have to fuss with it before you go to bed.

Hide important items in plain sight

If you sleep with only a comforter but your mate needs at least two blankets to keep from freezing, store extra blankets where they're easily accessible. In fact, you can put out the blankets in the morning and ask your mate to put them away when making the bed. Other extras to keep close to your bed include pillows and an orthopedic mattress, if your mate has back problems.

Send a clear message

Leave a pad and pencil on each nightstand so you and your mate can jot down information that the other person needs to know. This is a better system than waking your mate up with a phone call. If the kids need to be picked up at school or if the plumber is coming at noon, it's better for your mate to know that in advance than to be awakened by a phone or doorbell.

Corral the kids

If your mate works the third shift and sleeps during the day, send the kids to day care or to stay with a relative. Otherwise, they'll probably wake your mate when they get home from school, which can create an unhappy situation for all parties involved.

If day care isn't an option for you, perhaps your mate could stay awake until you get home. Then you can watch the kids while your sweetie sleeps.

On the Road Again

If you or your mate frequently travels on business, it disrupts the family schedule, much as if one of you worked different hours. The last thing either of you wants to do is spend a lot of time packing and unpacking, plus catching up on messages and other business. You'd probably rather just relax and enjoy the family.

To simplify pre- and post-trip preparations and to maintain your day-to-day routine in your mate's absence, give these tips a try.

Set aside travel stuff

You don't need two complete, separate wardrobes. Yet having spares of certain items set aside for trips can shorten your packing time. These items may include toiletries, an electric razor, and a hair dryer.

Sleep on schedule

When your mate goes on a trip, maintain your normal bedtime routine. Don't watch television or listen to an mp3 player while you're in bed because "the house seems so quiet." If you become accustomed to such background noise, you may have trouble falling asleep without it when your mate returns home. This can cause problems for both of you if your mate can't sleep with the TV or music on.

The Simplest of the Simple

Your bedroom is where you relax and replenish your energy every evening in preparation for the busy day ahead. This is why it needs to be the simplest room in your home. To make it so, follow these simple strategies:

- Remove all of the noisemakers from your bedroom. This includes the television and radio.
- Keep a nightstand on each side of your bed—one for you, one for your mate.
- Use a shoe bag to store shoes in your closet, uncluttering the closet floor.
- Remove all of your old clothes from your dresser and chest of drawers.
- Group similar articles of clothing together in your closet.
- Hang up clean clothes and put dirty clothes in the hamper immediately.
- Store extra blankets and pillows in the guest bedroom.
- Compare prices when purchasing a mattress. Don't pay extra for pretty ticking. Then use a mattress cover to protect the ticking.
- Choose the right pillow types for you and your mate for a better night's rest.
- If you or your mate travels frequently, create an extra set of toiletries only for traveling. This saves time when packing.

Chapter 8

The Kid's Bedroom

Creating Order Where Parents Fear to Tread

Your first memory of the movie *E.T.* will always be that cute little rubber-necked alien. Yet the megahit movie also memorialized the rampant overmaterialism and disorganization that plagues so many children's bedrooms today. In every bedroom scene, and often in other rooms throughout the house, the film shows toys, games, sports equipment, dolls, and knickknacks strewn about as if anyplace and everyplace were suitable resting places.

Hmm. Now let's talk about *your* child's bedroom.

Simplifying your child's bedroom is no light task. When organizing your own bedroom, you had a broad measure of control over what you did. Simplifying was your responsibility, so essentially you could arrange things the best possible way for you.

You may be thinking that, although it's your child's room, you should still have control over what goes on. This is true, to a point. But it's a delicate situation. You want your child to realize that this is his room and he has the responsibility for taking care of it. Yet, your child needs to actually *take* responsibility, and not do whatever he wants—or do nothing if he wants.

Teach your child responsibility when he's young. Waiting until your child is a teenager will present problems. Aside from the potential conflicts and arguments, your child may not believe that taking care of his room is his responsibility. Whatever you do, treat your young child like a human being who deserves respect. You wouldn't tell an adult roommate bluntly, "Pick up your clothes." Nor would you use the old "Because I said so!" line of reasoning. You would most likely treat a peer with respect. Use the same approach in your relationship with your child.

This chapter provides tips on simplifying your child's bedroom and encouraging your child to take responsibility for his actions. Covering every age group would not be practical, so much of our emphasis here is on kids from six to ten years old.

Toy Tactics

From the looks of your kids' rooms, Santa Claus has been good to your children over the years. There are tons of toys on the floor, and there are dozens more lying around every other room in the house. You probably ask yourself, "Does my daughter need 15 Barbies?" or, "Where did this fleet of toy trucks come from?"

Keeping this avalanche of toys in order seems impossible. Do your children really appreciate and take care of all the toys they have? Even if you could get them all picked up, where would you keep them? And what's a reasonable way to get all of the old toys out from under foot?

Managing the Toy Menagerie

Here are ideas for bringing some order to the overabundance of toys.

Skip the trip gifts

Regardless of whether you or the proud grandparents are doing the buying, your child doesn't need a new toy every time someone goes to the store or returns from a trip. Children can easily come to expect gifts and take them for granted. They may love a toy for a few days, then decide it's no fun anymore. So if you give a gift after every trip, watch out—this leads to anything but simplicity. Remember: less expense and less clutter yield less to do. Make your return the "gift" by being a great parent.

Weed out the old

If little Tommy's room looks like the toy section of a major department store, it's probably time to clear out some things. If there are older items that your child doesn't play with any more, pass these toys down to someone who wants them—a younger sibling or another family's kids, for instance. Let your child help pick out what goes and what stays.

Rotate the regulars

Pack up several toys into a cardboard box and stow them in the basement for a few months. When you return these toys to the playroom, your kids will feel like the toys are brand-new. With fewer toys around the house, you'll have less clutter and your kids will have an easier time deciding what to play with.

Make it clear

Clear plastic storage containers are a godsend to any child's room. They can hold virtually any kind of toy, they're durable, and they stack easily. What's more, your child can see through the plastic and find exactly what she's looking for without having to dig through boxes of toys.

Large plastic crates are another good storage option, especially for that mountain of sports equipment that winds up all over the floor. Basketballs, footballs, jump ropes, and such can be kept together in one crate that is designated for sports equipment only. Place the crate in a corner of the bedroom. If you need extra space for all of your child's equipment, buy a second crate and stack it on top of the first.

Control confusion with color coding

Color coding is an easy method for keeping items straight in your child's room. Buy small colored stickers to put on toys and the plastic storage containers that the toys belong in. When a child sees a blue sticker on a toy truck, for instance, he knows the truck belongs in the storage container with a blue sticker on it. With fewer decisions to make, your child's cleanup time should go faster.

If you have more than one child sharing the room, color coding helps to keep each child's toys separate and just might cut down on the arguments.

Plant toy boxes

Keep toy boxes or large plastic containers in various rooms all over your home. With a bin always at hand, you and your kids won't have to walk all over the house to put toys away. And your children will love having toys to play with no matter where they go in the house.

Assign some toys to the car

Keep a few small toys ensconced in your car at all times. Since they haven't been playing with these toys day in and day out, your kids will love having something "new" to play with when they join you for a drive. Not only will you have a quieter trip, but this technique will also cut down on the number of things you need to bring out of the house for the drive.

Finding Harmony with Stereos, Televisions, and More

Kids today have access to many more forms of communication than you did at their age. This is good and bad. Computers are wonderful learning tools, exposing your child to knowledge with the touch of a key. That's practical—it saves the time and effort of going to the library. But overuse of a personal computer or television can be hard to control. If your child has a television and DVD player in his room, it's important that you have the means to keep track of what he's watching when he's in his room alone.

Favor family time

As a parent, you want the best for your kids. Electronic equipment, like video games and stereos, are nice gifts, but you should insist that your kids spend some part of their day with you, far from the reach of headphones, joysticks, and remote controls. If possible, try eating your evening meal together so you can see your children and actually spend quality "unplugged" time with them. Talk is cheap and simple. (This means no radio, no television, and no mp3 player for you, too.)

Exercise parental controls

Most cable systems offer some kind of parental control. But don't leave all of your decision making to the TV industry's and movie industry's assessment of programming. Just because a program is rated PG doesn't mean it's suitable for your child to watch. Watch the beginning of the shows your children want to see. You'll have a sense of the tone and quality of the programming after only one minute.

Tighten your control

If your home has a computer with access to the Internet, there are parental controls to help you restrict the Web sites that your child visits. But remember, these controls aren't difficult to circumvent. Your child can probably figure out how to bypass many of these controls in less than 30 minutes. Internet providers urge parents not to depend on such systems. America Online posts a message reminding its users that "no system of controls makes up for good old-fashioned parental supervision." There's no substitute for your going into your child's room to see what she is up to.

Reduce the racket

If you can hear your kid's stereo two blocks away, it's past the time to turn down the volume. When children are home alone, they tend to turn the volume up to dangerous levels. If the stereo is too loud, they risk hearing loss, not to mention bothering the neighbors.

Don't take headphones for granted either. They can actually be worse than the stereo. With headphones, the sound is being projected directly into the child's ears, and this can cause permanent damage more quickly than a loud stereo can.

Try talking to your child about the risk of hearing loss and the possibility of paying a hefty fine for disturbing the peace (if your local government has such an ordinance). If he still resists turning down the volume, perhaps the only thing you can do is take away his stereo or headset.

Finessing the Furnishings

A child's bedroom may be largely his own domain, but the simplicity of this venue is influenced directly by the furnishings supplied by the adults in the family. For example, if you want to see a child routinely put away all of those planes, trains, and Batmobiles, give serious consideration to the storage spaces you've provided.

So let's take a look at the furniture, closets, and wall and floor coverings—all of the infrastructure of your kid's bedroom.

Clearing Out the Dresser Drawer Jungle

The previous chapter helped you get your own dresser drawers organized. Now it's time to help your child with the same thing. Encourage your child to take responsibility for her dresser and to make sure clean clothes are stored there. Remember: When you leave it up to your kids to handle their own clothes, they're probably not going to be as neat as you want them to be. That's all right. Don't arrange things for them. Straightening up your child's dresser convinces her that she can't do it right or that her parents are going to do it anyway, so she needn't bother.

Take Tom Thumb's perspective

You'd be amazed at how many people disregard the fact that their children are small. Your small child probably can't reach most of the drawers in a standard-size dresser. Even if he can reach them, he probably is not strong enough to pull the drawers out far enough, reach over, and get what he needs. Use lower furniture and

dressers if you expect your small children to pick up after themselves. If they can't reach the drawers, how are they supposed to put things in them?

Cluster those pants

Group similar clothing items in the same drawer. This will make it easier when you put away the clean clothes. And when your kids are old enough to put away their own clothes, they will have a clearer idea of where everything goes. If your kid wants the blue pajamas in the bottom drawer, put all of the pajamas in the bottom drawer.

Unfurl fewer folds

Folding clothes is a tedious job for anyone, but especially for a small child. A child with even the best coordination may have problems folding socks or T-shirts. Then again, why do items like socks or T-shirts need to be folded in the first place? (Surely you're not concerned about wrinkling these items.) It will be much easier and less frustrating for a kid to place socks together in piles or lay T-shirts in a drawer without folding them perfectly.

If you want your child to learn this task, bring him into the fold slowly. Start him off with easy-to-fold items like shorts or jeans.

Save a Bundle on Furniture

Furniture doesn't have to be replaced yearly, but it can still put a crunch on your wallet, especially if you finance the purchase. Most parents want nice things for their children, but there comes a point when wanting stops and economics takes over. Perhaps you're at that point right now, or you will be soon. Let's focus for a moment on ways to economize your furniture purchases.

Forsake furniture financing

Make do with the furniture you have until you can afford to pay cash for new stuff. Paying cash for a less expensive set of kids' furniture is simply more prudent than financing a more expensive set. You really don't need a long-term partnership with the furniture store or credit card vendor. The interest you pay will make your purchase outrageously pricey.

Borrow from the grandparents

If your parents or in-laws have recently re-outfitted their home with new furniture, borrow the older furniture for your child's room. If you're not comfortable borrowing from relatives, offer to pay them for the furniture. Chances are, they won't ask anything near the amount that a furniture store would. You may get lucky and get some high-quality furniture.

Consider convertibles

Many furniture stores carry adjustable children's furniture that grows with your child. Cribs can be turned into twin beds, while changing tables convert to dressers. This is a novel idea, but there is a catch. Be sure to compare prices. Sometimes, buying adjustable furniture is more expensive than buying each piece separately.

Lean toward laminates

If you have small children, it's important to use durable and easy-to-clean furniture. Laminated surfaces and good sturdy structures are essential. Laminates won't show nicks and scratches and other forms of abuse. And they are easy to clean if drawn or painted on.

Simply Stated

An inability to stay quiet . . . is one of the most conspicuous failings of mankind.

**—Walter Bagehot,
English economist and author**

Resist the characters

It pays to prefer the practical. Kids go crazy over beds shaped like cars or items featuring favorite cartoon characters or their heroes of the moment. Avoid buying furniture of this type. Children quickly outgrow these things and then want something new. Stay with practical furniture that can be used for several years.

One way to achieve a happy middle ground is to buy comforters or bedspreads with the favorite character. These can be changed and can be passed down to other children who will like them.

Strategies for Tight Spaces

You've tried all of the storage bin and closet tricks, and you still have a space problem in your child's bedroom? Parents have an inalienable right to a clear path through a kid's bedroom, without having to dance some twisted route around furniture, toy containers, and whatnot. Even if you have two children sharing the same bedroom, there are clever ways to make maximum use of the space.

Bunk up

Many kids find the prospect of bunk beds a marvelous adventure. For you, they're a great way to position two beds in the space normally occupied by just one. Your only quandary will be deciding who gets the top bunk. If both kids want it, flip a coin to see who gets it for the first month, and then trade off.

Measure before you bunk

Before you put your children in a bunk bed, measure the space between the guard rail and the mattress or bed frame. This space should be no more than 3½ inches, because a smaller child can fall through and become suspended by his head. 36,000 children are treated for bunk bed-related injuries per year, mostly due to falls, according to a 2008 investigation by the center for injury Research and Policy of the Research Institute at Nationwide Children's Hospital in Columbus, Ohio "Choose bunk beds with guard rails that are firmly attached to the bed structure, and don't allow kids under six to sleep on the top bunk."

Hide a sliding bed

If you have no takers on the bunk beds but you still want to economize space, opt for a trundle, or pullout, bed. A trundle bed is made to fit underneath another bed when it is not in use. When needed, the trundle bed is pulled out and raised to create a second sleeping surface. This is a good option even when you have just one child per bedroom—it provides a place for friends to sleep when they spend the night.

Corner the beds

Save space by placing two twin beds at a right angle to each other against the walls in the corner instead of having them stick out into the middle of the floor, recommends author Arnold Friedmann in his book, *Commonsense Design.* You won't have anything to walk around when you're vacuuming, and your children will have lots of space in the middle of the bedroom for playing.

Now Hear This

When it's at full tilt, your child's stereo can easily exceed 90 decibels. But the federal government advises wearing earplugs, earmuffs, or other hearing protection whenever you are exposed to 85 decibels for a period of more than a few hours. Some experts say that even levels as low as 70 decibels can damage your hearing. (Every step up of 10 decibels reflects a tenfold increase in sound. So 100 decibels is 10 times louder than 90 decibels.)

So share with your child the following roster of decibel levels, provided by the Better Hearing Institute in Washington, D.C. Point out where the danger zone is. Let's hope the message comes through loud and clear:

20 decibels:	watch ticking
30 decibels:	whispering, library
40 decibels:	leaves rustling, refrigerator
50 decibels:	average home, neighborhood street
60 decibels:	normal conversation, dishwasher, microwave
70 decibels:	car, alarm clock, city traffic
80 decibels:	garbage disposal, vacuum cleaner, outboard motor
85 decibels:	factory, electric shaver, screaming child
90 decibels:	passing motorcycle, lawn mower
100 decibels:	hair dryer, diesel truck, subway train, helicopter, chain saw
110 decibels:	car horn, snowblower
120 decibels:	rock concert, prop plane
130 decibels:	jet engine 100 feet away, air raid siren
140 decibels:	shotgun blast

Designate desk space

Sooner or later, your child will need a desk and possibly a computer table. Plan for it now. It's nice to put the desk near a window so your child can take a break every once in a while and look outside. This is important if your child will be using the computer often. After staring at the screen for an hour, the kid needs to have something to focus on at a distance, like trees.

The desk can also hold items that a nightstand would normally hold, which will save you some space if things are tight.

Convert an armoire

As with your own bedroom, look for an inexpensive armoire at flea markets or auctions. An armoire can be converted into a computer desk by adding some shelves (if they don't already exist) and installing a pullout drawer to hold the keyboard. The armoire will keep your child's computer hidden and away from dust when not in use. Let your child pick out what color the armoire should be painted and let him help do the painting.

Banish bedside lamps

Avoid bedside lamps in a child's room. Bedside lamps are typically placed on a shelf or nightstand, and they're a hazard if knocked over. Instead, install wall lighting, which will save space and may even eliminate the need for a nightstand. If you don't like the idea of wall lighting, try overhead fixtures instead—but make sure the illumination is adequate. Here's a good rule of thumb: For each square foot of space in a kid's bedroom, you need one watt of lighting. So for a room measuring 15 feet by 18 feet, you'd want to use lightbulbs totaling 270 watts.

Wall Wisdom and Floor Foresight

Although not as difficult as painting the Sistine Chapel for four years on a scaffold on your back, decorating your child's room can be a complex proposition. You want something your child will enjoy, but also something that's not a hassle for you to install and maintain. The walls in your kid's room will get scratched, dented, inscribed, painted, and they will undergo other assorted stresses that are limited only by your child's imagination.

There's no need to make things more complicated for yourself by going overboard when decorating for your child. Smaller children in particular don't care if the walls are painted or wallpapered, as long as there are pictures of Barney, Hannah Montana, Dora, and Pooh and the gang.

Undo Rembrandt

Sooner or later, your child is going to have the brilliant inspiration to color on the walls of her bedroom. So prepare for this artistic event—paint her room in a bright, easy-to-clean color. Make sure that you tell your paint salesperson that you're painting a child's room. Oil-based paints and newer latex paints provide surfaces that make it easier to remove artistic endeavors.

Forget wallpaper

Aside from being a pain to hang, wallpaper is not practical in children's rooms. It's harder to get crayon and paint marks off wallpaper. Also, a five-year-old most likely will not want the same design on his wall that was there when he was a baby. Changing paint colors is easier and cheaper than hanging more wallpaper. Easy and cheap means simple.

a mess if a beanbag tears and the insides spill all over the floor. If you're afraid this may happen with your rambunctious crowd, stick with the large pillows with washable covers.

Conquering the Closet

Now that you can navigate around your child's bedroom, take a peek in the closet. Is it stacked floor to ceiling with a jumble of board games, stuffed animals, clothes, dolls, hockey sticks, and action figures?

Well, it's time for a little inner reflection. Are you and the grandparents buying a lot of things that your kid doesn't need or want? Have you been holding on to toys that your eight-year-old hasn't played with in four years? No wonder there's no room for clothes in your child's closet—look at all the wasted space and all the junk that is stored in there. Remember the principles in chapters 2 and 3—pare down.

Draw your own decor

If your child has a favorite cartoon or TV character, you can decorate her room with that character without paying outrageous prices. If you have a computer and modem, search the Internet for the characters your kid adores. Print out the pictures that you like, help you child color them, and post them in her room.

Pop the cork for posters

If you prefer not to have your children sticking posters and pictures all over the walls, buy a corkboard or many corkboards. Kids will want to hang pictures of their favorite actors, actresses, music stars, and more. Ultimately, you may want to invest in large floor-to-ceiling corkboards. But they can be costly, so weigh the pros and cons of letting your kids just hang things on the walls.

Soften the bedroom floor

Carpeting a child's bedroom is a frightening thought. There's a good chance it will get messed up (and terrorized) by all of the action figure toys rolling over it and juice drinks spilling on it. But you will still need some type of soft surface for your children to play on. You can purchase soft mats from children's stores that can be folded up and stored when not in use. Or simply buy a rug for use in the bedroom. A tightly looped rug in a dark color will work best for the type of abuse it may receive.

Buy beanbags and trusty pillows

Your child will spend much of his time on the floor, so besides a soft surface, get something to make playing games on the floor or watching television more comfortable. Large pillows and futons work well. Beanbags may be even a better choice because they're easy to clean. On the other hand, you'll have

Follow the fashion

From little mouths often springs fashion sense. Even young children know what they want to wear and what they don't like. If your child sees a sweater in the store and comments, "Mom, that's the ugliest thing I've ever seen," you can be sure it will get very little wear if you take it home anyway. Don't force the issue—leave that sweater in the store, even if you personally like the style and think the price is a bargain. Not only will you save money, but you'll save space in the closet and prevent lots of getting-dressed arguments.

Pack up the old, outdated, and outgrown

Growing children go through clothes like Bugs Bunny goes through carrots. Pack up the old clothes in boxes

or plastic containers. Put these on a high shelf in your child's closet. Once every six months (or more often if needed), donate the extras to charity, hold a yard sale, or pass them on to a friend with smaller kids.

Bag the shoes for easy reach

Hang your children's shoes in a shoe bag and hang the bag on the inside of the door at an appropriate height for your child to reach it. The child will be able to see exactly where each pair of shoes is, and the shoes won't be all over the floor. If your child outgrows the shoes, remove those shoes and store them with the other outgrown clothes. This will free up some space in the shoe bag for newer shoes.

Simply Stated

On the whole, the happiest people seem to be those who have no particular cause for being happy except that they are so.

—William R. Inge, English religious leader and author

Install a spare rod

Mount two clothes rods in your child's closet. The first rod should be standard height. The second rod, however, should be considerably lower so your younger children can pick out their own clothes and rehang clean ones. By mounting two rods, you double the space for hanging.

Shelve the games and puzzles

Install low shelves inside your child's closet. If you supply this extra storage space for games, puzzles, and whatnot, you'll not only ensure that those items aren't strewn all about the house, but your kids will have direct access to those items. You won't have to stop what you're doing to get a game for one of your children. Ah, the simple life.

Get a better box

Put toys and games with small pieces in plastic containers with snap-on lids. Then label the containers so that you and the kids will know what's in there. You've probably noticed that kids tend to drop and lose small things. Also, cardboard boxes have a life expectancy of six minutes in some kids' rooms.

Create a sports closet

If you like to participate in sports activities with your children, keep the sports equipment in a central location that is convenient for everyone and simple for you. A closet in the hallway, a spare bedroom, or the laundry room might be just the place. Use crates to organize related equipment. Make sure all of your budding athletes put the equipment back in its proper place after each use.

Play—But Play It Safe

Children like to explore forbidden places, and there may be little you can do to suppress the inquisitive nature of your child. But it's your responsibility to keep your children safe, so be aware that one of the most dangerous places you or your child will ever be is your own home. Take steps to ensure that your child's room and the toys you buy for your child are safe. Remember: There's nothing like an accident to complicate your life.

Go low with the heavy stuff

In your child's room, anything that's heavy needs to be as close to the floor as possible. Shelves won't do—heavy items can fall off a shelf at any time and seriously injure your child.

Soften the edges on your furniture

If the dresser or other furniture in your child's room has sharp corners or edges, get thee to a hardware store. Most stores carry rubber moldings that will cover the sharp edges of dressers and other furniture. If you can't find such moldings, many fabric stores carry felt material that you can tack or glue around the edges. Try to use the thickest material you can find. In addition to preventing your child from getting hurt, this will protect your furniture from getting scratched and dented.

Learn to save a life

Accidents can happen at any time, especially with children. Contact your local chapter of the American Red Cross and sign up for classes in infant and child CPR. In a few hours, you can learn enough to be a lifesaver.

When in Doubt, Be Strict

To raise a child with a high EQ, the emotional intelligence quotient, being strict pays off. *USA Today* reports that among 101 former Academic Team All Stars—high school seniors selected annually for high academic performance, talent, and community service—49 percent described their parents as stricter than other parents.

Inspiring Responsibility

Did you ever watch *The Cosby Show*? Mr. Huxtable once walked into his son's room to find clothes strewn about the floor, the bed, and the furniture, and hanging off every possible surface. Instead of getting angry, the father commented, "It's hard to find good help, isn't it?"

If your child thinks you're his personal maid service, then you need to make some adjustments to your employment status.

Encourage Your Child Early in the Game

The earlier you start encouraging your child to help around the house, the less trouble you will have persuading her to do her fair share. Here's how to teach younger children to grow into dependable older children.

Expect less than perfection

When your child is doing a chore, don't expect the job to be the same quality as if you were doing it. This is especially true when your child is beginning to help out around the house. Everyone, whether child or adult, has to learn the best way of doing things. Your child may have done his best, and you should reward him instead of criticizing because it's not up to adult standards.

Overexplain and undercomplain

Children think the world revolves around fun. If only it were true! Put yourself in your child's position. If you were five years old, would dirty dishes bother you? Probably not. When you instruct your child to do something, explain why you want him to do it and why it's important to the family. You'll get more cooperation this way.

Enlist your children early

Children learn by example. If you or your mate isn't doing a fair share of the chores around the house, you can't expect your child to do her share. Also, be careful that other siblings are doing fair shares. They probably won't all be doing the same chores—to be fair, give kids an equivalent amount of responsibility, based on age.

Retire permanently as maid

If your child knows you're going to pick up the room anyway, there's no motivation for him to take care of it. If a teenager is looking for an outfit to wear to a party and realizes that because he left it on the floor it hasn't been washed, he will be more likely to put the dirty clothes in their proper place.

Make a Clean Break from the Baby Clothes

A funny thing happens on the way to decorum. When you hold a yard sale, it's relatively easy, from an emotional standpoint, to sell your child's baby clothes if somebody wants them. When you sell items for cash, you feel pretty good.

When the crowds are gone and it's time to pack up the remaining clothes and give them to charity, watch out. There's a good chance you'll attempt to talk yourself into taking that clutter back into your home. "My goodness, I should hang on to these items for posterity rather than give them away," you might say. "When my child is an adult, she may open the box and appreciate them."

Instead, decide in advance of the yard sale what items of clothing you'll retain for posterity. Have empty boxes ready at the sale so that when the last shopper leaves, you can quickly load up the car and make your way to the nearest charity for drop-off.

Hand out the hampers

Put a laundry basket or clothes hamper in your child's room for dirty clothes. This gives your kid a specific place to put his clothes instead of all over the floor. Start this habit early with your child so she will learn responsibility for putting dirty items away.

Say "Thanks"

A little recognition will go a long way. When your child completes a task, show your appreciation. You don't need to bribe anyone with gifts or candy. Simply say, "Thank you. I appreciate your help." Your kid will feel that he has done well, and he will be encouraged to do more to please Mom and Dad.

Make the Work Fun

Cleaning up the bedroom does not have to be drudgery. Try out these ideas for making the work more fun, and things will soon be picking up.

Make it a game

There's no denying that cleaning up is a bore. If you make it a game, however, kids will throw their all into it. To make this duty a race, set the kitchen timer to ring after a reasonable amount of time, and watch your child scramble to beat the bell. Turn cleanup time into a scavenger hunt by hiding a prize somewhere amid the mess. Or turn it all into a play-acting game: For instance, pretend that she's straightening up a disheveled spaceship. ("I think the photon bombs go in the bin in the corner. . . .")

Straighten up with a song

When your child is older, let him listen to music (at a reasonable volume) while cleaning. He can sing, dance, and even impersonate others. Let your child pretend to be Mom or Dad while cleaning if it helps.

Check the chore chart

Once your child is old enough to read, you can develop a chore chart. A chore chart lists all the members of the family and days of the week. For each day of the week, write down the chores that your child needs to do. After the child is finished with the chore (and it meets approval), she can erase that item.

To increase her responsibility around the house, let her choose the chores she wants to do. If she would prefer dusting to washing dishes, let her dust. She will be more likely to stick with a chore that she would rather do than be forced to do something she hates. In any case, set up a system to which both of you agree ahead of time, so she will know what is expected of her.

Brush up on neatness

If your child helps to fix up a coatrack for the home, he will be more likely to use it. You can probably find an old coatrack at a flea market or discount furniture store. If not, see if grandma and grandpa have one they will give you or if a family member will make one for you.

Make sure the coatrack has been stripped or isn't painted. Let your child pick out what color he wants the coatrack to be, and let him help do the actual painting. So what if it's not a professional job? The kid will like it and feel like it belongs to him.

When Your Family Grows

If you're going to have a baby soon or if you recently had one, you know your life is much more complicated than it was a few months ago. Babies are wonderful, but the truth is your life will never be the same. Your feelings about a new baby are overwhelming enough—don't complicate the situation by making your nursery a burden. Arrange everything in the nursery so it's easy for you to maneuver in and clean.

Making the Big Arrival a Little Simpler

In all the excitement, you may want the best of everything for the nursery, including furniture and accessories. This is fine if you can afford it. If you can't, you can still have a nice nursery on a budget. These ideas will make your life smoother during your first few months with a new baby.

Go bright, but durable

Bright, contrasting colors will stimulate your young child better than subtle colors. Wallpaper is fine for a nursery,

too, but remember that a babyish choice won't be suitable forever. Pick a look that your child will be happy with for several years.

Hanker for hand-me-downs

It's perfectly acceptable to use hand-me-down furniture for your nursery. Hand-me-downs that are safe and in good condition will save you considerable sums. Your one-month-old won't notice, won't care, won't remember, and won't even comment about the fact that the crib has a maple finish while the dresser has an oak finish. Still, if not having new or matching furniture for the nursery is going to bother you, then follow your own instincts and go get it.

Create a high-speed nursery

Arrange your furniture so you have as little in the way as possible when you're attending to your baby's needs. Put the changing table close to the crib so you don't have to carry the baby far for changing after a nap. Also, keep a clear path from the door to the crib. If possible, position the crib so you can easily see it if you're down the hallway catching up on housework.

Be blissfully blunt

When you bring your baby home from the hospital, make it clear to all of your relatives and friends that you need some private time with your baby and mate after coming home from the hospital. Well-intentioned people tend to crowd into your home and offer help when all you want is some time to catch your breath and get your baby settled in his new nursery.

Sleep where it works

When you've just brought a baby home from the hospital, you may be unsure of where she should sleep. However well-appointed the nursery may be, you might still find it hard to leave her in a room by herself. Let your

baby sleep wherever all of you sleep best, suggest William Sears, MD, and Martha Sears in *The Discipline Book*. If your baby sleeps well alone, then it's all right for her to sleep alone. If she sleeps better in a bassinet beside your bed, that's fine also. Be flexible, knowing that the older the baby gets, the more she will sleep by herself.

Teach cause and effect

As your child gets older, provide him with toys that produce a specific effect when he plays with them. For example, some toys produce animal sounds when a certain animal button is pressed. Toys that squeak or play music are other options. Your child will learn that he is causing these actions, which will help his cognitive development.

Use a squirt bottle

When you wash your baby's hair, fill a squirt bottle with water and use it for rinsing. It provides enough pressure to rinse out shampoo, and there is less chance that shampoo will get in your baby's eyes. This is also good to use for bathing, but make sure you get all the soap off so your child's skin won't be irritated.

For Peace of Mind: Prevention

Safety in the nursery is a more subtle consideration than safety in an older child's room. If you're new at this, you may not realize something is dangerous until your child has had an accident. Think defensively—preventing injuries is a powerful form of simplifying your life. There are entire books on this subject, but here are a few tips to help you out.

Lay baby on his back

The American Academy of Pediatrics recommends placing a newborn on his side or back when he is sleeping. This sleeping position reduces the chance of SIDS (Sudden Infant Death Syndrome). Don't place your infant on pillows, comforters, or any other soft item while sleeping. He could roll over and suffocate.

Don't crowd the crib

The more toys and "comforting objects" you place in your baby's crib, the higher the risk that your child will suffocate while sleeping. You may think a stuffed animal will be comforting to a baby, but don't risk it. Try using other toys that can be attached to the crib but are safely out of reach of the sleeping baby.

Cut the strings

Remove all items and toys in the baby's room that have strings or elastic on them. Strangulation can occur if the baby rolls over and gets tangled in the cord. If you have blinds in your nursery, make sure the cord is kept far from the baby's reach.

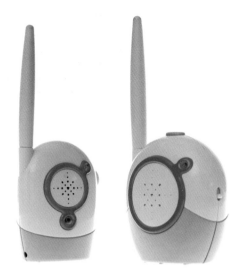

Anchor your accessories

If your baby is in a playpen or portable crib, make sure all sides are up and everything is properly secured. The mesh that is used in many playpens can form a loose pocket that an infant can roll into and get dangerously tangled up in. Follow manufacturers' instructions for securing the item—don't assume you've done it correctly.

Scrutinize secondhands

Secondhand furniture can save you a ton of money, but it can cost you a lot more if it's not good quality. If the crib or bassinet falls short of safety standards, you're putting your baby at risk. Babies can slip through the slats in some cribs. Don't purchase or borrow a crib if you can slide a soft drink can between the slats.

The Art of Persuasion

Persuading your child to pick up after himself is certainly a challenge. Here are some tips for keeping the communication simple:

- When giving your child instructions about chores, avoid dictating. Yes, it's important that you make her realize it's her responsibility, but saying "Do it because I said so" will make your child resentful.
- Supervise the chores your child performs to help him learn the correct and easiest way of doing the work. Be careful not to criticize harshly if the child is not working up to par.
- Removing old clothes and toys from your child's room is a good idea for maximizing the space in the room. But make sure you discuss with your child what clothes and toys are expendable. You wouldn't want someone to throw out your things, would you?

Monitor your baby

A body can't be in two places at once, regardless of how much you may need or want to be. So set up a baby monitor, which will allow you to go about your daily activities while the baby is napping. Such units transmit any sounds your baby makes to a unit you keep with you. Not only will you get a lot more done around the house but you'll also find that the monitor provides wonderful peace of mind. Be sure to keep fresh batteries in the monitor.

Monitor your baby's mouth

Since babies will stick anything and everything in their mouths, only buy toys that they can chew and suck on without danger. Look for large, nontoxic playthings with no small or removable parts. Make sure they're fully water-immersible for easy cleaning.

The Simplest of the Simple

Here's the nut of it—the most basic tips for making your children's bedrooms more manageable:

- Put a halt to excessive toy buying.
- Supervise your children's television viewing habits.
- Use plastic storage containers for toys.
- Keep similar clothing items together in dresser drawers.
- Use bunk beds when space is sparse.
- Pack up old clothes and shoes that are no longer used.
- Don't expect perfection from a child performing chores.
- Don't do your children's chores for them.
- Keep toys out of your baby's crib.
- Keep a baby monitor in your child's nursery.
- Throw out toys that are old and worn out.

Chapter 9	# Laundry Logic

Lessons to Lighten the Load

Think back to a time when someone else washed, dried, and ironed your clothes. Ah, those were the days . . . at least for you. The person who did your laundry—most likely your mom—probably had a different opinion. Washing clothes was more difficult a generation ago than it is today. State-of-the-art washing machines and dryers are readily available. If you don't have them in your home, then you can go to a nearby laundromat.

While you enjoy conveniences that were not available to your parents or grandparents, you also have to deal with many more demands on your time. You probably squeeze more tasks into one day than they would have ever thought possible.

So even if your mother did all the laundry by herself, you needn't do the same. Your mate and your children can and should help you. How do you persuade them to pitch in? By making their part of the job so fast and easy that it becomes second nature to them.

Even if you live alone and don't have any helping hands available to you, you can still make wash day much less of a chore. You'll save yourself time and effort simply by applying some of the tips below.

Getting Started

Probably the most important step in doing laundry occurs before you even open the lid to the washing machine. You have to round up everything that needs cleaning, weed out the dry cleaning, then divvy up the remainder into loads. It may not be high science, but it can get tricky, especially with so many new fabrics on the market.

Sorting Made Simple

Since washers and dryers have preset cycles, you can't do much to make them work faster. But you can save a lot of time and effort on the front-end tasks—the gathering and sorting. This is where you can enlist the help of your family.

Every member of your household, with the exception of very young children, should be able to deliver their dirty clothes and linens to the laundry room. To get them in the habit of doing so, employ these techniques.

Wear it again, Sam

The first and foremost rule of laundry management: If it isn't dirty, don't wash it. Sure, it seems obvious. Still, many of us automatically throw clothes in the hamper, whether or not they actually need laundering. If you've worn a shirt for only a few hours and it doesn't appear soiled, hang it back in the closet. This cuts down your laundry, and extends the life of your washer and dryer to boot. Machines that do four or fewer loads each week require repairs half as often as machines that do eight or more loads each week.

Collect laundry on the spot

Give each person in your home a hamper, clothes basket, or laundry bag to collect dirty clothes and linens. This helps discourage anyone from using a bedroom chair or the floor of the bedroom closet as a laundry collection site.

Divide and conquer

In the laundry room, have separate hampers for whites, colors, towels, and other items that you wash frequently. Then on wash day, everyone can place their clothes and linens in the appropriate hampers. By having each person do his own sorting, you dramatically cut your preparation time.

Arrange for delivery

If you don't have a set wash day each week, you may want to instruct family members to take their laundry directly to the laundry room rather than collecting it in a hamper. That way, whenever you decide to wash, you won't have to walk from room to room collecting laundry first.

Separate dry cleaning

Designate a hamper or laundry bag for items that are dry-clean-only. Keep it in your laundry room, but make sure that it's clearly marked or sitting by itself so no one tosses in machine-washables by mistake. Then when you make your trip to the dry cleaner, everything will be in one spot ready to go.

Leave no pocket unchecked

Remind everyone in your family to clean out their pockets before sorting their clothes. This simple step can prevent a mishap with a pen that breaks and leaks ink on an entire load of wash, or a tissue that shreds and clings to clothes. Also have everyone remove shoulder pads, turn down cuffs, and button all buttons. That way, you can fold clothes immediately after drying.

Zip up zippers

Open zippers, flung about at high speeds during the wash and spin cycles, can snag and tear other clothes. Instruct your crew to close the zippers on their garments before sorting.

Hold everyone accountable

If your daughter's favorite dry-clean-only outfit gets ruined when it's tossed in the washing machine by mistake, she will probably be more careful the next time she separates her clothes. Yes, you'll lose money on the outfit, but you'll more than make up for it in the long run because you'll save time by not having to double-check everyone's sorting.

Make washing sheets easy

You may want to collect and wash everyone's bed linens on the same day rather than on different days. They're likely to be equally dirty anyway, especially in the summertime. By washing bedsheets all at once, you won't have to track which you've done and which you need to do.

Learning the Lexicon of Labels

These days, you almost need to be a detective to determine the best way to clean your clothes. Sometimes even the manufacturers don't know for sure. They tend to rely on the recommendations of the mills that provide the fabrics, explains Alice Laban, spokesperson for the International Fabricare Institute, an association of dry cleaners and launderers that evaluates the accuracy of care instructions for clothes. "Unfortunately, there is little consistency in some testing done at mills," Laban says. "Some mills test only one bolt of fabric out of many."

The clothing labels themselves tend to give cryptic instructions about fabric care. At least in this case, a little information is better than none. As long as you know the type of fabric you're working with and you use your common sense, you should do just fine most of the time.

Do your homework

Even though they may not tell you much, reading labels remains your best opening move in the laundry game. Many a person has ruined a perfectly good article of clothing by not checking its label before laundering. If you see the words "machine wash," consider yourself in the clear to do just that. The one possible exception is garments made from delicate fabrics, which you may want to have dry-cleaned instead.

Be aware before you buy

Most people have at one time or another bought an article of clothing that turned out to be more trouble to care for than it was worth. For instance, you may buy a pair of tan pants to go with many shirts or blouses in your wardrobe, only to realize that they're dry-clean-only. To avoid this expense, you may end up wearing the pants only occasionally, in which case you're not getting your

---

For small families, once (a week) is enough

Why do laundry more often than you have to? By designating one day of the week as wash day, you'll be sure to have full loads. You won't waste time and water on half-loads. And if you cut back by one load per week, you'll save money on your electric bill and prevent unnecessary wear and tear on your washer and dryer.

To get from one wash day to the next without running out of clean clothes and linens, you'll need to do a little advance planning.

- Have enough towels and washcloths to last each family member one week.
- Have enough pairs of socks and underwear to last each family member one week.
- Buy everyday wear such as T-shirts in quantity. Often, T-shirts are sold in packs of three in discount stores. Purchase a couple of packs, and you'll be set for an entire week.
- If you frequently wear a particular article of clothing, buy a second, similarly styled garment in a different color to go with the same clothes as the first one. That way, you can mix and match to create new outfits for every day of the week.

money's worth from them. Or you may take a chance on machine washing, which could ruin the pants and waste money in the process.

Heed the hidden meaning

The Federal Trade Commission requires that some type of "satisfactory label" appear in every garment sold in the United States. Satisfactory means that the method of care "should be tested and work for the entire garment—including buttons, fringe, shoulder pads, and linings." In other words, a label may tell you to dry-clean a garment just because it has fancy buttons or fringe. This can run into a lot of money.

Selecting the Best Fabrics

Some clothing labels read like road construction signs: they tell you what to do, but not why. For instance, why must wool be dry-cleaned? And why must spandex be line dried rather than machine dried?

The following tips evaluate the most popular natural fabrics on the market. They'll tell you which are most durable and easy to care for and which are too delicate to be practical.

Count on cotton

Cotton reigns as one of the most popular and readily available fibers in the world. Cotton garments absorb wetness from the body, making them much more comfortable than most synthetic garments. Plus, cotton cloth can be manufactured and dyed very inexpensively, which explains its popularity among textile manufacturers.

Cotton goods tend to pucker when drying and are prone to wrinkling. For less wrinkling, add fabric softener to the wash or buy garments with a permanent-press finish.

Deciphering Fabric Care Labels

You may be a little confused as to what some labels mean. Or perhaps you're not sure what to do with a garment that is "hand wash only." The following chart, from the American Apparel Manufacturers Association, translates common label lingo into simple instructions for proper fabric care.

When The Label Says . . .	It Means . . .	When The Label Says . . .	It Means . . .
Machine Wash		**Machine Dry**	
Delicate/gentle cycle	Use the appropriate machine setting; otherwise, wash by hand.	Drip-dry	Hang up wet and allow to dry with hand shaping only.
Durable/permanent press	Use the appropriate machine setting or the warm wash/cold rinse/short spin cycle.	Dry flat	Lay the garment on a flat surface.
		Line-dry	Hang up damp and allow to dry.
Machine wash	Wash by any customary method, including commercial laundering and dry-cleaning.	No wring	Drip-dry or dry flat.
No chlorine bleach	Do not use chlorine bleach. Oxygen bleach is acceptable.	Tumble dry	Dry in a tumble dryer at the specified setting: high, medium, low, or no heat.
No spin	Remove before the machine's final spin cycle.	Tumble dry/remove promptly	Same as above, but in the absence of a cool-down cycle, remove at once when the tumbling stops.
Wash separately	Wash alone or with like colors.		
Non-Machine Wash		**Iron**	
Dry-clean only	Have the garment professionally dry-cleaned.	Cool iron	Set the iron at its lowest setting.
Hand wash	Launder only by hand in lukewarm water, or dry-clean.	Iron damp	Dampen the garment before ironing.
		Steam iron	Iron or press with steam.
Hand wash only	Same as above, but do not dry-clean.	Warm iron	Set the iron to its medium setting.

Line up for linen

Linen is a natural fiber in a class similar to cotton. It lasts longer and holds its shape better than cotton. It also costs more and wrinkles more, which means that linen garments require a lot of ironing. Look for linen blends as well as linen garments with a permanent-press finish. By comparison, these require little or no ironing.

Treat silk sensitively

Easy-care silk has become very popular in recent years. But usually, the cheaper the garment, the less durable and the more likely to fade. Silk is a delicate natural fiber that should always be dry-cleaned, regardless of what the label says. Hand washing or machine washing easy-care silk garments causes the fabric to fade or lose its shape.

Warily approach wool

Wool is one of the most resilient natural fibers, but it's not without problems. It shrinks considerably when it gets wet. Never machine wash a wool garment. If you do, a Barbie doll couldn't squeeze into it (okay, it wouldn't shrink that much, but you get the idea). Always dry-clean.

Washing Machine Mastery

Not long after moving into his first apartment, a young man threw his leather jacket and snakeskin boots into the washing machine. Needless to say, neither item survived the experience.

Not to poke fun at the young man's loss, but most of us know better than to do what he did. Still, we can all learn a thing or two about washing clothes and linens—simple strategies that can save us time and money and, in the long run, make doing laundry less of a chore.

A Laundry List of Tasks

Do clothes and linens appear dirty and dingy even after you take them out of the washer? Don't blame the machine. With a bit of laundry room know-how, you can get just about anything cleaner and brighter than brand-new.

Pretreat the tough stuff

If an item has a dried or particularly nasty stain, one cycle in the washing machine probably won't get it clean. Try a stain-removing pretreatment product that contains enzymes (the label will tell you the ingredients). Enzymes work well in removing protein-based

stains such as dirt, food, and blood. Soak the garment for at least 30 minutes before washing.

Temper your water temperature

Most laundry detergents are formulated to clean well at temperatures above 60°F. So washing in warm or hot water will likely produce better results than washing in cold water. Warm water is even better than hot because it doesn't require as much energy to heat it.

Use cold water to wash bright colors as well as to rinse all laundry. Warm or hot water makes colors fade more quickly.

Avoid an overload

Putting too much laundry in your washing machine at once prevents clothes and linens from coming clean. Overloading a washer is bad for many reasons. Your clothes don't circulate well, which decreases cleaning. Decreased cleaning leads to rewashing loads. And rewashing puts unnecessary wear and tear on your washing machine. Your washer could break down, and then you'd be out a lot more money than if you had just done an extra load.

Stick with softener

Fabric softener is important because it reduces static and makes your clothes softer. Some say that dryer sheets work better than liquid products because the liquid is diluted with water. This may be true, although we don't yet have any scientific evidence that it is. For now, use the product that is more economical and convenient for you.

No matter what its form, fabric softener may spot your clothes. If this happens, rewash the garments immediately.

Bleach with the best of them

At some point in your life, you've probably had a bad encounter with bleach. Chlorine bleach destroys, or at least spots, colored clothing and linens. If you must use bleach on a colored fabric, choose a product that is oxygen-based. (The label should say "color-safe.") It is safer than chlorine bleach, although not as effective in removing stains.

Clean delicates with a gentle hand

For delicate clothes, hand washing is a good alternative to machine washing. It provides little agitation to damage fabrics. When you hand wash an item, gently move it through the water to disperse the detergent. Use a product specially formulated for delicate fabrics. Stronger detergents can fade or damage more fragile clothing.

Leave big stuff for the coin laundry

Large items such as comforters, quilts, and sleeping bags should be washed in a large-capacity washer, which you'll find at the local coin laundry. Standard-size washing machines are not designed to handle such items. If you repeatedly use your machine for this purpose, it is more likely to break down.

Souping Up Your Soap

All detergents, regardless of price, work on the same principle. During the wash cycle, they break down into microscopic structures called micelles (not your cells, micelles). The micelles encapsulate dirt and grease and suspend them in the water so they can't be redeposited on your laundry.

No matter which detergent you choose, you can maximize its cleansing power just by following this advice.

Be generous with the suds

If you don't use the right amount of detergent when washing your clothes, you may be wasting water and time. Extra-dirty items and full loads require more detergent than usual. This may seem like a waste, but it's better than having to rewash laundry because it didn't get clean the first time around.

Account for hard water

If you have hard water (water with excess calcium and magnesium), you'll most likely need to use extra detergent. The minerals bind with the detergent and partially deactivate it, producing what you probably know as soap scum. If you can't afford a water filtration system for your home, you'll need extra detergent to adequately clean your clothes.

Add a little less

Many detergents now on the market come in ultra concentrations. This means you don't need to use as much for a standard-size load. You may have a tendency to add a little more simply because the recommended amount seems too small to do the job. You're throwing away your money when you do this, because ultra concentration detergents are usually more expensive per ounce. If you're going to use more of a product than necessary, you may as well go back to a standard concentration detergent.

Don't let foam fool you

You may think that the more a laundry detergent foams, the better it cleans. This doesn't always hold true. Some products are formulated not to foam so much. They work well in front-loading washing machines because of the agitation. They're also appropriate for hard water since the minerals in the water resist foaming anyway. As long as you're following the instructions on the product's label, don't worry if your suds subside.

See Spot Fade—Fade, Spot, Fade

Most clothing stains easily come out with regular laundry detergent—one of the small miracles of modern technology. Still, some stains are a bit more difficult to remove. Coincidentally, they always seem to show up on your favorite clothes. The following remedies can leave almost any garment spotless.

Note: Test each remedy on the inside of a seam. That way, if it causes the color to fade, no one else will notice. If none of these homemade spot removers works, then take the garment to your dry cleaner.

Outwit alcohol

A stain caused by a spilled alcoholic beverage quickly disappears with the help of a glycerin solution. You can buy glycerin in most grocery stores and drugstores. Just add a few tablespoons to cold water, then soak the affected garment. After 20 minutes or so, remove the garment and put it in fresh cold water with ½ cup of vinegar. Of course, if the fabric is dry-clean-only, take the garment to the cleaners instead of trying to get the stain out yourself.

Bleach the bleed

Most everyone has had the dye from one garment bleed onto another, if not onto a whole load. For a white item, try removing the bleed with chlorine bleach. For a colored item, try rewashing it immediately. Don't just throw the discolored garment in the dryer—the heat will cause the dye to set.

If the bleed lingers after the second washing, you can salvage the item by making it a darker color. You can buy fabric dyes inexpensively in most grocery stores. Just follow the product instructions.

Try a little tenderness

To remove a bloodstain from fabric, coat the spot with a meat tenderizer paste. Simply mix a tiny amount of meat tenderizer (any brand will do) with cold water, then apply the paste directly to the stain. After about 15 minutes, sponge off the paste and wash the garment as you normally would.

Why does meat tenderizer work? It contains enzymes that break down proteins, and a bloodstain contains proteins.

Avoiding Laundry Quandaries

Here are some of the most common laundry problems, along with some simple, quick ways to solve them.

Problem	Cause	Solution
Brown stains	Bleach, detergent, or soap reacting with iron or manganese in the water	Install an iron filter on your water system; use a water conditioner in both the wash and rinse cycles; don't use chlorine bleach
Holes, snags	Excessive wear	Make all repairs before washing an item; fasten hooks, close zippers, and remove pins before putting items in the washer
Tears	Improper use of bleach	Always dilute chlorine bleach before adding it to water
Gray and dingy fabrics	Incorrect sorting, insufficient detergent, or water temperature too low	Follow proper sorting and washing techniques
Greasy spots	Fabric softener sheets in the dryer with lightweight fabrics	Use liquid softener when cleaning delicate fabrics; use a lower temperature setting in the dryer; remove greasy spots by rubbing in liquid detergent and washing again
	Undiluted fabric softener coming into contact with fabric	Dilute liquid fabric softener before adding it to the rinse cycle
Harsh-feeling fabrics	Hard water	Increase the amount of detergent; install a mechanical water softener; use a water-conditioning product
	Inadequate spin speed	Increase spin speed; check to make sure the load is balanced so that the spin can reach its maximum speed
Linting	Improper use of fabric softener	Do not add softener directly to wash water unless specifically directed to do so
	Not enough detergent	Increase the amount of detergent to help hold lint in suspension so it can be flushed down the drain
	Overloaded washer	Reduce the load size or increase the water level so the wash can circulate freely
Yellowing	Incomplete removal of soil, especially body oils	Pretreat heavily soiled areas; increase the amount of detergent; use bleach and hotter water

Clean up after baby

If you've ever had a baby spit up formula on you, you know that removing the stain—and the smell—is difficult. The quickest and easiest solution is to dab the area with a baby wipe. These wipes are gentle enough to be safe for most fibers, and they're certainly more convenient and cost-effective than taking the garment to the dry cleaner.

Cut the grass

To clean a grass stain, first sponge the stain with rubbing alcohol, then wipe the area with cold water. The alcohol can fade fabric, so be sure to test it on the inside of a seam before applying it to the stain. If the color doesn't hold, then try sponging the stain with vinegar and cold water instead.

Unstick gum

One of the easiest and most convenient ways to remove gum from clothing and hair is to rub the area with peanut butter. The peanut butter disintegrates the gum so it comes out easily. Then all you have to do is wash the garment or your hair.

Handle with Care

Clothing can cost a bundle these days. The only way to fully justify the expense is to get as much wear from a garment as possible. Of course, if it fades or otherwise self-destructs after a few washings, that's money down the drain. So you have all the more reason to exercise caution with the clothes you choose.

- Be careful with clothing that you buy in discount retail stores. Some of these stores sell low-quality garments that quickly fade or tear after a few washings. The clothes are made to look good in the store, but that's about as long as many of them do. In the long run, you'll spend more money on inexpensive garments that don't last than on one well-made, higher-priced item.
- If you're concerned that a garment is too delicate to be machine washed even though the label says it's washable, take it to the dry cleaner instead. The exception: A garment labeled "machine wash only" should never be dry-cleaned. The color is probably sensitive to solvents, in which case the garment would be ruined.
- While saving money is a good thing, you don't want to cut corners when it comes to removing stains. If you try a few home remedies (after testing each one for colorfastness) to no avail, take the garment to the dry cleaner.

Finishing Touches

The main purpose of doing laundry is to get your clothes and linens clean. Once you've accomplished that, you're more than halfway done. You can make the rest of the job, including drying and ironing, go as quickly and easily.

For Best Results, Dry Wisely

Years ago, folks had no choice but to hang soaking-wet laundry outside to dry. If they were lucky enough, the sun was actually shining.

Today, while some folks still prefer line drying, many others opt for the automatic dryer. To be sure, line drying costs less. But it also is more labor-intensive and time-consuming. And machine drying tends to leave clothes and linens softer and more comfortable.

If you use an automatic dryer, apply the following strategies for best results.

Select the right setting

Your dryer has more than one temperature setting. Choosing the correct one not only decreases wrinkling but also saves time and money (on your electric bill, that

is). Plus, certain fabrics—including permanent press and delicates—should never be exposed to high heat. Check your owner's manual for suggested settings.

Shake, shake, shake

When you remove items from your washing machine, shake them out before you put them in the dryer. This may seem trivial, but it makes sense in many ways. Shaking untangles clothing and decreases drying time. It also protects clothing. A shirt that gets tangled up with a pair of jeans can become very wrinkled or even damaged during the drying process.

Overcome overloads

As with your washing machine, refrain from overloading your dryer. Too many clothes make the appliance work harder, which could break its belts. Overloading also increases drying time, which adds up on your electric bill. And it causes wrinkling, which leaves you little choice but to waste time ironing things you normally wouldn't.

Take a big hint for small loads

Have you ever noticed that small loads—when the dryer is, say, less than half full—sometimes take longer to dry than large loads? Small loads don't tumble as well, which increases drying time (not to mention wrinkling). You actually save time and money by adding an item or two. So when you have a small load, throw in a few pillow cases or towels.

Empty promptly

Removing clothes from the dryer as soon as their cycle ends prevents them from wrinkling excessively. It also eliminates the chance that you'll forget about them and leave them in the dryer until you're looking for a certain shirt or pair of slacks.

Divvy up the duties

Make each family member responsible for removing his clothes from the dryer, folding them, and putting them away. Or establish a policy that whoever empties the dryer folds everything and leaves the items stacked in the laundry room for the owners to pick up and put away. As long as the items are immediately removed from the dryer and folded, they shouldn't wrinkle much.

Lay down the law on lint

Make sure you or someone in your family clears the lint filter after each dryer cycle (not a major undertaking by any stretch of the imagination). A clean filter helps air circulate more efficiently, so clothes require less time to dry. A clean filter also puts less stress on the dryer, which may help it last longer.

Iron Like a Pro

You iron to get rid of wrinkles. What causes them, anyway? A wrinkle occurs when the moisture in air bonds with the fibers in fabric. The bonds lock the fibers in place. You'd never see another wrinkle if the air had no moisture.

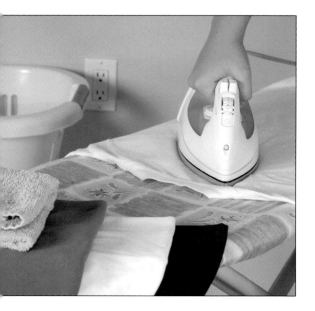

and other hard-to-reach areas. Lift each leg and iron the inside of the crotch.

Slide the pants off the ironing board. Holding them at the cuffs with the inseams matched up, hang them straight down to find the old creases. Lay one leg flat so that the waistband is at the wide end of the ironing board. Using long strokes on the damp towel, iron downward from below the seat to the cuffs. Repeat with the other leg.

Laundering Whites and Darks

If your whites look more dingy and your darks get more faded every time you wash them, these tips can make them look like brand-new again.

- Wash white synthetics only with other white fabrics.
- Soak white socks in baking soda and water to help loosen dirt before washing. Or boil them in water containing a lemon slice.
- To brighten white handkerchiefs, add a touch of cream of tartar to the wash water.
- Wash darks separately to avoid deposits of light-colored lint. Turning the garments inside out before washing also helps.
- To restore the color to black lingerie and other black garments, add bluing, coffee, or strong tea to the rinse water.
- Wash and dry jeans inside out to keep them from fading.

The best way to get rid of a wrinkle is to add *more* moisture—from a steam iron, for example, or a steamed-up bathroom. This changes the bonds so that the fibers assume more desirable positions, such as sharp creases and smooth straightaways.

These iron-clad tips can keep ironing simple.

Dial down for delicates

If you have many items to iron, start with delicate fabrics, which require the lowest heat setting. Otherwise, you'll have to wait for the iron to cool down, which only wastes time. Never cut corners by pressing delicates on a higher setting. You risk permanently damaging the garments.

Add foil to save toil

Put a piece of aluminum foil, shiny side up, between the ironing board and the pad. The foil reflects the heat back up toward the garments, so ironing goes faster. Remove the foil when you're done.

Note: This technique is not appropriate for delicates and other items that require a low heat setting.

Follow direction

When you iron, always go with the weave of the fabric. This prevents the fabric from folding and puckering, so it doesn't take as long to press. Plus, the fabric is less likely to stretch.

Trim time on trousers

You can iron cotton trousers in less than five minutes by using this technique recommended by Paul Buckter, manager of At His Service, a valet service at Bloomingdales in New York City. Begin by laying the trousers on an ironing board and placing a slightly damp hand towel over the waistband. Using long downward strokes, press the waistband and pleats. Work the pants around the narrow end of the ironing board to iron the pockets

For linens, just add water

To iron linens, sprinkle the fabric with water, then roll up the garment in a slightly damp (not soaking wet) towel. Allow the roll to sit for 10 to 15 minutes at room temperature. Unroll the towel and press the garment on the setting for linen.

Get steamed

You can remove wrinkles from many types of clothing just by hanging them in the bathroom. Run very hot water in the shower, hang your garments on the shower curtain rod, then close the door. The steam will smooth out the wrinkles. Keep in mind, though, that your clothes won't look pressed. They'll just look less wrinkled. Fabrics made from natural fibers respond better to steaming than fabrics made from synthetic fibers.

Seek smart substitutes

When you're traveling or when you have just one or two items to press, set up a makeshift ironing board by covering a countertop or desk with newspapers and laying a towel over top. If the newspapers slide around, place them in a pillowcase and tuck the end of the pillowcase under before covering with the towel. Remember to unplug the iron when you're finished: Leaving a hot iron unattended near paper of any kind is a fire hazard.

Remove any ribbons

Ribbons on dresses and blouses can be difficult to press, especially if they're small. Instead of trying to run the iron back and forth, set it on top of the ribbon and gently pull the ribbon through. If this doesn't help and you really want to save yourself the trouble, cut off the ribbon.

Call on the pros

Take expensive clothes made from wool, synthetics, and other blends to a professional dry cleaner for pressing. This may seem inconvenient, but at least you won't risk ruining a garment. Call local cleaners to find out whether any of them pick up and deliver. Door-to-door service can save you time and hassle.

The Well-Appointed Laundry Room

A properly outfitted laundry room makes tackling the laundry that much easier. Without efficiently functioning equipment and a few at-your-fingertips accessories, all the detergent in the world won't get the job done. This section is intended to help you make your laundry room as user-friendly as possible.

Buying the Right Appliances

When you consider that an average washing machine uses 15,597 gallons of water a year, which is the Maytag Company's estimate, it's a wonder that the appliance doesn't have to be replaced more often. To be sure, washers and dryers last a long time. You can make them last even longer just by decreasing everyday wear and tear. Whether you're in the market for new appliances or you want to extend the life of the ones you have, these tips can help.

How Complex Can It Get

Daunted by Detergents: The average supermarket devotes an entire aisle to detergents and other laundry products. They come in all varieties—with bleach or without; environmentally friendly or, one supposes, environmentally unfriendly; liquid, powder, or tablet; and so on. Here are some of the popular brands:

Arm & Hammer	Gain
All	Method
Biz	Oxi Clear
Cheer	Purex
Dauny	Tide
Fab	Woolite

Homemade Stain Removers

Stumped by a stubborn stain? Rub it out with one of these easy-to-make, proven-to-work home remedies.

- For non-oily stains on washable fabrics (except acetate, acrylic, silk, spandex, and washable wool), mix equal parts ammonia, dishwashing liquid, and water in a squeeze bottle. Shake the mixture well, squirt it on the spot, and work it in. Let the garment set for several minutes, then rinse with water. This mixture works well on blood, milk, perspiration, and urine stains. For beverage, fruit, and grass stains, replace the ammonia with vinegar.

- For oily stains on washable fabrics (except acetate, rayon, and triacetate), mix 1 tablespoon glycerin (a grease cutter), 1 tablespoon dishwashing liquid, and 8 tablespoons water in a squeeze bottle. Follow the same steps as above. Glycerin products are usually stocked with the soap products in many supermarkets. Ask a clerk to help you find them.

Stick with the basics

To clean and dry laundry, no-frills washers and dryers work just as well as the bells-and-whistles models. The only options you need on your washer are a water level selector, a temperature selector, and normal, gentle, and permanent-press cycle selectors. On your dryer, all you need are normal, gentle, and permanent-press timers. Most of these features are standard. Others cost extra and are more expensive to fix when they break.

Measure twice, buy once

Most washers and dryers, whether freestanding or stackable, are 27 inches wide. So make sure you have enough room for them before you buy. While you're at it, verify your power source, too. This is especially important if you rent your residence and are unsure of the power connection and voltage. While most washers and dryers operate on 120 volts, some need 220 volts.

Select the right style

Washing machines come in top-loading and front-loading models. If you have limited space in which to place your washer, a top-loader may be your only option. On the other hand, if you have ample space available, check out the pros and cons of both models before you buy. Front-loading washing machines use less water, but typically they are more expensive and hold smaller loads than top-loading machines.

Use used goods

If someone in your family is buying new appliances, perhaps he'll loan you the old ones or sell them to you inexpensively. Granted, you won't have any type of warranty or guarantee. But paying next to nothing for a washer or dryer that's in reasonably good shape will more than offset the cost of small repairs.

Go the direct route

When installing your dryer, use the straightest and shortest line possible for the venting duct. Straighter lines seldom clog with lint, and they cut down on fire hazards. Inspect the outside vent to make sure that no small critters have crawled in and made themselves at home (yes, this has actually happened).

Stay on the level

Install your dryer on a one-foot-high platform. That way, you won't have to bend over as far when loading and unloading laundry. Make sure the platform is made from some material other than wood. Wood is a fire hazard and shouldn't be used to house a dryer. A high-density plastic will work better.

More Hints for Laundry Management

You can simplify your laundry room even more just by keeping some essentials close at hand.

Add a table

If you have enough space in your laundry room, set up a small table on which you can fold your clothes immediately after they come out of the dryer. Leave the folded clothes on the table so family members can come by and pick them up. You can place your hampers underneath the table or install a pull-down ironing board to maximize space in a small laundry room.

> ### Simply Stated
>
> *Make hay while the sun shines.*
> **—English proverb**

Stash the trash

A trash can is a laundry room necessity. Whether you're disposing of lint, used dryer sheets, or empty detergent boxes, you'll find that having a trash can at hand is much more convenient than having to travel to another room to dispose of garbage.

Hang 'em high

Keep an ample supply of clothes hangers in the laundry room. You'll always have a few items that you want to hang up instead of folding. Dress pants and jeans, for example, can be put on hangers and placed on hooks attached to the laundry room wall. For simplicity, you may want to assign a hook to each family member.

Stifle the stench

If you use hampers, place a box of baking soda in each one to absorb moisture and eliminate odor. This is especially helpful if you allow laundry to collect for a few days before you wash it.

> ### I Came, I Saw, I Ironed
>
> If you think ironing is a chore now, then you have to pity the ancient Romans. They used a flat metal mallet to literally hammer the wrinkles out of clothing. It worked—crudely and loudly. ("Hey! No ironing before 8:00 in the morning!") The first iron, as we know it, was patented in 1882. It weighed so much that it probably didn't seem much better than the irons of the ancients.

The Simplest of the Simple

You can streamline your laundry chores considerably by applying these basic guidelines:

- Put separate hampers in your laundry room for whites, colors, towels, and other items to simplify sorting.
- Use your judgment when laundering delicate fabrics. When in doubt, have an item dry-cleaned.
- Be careful not to overload your washer or dryer.
- Use the correct amount of detergent for the particular load size and water level.
- Use baby wipes to clean stains from baby formula off most fabrics.
- Quickly remove clothes from the dryer to minimize wrinkling.
- Put away everyday clothing—those garments that you wear only around the house—without folding.
- Hang wrinkled clothing in the bathroom while you take a hot shower. The steam from the shower will remove the wrinkles.
- When replacing your washer and dryer, buy only basic models with standard features.
- Keep a trash can in the laundry room.

Chapter 10

Storage and More

*Making the Most
of Your Basement and Attic*

Here's a thought worth pondering: Using your basement to its fullest potential can help simplify the rest of your home. For instance, if you set aside your basement for storage, you'll free up valuable space upstairs. If you prefer to remodel your basement, you'll have another functional level in your home. You'll gain a brand-new family room, home office, or home business location—and increase the value of your property, too.

You may even decide to take remodeling a step further, converting your basement into living space that you can rent out. In this case, you'll need to make sure that all of the piping and wiring is in good condition and that other amenities are installed, which may require putting in a bit more work than you would for a room that only your family will use. It probably requires spending more money, too, unless your basement is in tip-top condition to begin with. Of course, by renting out the basement, you'll receive monthly payments that should qauickly offset the cost of remodeling and, in time, bring in extra income for your family.

This chapter explores your many options for making the most of your basement. It offers suggestions for organized, accessible storage and advice for simple, successful remodeling and finishing.

Because the attic presents its own opportunities for expanded storage and living space, ideas for fixing up this part of your home are included in this chapter as well.

Looking for Trouble

From a purely structural standpoint, a basement provides a foundation for a home. Yet not every home has one. Some older dwellings have little more than crawl spaces. Others have only partial basements. Newer dwellings are more likely to have full basements that extend the full length and width of the first floor.

As convenient and versatile as a basement is, it can also be the source of considerable trouble for the homeowner. Unless problems are caught early, they can end up costing a chunk of change to repair.

Keeping Your Goods Dry

Moisture is the most common problem to plague basements, especially in older dwellings. If you're shopping around for another home, make a point of carefully examining the basement for evidence of existing moisture or water damage. If you find a home you like, ask an independent home inspector of your choice—not the seller's—to check out the basement before you make a commitment to buy. That way, you'll avoid having to spend your money on repairs sometime down the road. (To locate a qualified home inspector in your area, contact the National Association of Home Inspectors at www.nahi.org.)

If you're planning to sell your home, keep in mind that it will lose value if any moisture problem isn't taken care of. The National Association of Home Builders estimates that 95 percent of wet basements can be dried up easily and inexpensively.

To ensure that your basement passes moisture muster, follow this advice.

Give the walls a good once-over

If a wall in your basement shows signs of mildew, it may have small cracks. Look for the cracks yourself. If you can't find them, hire an independent home inspector to locate them. Once the cracks are found, they should be filled with patching (hydraulic) cement. The extra money you spend now may save hundreds or thousands of dollars later on, when you'd have to replace rotted wood because of water damage.

Consider the source

If you have dampness in your basement, hang a mirror on one of walls. Check it the next morning. If the mirror is moist or fogged over, you have condensation, which can be remedied with a dehumidifier. If the mirror is dry and the wall is damp, you're dealing with seepage, and you need to look for cracks in the walls.

Defeat dampness decisively

Rising damp lines—dark, wavy lines that appear on concrete walls right above the basement floor—result as moisture seeps into the concrete and rises up through the pores, according to *Popular Mechanics* magazine. The lines are a cause for concern only if you want to finish the walls. You can make the walls look nicer simply by applying a masonry paint designed for damp situations.

Assess the incline

"Make sure the ground slopes away from the house, or surface water from rain or melting snow will accumulate around the foundation," says Norman Becker, an engineer in Greensboro, North Carolina. "If you still have a moisture problem, you should coat the interior surface of the foundation walls with a cement-based sealer such as Thoroseal."

Many home improvement stores carry Thoroseal. If you can't find it, write to the manufacturer, Thoro Systems Products at www.thorosystem.com.

Redirect rainfall

If your basement is relatively dry, then some basic maintenance will ensure that it stays that way. Keep your outside gutters clean so that they don't overflow and make sure downspouts lead a good distance away from the house or empty into dry wells.

Preventing Other Lower-Level Problems

Perhaps because they stand partially or fully below ground, basements are susceptible to other problems besides moisture. To outwit these lower-level woes, try the following tips.

Use activated charcoal to absorb foul basement odors.

Soak up the smell

Even if your basement doesn't have a moisture problem, it may still have a musty smell if it isn't used often or isn't properly ventilated. You can get rid of the odor quickly and easily with activated charcoal, which is sold in most drugstores. If the odor persists, you may indeed have an undetected moisture problem that should be taken care of.

Drown septic stench

If your basement smells like sewage, first check the pipes, ducts, vents, and other openings to see whether sewage has backed up. If that isn't the problem, then check any toilets and sinks in your basement. If these fixtures haven't been used for a while, the water in the trap (which provides a barrier to sewer gas) has probably evaporated. You can alleviate the problem by pouring water down the drain to fill the trap.

Arrest those pests

Termites and carpenter ants can wreak havoc in your basement as well as in other areas of your home. Termites eat wood, leaving behind shards as evidence. Carpenter ants, on the other hand, tunnel into wood to make their nests. Small piles of sawdust tip you off to their presence.

> ### Simply Stated
>
> *I counted two and seventy stenches,*
> *All well defined, and several stinks!*
> —**Samuel Taylor Coleridge,**
> **English poet, in Cologne**

Both insects love moisture, so your best bet for preventing an invasion is to keep your basement dry. If your home is already infested, don't waste time—consult a pest control service.

Rats (the rodents that introduced the bubonic plague to fourteenth-century Europe) would love to make your basement their home. Let them know they're unwelcome by installing an ultrasonic device, which emits high-frequency sounds that they can't stand. You'll find these devices in home improvement stores and online.

Eradicate radon

Colorless and odorless, radon gas may be responsible for as many as 100 of the lung cancer deaths that occur in the United States each day, according to the Environmental Protection Agency. The gas can seep from the ground into your home through cracks in the basement walls. Radon testing kits are available at nominal prices in home improvement stores. If the test results indicate that you do have radon gas, hire a contractor to remove the gas, seal all the cracks, and waterproof your basement. This is a job best left to a professional.

Putting Safety First

Just like any other area of your home, your basement should be well-protected. So as you repair any moisture problems or other damage, you may also want to install appropriate security devices.

Lay out the unwelcome mat

If your basement has an outside entrance, keep it locked and well-lit. Strong framing and dead bolts are musts.

Look at it this way: If you can pick the lock on your own basement door, a burglar can do the same—only much faster and more quietly.

If you own a dog, consider keeping him in the basement at night. That way, he can alert you to prowlers.

Protect your panes

Basement windows are perfect targets for break-ins because they're just above the ground. Securely lock each window, and install a steel bar across its width. The bar will prevent an intruder from crawling through the window. You may also want to install metal grating or a metal gate, which makes picking the lock more difficult.

Be liberal with lighting

Basements aren't usually well-lit, so installing extra fixtures should be a top priority. They'll discourage intruders, and they'll come in handy if you plan to use your basement as an office or a workshop. Rather than leaving a light on all night, invest in an outdoor sensor light that goes on automatically when it detects motion. You can prepare for the installation of extra lighting while working on any structural modifications in your basement.

More in Store

If you're not otherwise using your basement, it could be the perfect place to keep items that you don't have room for upstairs. In fact, many people purchase homes with basements just for the extra storage space.

Everything in Its Place

To keep your basement organized, you will likely need to add some shelves and other storage receptacles. Many basements are simply open, unfinished rooms with little or no storage. If you just pile everything on the floor, you'll eventually run out of room to walk. Besides, if a pipe bursts or the basement floods, most of what is sitting on the floor will be ruined.

You can buy ready-made storage units in discount retail stores. But since these units usually have to be assembled anyway, you may find do-it-yourself storage easier and less expensive.

The following measures can help ensure that everything in your basement has its proper place.

Negotiate for a cupboard

If one of your relatives or friends has experience with woodworking, ask him to build a storage cabinet for you. A handcrafted cabinet will likely be sturdier and last longer than a store-bought version.

Scrap the cardboard

Use plastic crates rather than cardboard boxes to store items. Plastic is more durable and extremely difficult to

break. If you buy clear plastic crates, you don't have to open each one to see what's inside.

If you've already amassed a collection of cardboard boxes, go ahead and use them. Write the contents of each box on the outside so you can find items more easily.

Get hooked on shelving

If your basement has no shelves, consider installing a few yourself. Simply fasten four S hooks to the ceiling or ceiling beams and four more to the shelf corners, then use lengths of chain to hang the shelf. Or attach one shelf directly to a wall, then hang another from it using S hooks and chains. The hooks are easy to remove, relocate, and adjust.

How Do You Find a Stud?

In construction parlance, studs are vertical boards in walls. They're usually spaced 16 inches apart, although in newer houses they may be 24 inches apart. The best place to look for a stud is not around a door or window opening or at the end of a wall but in the center.

If you don't have a magnetic stud finder, which locates nails in the studs, try one of the following methods:

- Knock on the wall. A stud will make a solid thunk, compared with the hollow sound of a wall.
- Check the baseboard. Nail heads are usually driven into a stud's center.
- Remove the faceplate of an outlet. The box behind it is usually nailed to a stud.

Hang 'em just high enough

If you attach shelves directly to the basement walls, position them so that they're accessible to the person who will be using them the most. The person should be able to view the entire contents of each shelf—including items stuck in the back—and to retrieve items without standing on tiptoes or a stool.

Give yourself a leg up

If your basement already has shelving that's higher than you can reach, keep a small step ladder close by. That way, you don't have to tote a kitchen chair or step stool downstairs every time you need something.

> ### Simply Stated
>
> *Things don't turn up in this world until somebody turns them up.*
>
> **—James A. Garfield,**
> **Twentieth president of the United States**

Fall for a line

If you line-dry your laundry—either by choice or by necessity—you probably know that a sudden downpour can make a mess of several hours' work. To solve this problem, hang a clothes rod or short clothesline in your basement. You'll have a safe, dry place to hang your laundry on days when the weather proves uncooperative.

Mark the spot

Once you've organized your basement the way you want it, create an inventory list and hang it on your basement door. The list will tell you at a glance where to find whatever it is that you're seeking. If you have a family, you can turn the list into a detailed grid or map that others in your household can use. If you live by yourself, your list may be more general, consisting of just enough information to direct you to your spare set of dishes three years from now when you need them.

Show your colors

You can make finding items in your basement even easier by color-coding crates and other storage containers. Assign each family member a color, then put everything belonging to that person in appropriately colored containers. Stick with the color designations—don't let your son talk you into changing from green to blue. Such a switch will only complicate matters.

What Belongs in Your Basement?

Try to go through everything in your basement once or twice a year to weed out items that you can sell, give away, or toss out. There's no need to keep something that you're not going to use or to let stuff pile up year after year. It just makes cleanup a lot more difficult and time-consuming.

Once you've emptied your basement of what you don't want, you have a perfect opportunity to organize what's left. That way, you can find any item you need right when you need it.

So what—and how—should you stow down below? Here are some suggestions.

Capitalize on quantity

If you get a good deal on nonperishable bulk items such as toilet paper and cereal, store the extras in a clean, dry area of your basement. Organize the items room by room, storing all kitchen supplies together, all bathroom supplies together, and so on.

Employ natural refrigeration

Basements are generally cool (unless they're directly heated), which makes them ideal for storing fresh fruits and vegetables as well as canned goods. If you use your basement for this purpose, just make sure that it has good air circulation. Also, frequently check fresh produce for spoilage so your basement—and, subsequently, your whole house—doesn't start smelling like rotten tomatoes.

Go for the big chill

If the freezer in your refrigerator is almost always filled to capacity, then consider putting a stand-alone freezer in your basement. This appliance can come in handy, especially for people who buy meat in bulk. And by having the freezer in the basement, the food inside won't spoil as quickly in the event of a power outage, because the basement tends to be cooler than the rest of the house.

Before installing a freezer, make sure that any moisture problems in your basement have been corrected. To be on the safe side, you may want to set the freezer on a platform so it won't create an electrical hazard if a pipe bursts or the basement floods.

Keep furnishings under wraps

You may have some old but still usable furniture that you're planning to pass on to your child or grandchild when he goes away to college or gets his first apartment. Cover these items with plastic and store them in a dry area of the basement.

Shop at home

The basement is a good place to store all the duplicate wedding or housewarming gifts that you receive. Then when you're invited to a similar event, you can go through your supply of extras and select something appropriate to give. It sure beats returning gifts. Simply attach a name card to each item showing who bought it for you. Don't make the grand social faux pas of giving a toaster back to the person who gave it to you!

Derailing the Dangers

If your basement serves as a dumping ground for items that you can't store anywhere else, you may unwittingly be endangering your and your family's safety. Strong solvents and cleaners, for example, create a fire hazard when stored near combustible materials. And if the solvent containers aren't tightly closed, fumes can seep into your upstairs living area. Such situations can complicate your life in dreadful ways.

So be careful when storing items in your basement. If you consider something too hazardous to keep elsewhere in your home, then it most likely is a hazard in your basement as well. The following guidelines can help you decide what can stay and what should go.

Remove fuel for flames

Most people have flammable liquids (such as gasoline and paint thinner) in the basement or garage. Although neither place is ideal, the garage is a better choice. Avoid keeping flammables anywhere in your house.

If you have no other option besides the basement, at least be sure to put some distance between the flammable liquids and any heat source. And never, ever store gasoline in your house. The fumes can escape, and if they become concentrated enough, they can ignite with nothing more than a spark. Your house would literally explode.

Put old rags in their place

Paint-stained and oil-stained rags left lying around are fire hazards. Ideally, you should get rid of them—but don't just throw them in the trash. Stuff them into a tin can (preferably one with a lid) or a resealable plastic bag. Forget paper bags, though: The combination of paper and paint or oil is highly combustible.

If you're storing the rags for some reason, put them in metal containers that are outside or in an outbuilding. If you must keep the containers inside, move them away from heat sources.

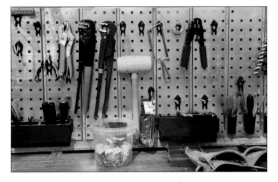

Abandon the paper trail

Stacks of newspapers and magazines in cardboard boxes are highly combustible. If a fire started in your basement, these items would help the flames quickly spread. In such a situation, you could do little more than escape to safety. The same goes for old wooden furniture.

Stow away power tools

Lock up all of your power tools when you're not using them. This keeps them out of the hands of curious children and also out of the view of potential burglars, who may look through basement windows to check out the loot.

Keep out kids

If you have a toddler, consider putting a childproof lock on your basement door. You can buy a lock that mounts high, where kids can't reach it. It will prevent your child from opening the basement door and falling down the steps. You may also want to install gates to keep your child out of certain areas of the basement.

> **Simply Stated**
>
> *No money is better spent than what is laid out for domestic satisfaction.*
> **—Samuel Johnson, English author**

Room to Grow

Of course, you may need only a portion of your basement for storage. So what should you do with all that leftover space?

Well, you could expand your home's living quarters by converting part or all of your basement into an extra room. In fact, if you've thought about building an addition to your house but found the costs prohibitive, you may be able to save money by remodeling the basement into what you desire. After all, the basic structure already exists, so you wouldn't have to start from scratch.

Pondering the Possibilities

The hardest part of remodeling your basement may be deciding exactly what you want to do with it. Ask yourself, "If I were building a new house, what type of room would I add that I don't currently have?"

To get the ball rolling, read through the following possibilities. Perhaps you'll find one you like—or you'll come up with an idea of your own.

Let the kids romp

Some families designate the basement as a play area for their children. This can be a good idea for many reasons.

The upstairs won't get as cluttered with toys and books, so you won't spend as much time cleaning up. Plus, the play area will be hidden from view, so if the kids don't pick up their toys, you don't have to worry about your house looking messy. After all, this is your children's room. If they don't mind the mess, you need not either.

Of course, for your kids to use the basement, they should be old enough to navigate the stairs and to turn the lights on and off. Otherwise, they could get hurt if you're not around to supervise.

"Rec" the room

As your kids get older, or if only adults live in your home, you may prefer to convert your basement into a recreation room. Some families outfit such rooms with entertainment centers, pool tables, and other grown-up toys. This way, everyone can enjoy the space. It may even become an unofficial meeting place where the entire family spends time together.

Seize a photo opportunity

Photographers—amateurs and professionals alike—sometimes like to have their own darkrooms for developing photographs. The basement is an ideal place for a darkroom because it's cool and dark. Also, since the basement is more private, you'll have less chance of someone ruining your pictures by walking in on you.

Build a laundry down below

If you currently have a laundry room upstairs, moving it into the basement will free up space for a large closet or even a second bathroom. The downside, of course, is that the laundry room won't be as convenient. You'll have to do a lot of running up and down the stairs.

If you do decide to build a laundry room in your basement, remember to set your washer and dryer on a platform. This will protect the appliances in case a pipe bursts or the basement floods.

Peruse in privacy

Provided your basement has no moisture problems, consider turning it into a small library or study. You can escape the television and other distractions and enjoy some quiet time with less chance of an interruption. You may want to build bookcases into the walls or set up a few ready-made, freestanding bookcases.

Set up shop

Many small businesses start in the home. For instance, if you have enough empty space in your basement to accommodate woodworking tools, you can try your hand at making crafts or—on a larger scale—furniture. If woodworking isn't your specialty, you have almost unlimited options to explore.

Before you go this route, however, make sure that having a business in your home is practical. For instance, does your basement have an outside entrance so customers don't have to walk through your living quarters? Always troubleshoot potential problems when beginning a home business.

Establish a satellite office

Many people now have the option of telecommuting, that is, working from their homes. If you do this, you'll want your home office to be every bit as efficient as a corporate office is. Your basement may be a suitable space for an office as it offers a quiet environment that is somewhat separate from the rest of your home.

If you need a computer, first check your basement for moisture. Correct any problem before you install expensive electrical equipment.

Baby your bottles

If you happen to be a wine aficionado, you may want to build a wine cellar in your basement. For this to work, your basement must have a consistent temperature that

---

Reality Check

Remodeling any part of your home can be exciting. The finished product will give you a source of pride that you can show off to other people. Enjoy the enthusiasm—but be careful to not get so carried away that your new project becomes your new nightmare.

- Make all necessary repairs to your basement, even if they seem expensive. If you ignore a problem, it is going to get worse and cost a lot more in the long run.
- Just because you want your basement to be your new den doesn't mean that you have to pursue the project at all costs. Set a realistic budget and stick with it. If it looks like the project is going to be too expensive, scrap it and consider an alternative.
- Doing most of the work yourself can save you a bundle of money. If you're not sure what you're doing, however, it can cost you more in the long run, when you have to hire a professional to correct your mistakes.
- Many people remodel or finish their basements in expectation of huge payoffs when they sell their homes. It's true that a finished basement increases property value. But if you sink thousands of dollars into your basement, don't expect to get every last cent back. After all, the people who buy your home may want the basement just for storage.

is slightly cooler than room temperature. You can use milk crates as inexpensive wine racks, suggests Terence Conran, author of the *New House Book*. Simply turn the crates on their sides.

To make the most of your available space, stack the crates underneath your basement steps. Or build a storage unit to fit beneath the steps.

Before You Begin . . .

Once you have some idea of what you want to do with your basement space, you need to evaluate your plan in practical terms. Many homeowners get excited about the prospect of remodeling, invest lots of time and money in doing the work, then barely use the new room. The costs you incur should be directly proportional to the amount of time you'll spend in your finished basement. In other words, if you don't expect to be downstairs much, then don't shell out a lot of money to fix it up.

With that in mind, use the following guidelines to assess just how much work you'll have to do to transform your basement into the room you want.

Size up the space

Before you do anything else, check out your local building codes. They may impose certain standards for residences. For example, building codes may require homes to have a certain amount of headroom—usually 7½ feet

from floor to ceiling. If space is a problem, you want to know about it up front.

Even if your basement meets code, however, you may not have enough room for comfort. For instance, if you're turning your basement into a home gym, you need adequate space for a treadmill, a weight bench, and any other exercise equipment you purchase.

Note what's available

Examine the accessibility of lighting and ventilation. Does your basement have adequate light sources, or will you need to rewire for electricity? Does your basement have windows for ventilation? This is especially important if you intend to keep any electrical equipment or musical instruments downstairs. These items can easily rust, warp, or stain in a damp environment without adequate air circulation.

Also, if you're planning to start a small business in your basement, you may want to install an outside entrance if you don't already have one. That way, patrons won't have to walk through the rest of your home to get to you.

Turn down the volume

Because of their construction and location, basements seem especially prone to echoes and excessive sound. "Soft" interiors—carpeting on the floor, tapestries on the walls—lessen the noise and office partitions absorb some of the sound. A suspended ceiling may also help.

Run hot and cold

If you're converting your basement into a family room, an office, or another room where you and your family will spend a lot of time, you will need adequate heating and air-conditioning systems. There's a good chance that the heating system you already have will be sufficient. If not, you may have to run ducts into each downstairs room. Make sure the heating system you choose is efficient so you won't be throwing away money when you pay your electric bill each month. New systems come with efficiency ratings so you can compare before you buy.

Set a limit

In the movie *The Money Pit*, Tom Hanks and Shelly Long end up paying much more than they bargained for to fix up an old house in a New York City suburb. Establish a budget before you start remodeling, then stick with it.

Consider the alternatives

Develop a backup plan just in case the original falls through because of unforeseen problems. For example, building code restrictions may rule out the possibility of building a family room. But you may be able to install a laundry room, bathroom, or shower. So even though your first plan doesn't work out, you can still use the basement for something your family needs.

Shaping Up Your Living Space

Okay, you have a remodeling plan and the all clear to move ahead with it. What next?

Here's a rundown of some of the tasks that may come up during your remodeling project. Keep in mind that this is only an overview. For more information and suggestions, you may want to consult a remodeling expert at your local hardware or home improvement store.

Cozy up to the proper insulation

If you're transforming your basement into a family room or an extra bedroom, you may need to install insulation to hold in the heat. You can use rigid polystyrene board insulation or batt insulation (the fluffy stuff). You may also want to put a vapor barrier on the insulation, either facing into the room or against the foundation wall itself (or maybe even on both sides). Where you place the barrier depends on the climate in which you live. If you're unsure, ask the insulation specialist at your local home improvement center.

Drop your ceiling

A suspended ceiling definitely has some advantages over a traditional ceiling. It serves as a sound barrier between the basement and the rest of the house. Plus, it conceals ducts, pipes, and cables so they're out of sight but readily accessible for repairs. If an overhead pipe should develop a leak, repairing it will be only a minor inconvenience rather than a costly, labor-intensive task.

Paint for posterity

A burst water pipe can ruin wallboard and carpeting in your basement. So consider painting the walls and floors instead. Likewise, if you prefer a traditional ceiling over a suspended one, you'll need to paint or stain it. The easiest way to do this is with a spray gun, which you can rent from a hardware or equipment supply store. For walls and floors, use latex masonry paint or waterproofing/damp-proofing paint.

Get fired up

If you have a fireplace upstairs, you may be able to install one downstairs as well. Either way, remember to have your fireplace cleaned and checked every year. Creosote can build up and create a substantial fire hazard.

If your fireplace has stood idle for a long time, call in a professional to inspect it before you use it.

Furnishing with Family in Mind

A family room is used extensively and can quickly become cluttered and disorganized. For these reasons, you'll want to pay particular attention to its design and decor. The following tips can help you outfit your basement family room simply and inexpensively—for durability, comfort, and style.

Raid your relatives' homes

Since you don't want to spend a lot of money on new furniture for your family room (especially after the expense of building it), ask relatives whether they have any pieces that you could borrow or buy from them. Even if you have to buy it, it won't be as expensive as store-bought sofas and chairs. And remember: get only as much furniture as you really need. Extra pieces just collect dust and dirt.

Put the fridge within reach

If you and your family have a habit of munching in front of the television, consider installing a small dormitory-style refrigerator in the family room. Use it to store snacks and drinks so that you don't have to run upstairs to the kitchen every time you want to get something to eat.

Put everything in its place

Some homes have televisions and DVD players in the living room and every bedroom. If this describes your home, try assigning DVDs, video games, and similar items to specific rooms. For example, select the DVDs and games that you want in your family room, then keep them there. Ask family members not to tote them elsewhere in your home.

Also, store at least one blank tape downstairs so you don't have to search the entire house for one when you want to record something.

Stow toys downstairs

If you have children or grandchildren, the same rule applies to their toys as to DVDs and video games. Store some of their playthings in a toy box in the family room, and make sure they stay there. Remind the kids not to drag stuff downstairs from upstairs. This can help keep your family room uncluttered.

Make cleanup convenient

Toting a vacuum cleaner and cleaning supplies all around your home can be very aggravating. You may want to install a small closet in your family room and use it to store extra cleaning equipment. You'll save time—and your back will thank you for not carrying a vacuum up and down the stairs.

Also, you can do yourself a big favor by encouraging family members to pick up after themselves before they leave the family room.

Room to Rent

Finishing your basement increases the value of your home, so it will fetch a higher price if you decide to sell. But you don't have to wait until you move for your basement to generate income. It can earn money now, while you're still living there, if you fix it up to rent out.

Creating a Whole New Unit

If you're thinking of converting your basement into a rental unit, your first step is to go to your local library and read up on the legal rights and responsibilities of both landlord and tenant. Many people rent out property to others without fully understanding all of the issues that can arise. For instance, what is your legal obligation if your tenant injures himself on your property? Or if water leaks through the floor of your living quarters and ruins your tenant's personal belongings?

Once you know what to expect, you can proceed with plans to transform your basement into an apartment. Be sure to consider the following when preparing the space for occupancy.

Enter from the outside

Even though your tenant will be renting part of your house, there's no need for you to see him very often—and vice versa. Just ask him to use the outside entrance to your basement. He can come and go as he pleases, and he won't bother you if he comes in at 3:00 in the morning. Install a dead bolt on the door and keep an extra key in case your tenant locks himself out.

Provide a private potty

You'll want your tenant to have his own bathroom. A shower, toilet, and sink should suffice. If these fixtures are already installed, make sure they're functioning properly, with no clogs to cause foul odors or backups.

Rather than wallpapering, paint the bathroom with a latex or an oil-based paint for ease of cleaning. Also, use a dark shade of floor covering, which won't show stains or dirt.

Opt for a cozy kitchen

As with the bathroom, a small and simple kitchen should do just fine. Since you're renting to one person (or perhaps a couple), your tenant won't need a lot of kitchen space. An open kitchen with a small refrigerator, a range, a sink, and a few cabinets should do. If you want, you can install a breakfast nook or a small table against one of the walls so your tenant won't have to buy one of his own.

Phone alone

A separate phone line for your tenant is an absolute necessity. You don't want your tenant running up a large long-distance phone bill that you are legally responsible for paying. Also, your tenant may need an extra hookup for Internet access.

Make the connection

The person who rents your basement may or may not have a washer and dryer. To be on the safe side, install connections for these appliances anyway. Your tenant will appreciate the convenience—and you will enjoy peace of mind knowing that your tenant isn't sneaking

upstairs to use your machines. You can raise the rent a few dollars to cover the costs of the electricity and water.

Dollar-Wise Decorating

Once you have the apartment in live-in condition, you have to decide how much additional decorating you want to do. Use the following guidelines as your gauge.

Spend on remnants

Most do-it-yourself home centers sell carpet remnants at reasonable prices. (If you happen to live near a college or university, you may be able to pick up remnants at the start of the school year, when vendors hawk them to students living in dormitories.) For rental units, remnants work better than wall-to-wall carpeting. If a tenant trashes the carpets, you won't lose a lot of money.

Granted, carpet pieces don't keep the floor as uniformly warm as wall-to-wall. You can make it up to your tenant by giving him a pair of warm, fuzzy bedroom slippers.

Furnish in your favor

One advantage to renting out your basement is that you don't have to buy furniture. Tenants typically bring their own. But if you prefer to provide some basic furnishings, refrain from spending huge sums of money on them. Anyone who has rental experience can tell you that one bad tenant will tear up everything you have. If you don't invest much, you won't lose much.

Clear the air

Regardless of how you feel about smoking, don't rent your basement to a smoker. A careless person may fall asleep with a cigarette in his hand or throw a cigarette butt in the trash, either of which can lead to a fire. The object is to make money off your basement, not to let a tenant burn down your house.

Of course, asking a person outright whether he smokes and denying him housing if he says that he does may leave you battling charges of discrimination. To avoid such a legal entanglement, have all potential tenants fill out a simple application form that includes a question about smoking. Also request references. This way, you can discreetly choose a nonsmoker.

Going Over Your Head

Like your basement, your attic can come in handy when you need extra storage or living space. There's plenty of room to expand, provided you use every inch wisely.

Stowing for Space

If you're like most folks, your attic is already piled to the rafters with stuff. Did you ever ask yourself whether the floor is sturdy enough to hold all that extra weight? Or whether rodents or other pests might destroy any valuables you have stashed up there? Perhaps some items belong in a safe-deposit box rather than a cardboard box.

To organize your attic and keep your belongings in good condition, take these suggestions to heart.

Put pests out to pasture

Before you store anything in your attic—especially clothing—you need to get rid of rodents and other unwelcome guests. Consult a professional exterminator and follow his advice for keeping not only your attic but your entire home pest-free.

Log every location

If you use your attic strictly for storage, post an inventory list somewhere up there. That way, other family members will know where you've put the holiday decorations, for example. The list doesn't have to be detailed. As long as it describes the basic location of an item, people should have few problems finding what they need.

Label boxes and crates

Reinforced cardboard boxes and plastic crates are the most popular container types for attic storage. (Cedar chests are also common, although some of these can be very heavy.) Indicate on each container what is inside. Or as an alternative, color-code the containers. For instance, put all of your holiday decorations in red crates, all your off-season clothes in blue crates, and so on.

Go on a roll

If you're in the habit of putting too much stuff in your storage crates, you may have a hard time lifting them. In this case, you may want to buy crates with rollers or attach rollers to crates yourself. You can purchase rollers in most hardware and home improvement stores. They're easily fastened with Krazy Glue or Super Glue.

Raise the rafters

Instead of putting your clothes in boxes, hang them in your attic. You can easily install a wooden or metal rod across rafters, creating a makeshift closet. Be sure to put the clothing in some sort of plastic cover. The cover will prevent your clothes from inheriting the attic's musty smell. It also deters rodents and other pests.

Consider shelves

Hang adjustable shelves from the rafters and ceiling to store small items. You can also hang plastic-coated wire baskets, which are available in discount retail stores and home improvement stores.

If you still have stuff to store, get rid of it. You're drowning in a sea of clutter.

Stretching Your Living Space

Whether you need an extra bedroom or a study, you may want to consider converting your attic. In fact, if you don't have a basement, your attic may be your only option for expansion—especially if you lack the room or the finances to build an addition onto your home.

If you decide to fix up your attic, first check for structural problems and correct them. Then decide how you can best utilize the space. Attics aren't known for being roomy, so you'll want to take advantage of every inch that you have available.

The following ideas can help you make your attic livable.

Verify the ventilation

Moisture problems can be just as serious in the attic as in the basement. In fact, the two are closely related. The damp air rises from the basement through each floor of your home until it reaches the attic, where it becomes trapped.

If you notice moisture in your attic, first check for problems in your basement. If everything seems okay there, then take steps to increase the airflow upstairs. Try setting a 20-inch-wide electric fan in the doorway to the attic to draw air from the rest of the house. Run the fan whenever you feel it's necessary. If it doesn't help, call in a professional to assess the situation.

Outwit water

When the roof sheathing in your attic frosts over, dampness in the basement may be to blame. You can reduce the frost by installing a vapor barrier beneath the insulation (This won't correct the moisture problem in the basement, however).

Bring in the reinforcements

If your attic wasn't built as living space, you may need to strengthen the floor by adding thicker joists. You may also need to add insulation between the floorboards and the rafters. Extra insulation ensures that the attic stays warm in the winter and cool in the summer.

Lay down a new floor

If your attic has no floor to speak of, you can make one by installing plywood panels. You will probably need at least two or three panels, each ⅝- to ¾-inch thick. For increased support, make sure that each panel covers at least three ceiling joists.

Let the sunshine in

Skylights invite natural light into your attic where more is needed. They also help heat the attic and make it

appear more spacious. Manufacturers size skylights to fit common rafter spacings. By purchasing units that fit neatly within two or three rafter bays, you can minimize the number of rafters that must be cut. You can choose from fixed skylights and ventilated skylights, the latter of which open to improve air circulation.

Enjoy your flight

Your attic may have only a pull-down ladder for access. If you want to use the attic as living space, you'll need to trade in that ladder for a flight of stairs. A spiral staircase may be most practical because it takes up the least amount of space. But even it may not work if you have a narrow hallway (Keep in mind that a staircase will take up space not only in the attic but on the floor immediately below as well). In that case, your best bet is to ask a professional what your options are.

Take a powder—upstairs

Planning to build an extra bathroom in your attic? Your first step is to examine the plumbing and the floor to ensure that both can support the additional bathroom fixtures. Then position the fixtures in their proper places to make the most of the available space. Put the bathtub and sink beneath a sloped ceiling. And instead of positioning a small mirror over the sink, hang a full-length one behind the door. Or install a mirror with an accordion-like extension handle, which you can pull out when you need it.

The Simplest of the Simple

With efficient use of the available space, you can transform your basement or attic into one of your home's greatest assets. As you do, keep the following guidelines in mind:

- Fill in all cracks from water damage in your basement.
- Store items in sturdy plastic crates or reinforced cardboard boxes in the basement or attic.
- Designate a clean, dry area of your basement for items that you buy in bulk.
- Remove all flammable liquids from the basement.
- Set up a home gym in your basement, or clean out an area where you can do aerobics.
- When remodeling, establish a budget and stick with it.
- Paint the floor of your finished basement instead of carpeting it.
- Keep extra cleaning supplies downstairs.
- Maintain an inventory list of items that you've stored in the basement or attic.

Chapter 11

Retooling the Garage

A Practical Plan to Maximize Space
and Minimize Maintenance

You can tell a lot about a family by looking in its garage. One quick glance will reveal whether household members are organizers or pack rats—or simply overwhelmed by all the junk cluttering the space where they once parked their cars.

The attached or unattached garage is a room, just like the kitchen or bedroom. On a typical day, more people probably pass through the garage than through the bedroom. Because the garage is such a high-traffic area, keeping it organized and safe is critical. Storing hazardous items there isn't necessarily any safer than storing them inside your home. If you must stow them in the garage, then do it safely.

This chapter includes storage tips for your garage that build upon ideas from previous chapters. It also proposes a six-month checkup for your entire home to ensure that everything is in good working order. From the basement through the attic and out into the garage, a number of structural features need to be examined periodically both to protect your family and to preserve the value of your home in the long run.

Not Just for Cars Anymore

Organizing your garage doesn't have to be painful. The key, as with all your rooms, is to break down the work into manageable parts and enlist help from those around you. You may even want to make family members responsible for sorting through their own belongings, throwing out what they don't want, and properly storing what they do.

Don't cram your garage with stuff as if it were some kind of catchall. Store items with care and keep the dangerous ones out of the reach of children. A little organization can go a long way. You may even be able to get your car back inside.

Sorting through Stuff

The longer you've lived in your home, the greater the odds that your garage has become a disaster area. You can restore the space to its former neat-as-a-pin glory by following this advice. (If you're moving into a new home, you can use these tips to create an organized garage from the outset.)

Start from scratch

Cleaning and organizing are nearly impossible when items are stacked from floor to ceiling. Recruit family members and anyone else who is available to completely empty your garage. Pick a nice weekend so stuff won't get rained on while it's sitting in your driveway. Once everything is outside, sweep the floor and make any structural repairs that are necessary. Paint if you need to.

Trash all the junk

Once you've moved everything out of the garage, you and your helpers can go through it all and pick out what can be thrown out or given away. Or pick out only what you want to keep, meaning that what's left can be tossed.

In either case, a simple three-pile system will work best. Separate everything into three piles. The first pile is for the items that will go back into the garage. The second pile is for the items that will be thrown out. The third pile is for items that are too good to throw out but that you don't want to keep anymore. This pile includes things that can be given away or sold at a garage sale.

Simply Stated

I go at what I am about as if there was nothing else in the world for the time being.

—Charles Kingsley, English author and clergyman

Divide and reconquer

Separate all the items that will go back in your garage into categories. Sports equipment may go in one category, while tools go in another. Once you're done sorting, combine piles of related items if you can. For instance, put small tools such as the hammer and screwdriver with the nails and screws, or put the rake and edge-trimmer with the lawn mower.

Consolidate collections in containers

If the items in one pile belong to various family members, store each person's belongings in a different color container. That way, there's no confusion as to what belongs to whom. You may have some things that won't fit into storage containers. In this case, put colored stickers on the objects so they can be identified.

Stake your claim

This is the difficult part, which will require a lot of compromising. Mom might want her gardening items near the garage door, where they'll be accessible to her, while Dad wants his tools and workbench in the same area. Look at the situation rationally. Should certain items be near the door to the house because they're used more often? Are some things too bulky to be kept near the door without blocking access?

Give your garage a chance to breathe

Your garage will get hot in the summer, just like the rest of your home. Make sure the space has adequate ventilation, especially if you're storing chemicals and cleaners there.

Sell your trash

If you have many items in the too-good-to-throw-away pile, plan a garage sale as soon as possible. If you put it off, those things will likely find their way back into the garage, which defeats the purpose of removing them to begin with.

Organizing Inch by Inch

Anyone who has ever cleaned out a garage knows how quickly it can become cluttered again. One way to prevent this is to make sure that every item has a designated storage space. Here are some suggestions.

Install shelves and cabinets

If you simply set all your belongings on the floor of your garage, you'll barely have space to walk around, let alone park the family vehicles. Instead, purchase some ready-made shelves and cabinets to hang in the garage. Cabinets are especially handy because they keep items out of the reach of children and out of the sight of snooping thieves.

Store flammables with care

If you have hazardous products—especially flammable liquids—in your garage, purchase a small fire-safe cabinet to store them in. You'll find such cabinets in home improvement stores.

Take advantage of cans

Since your garage doesn't need to be pretty, hang empty coffee cans or soup cans on the wall to hold small items such as nails and screws. Fasten the cans directly to the wall or to a pegboard. Position them high enough that children can't reach them.

Fix It Fast, Fix It Right

Who wants to call in a professional for every minor household repair? With the right tools, you can handle many jobs on your own. You'll save money—and avoid the hassle of waiting around for the repairman.

The following tools will take care of most do-it-yourself projects. Buy only the best. Cheap tools can be harder to use and may need to be replaced often.

Adjustable wrench	Nail set
Block plane	Paintbrushes
Carpenter's square	Plunger
Caulking gun	Pry bar
Cold chisel	Putty knife
Combination square	Receptacle tester
Crosscut saw	Screwdriver set
Drill and bits	Slip-joint pliers
Flat file	Staple gun
Hacksaw	Tape measure
Hammer	Triangular trowel
Keyhole saw	Utility knife
Level	Wire brush
Long-nose pliers	Wood chisel

Capitalize on plastic

Plastic storage containers are great for organizing small items. Containers with small compartments can be used to house anything from bolts to thumbtacks. This is convenient because if you drop the container, it won't break and spill its contents all over creation.

Elevate your drop cloth

If you have a workshop in the garage, install a few wooden or metal racks for holding dirty rags. Such racks are also convenient places to keep drop cloths so you won't lose them and need to buy new ones the next time you change your oil or paint your walls. Racks can be used to hold most large drapeable items for easy access when you're doing yard work or cleaning the garage.

Cork it

Corkboard is functional for the garage because it's so versatile. You can stick many things on corkboard, from blueprints to instructions for making that birdhouse you've been wanting to find time to work on. All the paperwork will be out of your way but accessible. You can purchase corkboard in any home improvement or discount retail store. Make sure to keep the pushpins out of the reach of children.

Position it with pegboard

Pegboard can be your best ally in the garage. There's virtually nothing lightweight that you can't hang on pegboard. If you have a workbench, install pegboard over the bench for hanging small hand tools. If you're a mechanic, you can mount pegboard on one whole wall and hang sockets, wrenches, or whatever automotive tools you'll need. You can also hang garden tools and accessories where they'll be accessible when you need them.

Hang bicycles

Install heavy-duty rods or hooks in your garage wall for storing the family bicycles. Keep the rods or hooks low to the ground so children can reach them. That way, a child can put away his own bike—even if it's heavy—by lifting it one wheel at a time.

Rest your equipment in a hammock

If you have an old hammock lying around your garage, hang it up and use it to store sports equipment. Soccer balls, basketballs, footballs, and other sports equipment will fit nicely and won't fall out. If you don't have a hammock, most hardware stores carry mesh material that can serve the same purpose. Hang it across a corner at a height low enough that it will be available to anyone who needs to reach something.

Balance your garden tools

Purchase a heavy-duty plastic garbage can on wheels for storing long-handled yard and garden tools, such as rakes and hoes. Glue or drill hooks onto the inside of

the garbage can, and attach smaller tools to the hooks. Always balance the tools so you won't overload anything and cause the can to tip over. With everything so compact and in one place, all you have to do is drag the garbage can with you around the yard or garden.

Keep garbage cans convenient

Storing garbage cans in an attached garage means you don't have to trudge outside—especially when it rains—to dispose of household refuse. Even if your garage is freestanding, keeping garbage cans there will discourage scavenging animals from rooting through your trash and making a major mess in the process. Keep the lids tightly closed at all times to contain any foul smells that may develop between garbage pickup days. Sprinkling baking soda on top of the trash also minimizes odors.

Recycle your refuse

Put containers for newspapers, aluminum cans, plastics, and other recyclables in the garage. The containers can sit against a wall so they take up little space. Also, they'll be closer to the driveway when pickup day rolls around.

Exploring Your Options

Once you've cleaned out and organized your garage, you may discover that you actually have extra space. What shall you do with it? Well, a little creativity can go a long way. Your only guideline is to use the space to its fullest potential and make your life easier in the process. Consider these ideas.

Work handily at a handy workbench

Even if you already have a workbench in your basement, think about installing a second one in your garage. You'll have better ventilation there, which is important for tasks

such as painting and staining. You'll also have an extra flat, solid work surface for tasks such as sawing and drafting. Keep the workbench against the wall when you're not using it, and then pull it out when you need more room.

Restore your antiques yourself

A garage is a convenient place for restoring antiques or refinishing newer items. If you're using strong chemicals or solvents, you can open the garage door for ventilation. This is much better than working in the basement, where the chemical fumes can escape to the main floor of your home.

Keep the garage a garage

Think twice before converting your garage into a family room or another living space. Generally, a full-size garage adds more value to your home in case you ever decide to sell. Plus, you'd lose all that storage space and you'd have to park your cars outside. If you live in the northern United States, you know how nice it is to get in your car on a cold winter morning and not have to scrape the windshield before leaving home. Ask yourself if an extra room is worth the sacrifice.

Prudent Protection

Have you ever thought of your garage as a dangerous place? A garage or carport is among the most hazardous areas in the home, according to the National Safety Council. On average, garage mishaps annually accounted for more than 19,000 of the injuries treated in hospitals.

Outsmarting Stains and Spills

Keeping the garage clean doesn't seem like that difficult of a task. After all, a garage is just a large room with a concrete or asphalt floor. But because of all the stuff you store there, it's especially susceptible to spills, stains,

and other messes. These are not only unsightly, they're unsafe, too. For fast and easy cleanup, try these tips.

Seal the floor

Coating your garage floor with a protective sealant makes cleaning up oil and other spills easier. It also helps the floor last longer. You can buy sealant in any home improvement store. When you apply it, make sure you have adequate ventilation and a moderate outside temperature (70 to 80 °F).

Get out, spot

If your garage has an asphalt or concrete floor that isn't protected by sealant, removing an oil stain can be a challenge. Even using water and detergent can leave a

residual stain. The next time you're faced with this problem, use paint thinner or mineral spirits. Pour a small amount on the stain, scrub it in, and sprinkle cat litter over top. Let it sit for 30 minutes, then sweep it up.

Swab spilled antifreeze

Besides being bad for the environment, antifreeze containing ethylene glycol can poison the family pets. It has a sweet taste that appeals to animals. Even a small amount can kill them. Switch to an antifreeze without ethylene glycol (the label will tell you what the ingredients are). Also, keep all containers of antifreeze tightly sealed, no matter what their active ingredients are, and clean up any spills immediately.

Protect paint from peeling

Your water pipes aren't the only fixtures that can freeze and burst in wintertime. Some common household products will also freeze if they're stored in a garage that isn't heated. Paints, caulks, and certain adhesives should be put in an area where they will stay warm, or they should be disposed of at a local refuse center.

Detox daintily

The average home contains more than 100 pounds of hazardous products and hazardous household waste, according to Sharon Rehder, author of The Household Side of Hazardous Waste. Most of it can be found in the garage, though some may be stored under kitchen and bathroom sinks as well as in basements. Always dispose of hazardous materials properly. If you're unsure about how to do it, call your local waste management department or the local office of the Environmental Protection Agency.

Go green

There are many environmentally friendly solvents and cleaners on the market. Switch to these products if you haven't already. They're safer for your family and for the world around you.

Ensuring Safety

Beyond clearing pathways and properly storing cleaning products and other chemicals, the following measures can help you keep your garage safe and secure.

Batten down the hatches

Keep your garage door closed and locked at all times, unless you're working in your garage and need extra ventilation. An open door is an open invitation to curious kids or animals or, even worse, burglars. A locked garage door, on the other hand, provides extra security—especially if you have an attached garage that provides access to your home. Doubling up your protection never hurts.

See the light

Always use bright lighting in your garage. It makes finding things easier, especially at night. It also prevents you from tripping and falling over an object that isn't where it should be. Install switches inside your home to turn on all the garage lights, inside and out. You'll have a better view of what's going on outside without leaving the security of your home.

Sense any motion

Many floodlights come equipped with motion sensors that go on and stay on for a few minutes when someone or something crosses their paths. Having motion sensors outside the garage is a good idea because they'll illuminate your home and yard when you pull into the driveway. You can check out the area before you step out of your car. Don't panic the first few times the lights go on when you're home alone. An animal may have walked into the sensors' path and triggered the lights.

Slam the door on danger

If your garage is attached to your home, you need a fire-safe door between the two. It will prevent a small garage fire from spreading to your living quarters. A fire-safe door costs $200 to $1000. Choose one that has a rating of 90 or above (The rating is usually mentioned in the literature that comes with the door. If it isn't, ask the

Hazards In Your House

A variety of common household products can create serious health and safety risks if stored improperly. If you have any of the following in your home, read the label for storage instructions.

Property	Description	Products
Corrosive	An acid or alkaline chemical that dissolves materials	Acids, car batteries, drain cleaners, oven cleaners, pool chemicals
Ignitable	A material that catches fire easily	Gasoline, oil-based paints, paint thinners, solvents, wood preservatives
Reactive	A material that explodes or reacts violently	Aerosols, pool chemicals
Toxic	A poison or other substance that can harm humans when eaten, inhaled, or absorbed through the skin	Antifreeze, car batteries, disinfectants, household batteries, mercury, moth balls, pesticides, solvents, wood preservatives

salesperson). A 90 means that the door can withstand flames for at least 90 minutes. The door usually comes with all the parts necessary for do-it-yourself installation. But if you're not mechanically inclined, hire a professional to do the job.

Get an eyeful

If the door from your garage into your home doesn't have a window, install a peephole instead. You can discreetly check out any noises and quickly determine what or who is causing the commotion. If you suspect that you have an intruder, you can call the police and get yourself to safety.

Fight fire before the fire

If you have paper or wood that you're not using, dispose of it rather than letting it lie around in your garage. These materials dry out with age, and they'll ignite quite easily. The situation becomes even more combustible when oil- or gasoline-soaked rags are stored nearby. Stuff rags into a tin can (preferably one with a lid) or a resealable plastic bag before throwing them away.

Lock up hazardous gadgets

Be careful when storing power tools and other items that you don't want children to handle. Lock the items in cabinets or storage containers so kids can't get at them. Same goes for toolboxes.

Evict vagrant varmints

Raccoons, rats, bats, birds, and snakes would all love to make themselves at home in your garage. After all, it's warm and cozy in the winter and cool and shady in the summer. Frequently check your garage for uninvited guests, especially in the summer months. These creatures can bite or carry and spread diseases.

Unblock the fuse box

If your fuse box is in the garage, be careful not to stack items up against it. If you have an emergency in your home and you need to shut off the power quickly, you don't want to waste time digging through assorted stuff to reach the fuse box.

Avoid drowning in a sea of cords

Once you use an extension cord for the first time, you can never rewind it as tightly as it was wound to begin with. To keep longer cords in order, wind them as tightly as possible and secure them with thick rubber bands. For shorter cords, wind them and slip them into empty cardboard tubes. You can store the cords in one drawer, and they won't become tangled up with each other.

Nail your tires to the wall

If you have old tires that you don't know what to do with, cut them into strips and nail the strips to the garage walls so that they're level with your car's bumpers and doors. The rubber will protect your car should someone bump a wall when driving in or out of the garage or opening a car door. If you don't want to use old tires, your local home improvement store carries molding that you may find more to your liking.

Showing You the Door

Your garage door is the largest moving object in your home. Some doors weigh hundreds of pounds and, unless properly maintained, can injure a member of your family. Children will try to beat an automatic garage door as it's coming down, and many end up in the hospital as a result. Don't let this happen in your family. Install a garage door that meets current safety standards and practice preventive maintenance.

Give it a good once-over

Your garage door is like any other tool or appliance. It needs a little extra attention every now and then to ensure good operation. On segmented or sectional doors, lubricate all of the connecting hinges with 20-weight oil. On manual doors, lubricate the large pivot hinges on each side with an all-purpose grease. If the garage door manufacturer has provided specific maintenance instructions, follow them to keep the door moving smoothly.

Replace every piece

If you notice that your garage door is missing a bolt, immediately install a replacement bolt. Otherwise, the door could malfunction and injure someone in the process. If you find a bolt but aren't sure where it belongs, call in a professional to inspect the door and make the necessary repair. You can probably find someone through your local home improvement center.

Construct a complex combination

Professional thieves have ways of unlocking your automatic or manual garage door. A chain and combination lock will make them work extra hard because it prevents them from raising the door. You can buy this hardware in home improvement stores. Loop the chain so that it immobilizes the door, then fasten it with the lock. Use this setup when you're going to be away for an extended period of time (on vacation, for example), so you know your garage—and your home—is safe and secure.

Block the roll

As an alternative to a chain and combination lock, try a padlock roller bracket. It blocks the garage door roller so the door can't be raised. The bracket is sold in home improvement stores. Installing a padlock roller bracket, which is specifically designed for blocking, is much better and safer than using a homemade blocking device. If the object you use to impede the roller isn't securely in place, someone could get hurt.

Small animals and rodents will try to make a home in your warm garage.

Update your door opener

Back in 1992, Underwriters Laboratories (UL) issued safety standards for automatic garage door openers. The standards required all door openers manufactured after January 1, 1993, to be equipped with noncontact sensors. The sensors detect when a person or object is in a garage door's path and prevent the door from closing. If your door opener was made before 1993, you can retrofit it with a noncontact sensor. It's easy to install. Look for one in home improvement stores.

More Door Diagnostics

Test your automatic garage door regularly. A new door can be checked every few months. An older door—one manufactured before 1982—should be checked every month. Here's what to do.

Stop on a block

Automatic garage doors that fail to stop and reverse after contact are dangerous. To test your door, place a two-inch block of wood where the door meets the ground. If the door doesn't reverse when it touches the wood, disconnect the garage door opener and have it serviced or replaced.

Check if its slip is showing

The ability of an automatic garage door to stay put is just as important as its ability to reverse. To make sure your door won't slip, disconnect your garage door opener and manually raise the door to a height of three to four feet. Then let go of the door and quickly move out of the way. (In fact, make sure everyone—especially a child—has cleared the area before you let go.) The door should stay put and not slip back down. If it does slide closed on its own, it needs to be refitted. This is a fairly easy do-it-yourself job; ask for advice at your local home improvement center.

Play the straight man

While the garage door opener is disconnected, eyeball the open door and notice whether it hangs evenly. Any imbalance or lopsidedness may cause the door opener to push or pull so hard that the door closes with excessive force. If your garage door appears crooked or uneven, have it repaired or replaced immediately.

> ### Simply Stated
>
> *I would rather be able to appreciate things I cannot have than to have things I am not able to appreciate.*
>
> **—Elbert Hubbard,
> American author**

What Are Your Options?

The garage can easily become a repository for items that don't seem to belong anywhere else in your home. Over time, this creates a tremendous amount of clutter that's unseemly and unsafe. You can avoid this situation simply by maximizing storage space in other areas of your home.

Putting Stuff in Its Place

These days, there is a gizmo or gadget for just about any purpose that you can imagine. These playthings seem nifty in the store, but once you get them home, you realize that you don't have anywhere to put them. An obvious solution to the problem would be to not buy the stuff in the first place. But that's no fun. So here are some ideas for maximizing storage space throughout your home.

Save space with stackable shelves

If your cabinets and closets have only a few shelves, why not add a few more? Many discount retail stores sell stackable shelving units. Larger units have stacked and pull-out shelves for sweaters, shorts, T-shirts, shoes, and so on. Smaller units are designed to fit on the shelves in kitchen cabinets. They have compartments for dinner plates, saucers, and bowls so you can keep all of these items on one shelf instead of taking up two or three.

Let your door do double duty

You can use the space behind the doors in your home to store small items that you don't often use. The doors of bedrooms, bathrooms, and home offices are especially ideal, since their backs are not visible to anyone other than the rooms' occupants. You can hang small-width, wire-covered baskets behind each door and store items such as hair bows, brushes, notepads, and paper clips. Don't use baskets that make the door stand away from the wall.

Bury it under the bed

Don't be ashamed to hide things under your bed. It's a good storage space where no one ever looks. Use zippered plastic bags and particleboard drawers to store clothes and other items that you don't want small pets getting into. If you have only large cardboard boxes, cut them down so that they fit under the bed. Cover the boxes with contact paper so that they will hold up better.

Give your tools a lift

If you have a utility room in your home, hammer long galvanized nails into the wall so you can hang up items such as garden tools, brooms, and mops. That way, they won't be leaning against the wall, where they can easily fall over. For heavier equipment such as shovels and weed-eaters, hang heavy-duty hooks into wall studs.

Home in on the hot-water heater

If you have a house or an apartment where the hot-water heater is in its own closet, you can use that space for storage. It's a great place to put the vacuum cleaner, because it's out of everyone's way. It's also ideal for lightbulbs, window screens, extension cords, and other household goods. Just make sure that nothing lies across piping or electrical work. Also, be careful not to store chemicals or cleaners near the hot-water heater, in case they spill or leak.

Get after the rafters

The exposed rafters of any unfinished basement are good for hanging long, lightweight items such as skis or garden equipment such as rakes and hoes. Hang these items low enough that you can easily reach them, but not so low that they become safety hazards to the taller members of your family. To hang heavier items, you may have to reinforce the rafters.

Bikes can be easily stored by hanging them from the garage rafters.

Access your attic

You can buy or build shelving units to fit in your attic. Buy units that have deep shelves, so you can stack items. Install rods across the rafters for hanging clothes in plastic garment bags. Also, use furniture that you already have in your attic to hold other things. For instance, an old bookcase can house out-of-season sweaters and other clothing as well as books. Store as many items as you can around the perimeter of your attic so that you have a clear walking path.

The Best-Kept Secrets

Some of the following storage areas may remind you of the secret compartments and hidden rooms of the homes in murder mystery novels. Storing objects in your home certainly isn't a crime. Not taking advantage of every inch of space ought to be.

Unseal the staircase

The space underneath a staircase is often sealed off and unused. Add a door, and you have an extra closet. Install some shelves, and you have a pantry or even a library. Use your imagination.

Saving Space

Simplifying your garage takes some effort but it shouldn't feel like hard work. If it does, then maybe you need to step back and reassess your approach to the project. Remember, just because you have all that space doesn't mean that you have to fill it. Here's a good rule of thumb: If parking your cars in your garage leaves you no room to walk around, you're saving too much stuff.

Stack extras in the soffit

If your kitchen cabinets are attached to your ceiling by a soffit, you can use this space for storing bulky pots and pans or china that you seldom use. Before you do this, make sure that your cabinets are strong enough to hold the extra weight. You can leave the soffit open or enclose it with regular cabinet doors. If you have decorative pots and pans, this is a good place to store them so everyone can see them.

Sit on extra space

If you have a bay window in your home, install a window seat with a hinged top. This creates a built-in chest in which you can store curtains, decorations, or whatever you like.

Keep storage secret

When you find a hidden storage area in your home, you don't have to tell other family members about it. Instead, use it as a hiding place for gifts and other surprises.

Seasonal Cleaning

Your home needs regular checkups—ideally every six months, when the weather changes significantly. By spending as little as two weekends a year on routine preventive maintenance, you help preserve the structural soundness of your home and extend the life of the heating and air-conditioning units and other fixtures. You'll keep breakdowns to a minimum, and you'll be able to set aside money for anticipated future repairs.

Getting Wise to Warm Weather

The arrival of spring presents the perfect opportunity to give your home a once-over and make sure everything is functional. Here's a checklist to help you get started.

Review your roofing

Cold winter weather can do a number on your roof, so spring is a good time to check for damage. Water spots on the ceilings inside your home are telltale signs of leaks. Also look for buckled shingles and rotted wood. You may want to hire a professional roofer to check your shingles, especially if your roof is covered under a warranty or service agreement.

Gut the gutters

Cleaning out your gutters and checking downspouts can prevent a number of household problems. If water does not flow freely through your gutters, it may back up and leak into your house or damage the exterior. If water from the downspout drains toward your house instead of away from it, it may damage your foundation.

Gear up for a good paint job

Because it's neither too hot nor too cold, early spring is the perfect time to paint the exterior of your home. Doing the job yourself will save a bundle of money. But if balancing on a ladder isn't your cup of tea, by all means hire a professional.

Tidy up the siding

Wood siding needs to be stained every few years. Don't neglect this job. Unstained wood splits and cracks and may cost you a lot of money in the long run.

Clean your windows to the world

When the weather starts to get warmer, thoroughly clean the outside of all windows, along with their screens. There are new cleaners on the market that you can attach directly to your outdoor hose, so you don't have to climb a ladder and risk hurting yourself. If you removed the screens in the winter, put them back up now. Repair or replace any damaged windows and screens.

Reinvigorate the interior

Springtime is the right time for heavy-duty painting inside your home. You can open all of the windows for ventilation, which will also help the paint dry quickly. Even if you don't need to paint, wash all of your walls and examine them for mildew. If you notice any, hire a professional to check for water damage and other moisture problems in your home.

Click on the AC

Have your household air-conditioning system serviced every year before you turn it on. The compressor needs to be checked and the filters need to be replaced. If your system has reusable filters, they should be cleaned. Also, dust off window air-conditioning units before turning them on, especially if they've been in storage over the winter. Otherwise, you're likely to be blasted with dust.

Drain your drains

Even if you're not having any problems with your household drains, inspect them at least once a year. Kitchen sink drains are the worst because food can get lodged in the pipes and cause clogs. (Rice is especially problematic because it swells up.) Use a wire hook to check for obstructions. If you find one, try to break it down with a solution of vinegar and baking soda.

If that doesn't help, try plunging the drain. If the clog still won't budge, you may need to call in a plumber. Use strong cleaners to unclog drains only as a last resort. These products are harmful to the environment and tend to kill the good bacteria in your sewage and septic systems. Such bacteria work on your behalf to break down and liquefy solid wastes.

Break out the barbecue

Thoroughly clean all outdoor equipment that has been in storage over the winter. Check for wear and tear on lawn furniture and rusting on the propane tank of the grill. Also, check out the kids' swing set and other outside toys to make sure they're still safe.

Coming In from the Cold

When temperatures start to tumble in the fall, check your house to make sure that it's ready for the harsh weather ahead.

Store summer sundries

Pack up and put away children's outdoor toys so that they won't rust or become damaged by the winter weather. The same goes for other household equipment that won't be used in the wintertime, such as window air-conditioning units. Clean each item and make any necessary repairs before putting it away. That way, it'll be ready to go in the spring. Cover and seal all outdoor air-conditioning units that can't be stored inside.

> ### Simply Stated
>
> *In putting off what one has to do, one runs the risk of never being able to do it.*
> —**Charles-Pierre Baudelaire,
> French poet**

Trim the trees

Check trees and large bushes to make sure that their branches aren't hitting the sides of the house or hanging over the roof. Winter wind and ice storms can break off branches, causing damage to your home. Hire professionals to do any trimming. They have the right equipment and know the proper safety procedures for big jobs.

Weatherize the windows

Replace damaged window panes and rotted window seals before cold weather arrives. Much of the heat inside your home escapes through the windows, and you pay for it many times over in high electricity bills. Check the weather stripping around windows and recaulk if necessary. Consider installing storm windows to keep the heat inside your home and save energy.

Seal off the garage

If your garage is attached to your home, make sure the door that leads from the garage into the house has weather stripping around it. Otherwise, cold air can leak from the garage into your home. Also, store all paints and chemicals in areas where they won't freeze.

Diminish debris in ducts

As with your air-conditioning system, have your furnace professionally serviced before using it. Clean all duct-work of debris and change the filter. Also, clear the area around your furnace, especially of cardboard and paper products, which are fire hazards.

Fix up the fireplace

Hire a professional to clean your fireplace and chimney. All manner of debris can settle into your fireplace, never mind the birds and other critters that may call your chimney home. Check the flashing and secure it if it's loose. If you have more than one fireplace, have all of them checked—not just the one that your family uses the most.

Check out your detectors

Make sure that your smoke detectors are functioning properly. Check and change the batteries if necessary. If the detectors still don't work, buy new ones. Install them on each floor of your home, near the bedrooms and the kitchen. If you use your fireplace frequently, install carbon monoxide detectors in the same areas as the smoke detectors.

Fuss with your faucets

When cold weather approaches, close the shut-off valves and completely drain all the outdoor faucets. Water left in the faucets may cause the fixtures or pipes to freeze and burst. Leaking faucets waste water and can increase your water bill.

Add moisture to indoor air

Cold winter air can dry out your skin and your respiratory tract. A humidifier can alleviate the problem.

Before you run it, clean the filter as well as any reservoirs that may still hold water. Avoid using dirty or old water in a humidifier, especially if anyone in the household has allergies or is sensitive to mold or mildew.

Inspect the outlets

Room by room, check each electrical outlet to make sure that it's securely fastened to the wall and not over-loaded. While you're at it, make sure that all the plugs are grounded—that is, they have three prongs. Don't used old or hand-me-down electrical appliances with plugs that aren't grounded. They're fire hazards.

The Simplest of the Simple

To keep your garage—and the rest of your home—ship-shape, apply these super-simple strategies:

- Remove everything from your garage, then throw or give away what you don't need or want to retain.
- Keep small items (nails, screws, washers, and the like) in empty soup or coffee cans or in small plastic containers.
- Install pegboard on the walls of your garage for hanging up small hand tools and other items.
- Clean up any spills on the floor of your garage immediately.
- Keep the garage door locked at all times.
- Store extra items under the bed in boxes.
- Clean your gutters and check your roof for leaks at least once a year.

Chapter 12

Calling All Cars

The Keys to Hassle-Free Auto Ownership

Nothing represents freedom quite like a car. It enables you to take off virtually any time the mood strikes. It gets you where you want to go, whether across town or across the country.

Unless, of course, it breaks down. If your car has ever left you stranded, you know how frightening and infuriating it can be. It's the ultimate betrayal of man (or woman) by machine. In most cases, though, it doesn't have to happen.

Routine maintenance can help keep your car running smoothly for thousands of miles. And if it does start making odd noises or handling differently, it needs to be serviced. The problem won't just go away.

Besides giving you peace of mind, taking care of your car benefits your pocketbook. After all, a car is a huge investment. Depending what make and model you choose, you can pay as much as you would have paid for a house years ago. That's reason enough to get as many miles from your car as possible.

All this can make car ownership seem like more trouble than it's worth. It doesn't have to be. As this chapter shows, you can buy or lease, outfit, and maintain an auto without losing your shirt—or your sanity.

To Buy or Not to Buy

When one auto manufacturer introduced a "no hassle, no haggle" car-pricing policy, some customers insisted on wheeling and dealing anyway. They couldn't shake the mindset that price is always negotiable, at least where cars are concerned.

Few people actually enjoy negotiating. Thankfully, the Internet and auto malls have changed the way many people purchase cars. Preparation is still your best weapon in buying wisely. Whether you intend to buy (or lease), the strategies in this section will help you get the vehicle you want at a price you can afford.

As Good as New

Many people steer clear of used cars because they "don't want to buy someone else's trouble." If you shop smart, you don't have to. Here's what you need to know.

Do your homework

Decide what type of car you want before you do a lot of looking around. Peruse publications such as *Car and Driver* and *Consumer Reports* for unbiased information on the advantages and disadvantages of various makes and models.

Track down a three-year-old

car will lose between 15 percent and 20 percent of its value each year according to Bankrate.com. A car in its second year will be worth 80 percent to 85 percent of its first year value and a car in its third year will be worth 80 percent to 85 percent of its second-year value. So shop around for a well-maintained, regularly serviced three-year-old car with low mileage—fewer than 60,000 miles, or 20,000 miles a year.

Deal with the owner, not with a dealer

In most cases, you're better off buying a used car from a private party rather than from a dealer. You can talk one-on-one with the car's driver and examine all the maintenance records (if the seller says that he doesn't have the maintenance records, the car isn't for you). Arrange to meet the seller at his home. If other cars in the garage and driveway are neat and well-maintained, chances are that the one you want to buy is in good shape as well.

Go straight to the source

If you're buying a used car from a dealership, insist on speaking with the car's previous owner. This person will most likely give you the straight scoop on the vehicle because he no longer has a financial interest in its sale. If the salesperson is reluctant to put you in touch with the former owner, walk off the lot.

Look into leases

The best thing about a previously leased vehicle is that most lease agreements include stringent service requirements. Most also limit mileage to about 12,000 miles a year. In effect, you're virtually guaranteed a well-maintained, low-mileage car. And since most previously leased vehicles are at least three years old, you can usually get a good deal.

Steer clear of rentals

Many people think that buying rental cars is a good idea, especially since these vehicles often have fewer than 10,000 miles on them. Keep in mind, though, that a rental car has been driven by scores of people, few of whom took good care of it. Make sure that it received regular servicing.

Take the car for a checkup

Any dealer or owner who is confident that he's selling a good, reliable used vehicle should have no problem with your taking the car to your mechanic. Or if you feel more comfortable, invite your mechanic to go with you to look at the car. He can at least give it a quick overview and check for rust and other less obvious problems.

Knock off 15 percent

As a general rule, when making an offer on a used car, start at about 15 percent less than the asking price. This counterbalances any padding that the seller may have tacked on to the price in anticipation of negotiation. You can also gauge your offer by comparing it with the list price in the *National Automobile Dealers Association Official Used Car Guide* or the *Kelley Blue Book Used Car Guide.*

Straight off the Assembly Line

New cars usually require a bit more wheeling and dealing than used cars. Don't let that discourage you. Follow this advice, and you'll handle negotiations like a pro.

Ignore the number in the window

The dealer would love for you to pay the sticker price for a new car. He'd make a huge profit because the sticker price far exceeds what he actually paid. Here again, doing your homework is important. Know what a new car is worth, and be prepared to negotiate. If you can't get the deal you want at one dealership, go to another.

Find out the invoice

The dealer invoice is lower—sometimes 7 to 25 percent lower—than the sticker price. And the dealer may pay even less than invoice depending on the situation. Annually updated guides, such as *Edmund's New Car Price Guide,* list the dealer invoice price for every make and model with all options.

Shop late, pay less

Shopping late in the day or, even better, late in the month may get you a better deal on a new car. At the end of the day, salespeople are tired and anxious to go home, so they're less likely to haggle over price. At the end of the month, they may be desperate for a sale if they haven't met their monthly quotas or are trying to earn bonuses.

Skip the hype

If a car manufacturer or dealer is promoting a big sale, wait until it's over to buy a new car. During a sale, you may think that you're getting a good deal and be less likely to negotiate price. And the dealer will be less willing to wheel and deal because you're already getting the car "on sale."

Skip the details

Most new-car dealers add on charges for paint sealant, fabric protectant, and other detailing. Don't fall for these "extras." You're paying enough for the vehicle without putting up an additional $150 to $250 for a clear coat. Tell the salesperson to subtract the charges or forget the deal.

Keys to a Great Deal

In the market for a new car? You can take the hassle out of the haggle with these savvy showroom strategies:

- Go to the showroom prepared. Before you go, read several car magazines and choose three or four cars that are within your price range and that include the features you need.
- Take other people with you only if they have direct involvement in your purchasing decision.
- Deal only with salespeople with whom you feel comfortable.
- Get complete and satisfactory answers to all of your questions.
- Give any car that you're considering a thorough road test under the same conditions in which you will be driving it.
- Buy the car you want if it handles perfectly, the price is right, and you like the overall deal.

Live without luxury options

Unless you get a spectacular deal on a new car, luxury options such as leather seats and convertible roofs can cost you far more than they're worth. If you live in the northern United States, for instance, you only have about three months each year when you can actually put the car's top down. And that's only if the weather cooperates.

Extend your wallet, not your warranty

The dealer assures you that you're getting a quality new vehicle that you'll drive for thousands of problem-free miles. Then in almost the same breath, he suggests that you buy the extended warranty—just in case. The catch is, most extended warranties don't cover the types of mechanical problems that are most likely to occur.

You're better off taking the money and putting it in your savings account. That way, you earn interest—and you'll have funds set aside for any necessary repairs.

Love It? Lease It

When you buy a car, you can sell it at any time. When you lease a car, you make a 24- to 48-month commitment. You can always break the lease—but you'll shell out big bucks to do it, in terms of payments and outstanding penalties.

If you decide that a lease agreement is for you, these tips can guarantee you the best deal.

Be prepared to bargain

Just because you're leasing a car doesn't mean that the price is set in stone. While some dealerships won't budge on their rates, others will. To get the best rate, negotiate as if you were planning to buy the vehicle. Then when you and the salesperson agree on a price, inform her that you want to lease instead. If the salesperson attempts to withdraw the deal, take your business elsewhere.

Go for the short haul

Stick with lease agreements of 36 months or less. After all, if you're going to lease a car for a longer period, then why not buy it instead? At least the car will be yours in four years or so. If you want, you can sell it and put the cash toward your next car.

Buy extra miles

Most lease agreements restrict the number of miles that you can put on a car each year. If you think you'll be close to but not quite under the limit, buy extra miles up front, before you sign the paperwork. Be aware, though, that if you don't use the miles, you lose your money. And if you exceed your annual mileage allotment and your extra miles, you'll have to pay a penalty.

Carefree Auto Care

Whether you buy or lease it, your vehicle represents a huge financial investment on your part. You want to make sure that it lasts at least as long as your payments do—and, hopefully, much longer. Preventive maintenance is key.

Make like a Mechanic

Your car needs periodic checkups, even if it's brand-new. Here's what the automotive experts advise.

Change the oil at regular intervals

How often you need to change your car's oil depends on how much you drive your car. For the average driver, an oil change every 3,000 miles should keep a car's engine in mint condition.

For long distances, switch to synthetics

Synthetic oils can withstand much higher temperatures than petroleum-based oils. They also stay cleaner and maintain their viscosity (thickness) longer. All of these qualities make synthetics the better choice for long-distance driving.

Subtract the additives

"Oil additives are stopgap measures for cars that really need mechanical attention," explains David McManness, a mechanic and former vocational school auto-shop instructor. "The typical additive just makes the oil thicker

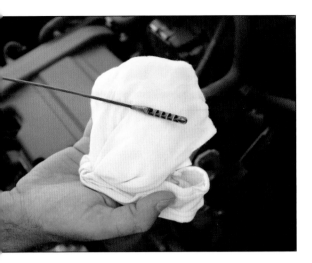

so it fills the gaps between worn parts. This keeps an engine that's essentially shot running a little longer."

Take a whiff

If your car has an automatic transmission, McManness also recommends smelling the transmission fluid for signs of a problem. Just remove the transmission dipstick and sniff it. A burnt odor means that your car needs a mechanic's attention. Sniff the dipstick when your car is running well, too, so you have a comparison scent.

Pick premium to placate the ping

"There is no more energy in a gallon of premium gas than in a gallon of regular," notes *Road and Track* magazine. "The main difference between the grades is octane—the resistance to ping. If your car engine pings, you'll hear a rattling, metallic sound when you accelerate. Ping can damage an engine if it's allowed to go on too long. A higher-octane gasoline might solve the problem."

Pick the popular spots for refueling

"The busiest gas station may be your best bet, regardless of the brand name on the sign," according to Bruce Black a former manager for Pilot Oil Company. "I steer clear of shabby stations that look like they don't sell much gas. When gasoline storage tanks sit almost empty for extended periods, water can condense inside, fouling the gas."

Monitor your fuel consumption

Here's an easy way to calculate how many miles you're getting per gallon of gas: The next time you fill 'er up, reset your car's trip odometer to zero. Then when you fill up again, write down the trip odometer reading as well as the amount of gas you buy. Divide the number of miles you've driven by the number of gallons of gas you need, then compare your answer with your car's estimated optimum gas mileage (it should be listed in your owner's manual). If your actual miles per gallon figure isn't quite up to snuff, it could be because of underinflated tires, dragging brakes, a failing transmission, or some other problem. You'd better have your mechanic check it out.

Unclog your fuel line

"Fuel filters are cheaper than fuel injectors," says Greg Parham, owner of Import Connection car dealership in Arden, North Carolina. "If you don't change the filter at regular intervals, the small orifices of the injectors may get plugged up. Many people seem to think that the only time to worry about the filter is when it clogs up and the engine stops. But if you wait that long, you'll be looking at a very big repair bill for the injector. Change the fuel filter at least every 15,000 miles."

Favor fat tires

Your owner's manual probably has a list of recommended tire sizes for your car. The first is the size that's put on in the factory; the others are considered optional. When you need new tires, purchase the next size up from the factory size. The larger diameter improves fuel economy and reduces engine wear. Bigger tires also ride better and last longer.

Investigate odd noises

When pings and sputters emanate from beneath the hood of your car, have them checked out right away. They may indicate a problem, and ignoring them will only cost you more money—and more hassle—in the long run. Take your car to a reputable mechanic whom you trust.

By All Means, Keep It Clean

Maintaining a shiny, spotless vehicle is not merely a matter of aesthetics. It is also pleasing to your pocketbook. How so? A clean car lasts longer and thus has a higher resale value if you decide to sell it.

Driving a dirty car, on the other hand, can cost you in a big way. If your brake lights are coated with a thick layer of filth, for instance, the motorists behind you may not notice that you're stopping until it's too late. Similarly, a crud-covered windshield impairs your view and may contribute to an accident.

Don't worry: washing, waxing, and detailing your car needn't take all day or cost a lot of money. These simple strategies can help you keep your chassis looking classy.

Soap it yourself

The best and usually cheapest way to wash your car is by hand. You need only a detergent made specifically for cars. Skip the dishwashing liquid as well as the special cleaners for vinyl roofs, whitewall tires, and so forth. Just one product will do.

If you prefer the convenience of an automatic car wash, choose one that's brushless. Over time, the brushes can scratch your car's paint and dull the finish.

Wash the mats, too

Rubber or flexible plastic floor mats are easy to clean. Take them out of your car and wash them with car detergent. You may need to scrub them a bit with a nylon brush to remove all of the dirt. If you wash the mats first and hang them out in the sun, they'll be almost dry by the time you're finished cleaning the rest of your car.

Time for a Tune-Up

Pay attention to any of the following. They're your cues to take your car in for a tune-up.

- Difficulty starting
- Frequent stalling
- Knocking noise (usually when climbing a hill)
- Loss of power
- Poor gas mileage
- "Dieseling": the engine sputters after the ignition is shut off
- Exhaust odor: the catalytic converter smells like rotten eggs
- Rough running: the car shakes when idling or accelerating

Clean the windows with vinegar

Rather than buying an expensive window cleaner for your car, you can make your own in your kitchen. Mix two or three tablespoons of vinegar in a gallon of warm water. Dip a cloth in the solution and wipe each car window. Then go back over the windows with a clean, dry cloth.

Polish your chrome

While few new cars come equipped with chrome bumpers, plenty of older beauties have them. Simply wiping off the bumpers won't do because they're subject to rust. To really make chrome shine, dip a wet sponge into baking soda and rub it on the bumpers. Let it set, and then rinse it off and dry the chrome with a soft cloth.

Make sure your fuel filter is clean so your car runs properly.

Spiff up your seats

If you have vinyl or leather upholstery, you can probably wipe up stains and spills with plain old soap and water. To clean cloth upholstery, the folks who make Eureka vacuums have come up with this recipe: Combine ¼ cup of white dishwashing liquid with one cup of warm water. Whip the mixture with an egg beater until it forms a stiff foam. Spread the foam over the stain with a sponge, using circular, overlapping strokes. Let it dry, then vacuum.

Take your Dodge for a dip

If you're planning to spend the day at an oceanfront beach, be sure to wash your car before you head for home. Otherwise, the salt in the air can cause your car to rust over time.

Outfitting Your Auto

If you're like most people, you probably spend a lot of time in your car, whether you're commuting to work, running errands, or shuttling the kids to their various activities. You're entitled to ride in comfort and style, and you also want to be prepared for any situation that may arise while you're on the road. The tips in this section will help you do both.

Things to Have on Hand

Every new vehicle comes equipped with a spare tire. It's the manufacturer's way of preparing a motorist for one of the most common (and most annoying) roadside emergencies. But are you ready for other more common emergencies, like getting lost or locking your keys in the car? You will be, if you follow this advice.

Chart your course

Stock your glove compartment with a supply of maps for the states and cities in which you most often travel. If you're planning a cross-country drive, invest in a wire-bound atlas that shows the main roads and side roads in every state. Or simply install a GPS, but watch out because dependency on a GPS can leave you lost, even in your own community.

Make change

Keep a roll of quarters and a roll of dimes someplace in your car where you can quickly and easily reach them. That way, you're prepared for any toll roads and bridges that you may encounter in unfamiliar territory. You'll also have coins for pay phones and vending machines.

Keep spare keys at hand

Carry an extra car key in your purse or wallet or buy a magnetic key case to conceal the spare somewhere underneath your car. If you lose your keys or simply lock yourself out, you can open the car door without calling a locksmith or, worse, breaking a window. Keep an extra set of house keys in your car, too—just in case.

Brother, Can You Spare a Tire?

When people get flat tires, they usually call for roadside assistance or rely on a Good Samaritan for help. You can save yourself the wait and be on your way in no time by learning how to change a tire yourself. Use the following tips to help you get back on the road safely:

- Before you do anything else, make sure that your car is parked on level ground. If it isn't, don't attempt to change the tire yourself. Call for a tow truck instead.
- Put the car in park and engage the emergency brake.
- Read your owner's manual for proper positioning of the jack. Never place the jack on a car part that can bend or break.
- Using bricks, a flat board, or even a thick tree branch—whatever is sturdy and close at hand—brace the wheels on the end of the car that is not being elevated. This will keep the car from rolling.

As an alternative to changing a tire yourself, keep an aerosol inflation product in your trunk. Available in auto supply and discount retail stores, this product should enable you to drive to the nearest service station, where your tire can be repaired. Tell the mechanic that you used an inflation product.

Workplace on Wheels

For a growing number of professionals, the car doubles as an office. Manufacturers know this, and they've developed an assortment of car accessories for the pro on the go. You can outfit your vehicle with mini-clipboards that attach to the dashboard with suction cups or mini-desks that fit the passenger seat. With so many options to choose from, you can custom-design a mobile office that's functional and safe.

Put your car on call

If you have a long commute and do lots of sitting in traffic, you may as well take advantage of the time and use your cell phone. (To be safe, use the phone only when you're stopped or moving intermittently, as in a highly congested area.) Try to limit your car calls, though. At some point, they start making your life more complicated rather than less.

Pack a pouch

Keep a zippered pouch in your car for items such as pens, pencils, notepads, envelopes, and stamps. Why stamps? You never know when you'll need one. You may drive by the corner mailbox to drop off a bill, only to realize that it doesn't have proper postage. If you don't have a stamp with you, you'll have to run home or to the post office to get one.

Stow banking supplies

Keep a few deposit slips or deposit envelopes in your car so you can complete them before you get to the bank or ATM. The less time you spend in front of an ATM with cash or checks in your hand, the safer you'll be.

Duplicate documents

Photocopy your registration, insurance information, maintenance records, and other important documents pertaining to your vehicle. Keep the copies in your car. That way, you'll have backups in case something happens to the originals.

Also write down your credit card account numbers and the phone numbers of the issuing companies. Conceal the list someplace in your car. Then if your purse or wallet gets lost or stolen, you can quickly contact the issuing companies and cancel the cards.

Curbing In-Car Clutter

These days, most cars come with all sorts of clever design features for storing stuff. Still, we can't seem to resist the urge to throw things on the backseat or the floor. This is fine—until you need a particular item. Then you're pulling up the seat cushions and ripping out the floor mats in a panic. Fortunately, there is a better way.

Using the Backseat and Trunk Wisely

Why put something in the backseat when you have an entire trunk at your disposal? Convenience, most likely. The trouble is, your backseat and all of its contents are visible to passersby. If you leave valuable items in plain sight, you're just inviting trouble. If a thief happens to see the items, all he has to do is break a window, reach inside, and grab. A car alarm won't necessarily deter him, either. He'll just wait until no one is around and take off before anyone catches sight of him. So exercise common sense and follow these guidelines.

Cover up the goods

When possible, lock valuables in your trunk or even your glove compartment. If you have no choice but to put them in your backseat, conceal them before you leave your car. Slide them under the front seats or floor mats, or cover them with your coat or a blanket.

Over the Top, under the Hood

In the market for a new mechanic? You want someone who:

- Is certified by the National Institute for Automotive Service Excellence.
- Has at least 10 years' experience in auto repair and is employed at a facility that has been operating for at least five years.
- Is known for doing good work on the model car you own (ask family members, friends, and coworkers for referrals).
- Offers a guarantee and warranty on parts for a minimum of 90 days or 3,000 miles.
- Can clearly explain problems to you and offers viable solutions.
- Gives an itemized estimate for parts and labor.
- Calls for your approval before doing extra work that increases the original estimate by 10 percent or more.

Be secretive

Avoid putting valuables into your trunk while in a highly visible location, then leaving your car unattended. One woman locked her purse in her trunk before going into a mall. When she returned, she discovered that someone had pried open her trunk with a crowbar. You never know who's sitting in the parking lot watching and waiting to do dirty work.

If you are at a mall, rather than taking packages to your car and going back inside to continue shopping, ask the store clerk to hold your purchases until you're ready to leave. Or take someone with you to help you carry your shopping bags. Whatever you do, try not to make extra trips to your car.

Be ready for anything

Stock your trunk with the following supplies: a first-aid kit, extra tissues, a heavy blanket, flares, a flashlight, an umbrella, and jumper cables. You may want to throw in a few nonperishable food items, too, in case you get stuck somewhere overnight. Just remember to replace the food every now and then. Even vanilla wafers don't last forever.

Get your shirt together

If you work out regularly (and you should), keep a spare gym bag in your trunk. Pack it with exercise clothing, an extra T-shirt, socks, underwear, and a toothbrush. Even though you may usually carry these items with you, there may come a time when you forget. With the spare bag in your trunk, you won't have to drive back home to pick up your regular bag—or skip your workout altogether.

> **Simply Stated**
>
> *These days a man doesn't know if he's driving a car or an animal. Mustang, Jaguar, Cougar, Pinto . . . silly!*
> —**From the movie *Harry and Tonto* (1974)**

Making Room in the Glove Compartment

Glove compartments come in all shapes and sizes. Still, they have at least one thing in common: a lot of clutter and junk. You really need only a few items in there—namely, your vehicle registration, insurance information, owner's manual, and a small flashlight. You can put all your other stuff elsewhere, like in the console between the front seats (most newer cars have one).

By keeping your glove compartment clean and organized, you may discover that you have more room than you think. Just remember that you want to reserve this space for the most important items—the things you need right at your fingertips.

Empty it out

The glove compartment is not a trash can or a semipermanent home for unnecessary receipts and other papers. If the items you have thrown in there are important, take them in your house and put them in a folder where you can find them. You should be able to close your glove compartment door with ease. If you can't, then it's time to clean.

Bag the small stuff

Pens, coins, and other small items can be difficult to find when they're randomly tossed in the glove compartment. Put them in clear plastic cases or bags so that they won't roll around and so you can see the contents and easily pick out what you're looking for.

Organize your audio

One sign of disorganization is looking into your car and seeing 25 CDs lying around. Select two or three favorites and put them in your glove compartment. They're in less danger of breaking when stored, and they are easier to find. Take the rest of your audio collection in the house. You can periodically switch CDs if you want to.

Stow spare shades

Keep an extra pair of sunglasses in your glove compartment (in a glasses case, of course). When a gloomy day gives way to glorious rays, you'll be prepared. You'll also minimize sun glare, which often contributes to accidents.

Don't forget your gloves

If you live in a cold climate, make sure that you keep an extra pair of gloves in the glove compartment during the winter months. That way, you'll never have to scrape your windows in below-freezing temperatures with bare hands.

Behind the Wheel

Unless you're a collector, you don't buy a car just to keep it running and looking good. You buy it to drive it—to get you from one place to another. And the truth is, even the best-maintained, cleanest, most organized vehicle operates only as well as the person behind the wheel.

A competent motorist abides by the rules of the road and stays in control of her auto at all times. She doesn't act aggressively, nor does she make maneuvers that could cause accidents. In short, she does what she can to keep her commute simple and stress-free.

Faring in Foul Weather

Poor driving conditions challenge even the best of drivers. By keeping your car in good condition and knowing how to respond in various situations, you can navigate just about anything that Mother Nature throws at you.

Wake up before your time

If the meteorologist on the 11 PM news predicts rain or snow for the morning commute, set your alarm to go off a half-hour early. This will give you enough time to get to work without driving too fast for road conditions.

Ride the hydroplane

When the roads are wet, conditions are ripe for hydroplaning. According to the National Safety Council, this phenomenon occurs when water causes your car's tires to lose contact with the road. Your car may feel as though it's gliding or out of control.

If you think that you're hydroplaning, resist the urge to slam on the brakes. Instead, take your foot off the gas pedal and let your car slow down naturally. This allows your tires and the pavement to reconnect gradually and prevents sliding.

Allow plenty of room

When it rains or snows, leave twice as much space between you and the car in front of you as you usually do. This means two car lengths for every 10 miles per hour. This is a good idea at any time, but it is especially important in bad weather. If the driver in front of you slams on his brakes, you'll need an adequate distance to slow down safely. If you slam on your brakes, too, you may initiate a chain-reaction wreck.

Take notice of trees

Drive slowly in areas where trees line the road. In colder temperatures, the trees may shade the road and prevent ice and snow from melting. Wet leaves also make the road surface slippery.

Regain traction

If your car gets stuck in the snow, the Bridgestone Winter Driving School in Steamboat Springs, Colorado, recommends this technique to get going again: Begin by applying light pressure to the gas to try to move your car forward. If your wheels start to spin, ease up on the gas but don't step on the brake. When you feel traction return, slowly accelerate to build forward momentum. Repeat the sequence as necessary until you've freed your car.

Pump to stop

To safely stop in the snow, firmly step on the brakes until you feel your wheels lock. Release the pedal immediately, then repeat. Continue until your car comes to a complete halt. If you have antilock brakes, all you have to do is firmly step on the pedal. Your car's computerized system can pump the brakes faster than you can do it manually.

Turn down your high beams

In a heavy fog, your first inclination may be to switch your headlights to high beams. This is dangerous because the moisture in the air causes the bright light to reflect back toward you. Use low beams and drive more slowly than usual.

Watch your wipers

Aside from the fact that worn-out windshield wipers tend to squeak like crazy, they're just plain dangerous. If your

---

Nine Ways to Cut Your Auto Insurance Costs

Auto insurance rates can vary dramatically depending on the car you drive, the company you select, and the coverage you request. To pare down your premium now, try these tips from the Insurance Information Institute:

Comparison shop. Rates vary greatly from one insurer to another. Identify the best three companies for you, then request quotes from each.

Ask for a higher deductible. Increasing your deductible from $200 to $500, for example, could reduce your collision and comprehensive premiums by 15 to 30 percent.

Drop certain coverage on older cars. Most experts say that if your car is worth less than $2,500, you're losing money by purchasing collision and comprehensive coverage.

Drive a low-profile car. Before you buy a car, check the insurance rates. Coverage usually costs more for models that are expensive to repair or that are frequently targeted by thieves.

Take advantage of low-mileage discounts. Some companies offer great discounts to those who drive fewer than a predetermined number of miles each year.

Consider insurance costs when relocating. Typically, insurance premiums are lowest in rural areas and highest in cities, where there is more traffic and more crime.

Mention your car's safety features. You may get special discounts for a car that's equipped with air bags or antitheft devices.

Ask about antilock brakes. Some states require insurers to give discounts for antilock brakes. Many companies have opted to offer these discounts nationwide.

Stand on your record. Some insurers offer discounts to policyholders who own more than one car, who've had no accidents within the past three years, or who are age 50 or older.

wipers aren't cleaning your windshield sufficiently, invest in new ones. You can pick them up at almost any auto parts store, depending on the make and model of your car. They're relatively inexpensive and easy to install.

Stay home

When bad weather strikes, this is the best advice of all. Yes, taking a day off may put you a bit behind in your work. But all things considered, isn't that better than being involved in an accident and facing months of car repair bills, if not hospital bills?

Driving Defensively

Every year, countless car mishaps are caused by pure carelessness. Remember that when you get behind the wheel, you're operating several thousand pounds of machinery. You must stay alert and in control at all times.

Buckle up

Wearing a seat belt has proven to be the most effective safety precaution that a motorist can take. It doubles your chances of surviving a car crash, according to statistics compiled by the National Highway Traffic Safety Administration. Each year in the United States, about 43,000 people die in car crashes, and another 2,900,000 are injured. If you are among the few drivers who still don't buckle up, please make it a lifetime habit.

Protect baby

All pregnant women should wear seat belts, the American College of Obstetricians and Gynecologists, based in Washington, D.C., strongly recommends. Position the belt underneath your belly rather than over top. If it rubs across your shoulders or breasts, purchase a clip that pulls back the shoulder restraint. These clips are sold in auto parts stores.

Ignore the anti-air-bag hype

Air bags pose a risk primarily for children and short adults. Children should always sit in the backseat. Shorter drivers should sit far enough from the air bag to minimize the potential for injury. What's "far enough?" "If you stretch out your arms, your wrists should touch the top rim of the steering wheel," says Lesley Hazleton, author of *Everything Women Always Wanted to Know about Cars.* If your wrists extend past the steering wheel, then you're sitting too close.

Defuse, then drive

"At least one survey has shown that one in every five drivers killed in auto accidents had some kind of emotional upset sometime during the previous six hours," says Ming T. Tsuan, MD, PhD, a professor of psychiatry. If you're angry or upset, wait until you cool down before getting behind the wheel.

Stay in when you're sick

People with the flu were found to have worse reaction times than people who've been drinking moderately, according to scientists for the Medical Research Council's Common Cold Unit in Salisbury, England. People with colds even flunked tests assessing hand–eye coordination. If you're under the weather, your best bet is to stay at home.

Groom yourself elsewhere

There's a good reason auto manufacturers don't put makeup mirrors in cars: You're not supposed to put on lipstick or shave when you're behind the wheel. Yet you see drivers doing this every day on I-95 along the East

---

Before You Jump-Start Your Car . . .

The American Automobile Association reports that in 2009, more than 30 million motorists requested assistance in jump-starting their cars. You can do the job yourself—provided you have access to another vehicle, of course. Here's how to proceed safely:

- Make sure the battery in the vehicle that's giving you a jump-start has at least as much voltage as your own. Most cars have a standard 12-volt battery.
- Position the cars so that their hoods are near each other. They shouldn't actually touch, however.
- Put each car in park if it's an automatic transmission and in neutral if it's a manual transmission. Then put on the emergency brake.
- Connect one end of the positive (red) cable to the dead battery's positive (+) terminal and the other end to the live battery's positive terminal.
- Connect one end of the negative (black) cable to the negative terminal (-) on the live battery and the other end of the negative cable to an unpainted metal part of the dead car's engine chassis.
- Start the engine of the car with the live battery and let it run for a few minutes.
- Turn on the ignition of the car with the dead battery. If the car doesn't start, recheck all of the cables to make sure they're properly connected. Then try again.
- When the jumped car has been running for several minutes, remove the jumper cables, reversing the order in which you attached them.
- Keep the jumped car running for at least 30 minutes. Then head to a service station and have the battery recharged.

Coast and the 410 Expressway along the West Coast. If you can't get completely ready before you walk out the door of your house in the morning, then you're not allowing enough time to do so. Make an effort to get out of bed at least 10 minutes earlier. That way, you'll be able to do all your grooming before you get in the car.

Avoid the rush

Invariably, traffic is at its heaviest on weekends. That's not the time to be out running errands. If your schedule allows, set aside one evening each week to do your running around. Then you can be at home with your family when everyone else hits the road.

What to Do If You're Pulled Over

Few things can make you break out in a cold sweat like the sight of a police car's flashing lights in your rearview mirror. Keep your cool and stay in control by heeding this advice:

- As soon as it's safe to do so, pull off to the right of the road.
- Put the car in park.
- Turn off your radio or stereo.
- Turn on the overhead interior light.
- Roll down the window about an inch.
- Calmly greet the officer.
- Announce to the officer what you're going to do—for example, "Let me get my registration from the glove compartment."
- Ask why you've been pulled over. A police officer is required to explain what you have done.
- Answer all questions candidly. Give your version of what occurred.

When he gets back in his car, the police officer is supposed to help you safely reenter traffic, usually by blocking the lane behind him so that you can proceed onto the road. If you want to stay on the side of the road for a few minutes, tell the officer. Hopefully, he will leave before you.

Simply Stated

Commuter—one who spends his life
In riding to and from his wife;
A man who shaves and takes a train
And then rides back to shave again.

—E. B. White, American author,
in "Commuter," *The Lady is Cold*

Become a member

If you do a lot of driving, consider joining an auto club. The American Automobile Association (AAA) is probably the best known of these clubs, although you'll find many others nationwide. Most require an annual membership fee. In return, you'll receive a number of benefits and services (such as roadside assistance and travel information), not to mention greater peace of mind.

Keeping the Kids Safe

Infants and small children must sit in safety seats when riding in motor vehicles. Proper installation of these seats is absolutely critical. Government statistics show that when used correctly, safety seats reduce the number of injuries to children in auto accidents by 67 percent and the number of deaths by 71 percent.

Face the right direction

Infants and toddlers should always sit in the backseats of cars. For infants, the safety seat should face rearward. For toddlers, the seat can face forward.

Angle the seat correctly

The angle of a safety seat is important in protecting a child from serious injury in an accident, advises the American Academy of Pediatrics, based in Elk Grove Village, Illinois. A rear-facing seat for infants should be positioned at a 45-degree angle. A forward-facing seat for toddlers can sit upright.

Use the belt

When installing a child safety seat, many folks don't know what to do with the seat belt. Does it wrap around or loop through the seat in some way? The best way to find out is to carefully read the owner's manual for your safety seat. Different seats have different ways of using a seat belt, so don't try to copy from someone else.

Test it yourself

Once you've read the owner's manual and you think you have the safety seat properly anchored, try rocking the seat back and forth (without a child in it, of course). Then yank it toward you as hard as you can. If the seat doesn't budge, then you've installed it correctly. If it does budge, reread the owner's manual and identify where the problem might be. Don't strap a child into the seat until you're certain that it's securely in place.

Get Ready for the Long Haul

Going far by car? If so, the American Automobile Association offers these tips to ensure a safe, stress-free journey:

- Verify that your tires' air pressure is within the suggested range. Check the spare, too. You never know when you'll need it.
- Check the levels of all the car's fluids, including the oil, coolant, and windshield washer fluid.
- Make sure that all of the lights—headlights, brake lights, hazard lights, and turn signals—are working.
- When you pack your car, be careful not to over-load it. A car's carrying capacity (in pounds) is usually listed on a sticker attached to the driver's door.
- Arrange luggage so that the driver's vision is unobstructed in every direction, including out the side and back windows.
- Carry a detailed map with your route clearly marked.

Tighten up

After you've correctly installed the safety seat in your car, you're ready to strap in the child. The position of the straps varies depending on the direction in which the seat is facing. Generally, the straps come from a lower position when the seat faces backward than when it faces forward (read the manual to be sure). The straps should fit snugly across the child, but be careful not to make them too tight.

Simplest of the Simple

Car ownership can get a whole lot easier. All you have to do is practice these principles:

- Whether buying or leasing a car, decide which make and model you want and set a budget before you go to a dealership.
- Change your oil regularly—every 3,000 miles is ideal.

- Keep maps in your car at all times.
- Keep a list of important phone numbers hidden in your car.
- Avoid leaving valuable items on the backseat of your car, in full view of passersby.
- Clean out your glove compartment.
- If you're hydroplaning, never slam on the brakes.
- Always wear a seat belt.
- Never get behind the wheel when you're angry, upset, or sick.

In Case of an Accident

Despite your best efforts to drive safely, you may someday find yourself involved in a fender bender. When it happens, you want to be prepared. Specifically, make sure that you collect the following information at the scene. It can save you a lot of headaches later on, especially when dealing with your insurance company.

Driver Information	Police Information
Name	Name of officer on the scene
Address	Badge number
Home and work phone numbers	Police department
Driver's license number	Phone number
Insurance Information	**Eyewitness Information**
Carrier/agent name	Name
Address	Address
Telephone number	Home and work phone numbers
Policy number and effective date	Notes (what she saw and when)
Vehicle Information	**Tow Truck Information**
Car year, make, and model	Company name
Vehicle identification number	Address
License plate number	Phone number
Registered owner's name	Driver number
Registered owner's address	Owner's name

Provide your vehicle and insurance information to the other driver and cooperate with the investigating police officer, but say no more than is absolutely necessary. Also, report the accident to your insurance company as soon as possible. Your insurer will tell you how to proceed.

Chapter 13   Slices of Life

Smart Solutions for Mastering
Special Situations and Events

Even if your life is running particularly smoothly, you're bound to encounter a wrinkle now and again. It could be temporary, like a last-minute request to host the family holiday dinner, or more permanent, like the arrival of a parent or sibling for an extended stay. Either way, your life can become seriously complicated—unless you have a plan of action.

This chapter prepares you to take on an array of unique, sometimes unanticipated, situations and events. You'll get tips on entertaining, putting up guests (both short-term and long-term), and even adopting a pet. No matter what the circumstance, you'll have the tools you need to handle it with confidence and ease.

Here Come the Ho-Ho-Holidays

The four weeks between Thanksgiving and Christmas are probably the most hectic of the year. Shopping for gifts, planning parties, and preparing meals leave you little time for your usual responsibilities—and even less time for yourself. You can survive the holiday season with your spirit and sanity intact. The secret, of course, is to simplify, simplify, simplify.

No-Fuss Festive Fare

The holidays mean food, and plenty of it. You can make your meal planning and preparation a whole lot easier—and avoid last-minute cooking catastrophes—just by following this advice.

Stock up early

Buy as much food as you can ahead of time. Many supermarkets run out of popular holiday-related items as the holidays approach. Plus, the prices of staples such as baker's chocolate and fresh coconut tend to increase. If the food won't spoil and if you have the space to store it, start buying what you need a month or so in advance.

Make meals ahead

Set aside a day in late November or early December to make an assortment of casseroles, soups, stews, and other freezer-worthy foods. Then when time is at a premium, you can reheat one of these dishes and get a healthful meal on the table in minutes.

Let someone cook for you

Many grocery stores and delis offer prepared holiday feasts complete with turkey, ham, and all the trimmings. Be sure to buy from vendors who use wholesome ingredients, not processed food. You may spend a little more than if you made it all by yourself, but you'll save a lot of time and hassle.

Beat the rush

Instead of serving the big family dinner on Christmas Day, plan it for the weekend before. That way, you get to enjoy the holiday, too. For meals on Christmas Day, simply reheat the leftovers.

Buddy up on desserts

Rather than doing all your holiday baking by yourself, organize a "treat team" to divvy up the duties. Each member of the team chooses a dessert and makes enough to share with the others. Everyone ends up with a supply of baked goods to last the entire holiday season.

Take a cookie shortcut

Rather than making oatmeal, chocolate, or sugar cookies from scratch, buy ready-to-bake cookie dough. Then decorate each cookie with chocolate chips, peanut butter chips, nuts—whatever tickles your family's taste buds.

'Tis a Gift to Be Simple

Finding the perfect present for each person on your holiday list can seem like a daunting task. Make it easier by shopping smarter. Here's how.

Take a hint

Maintain a year-round "wish list" for people who are hard to buy for. Then when one of these folks happens to mention how much she likes a particular item, make a note of it. By the time the holidays roll around, you'll have several can't-go-wrong gift ideas from which to choose.

About Those Gift Boxes . . .

Keeping every gift box that comes through your house can create a huge amount of clutter, not to mention a major fire hazard. Which ones should you retain, and which ones should you recycle? Here are some guidelines.

Collect computer boxes. Definitely keep boxes from computers, televisions, and other major electronics. They'll come in handy in case you have to send any equipment back to the manufacturer for repairs or upgrades. These boxes tend to be quite large, however, so use them to temporarily store other items rather than leaving them empty. Choose lightweight items that won't damage the box and can easily be unpacked if necessary.

Repackage parcels. Keep the box in which you receive any mail-order purchase until you're sure that you won't be sending the item back. Returning the item in the same box that it came in is much easier and cheaper than buying a new box.

Reuse packaging. Of course, you can always save clothing boxes and use them to wrap gifts when the next holiday or birthday rolls around. Refold each box, then store them all together in one place—maybe with the holiday gift wrap or decorations. Make sure you don't accumulate so many that the pile becomes unwieldy.

Give the gift that weighs next to nothing

Invariably, you'll forget to shop for someone until the last minute. When this happens, go with the trusty gift certificate. Some malls offer mallwide certificates with which the recipient can get whatever he wants at whatever store he prefers. Or you can give a certificate for a specialty shop that caters to the person's interests or hobbies.

Do dinner

Buying gifts for people you don't know especially well—coworkers, for example—can be difficult. It can also be expensive if you have a lot of co-workers. Instead of a traditional gift, plan an evening out at a restaurant or club of everyone's choice a week or two before the holidays. You pay only for your own dinner, and you get a fun night out on the town. This is also a good idea for couples who've just started dating and don't yet know each other very well.

Repackage would-be heirlooms

If you have children or grandchildren, here's a clever way to distribute small items that you want to keep in the family but that take up valuable space in your home. In addition to a "big" gift, give each child a small trinket wrapped and labeled "A family treasure for . . ." The kids will love it.

Shop sitting down

You can't beat mail-order catalogs and online shopping for convenience. As long as you get your orders placed sufficiently before the holidays, you should receive your purchases on time. If you're buying clothes, find out the correct sizes before you place your order. Otherwise, you'll spend the week after Christmas sending everything back.

Perfect your timing

If you're planning to do your holiday shopping at the local mall, plan your excursion for early in the week. Stores tend to be much less crowded on Mondays and Tuesdays than on weekends.

Buy two at once

While shopping for Christmas gifts, pick up birthday gifts for family members and friends whose special days are just a month or two away. You'll save yourself another trip to the mall. Just remember to keep all receipts and tags in case an item needs to be returned.

Bag it

Decorative bags are an attractive and easy way to wrap holiday gifts. Many discount retail stores carry inexpensive bags, tissue paper, and accessories. Also, save any bags that you receive, so you can reuse them.

If you'd rather not deal with wrapping at all, have someone else do it for you. Nonprofit organizations often set up gift-wrapping booths in malls as fund-raisers. And there's always the department store gift-wrapping section.

Buy up the bargains

You already know that most stores hold great sales on Christmas items a few days after the holiday. This is a good time to buy wrapping paper, Christmas cards, bows, boxes, and the like for next year. It's also a good time to buy Christmas crafts and art supplies. You'll have everything you need when you start on next year's crafts and ornaments.

Stress-Free Celebrating

Many people tend to put a lot of pressure on themselves during the holidays. If you're one of them, do what you can to keep all the goings-on in perspective. These tips can help.

Hire temporary help

If you need to, bring in a few helpers around the holidays to do the cooking and cleaning. You can probably find some responsible college students who need extra tuition money and are willing to lend a hand.

Dictate who decorates

Decorating for the holidays can be a lot of fun if everyone does his fair share. It's no fun having to do all the decorating yourself, as it quickly turns into a chore. Have each family member pick and choose what decorating they want to help with. If two people want to do one thing, let them share the task. As long as everyone in the family gets involved, holiday decorating should go smoothly.

Relax on the 26th

If holiday chores have you and your mate stressed out, plan to spend some quality time together the day after Christmas. Take off from work and ship the kids to Grandma's. Then just enjoy each other's company.

Simply Stated

There are some people who want to throw their arms around you simply because it is Christmas; there are other people who want to strangle you simply because it is Christmas.

**—Robert Lynd,
Anglo-Irish journalist,
in *The Book of This and That***

Give yourself a gift

Pamper yourself after the holiday season comes to a close. Treat yourself to a massage, a manicure, a makeover—whatever your heart desires. Just do something fun and relaxing, and don't let anyone intrude on it.

Let the Good Times Roll

If you've ever planned any kind of get-together, be it a birthday party or a wedding reception, you know how much work is involved—and how much can go wrong. Here's how to keep things simple and ensure an event that's spectacular.

The Best-Laid Plans

Most of the time, being prepared will make the difference between a good party and a bad one. The following hints may help you tie up some loose ends before your guests arrive.

Decide on the basics

Depending on what type of party you're having, you'll need to decide some general details in advance. The first thing you need to do is set a firm budget and stick to it. Next, you need to decide on a date, time, and place for the party. Will the party be formal or informal? Will it be indoors or outdoors? After you decide on these items, set up a calendar and circle important dates for things that need to be done ahead of time.

Book a date

If you need a caterer or photographer, you need to call them as soon as you decide on a firm date for the party. Due to weddings and other events, it may be difficult to find a reputable caterer and photographer during the months May through October. This is why reserving your date ahead of time is so important. Also, keep in mind that if you're reserving a caterer for an event such as a wedding reception, you may want to reserve the same caterer for the rehearsal dinner. Many people forget this until close to the wedding, long after the caterer has already been booked by another customer.

Get extra help

Approximately a month before the party, you may need to arrange for extra help. For example, if you have children who won't be attending the party, you'll need to find a babysitter and arrange for her to pick up the children a few hours before the party begins. If you need a bartender or entertainer, it's best to book him a month ahead of time. Recruit someone to help you address invitations so they'll be ready when you need to send them out. Don't try to do everything yourself.

Choose your duds

Choosing what to wear can be more difficult than planning the party. Purchasing the right outfit should be done a month before the occasion. If you buy it too soon, there's a chance you will lose or gain weight and the outfit won't fit anymore. If you wait until the week before, you may not have the time to get the needed alterations done. If you're going to wear something you already own, try it on to make sure it still fits and that no alterations or repairs need to be done.

Cook it before you serve it

If you plan on preparing the food by yourself instead of spending money on a caterer, practice cooking each new item you plan on serving ahead of time so that you are sure you can make it and you know it's appropriate for the party. If a dish is too difficult or expensive, nix it and make something else. If the food is reheatable, cook it ahead of time and freeze it so you'll have less to do the day of the party.

Pick your poison

If you're serving alcohol at your party, knowing what type of liquor your friends prefer will save you time and money when purchasing alcohol. If there will be too many guests to be able to narrow the list, one expert advises to stick with the basics and consult a salesperson at the liquor store about the amount you should purchase based on the number of people you expect at the party.

Check up on people

About a week before the party, contact everyone you've hired to ensure that all is going according to schedule. Double-checking reservations (especially with babysitters or bartenders) is always a good idea because someone may have forgotten or overbooked the day of your event. If this disaster happens, you'll still have one week to find someone else.

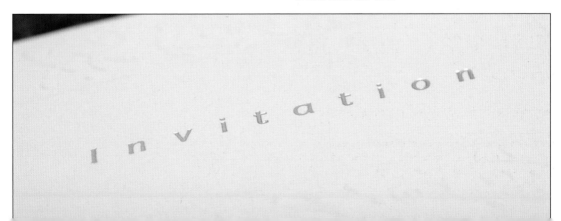

Identifying the Invitees

The more, the merrier, as the saying goes. Be careful, however, when letting friends bring guests you don't know. This is your party, so keep it in control.

Customize who's coming

If your next party is in honor of a specific person, design the guest list for that person. Invite people with whom the guest of honor will be comfortable. If the person is shy, stick to inviting guests you both know. If the person is more outgoing, invite a few people who are your acquaintances and with whom you feel the guest of honor will feel comfortable.

Encourage conversation

Position pieces of furniture at an angle to each other instead of head-on. This is less confrontational and will make your guests feel more comfortable. When arranging dining room seating, put those with common interests near each other but not necessarily next to each other. This setup encourages more people to participate in the conversation.

Invite some future friends

If you're holding a small party for a new neighbor or coworker, invite people whom you believe the newcomer will have something in common with as well as people with different interests. Invite those with common interests so that the guest of honor will get to know new people easily. Those with different interests may be equally fascinating, but a bit harder to get to know. Therefore, blending the two types together will expose your guest of honor to many different personality types and, hopefully, future friends.

The Well-Stocked Soiree

Do you have everything you need to pull off the perfect party? Use the following list to decide. These items are sometimes forgotten but oh-so-essential at many social gatherings.

Background music	Napkins
Bottle opener	Olives
Can opener	Paper or plastic
Coasters	cups
Coat hangers	Paper plates
Corkscrew	Paper towels
Dish towels	Place mats
Ice	Plastic drinking
Lemons	glasses
Limes	Tablecloth

Be firm when it comes to kids

Most parties that you have in your home are probably suitable for children of guests to attend, but there are those in which the kids should stay at home. If you're holding a party and prefer that children not come, let your guests know that and be firm with your decision. If you cave in and let one couple bring their child, other guests may be offended or upset that they weren't allowed to bring their kids.

We'll Have a Barrel of Fun

A party is supposed to be fun for everyone, right? Keep it that way by not losing your composure the day of a big party. If you've planned sufficiently, everything should be lined up and ready. Since you can't remember everything, recruit someone to double-check for you. If you're on your own, think positively and take some advice from the following hints.

Break out the fancy dishes

A day before the party, bring out all of the china, silverware, or crystal that you will need. Polish the silverware and make sure everything is washed and no pieces are nicked or cracked. Then, put all the items in a safe place where they won't get broken. If you're allowing smoking at the party, set out ashtrays ahead of time so that you don't forget.

Rearrange your space

Imagine your dining room or living room filled with people. If you anticipate a large crowd, you probably need to move some furniture around. You may even want to move some furniture out of the room. If so, enlist some help and temporarily move the furniture to an area where your guests won't see it.

Keep a wad of cash on hand

Invariably, there will be an emergency and you'll run out of something or something will break and need to be replaced before the party. Be prepared for this and have some cash available the day before the party. You'll also need it to tip people you've hired. Not everyone accepts credit cards, so be on the safe side and have an ample amount of cash stored in a safe place.

Clean your digs

You'll definitely need to clean your house either the day before the party or the morning of the party. Do a good cleaning job, not just a wipe down. After all, many people will be coming in and out of your house. Make sure you clean the entire house, not just the living and dining room. People will need to use the bathroom and getting there may mean walking past other rooms.

You may prefer to simply close the doors to rooms that you don't want your guests to see. But this can have the effect of making your guests feel unwelcome. Besides, cleaning up before your party makes cleaning up afterward much easier.

Manage the beforehand

Set out all your dishes and other needed items out the morning of the party, or at least as early as possible. Also, wash all dirty dishes and run the dishwasher the morning of the party so you will have a place to put the dirty party dishes after the meal. As early as possible, put out all the food that won't spoil, so you won't have to rush. After you get dressed, you can put the final items out before anyone arrives.

Company Is Coming

It's one thing when family or friends come to visit for the evening. They go home, you clean up, and your life is back to normal within hours. It's another thing entirely when those same folks decide to stay overnight or longer. Suddenly, you're faced with more people for whom you must cook, clean, entertain—and, of course, provide comfortable accommodations. You can do all of the above with calm and class.

Preparing for Overnight Guests

Whether your guest is a relative or a friend from out of town, have a few things prepared before his arrival. Here are a few basic tips to ensure that your guest will be comfortable.

Poll your guests

Ask overnight guests about their food and drink preferences. Chances are, you'll like some of the same things, so cooking for guests may not be such a chore. If you have guests who are picky, consider buying food ready-made at a deli to save yourself some time and effort.

Prepare for allergies

Some people may be sensitive to allergens in your home, including pet dander or dust. If you have company

Essential Amenities

If you're hosting overnight guests, make sure the bedroom they're using is outfitted with the following items. These will help guarantee your guests a comfortable stay:

Alarm clock or clock-radio
Bedding with all-cotton sheets, an extra blanket, and pillows
Bed lamp
Books and magazines
Closet or luggage rack
Pitcher for water and drinking glasses
Small bottles of shampoo and lotion
Soap
Towels and washcloths

coming, keep the pets in a separate room and clean thoroughly the day before their arrival. You want your guests to be comfortable, not sneezing their heads off.

Remember the little things

Keep extras such as shampoo, combs, and toothbrushes on hand for guests. Invariably, someone will forget something, and you should provide him with a small replacement. However, if a guest forgets clothing or something expensive, don't feel obligated to lend him something valuable that may get dirty or damaged. For instance, offer a clean but old shirt, not one of your workday best.

Live and Let Live-Ins

Sometimes, you may offer a relative or friend an extra dose of hospitality by allowing him to move in with you. Perhaps he is having personal problems and needs a place to stay until he can get back on his feet.

Having someone who's not part of the immediate family move in with you puts stress on everyone in the household. Sharing facilities and finding private time can become difficult. Be gracious about the situation. It won't be permanent (unless you let it be), and remember that this is your home and you're in charge. In cases where an elderly parent or grandparent will move in permanently, ensure that you make proper arrangements before this happens.

Stick to the time frame

Agree to the length of the stay before the guest arrives. If you agree to a two-month visit, hold firm to your decision. Mark it on a highly visible calendar. If the guest wants to extend his stay, don't allow him to if there have been conflicts during the course of the visit. Don't be concerned about stepping on his toes; after all, this is your home.

Lay down your laws, nicely

If someone is coming to stay with you for an extended period, you need to devise some rules. For example, younger guests should help with the cleaning chores or pay some part of the rent or grocery bills. Older guests, such as parents, call for a different arrangement. Make it clear to the parent that, although they are welcome to stay with you, this is your home and it will be run the way you see fit, not the way her home was run.

Nip conflicts in the bud

Don't let conflicts regarding guests (especially relatives) arise between you and your mate. This is your home, and you are allowing someone else to stay with you out of the goodness of your heart. If the guest is wearing out his welcome or causing problems, talk with your mate about it and try to come to a mutual agreement.

Entertaining with Restraint

On holidays and other special occasions, folks tend to go all out. It's a once-a-year or once-in-a-lifetime event, they figure, so why not do it up right?

Unfortunately, the combination of great plans and even greater expectations is a surefire recipe for stress. Instead, think simple. For example:

- If you're planning a party, aim for the understated and uncomplicated. Remember, you want your guests to feel relaxed and comfortable. They won't if they sense that you've spent more than you can comfortably afford.
- If a relative or friend announces that she's getting married or having a baby, weigh whether you have the time and money to plan the traditional shower. If you do, great. If not, don't feel obligated to take on the responsibility. Off-load it to someone else, then offer that person whatever support and assistance you can. Also lend a hand to the bride or mom-to-be as the need arises and as your time permits.
- For the holidays, feel free to buy one or two extra gifts. That way, you're prepared in case you receive a gift from a person that you left off your shopping list. One or two spares is fine. More than that is excessive.

Involve your guests

To avoid hurting the feelings of your guest, try to involve her in family activities. She will feel more like a part of the family and may have good ideas for family fun. Also, she can help you clean up afterward, which will free up time for you to do something else.

Kids and Kaboodle

If you see your kids only on the weekends, you know how precious this time together is. The hard part, of course, is getting started and staying prepared for emergencies.

Rolling Out the Welcome Mat

A custody agreement is difficult for all parties involved, especially the children. If your part of the agreement is having the children on the weekends, you may have problems adjusting to caring for your children on your own. From major things like keeping your home allergen-free for a child who has allergies to little things like buying the kinds of snacks they like, organizing your weekend for your children's comfort and your sanity can be a difficult job. To make things worse, your children may have to adjust to a new stepparent, which makes things harder on the family and the stepparent.

Childproof your home

Even if your children stay with you only on the weekends, make sure your home is safe for them. Remember to tie up loose phone cords, put plastic covers in electrical sockets, lock up household chemicals, and so on. Leave everything like this throughout the week so that you don't have to worry about it Friday evening before you pick them up.

Help your children to be bi-domicile

Buy some clothes and toys for your children and keep them at your house so the kids don't have to drag around suitcases. Providing a complete wardrobe, toys, and bathroom necessities will make your children feel like they're at home instead of at a hotel where they have to spend two or three weekends a month. Also, it will make life a bit easier for them if they don't have to pack and unpack several times each month.

Smooth the transition

Make yourself available to your children when they need you. Regardless of what your living agreement is, call your children frequently during the week and keep track of what's going on at school and how they're doing. Just because you only see your children on the weekends doesn't mean you have to be a second-class parent.

> **Simply Stated**
>
> *Even a minor event in the life of a child is an event of that child's world and thus a world event.*
>
> **—Gaston Bachelard, French scientist and philosopher**

Don't try to buy affection

If you see your children only on the weekends, don't try to make up for lost time by buying presents. Kids are smart. Even though they may enjoy getting presents, they can see your motive. You may mean well, but the best thing you can give your children is your time.

Avoid excessive child care

If you're only spending a few weekends a month with your children, focus on them during your time together. It's okay to leave them with a babysitter every now and then, but you're losing quality time when you do this. Try to schedule business dinners and dates during the week so the weekend is free for your kids.

Know emergency numbers

No one wants to think that an emergency may happen to one of their children. Unfortunately, accidents occur, and it's important to be prepared. Do you know what your children are allergic to? Do you know the name of the pediatrician? What's the insurance policy number? Do you know the number for the poison control center? Always have a list of emergency numbers handy.

Keep goodies on hand

If there are certain snacks that your children enjoy, keep these on hand. Make it a habit of purchasing these products when you go on your weekly grocery shopping trip. You won't spend your weekend at convenience stores picking up soda because you bought the wrong kind.

Mark your calendar

Write down important events and birthdays in the calendar you use at the office or the one you use the most. Few things are worse than forgetting a birthday or forgetting what day your daughter gets her report card. Write down events as soon as you learn of them, so you don't forget. You can use a specific color pen to color code so you can find activities at a glance. Or record them in your pocket organizer, if you have one.

Leave the office behind

As much as possible, avoid bringing work home from the office. Some days, you may have no choice. On those days, try to limit yourself to one hour of overtime. Then when you get home, your kids can have your undivided attention.

Sidestepping Parent Traps

Regardless of whether you're a veteran parent or a new stepparent, your relationship with your children will be tested at times. Whether because of problems with a spouse or ex, or an outside occurrence that has nothing to do with the children, sometimes parents take shortcuts or try to mold their children into who they want them to be. There's no perfect plan for parenting, but it's important to realize that your children are their own people with feelings and abilities separate from yours. Be aware of these feelings, and don't take them for granted.

Be nice to your ex

Don't argue with your ex-spouse around your children. This will only make them feel like they're being pulled in opposite directions between two people they love. It's not your kids' faults that you're arguing, so don't put them in the middle and force them to take sides.

> **Simply Stated**
>
> *The childhood shows the man,*
> *As morning shows the day.*
>
> **—John Milton, English poet, in *Paradise Regained***

Let prevailing rules prevail

Try to coordinate rules and discipline for your children with your ex, especially if there's a stepparent involved. If one of you is stricter on the children than the other, the children will learn to listen to one parent and not take the other parent seriously. The children may also come to resent the stricter parent.

Let your kids be kids

Don't try to change your children or stepchildren into who you want them to be. Accept them for who they are, now, at this age and work on building a relationship. As badly as you may want to mold the future Michael Jordan, your child may have Michelangelo in mind.

The Pet Set

In America alone, there are tens of millions of dogs and slightly more cats. Nearly three out of five households in America have at least one dog, not to mention those that have second dogs and other pets. Having a pet may serve many purposes—safety and security, companionship, and even stress reduction.

Picking the Perfect Companion

Adopting a pet is a long-term commitment. That's why it's so important to choose the right one for your family and your lifestyle. These tips can help.

Think about housing

Picking the ideal puppy or kitty is fun, but don't be taken in by those big droopy eyes and wagging tail. Before you shop, decide what type of dog or cat you want. Not necessarily what breed, but rather, what type of personality. A fun-loving, hyper dog needs to be able to run outside, whereas a laid-back, declawed cat should be kept indoors. Take the logistics into account before you take your pet home.

Prepare for pet problems

You may have your heart set on a certain breed when you're looking for a new pet. That's fine, but be aware that certain breeds are prone to specific health problems. This means you may spend a large amount of money on veterinary bills in the future. Before getting a new pet, call your local humane society to get specific information on breeds you may be interested in.

Give a mutt a chance

Consider adopting a mixed breed pet from an animal shelter. Mutts are less prone to health problems than purebreds are, although large dogs sometimes develop hip and joint problems. Pet-ownership thought for the day: Buy your pet from a pound and not only are you getting a new friend but you may be saving a life.

Roll Rover over

When selecting a pet, try a belly test, suggests Paul Donovan, DVM, a veterinarian and director of Alburtis Animal Hospital in Alburtis, Pennsylvania. "Pick a dog who appears healthy, roll him over on his back, and hold him there," says Donovan. "If he's a submissive dog, you should be able to hold him in that position without much struggle. A dog who's aggressive will probably fight to get out of that position."

Teaching Old Dogs New Tricks

You may prefer to let your dog be who he is and not worry about training. This is fine if your dog is well-behaved to begin with. However, if you have a wild mutt who thinks everyone who comes into your yard should be jumped on and slobbered over, a little training may be in order. Many professional agencies will train your dog for you, but if you find that impersonal or expensive, here are a few things you can do to calm a wild dog down.

Simply Stated

The great pleasure of a dog is that you may make a fool of yourself with him and not only will he not scold you, but he will make a fool of himself, too.

—Samuel Butler, English author

Pick a trainable dog

If you're looking for a dog you can easily train, your best bet may be to choose a submissive dog. "When we see a dog being submissive, we think he's afraid," says Liz Palika, a dog obedience trainer from Vista, California, and a columnist for *Dog Fancy* magazine. "In dog language, showing submissiveness doesn't mean fear or weakness. It acknowledges that you're the leader, which is the best message a dog owner can get from a pet. You can train a submissive dog with much less difficulty than a dog who isn't submissive."

Train on schedule

Consistency is the key to training your pooch. Using commands consistently can keep your dog from getting confused. It's also important to stay on a training schedule. If you skip a week between training sessions, don't expect your pet to readily remember lessons or pick up new concepts.

Bribe your pet

Bribery works as well with dogs as it does with some people. Your dog won't be easily trained if he's not having any fun. Keep treats on hand while training your

dog, advises dog trainer Mathilde DeCagney. "Treats can include toys and, of course, dog biscuits and snacks."

Train with a commanding voice

Most likely, your dog won't understand what you're saying to him. (If he does, you should think about going to Hollywood!) He will, however, understand your tone of voice. The tone of your voice is important when training your dog. When your dog does something good, encourage and reward him with a nicer, softer voice. When he does something bad, scold with a lower-pitched, louder voice. Your dog will learn to differentiate between the two, which will make training easier.

Housebreak at daybreak

Housebreaking is one of the most difficult ideas to convey to a dog. It's difficult for the dog, who just wants to relieve himself, and it's difficult for you when you have to clean up accidents on your new carpet. The easiest way to solve this problem is to put the animal on a schedule. Take him out after he wakes up from a nap, after he eats, or anytime he's too quiet or starts sniffing around excessively. When outside, only talk to the pet after he goes to the bathroom. Then praise him in a high-pitched voice.

Save your floor from the pooch's puddles

Every once in a while, your pet will have an accident on the floor. It's important that you clean the mess immediately to prevent permanent stains. For carpets, mix a paste of powdered laundry detergent and water and work it into the stain. Blot dry and flush with water. Let the spot dry, then vacuum the area.

Comfort your canine

Certain breeds of dogs are sensitive to loud noises such as sirens, thunder, and even loud voices. Helping your dog overcome his fear of loud noises should be done gradually, with a process that one veterinarian calls desensitization. Introduce your pet to a low-volume recording of the fear-inducing sound and reward him with praise and treats for relaxed behavior. If he does show signs of fright, don't reward him, as doing so encourages fearful behavior. Then gradually increase the volume of the noise and continue rewarding your dog when he remains calm, until he shows no signs of fear even at loud levels.

Get physical with your dog

Exercise is good for your pet's body as well as your body. Most pets need to be walked or played with at least once a day. Larger animals need more exercise, whereas smaller pets don't need as much. According to veterinarian David Alderton, DVM, author of *The Dog*, "If a dog doesn't settle down immediately after going for its daily walk, he hasn't walked far enough."

If you can't take your pet for a walk, at least engage in some play activity. Throw a ball or Frisbee up and down the steps or play another game in which your pet can get some exercise.

Living with Felines

Cats are much more independent and, in many cases, more self-sufficient than dogs. If you're a cat person, you know that despite the ease of care, there are also problems when sharing your life and home with a cat. Cats love to scratch. They'll scratch you, the carpet, the furniture, and whatever else is convenient. There's also a litter box to deal with. The thing will start to reek if it's not cleaned regularly. Despite the problems, if you can stay in control, cats make good pets.

Find an alternative scratching post

Your cat will undoubtedly prefer to scratch your furniture or drapes instead of a toy or scratching post you buy for him. Aside from keeping your cat out of the house or room, the most effective way to train him is the same way you would train a dog—positive reinforcement. Talk to Tabby with a stern voice when he's scratching something he's not supposed to and praise him in a soothing voice and pet him when he confines his claws to the right place.

Give your cat a pedicure

One option for controlling cat scratching is declawing. This should only be done after a careful consultation with a vet, because it limits much of a cat's behavior. Careful trimming is also an option, but most cats don't allow people to mess with their paws. Alternatively, you could try a product called Soft Paws—small pieces of vinyl that fit over the claw of each toe. This prevents scratching from damaging your furniture and carpet. Consult your vet to see if this product is right for your pet.

Simply Stated

When I play with my cat, who knows if I am not a pastime to her more than she is to me?

—Michel de Montaigne, French essayist

Soak the combatants

When your cats get into a catfight, it's usually over territory or a mate. The easiest way to stop a fight is to douse both participants with water. Cats hate getting wet. One way to curb unwanted behavior is to keep a filled water gun to squirt at the cat when he's scratching or otherwise doing something he's not supposed to do.

Make your cat feel at home

Most animals hate change, and this is especially true for cats. To make a move easier on your cat, take a few items with his smell and the smell of your family over to the new house or apartment and leave them there. This way, when the cat gets there, he'll find something he recognizes. Also, as soon as you move in, make sure your cat knows where his new litter box is.

Comb out the hairballs

Being the groomers that they are, cats tend to get hairballs, especially when they're shedding. The best protection against hairballs is constant grooming by you. Brush your cat at least once a day to remove loose hair. If your cat is still having a problem, there are glycerine-based products on the market that are formulated to lubricate hair so it passes through the digestive tract.

Hold the fish

Cats are susceptible to urinary tract infections and disorders, many of which are due to an increased amount of magnesium in the diet. Urinary tract problems can be serious health problems and, if left untreated, your cat may die. Fish is the culprit in some of these cases. Seafood-based cat foods are also problematic. Try to get your cat to eat other types of cat food, including the ones that are specially formulated for urinary tract health.

Outfoxing Fleas

Fleas are a big problem for pets and, by association, pet owners. Fleas put undue stress on your animal and invade your home. The best advice for getting rid of fleas comes from your veterinarian. He knows your pet's history and can determine the best medicine for him. Never give your pet pills or spray anything on him unless you know it's safe for him. Over-the-counter products can be particularly dangerous to an animal with allergies.

Decontaminate your dwelling

Getting fleas off your pet isn't the only problem you face in the battle against pests. You also have to get rid of the fleas around the pet's bedding and inside the house. This is no easy job. Sprays and powders simply don't work well because most of the fleas flee the area while it's being treated but don't stay gone long. You'll need to thoroughly bomb the inside of your home while your pet is being treated at the same time, so the pet won't bring in new fleas to reinfest the house.

Get into yard work

Fleas like humid areas, so if there are areas around your house where the grass is thick or where there is trash or wood stacked, these areas probably harbor fleas. Clean

---

Keeping Track of Your Pet

Recovering a lost pet is much easier if the animal is wearing a license. A second tag with your name and phone number can help even more. This goes for dogs as well as cats, who are more likely to roam free. More permanent means of pet identification include the following:

Microchip. This device contains an animal's address and phone number, along with other useful information. About the size of a grain of rice, the chip is implanted beneath the skin, in the scruff of the neck. It can then be read by a scanner that is often standard equipment in animal shelters and veterinary hospitals. Cost: about $60.

Tattoo. A pet owner's Social Security number or other identification number is tattooed on the animal, usually on the right inner thigh. Don't worry—the procedure isn't painful. Cost: about $35.

The American Kennel Club's Companion Animal Recovery maintains nationwide records of registered dogs with microchips or tattoos. If a dog is found and identified, the owner is contacted. To sign up for this program, you'll pay a one-time registration fee for each of your pets. Assistance dogs are eligible for free lifetime enrollment.

To find out more, contact the American Kennel Club at www.akc.org.

out any junk piles and keep the lawn cut as close to the ground as possible. Bright sunlight will kill fleas, so keep your yard mowed, especially around shaded areas that only briefly get sun. There are sprays on the market that are environmentally friendly and you may consider purchasing one of these products for your yard.

The Simplest of the Simple

Here's a list of easy tips to get you started on simplifying special situations:

- Buy Christmas dinner instead of making it from scratch.
- Shop for Christmas presents early in the day and early in the week.
- Hire some help for the holiday season.
- Stick to the budget when planning a party.
- Be respectful of houseguests.
- Stick to a firm time frame when allowing friends or relatives to move in with you for a period of time.
- Childproof your home, even if your children live there only on weekends.
- Buy your next pet from the pound.
- Be consistent when training animals.
- Buy your cat a scratching post.

PART THREE   **Streamline Home Paperwork**

Chapter 14

Business Basics

Setting Up a Home Office,
Step by Step

If you were to ask people what they would do if they could start over with their careers, many would say they'd establish their own businesses. Some might want flexible schedules so that they can have more family time. Others might want to make lots of money or be in charge of other people. All of these reasons share a single underlying principle: People want more control of their professional lives.

If you're the boss, you can make your own schedule. If you're the boss, you can put in a few hours in the morning and fly to Jamaica in the afternoon. Maybe the second example is a bit extreme. The point is, many people dream of owning a business simply because they're tired of being told what to do by others.

For more and more people, the workplace has moved from a city office building to the comfort of home. Each year, more Americans are starting new businesses than are having children or getting married, according to Paul Reynolds, PhD, who was chairman of entrepreneurial studies at Marquette University in Milwaukee for five years. At any given time, about 4 percent of the adult population is actively involved in trying to start a new business. In raw numbers, more than 7 million people are trying to start more than 3 million businesses. Some go it alone, while others team up.

"More than two-thirds keep their day job and launch a business part time . . . making the jump to full-time only when the business is up and running," asserts Dr. Reynolds. "The state of the economy seems to weigh less on the decision than their judgment about a specific business opportunity in a specific location." Nevertheless, as corporations continue to phase out full-time staff in favor of temporary and freelance employees, more home-based businesses and enterprises are bound to be started.

More than 17 million people work at home at least one day a week, and the majority of companies now allow some employees to telecommute, according to Gartner Dataquest. This number will probably grow in the future.

At first glance, working at home seems like a wonderful idea. However, working at home creates new complications and concerns, not the least of which is, where are you going to set up your office in your home?

If you are involved in a home enterprise or are telecommuting from home, read on. This chapter offers ideas on where to put your office, how to organize the office, what office items can make your life a bit easier, and what you can do to relieve some stress along the way.

Then again, maybe you just want to create a work space in your home where you can pay your bills and do other essential paperwork. The advice in this chapter will help you as well.

Decisions, Decisions

Perhaps the hardest part of setting up a home business is deciding whether or not you want to give it a go. Certainly, you should set goals up front, so you have a benchmark against which to evaluate your success in the future. But that's only the beginning of getting a business up and running.

Putting It on Paper

A certain amount of paperwork is required to establish a business—and to protect your financial interests. Be sure to take care of the following:

Make it legal

Before you invest a lot of money in your home business, be sure that it's okay for you to have a business to begin with. Many communities have laws and ordinances against certain types of home businesses in residential neighborhoods. Make a call to city hall and check the zoning laws and occupational license requirements before you start.

Insure a good future

Even if you have homeowner's insurance, it's not a bad idea to purchase extra insurance to cover business losses in the event of an accident. Check with different insurance companies before deciding on a policy. You may be eligible for a discount if you consolidate your homeowner's and business policy. The cost varies widely so shop around for the best price.

Put a tight lid on expenses

When you're in business for yourself, it's easy to let expenses get out of hand. You buy this, you order that, all with the underlying assumption that the expenditure

will pay off in terms of the business you'll be generating. Work at home with a budget or don't work at all.

Set the record straight

Most people with special talents and abilities know how to make their product, but many don't know how to market it and handle the bookkeeping. Since you'll probably be on a tight budget starting out, hiring a bookkeeper may be out of the question. If so, invest in bookkeeping software and have someone teach it to you. Or take a class or two online or at your local community college. Most community colleges have classes on running a small business that include tax-law information and basic accounting. Just knowing the basics will save you a lot of trouble in the future.

Measure your success

After you've been working for a year, divide your gross income by the amount of time you spend working to determine the dollar amount you make per hour. It may be considerably less than you expect and will make you rethink your business goals.

Finding Prime Property

Once you've decided to maintain a home office, the first big decision you need to make is where you're going to put your office. Ideally, you may have more than one area to choose from, but in reality, your choice may be limited. It's important to find an area that is quiet and not traveled through often by those in your family.

Your first choice for an office should be a room that can be yours and yours alone. If that's not practical or if you're just starting your business and don't need a large amount of room, steal some space from a room that's being used for another purpose. Although this is not an ideal situation, it can be done if it's your only option. With a little modification, almost any room can be transformed into a workable area.

Make a basement business place

If your basement is waterproof and finished, there may only be a small amount of work that needs to be done to touch up the place. The basement is an especially good choice as a work area if you have the type of business that requires a separate entrance. However, if you'll be receiving clients, more finishing will need to be done to convert your basement into a professional office. Ensure that all fixtures and electrical outlets are working properly, and set up a schedule with your family so you won't be bothered by excessive overhead noise when talking with clients.

Hide out in your attic

If all you need is a small office or work space, the attic may be the perfect place for you. Hidden from the rest of the household, you won't be bothered by noise and foot traffic. But you may have to find an easy way to access the space. Newer homes may provide staircases up to the attic, but some older homes have pulldown ladders that are difficult and dangerous to climb. Also, if it's not a finished attic, it may be too drafty in the winter and too hot in the summer for you to work there comfortably.

Simply Stated

For many people today, the stepladder of corporate life has been kicked out from under them. Even the wall the ladder was leaning on may be removed. Huge companies shrink to mere shells overnight. Mid-size companies start up, merge for a project, and metamorphose into something else to meet market demands.

—Gail Sheehy, American author, in *New Passages: Mapping Your Life Across Time*

Do your business in the bedroom

Many homes have spare bedrooms or studies that are ideal for a small office. This is much more cozy than using the basement or attic. Unfortunately, if you meet with clients, the bedroom office is impractical because your client won't be impressed if he has to walk through the house and pass your teenager's messy room just to get to the office.

Make your dining room convert

The dining room may be a good choice for an office, but only if you entertain infrequently—no one wants to move everything for a dinner party and then move everything back again afterward. Aside from being inconvenient, this also increases your probability of losing important paperwork when you're shifting things around. Also, the noise from the kitchen can be unbearable if you work when meals are being prepared.

Be prepared for bathroom breaks

You probably want to think about how convenient the bathroom is to your proposed work area. If the bathroom is on the opposite end of the house, well, that could be a long way. The closer you are to the bathroom, the less time you spend away from your desk.

A Work Space You Can Live With

You've decided where you want to put your office. Now comes the fun part: designing and accessorizing. Going overboard is all too easy. Start with the basics, and as your business grows, feel free to add on.

Getting Geared Up

You don't have to be an interior decorator to create a comfortable and professional office space. The only requirement is that you make logical decisions concerning the arrangement of items in your office. Organizing your desk and furniture in a way that is comfortable will help you get your work done in a shorter amount of time.

Stay at arm's reach

Anything that's used at least twice a day is best left within arm's reach or in a drawer close by. Other items you use less frequently may be stored in a drawer, filing cabinet, or desk so they're still close by but not in the way when you're working.

Box your way to success

With a little discipline, anyone can have a well-organized desk. A trick that works for some people is to use

priority boxes. More important papers go in one box and less important items go in another. Although the boxes take up space, at least papers won't be piled up all over the desk. When you start looking for an important paper, you'll know which box it's in and you won't have to waste time scouring the office.

Give yourself elbow room

To work most efficiently, give yourself plenty of room around your desk to move. Don't place filing cabinets or shelves so close that you keep bumping into them. Invest in a desk chair with rollers so you can move from one place to another and turn more easily. Also, leave excessive decorations off your desk. Your desk will crowd quickly enough without additional items cluttering the area.

Operate from your center

Some people organize their office into small work centers. For example, you could keep all communicating equipment such as the phone, computer, and printer in one area. Another example could be a mail center where you take care of all of the day's incoming mail and apply postage to outgoing mail.

Simplify your storage

If your desk and filing cabinets are packed full, consider hanging some shelves above your desk or at an angle to your desk. Make sure the shelves are sturdy and have plenty of support to hold the notebooks or journals that you may store overhead. However, before buying more storage containers or shelves, first see what you can take off the old ones to make space.

Avoid hanging supplies higher than you can reach from a sitting position at your desk. If you receive a telephone call requesting information from journals you've shelved, it will be easier and quicker to grab what you need without putting your customer on hold and making her wait longer than necessary.

Control your working climate

If you're the only one working in your home office, you have the luxury of being able to keep the temperature exactly how you want it. If the room is drafty, a small heater may be necessary for your maximum comfort. Also, a fan with a low-noise motor may be helpful in summer months so that you'll be comfortable and more productive.

An A-Plus for Organization

How do your organizational skills measure up? Ask yourself these five questions:

1. Are all of your file folders labeled?
2. Can you retrieve any paper from your files within one minute?
3. Can you file everything on your desk within thirty minutes?
4. Can you consolidate all of the backup materials for a report into a few folders?
5. Do you throw out marginally useful or outdated papers after two months?

If you've gotten a perfect score—that's five yes responses—congratulations. You're an organizational whiz. Any no responses? Now you know where you need to brush up.

Muffle the noise

It's difficult to concentrate on your work when you're being bombarded with noise from televisions, radios, banging pots and pans, and screaming children. It's impractical and unfair to put your family's personal time and habits on hold while you're setting up shop. To solve this problem, consider soundproofing or modular sound barriers to keep some of the unwanted noise out.

Adapt existing furniture

If you have extra furniture in storage, adapt it for use in your new home office. As long as it looks professional (in the event that you'll be receiving clients), it's better to save money to use for the business instead of spending it on expensive office furniture.

If you'll have heavy customer traffic, you may need to be more picky about what you use, but there are still a few items you can borrow from another room that will provide the function you need at little expense. Browse your house for chairs, tables, lamps, throw rugs, wall hangings, and other items that will make your work space more comfortable and functional.

The Brighter, the Better

Research indicates that increasing the amount of light in the workplace relieves depression and improves mood and productivity. Whether you will be drastically affected by a larger amount of light isn't the issue, but having an adequate amount of light and making sure the light is in the right place is important for your contentment. Traditional home lighting may be too dim to work by, and some types give off too much heat to work around comfortably. Be prepared to invest in a different lighting source if all you own are home lamps.

Let the sun shine in

If possible, position your desk near a window. The extra light will help increase your productivity and supply warmth on sunny days.

If you spend much of your time on the computer, it's necessary to give your eyes a break by looking at something in the distance. Make sure, however, that you don't spend more time daydreaming and looking out of the window than you do working.

Treat yourself to a window treatment

If sunlight floods your office during certain times of the day, buy an adjustable shade or blinds to modify the amount of light entering your room. Also investigate frosted glass windows. Because you can't look outside easily, it's less distracting, especially if you have a tendency to stare outside instead of doing your work.

An adequate desk lamp will make all the difference when you are working late at night.

Balance your light

The choice of light fixtures for your work area needs to provide a balance between the amount of light you need and the price you're willing to pay for electricity. You certainly need enough light to work efficiently, while an excessive amount will increase your electric bill. Wherever possible, use fluorescent lighting, which is more efficient than incandescent lighting and also lasts longer.

Hide your desk lighting

If you lack the desk space for a lamp, try adding fluorescent lighting strips underneath shelves or underneath a cabinet that may be over your computer. This type of lighting shines directly on the work surface without shadowing and doesn't take up valuable space. Also, this type of lighting doesn't produce an excessive amount of heat like other traditional lighting sources, so it may be more comfortable for you.

Everyday Office Essentials

Wander into one of those discount office supply stores and you're bound to see an abundance of gadgets and doodads that seem to scream, "Buy us!" When you're first starting up, though, you're better off spending money only on those items that you know you absolutely need—pens, pencils, a stapler, file folders, and the like. Save the gadgets and doodads for later.

Use one and only one calendar

Some people have separate professional and personal calendars, but this isn't necessary. Unless you're extremely organized, use only one calendar. Browse through it daily and enter all your important events in it. Even if your calendar is primarily for business, add personal appointments to it as well.

Secure a simple planner

Unless you travel often, you probably don't need an elaborate hard-copy day planner. This is especially true if you have a calendar in your office. Look around office supply stores to compare prices and contents of many different planners. In any case, don't spend a lot of money on a planner that provides more than you need.

Keep important numbers elsewhere

If you travel often, you'll need to maintain a list of important telephone numbers and addresses. Make sure you update and delete names from your list as needed. Make a backup list and keep it some place safe.

Get thee a good dictionary

If you're not a good speller, buy a dictionary so you can check words you're not sure about, rather than sending out correspondence with misspelled words. Although computer word-processing software programs have spell checkers, often these are inadequate, especially if your business is a specialty.

Stay on track with snack attacks

You'll save some time by keeping a small refrigerator in your home office to hold water, soda, and a few healthful snacks. You can also keep refreshments on hand for customers.

A Place for Everything

If you work alone in your office, every day is probably a busy day for you. Many of your tasks are special to your business, and you can't take shortcuts. Still, there are little things you can do to save time and effort. One of the most important, of course, is staying organized.

Taming the Paper Tiger

If you're not careful, paper can quickly overrun your work space, leaving you scrambling to find crucial documents amid all the throwaways. Keep important paperwork at your fingertips by filing it away.

Label what you file

Take 10 seconds to write or type a label for each folder, and watch your productivity increase. Avoid overcrowding your desk and filing cabinet—if your drawers are so clogged that you wrinkle papers every time you file something new, buy an extra filing cabinet, or better still, sort through all the papers and chuck what you no longer need.

File a little every darn day

Who likes to file paperwork? It's boring, but being organized can save you time and money. Set aside a few minutes at the end of the day to put items back in their proper places. You'll know where they are the next day and you won't waste time trying to figure out which pile you put them in.

Staple it together

If you have important items that relate to one customer or purpose, staple them together instead of using paper clips. Paper clips fall off, and you risk losing something that you'll need at another time. If you have an aversion to stapling, use clips that hold papers tightly together without punching a hole.

Make your office sparkle

At least once a month, thoroughly clean your office and go through all your files to remove what you don't need anymore. This is an important task because paperwork piles up so quickly. You can cut down on clutter by chucking things immediately, but you still need to do wholesale cleaning periodically.

Managing Snail Mail

Imagine a week without mail. The correspondence you receive is important, so handle the mail as quickly and easily as possible.

Create a tickler file

It's easy to forget important tasks when you're feeling overwhelmed. Create a rotating tickler file for each month and then four more for the current weeks (this week, next week, and so on). When important correspondence arrives, put it in the tickler file for the appropriate week or month. When that time rolls around, as you review your files, you can retrieve the items and take action.

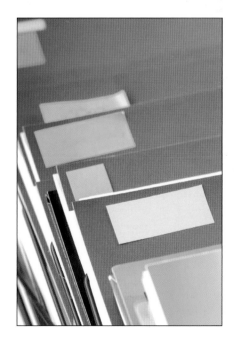

Use tickler files for the personal touch

To simplify personal correspondence such as birthday cards, if you happen to see a card that would be perfect for Aunt Martha, buy it and put it in the appropriate month in your tickler files. When that month rolls around, you'll remember Aunt Martha's birthday and you won't forget to send the card.

Rid yourself of pests

The best thing to do with unimportant mail is to throw it away immediately. Then it won't be piling up on your desk. You may receive mail that you don't need at that moment but feel you want to retain. In that case, put it in the tickler file for review closer to the time that it might be relevant to you.

Know your mailing options

Dealing with the postal service can be a somewhat easier experience if you know what services are available to you. In addition to first-class mail, which may take a few days or more for delivery, priority mail and express and parcel services are now available everywhere. Avoid sending items by overnight delivery unless absolutely necessary. The money you save by sending something first class as opposed to overnight may buy your lunch for the next day.

Slash open your mail

Using a letter opener will help save time, reduce paper cuts, and generate less mess. Keep the letter opener in a safe place when you're finished with it to prevent an accident.

More Options for Organizing

You may find yourself running out of space in your filing cabinets or drawers. When this happens, (as always) first examine what you can dispose of. If you still need extra space, store old files and paperwork in clear plastic storage containers. You can park these containers in another room of the house, or better yet, purchase a secure or fire-safe container to put your storage boxes in. Label boxes clearly to make it easy to refer to them in the future.

Stack your bins

Stackable bins are a common tool that are inexpensive. These bins can be used to house priority material or

---

Disconnecting Phone Solicitors

The Telemarketing and Consumer Fraud and Abuse Prevention Act, which became law in 1994, requires telemarketers to make certain disclosures when they contact you. Among other things, the callers must:

- Explain cost and quantity, either orally or in writing.
- Outline restrictions, limitations, or other conditions that may influence a consumer's decision to purchase the offered goods or services.
- Stipulate any no-refund policy at the outset.

In addition, the act contains a do-not-call provision that prohibits a telemarketer from contacting you once you indicate that you no longer accept phone solicitations by or on behalf of a particular business. Once you've given notice, any telemarketer who persists in soliciting you may face a civil penalty of up to $10,000 per violation. In most cases, just mentioning that you know about the do-not-call provision will stop a telemarketer cold.

For more information about this law, check out:

Bureau of Consumer Protection
Federal Trade Commission
www.ftc.gov
Direct Marketing Association
www.the-dma.org/telemarketing

---

simply to hold catalogs or reference material that you use often. The only downfall to stackable bins is difficulty in reaching papers that are in the middle of the bottom bin. Eliminate this problem by not overcrowding the bins and clearing them frequently.

Throw out the memo pads

If your desk looks like a sacrifice to the memo god, purchase a pocket recorder to record messages to yourself. Check the recorder in the morning when you go to work and in the evening before you quit for the day, so that you don't forget anything.

Tack messages on the bulletin board

If you need to clear space off your desk, post a small bulletin board over your desk so you can post important reminders for yourself or other people you have working with you. The only danger is that the bulletin board might be used for posting pictures or items that aren't important in a business sense. Clear the board every day so new messages catch your attention.

Tools of the Trade

As a home business owner, you'll rely on your telephone and your computer to keep you in touch with the outside world. Using both efficiently can save you time, money, and hassle.

Taking Control of the Telephone

You might feel like you're being controlled by the almighty telephone. Whatever your gripe, the telephone can be used to better serve you and your family.

Screen unwanted calls

Okay, maybe this isn't the nicest thing to do. Still, if your sweet (and talkative) Aunt Martha calls while you're working to tell you all about her vacation or her latest boyfriend, let it pass. Then call her back when you have more time and can pay attention.

Have someone else answer the phone

If you find yourself spending too much time talking instead of working, let an answering service take your calls. They can put through important calls and leave the others for another time.

Getting Personal with Your PC

Computers have speeded up information exchange and allowed people to get much more work done in a day than used to be possible. Unfortunately, along with computers comes a new set of problems.

Make backups

You never know when a natural or man-made disaster is going to destroy your computer or the information in it. To prevent losing all the precious information your business depends on, make disk backups of your data frequently. Keep backup disks in a fireproof cabinet or some other secure place for safekeeping. Also, further protect your PC by investing in a good power-surge protector. Some of these devices are better than others, so ask around before you buy, and always compare prices.

Purchase a picture-perfect monitor

If you'll be spending a lot of time at your computer, it pays to purchase a large flat screen moniter. This will help your eyesight and prevent you from becoming fatigued after several hours at the computer.

Cut down on background noise

In addition to extraneous noise in your home, office equipment gives off a fair amount of noise that can be distracting while you're trying to work. Consider placing a heat-resistant pad underneath the equipment to cut down on the noise and vibrations.

Avoid smoking up your computer

If you smoke, you already know that it's dangerous to your health. It can also be dangerous to computers, for several reasons. Beyond the obvious, cigarette smoke produces a buildup on computer equipment and disks that may corrupt them.

Open for Business

Once you have your office set up, you're ready to get to work. Remember, although you're in your own home, you are on the job. Conduct yourself like a professional and you're bound to succeed.

Counting the Hours

Establishing and sticking with a work schedule is imperative. You want to make every effort to keep your professional and personal lives separate.

Set up firm office hours

When you work in a traditional downtown office, you don't get much work done if your children, spouse, or friends are constantly calling or dropping by. The same applies if you work at home. Set up a work schedule that suits you, your clients, and your family and make every attempt to stick to it. You may have to find babysitters. Or you may need to have an answering service take personal calls while you're working.

Spare your neighbors

If you'll be receiving clients, it's necessary to plan your activities in a way that won't put a strain on relations with your neighbors. This is especially true if you live in a quiet neighborhood where the extra traffic will be a headache for others. Make sure there is adequate parking space for clients.

Handling Home Responsibilities

One potential drawback of working at home is the constant temptation to run errands, do chores, and take care of other personal business during your office hours. You can eliminate the need to do so by managing your home and family responsibilities more efficiently. Here's how.

Consolidate your activities

When running errands, combine what you do so the amount of time you spend away from work decreases. The same time that you pick up your dry cleaning, pick up a prescription from the pharmacist if you know you'll be needing it in a few days. You're already away from work and by getting this taken care of now, you won't waste more time or gas in the next few days.

Pain-Free Computing

Spending hours each day in front of a computer can leave you tense, achy, and downright miserable. In their book *Healthy Computing*, Ronald Harwin and Colin Haynes offer these tips for avoiding computer-related fatigue and injuries. *Note:* If you're experiencing severe symptoms, see your doctor.

- Monitor your posture. Slight headaches and backaches while working at a computer may indicate that you're not sitting properly.
- Check the position of your wrists and arms while typing on your keyboard. If your fingers are higher than your wrists, you're asking for trouble (in the form of a repetitive strain injury).
- Keep your work area uncluttered so that you can use your keyboard and mouse comfortably.
- Clean a dusty monitor screen.
- At least once each hour, drop your hands down to your sides. Gently shake your hands and fingers.
- If your shoulders feel tense, rotate them forward in a full circle four times. Then rotate each shoulder individually four times.
- Take periodic breaks from keyboarding—at least once every two hours and, ideally, once every 20 minutes.

Hire help for errands

When you're busy running a business, it's difficult to handle personal and family errands. Check with your local high school guidance counselor or job-placement center to see about hiring a teenager to run errands such as dropping off and picking up dry cleaning. You'll be amazed at the amount of work you can get done while others handle errands for you.

Make the business a family affair

If you have a teenager who has his driver's license, put him to work running errands for you. This will save time and money (since you probably won't pay your child as much as you would pay a stranger).

Take advantage of delivery services

If your budget allows, use delivery dry cleaning services, grocers, and, of course, delivery from restaurants you enjoy. The cost may seem steep at first, but when you consider the time you spend away from your office, the gas you use in your car to make the trips, and the vital calls you miss, it may be well worth the price.

All about Breaks

You know what they say about all work and no play. You'll be tired and stressed out and you'll start making careless mistakes in your work if you don't take a break. Get up and move around every once in a while. Get out of the office or even the house. Do whatever it takes to recharge your mental batteries.

Take a lunch break

You're allowed a lunch break like everyone else. Even if you don't leave home, move to another room and take some time for yourself.

Overcome yourself

Everyone has hobbies or activities they'd rather do than work. If you have a tendency to sneak over to the television or curl up with a good book instead of working, you may find yourself getting nothing done. If you need the extra motivation that a traditional office setting with strict hours requires, working in the home may not be for you.

The Simplest of the Simple

Setting up and maintaining a home office is easier if you apply these basic principles.

- Keep what you need close at hand.
- Adapt existing furniture.
- Update your calendar frequently.
- File papers every day.
- Use a cordless phone.
- Set up strict office hours.
- Take a lunch break every day.
- Get outside help.

How Much Will It Cost?

Starting your own business is a major financial commitment. To estimate how much money you'll need to get your enterprise off the ground, use the following checklist.

Start-Up Costs

Advertising
Cash
Deposits for public utilities
Equipment and fixtures (including installation)
Legal and professional fees
Licenses and permits
Remodeling and decorating
Starting inventory

Monthly Costs

Advertising
Deliveries
Insurance
Interest on any loans
Legal and professional fees
Maintenance
Salaries and other wages
Supplies
Taxes, including Social Security

Chapter 15

Money Mastery

Common-Cents Strategies
for Making Your Dollars Go Further

Everyone loves a good bargain, and retailers know it. To stay competitive, they keep coming up with new and innovative ways—newspaper coupons, special sales, frequent-buyer discounts, and more—to entice customers to patronize their businesses.

The real advantage for you is that you seldom have to pay full price for anything anymore, unless you want to. With a bit of investigation, preparation, and organization, you can get great deals on all kinds of personal and household goods.

The tips in this chapter will help you maximize the buying power of your dollars. No matter what your budget, you can get what you want at a price you can afford. Best of all, you can do it without a lot of headache and hassle

Bargains, Bargains Everywhere

If you want to save money when you shop, you first need to know how much you spend. This is easy enough: Write down all of your family's expenditures for one month. Then at the end of the month, add them up. Most folks are surprised by the figure they come up with. It's usually much higher than they expect. At least it provides motivation to shop smarter.

The Basics of Shopping Smart

Ready to simplify your shopping and save big? Here are some guidelines to get you started.

Visit warehouse wonderlands

Most warehouse clubs sell their merchandise at cost, according to a survey compiled by Mike Yorkey, author of *Saving Money Any Way You Can*. They earn their profits from the annual fees paid by vendors who display their goods there. So you'll find high-quality brand-name products at low prices as well as specials on necessities such as toilet paper and toothpaste. Many consumers find that one monthly trip to a warehouse club saves them time and money in the long run. If you don't already belong to one of these clubs, you'll pay a small membership fee when you join.

Go for broke

Watch for going-out-of-business and bankruptcy sales. You may be able to get some first-quality merchandise at a fraction of the original price. You probably won't be able to return items, though, so make sure that you get exactly what you want.

Plug in to a small outlet

Rather than automatically heading for the mall whenever you need something, check out off-the-beaten-path outlets and shopping centers. You'll likely find better deals on the items you're looking for. And because these stores tend to have less customer traffic, you'll spend less time waiting in lines.

Make a commitment

When you find a store with merchandise and prices that you like, patronize it as often as you can. The retailer may reward you for your loyalty with special discounts and gift certificates around the holidays. The same is true of mail-order and online catalogs.

Clothes-ing In on Great Deals

When it comes to buying clothes, the challenge is finding quality garments that fit, at a price you can afford. You can spend endless hours at the mall, browsing through every store. But there is a better way. For starters, try these tips.

Be a Johnny-come-lately

You can save lots of money by buying clothes right after the season ends rather than a month or two before it starts. Retailers are trying to get rid of old merchandise to make room for the new. Some retailers put before-season clothes on sale too, but usually the savings aren't that great.

Opt for irregulars

Many retailers significantly mark down clothes because of slight defects such as missing buttons or flaws in the fabric. Often, such defects are barely noticeable. Carefully inspect garments marked "irregular." If the problem is inconspicuous or repairable and the price is right, you've found a great deal—and a great addition to your wardrobe.

Shift to thrift

Kids grow so fast that they seldom get a chance to wear out their clothes before moving on to the next size. To avoid paying huge amounts of money for garments that will be worn only a few times, check out thrift stores such as Goodwill. You'll get inexpensive clothes in excellent condition.

A Supermarket Primary

The modern supermarket bears little resemblance to the corner store of a few decades ago. These days, you can get a can of green beans in one aisle and a pair of socks in another. "Picking up a few things" can take a good hour rather than mere minutes.

Can you shorten the amount of time you spend in the supermarket? The answer is, absolutely yes. By taking

five minutes out of your weekly schedule to plan your grocery run, you can save time, aggravation, and money.

Make one trip

Plan one big trip to the supermarket each week, rather than two or three small trips. Those small trips often turn into big time-wasters. You'll likely stop by the store after work, when everyone else is there, and end up doing a lot of waiting in line. Also, you may pick up more items than you need, because you won't have a list with you.

Do your grocery shopping before work, if you have time. Supermarkets tend to be least busy then. In general, the odder the hour when you go to the store, the less crowded it will be.

Designate a dollar figure

Before you even set foot in a supermarket, decide how much you want to spend. Your budget should cover the items that you need and allow for a few (but not too many) extras. By limiting your spending, you'll be less tempted to splurge on nonnecessities.

Keep a running list

Add items to your grocery list as they run out. If you wait to write up your list until just before you go to the store, you risk forgetting half the items that you really need.

Organize by aisle

How often do you get to the checkout only to realize that you've forgotten a particular item? You have to step out of line and backtrack through the store to get what you need. A better way is to organize your grocery list by aisle. You don't have to rewrite the list. Just number each item according to the aisle that it's found in.

Plan according to your palate

By creating weekly menus for your family, you know in advance what you'll need from the store to prepare each meal. You can use your menus to write up your weekly grocery list. And you won't get caught without important ingredients while you're cooking.

Go shopping in cyberspace

Choose from a list of groceries on a supermarket's Web site, and pay with your credit card. Then have the groceries delivered to your door, so you needn't leave your home.

Make people come to your door

Some supermarkets also offer delivery services within a certain radius of the stores. This is a good option if you don't have the time to do your own shopping and can afford the extra cost of delivery.

Cruising the Grocery Aisles

If you do your grocery shopping the old-fashioned way—by going to the store and pushing a cart up and down each aisle—you can still save big bucks. You don't necessarily have to clip coupons to do it, either (though you can if you want). Here are some alternatives.

Hang out with the best

If you have a choice, shop in a higher-quality supermarket—one that has more departments, stocks a greater variety of products, and offers more services to customers. You're guaranteed good merchandise, and in the long run, you'll get better value for your dollar.

Bring your own bags

Some supermarkets pay shoppers who bring their own bags. It's only a few cents per bag, but in the long run, those pennies can add up to nice savings. Also, by supplying your own bags, you won't have to deal with a stockpile at home (unless you use them for garbage or other household purposes). Some stores also collect bags for recycling.

Shop on a full stomach

You may have heard this before, but it's worth repeating. If you shop for groceries while you're hungry, you tend to buy items that you don't need—especially snack foods. This wastes money and, over time, may pack on a few extra pounds around your middle. Also, when you're hungry, you're more easily aggravated by minor annoyances like having to wait in line.

Look high, look low

Grocers tend to place the expensive or especially tempting items at eye level. If these items catch your eye first, you're more likely to choose them over more reasonably priced goods. Be aware of this and realize that you need to look around for the best buy.

Ignore the name

Store brands are less expensive than name brands. Most of the time, you can't tell the difference between the two—and sometimes the store brand is actually better. The packaging just isn't as fancy. Try store brands of various items and see which ones you like. You can save yourself a few pennies.

Think big

As a general rule, buying the economy or family sizes of nonperishable items such as laundry detergent and paper towels costs less. You'll pay more up front, of course, but you'll save on a per-use basis. Just remember to buy products because you need them, not because they're cheap. Otherwise, they're just going to take up space on your shelves.

Compare varieties

Vegetables and fruits come fresh, frozen, and canned. Compare prices before you decide which to buy. Canned corn, for instance, may cost less per serving than frozen or fresh. The store brand may be even cheaper.

See double

Many supermarkets double the face value of coupons up to a certain amount. So instead of getting 30 cents off a bar of soap, for instance, you'll get 60. This can add up to substantial savings over time. If you have to drive out of your way to get to a store that doubles coupons, the savings may not compensate for the inconvenience. Use your judgment.

Clip carefully

Manufacturers offer coupons as a way of enticing you to try their products. Never buy an item just because you have a coupon for it. Make sure it's something that you need.

Request a refund

Many manufacturers offer rebates to customers for purchasing their products. In most cases, all you have to do is fill in a coupon and send it to the manufacturer with proof of purchase. Depending on the product, you can get back a few bucks.

> **Simply Stated**
>
> *Americans are fascinated by their own love of shopping. This does not make them unique. It's just that they have more to buy than most other people on the planet.*
>
> —**Simon Hoggart,**
> **British journalist**

A Place for Every Paper

Invariably, all purchases come with paperwork. It could be something as simple as a receipt or as significant as a warranty. No matter what they are, you want to keep these documents organized so that you can find them when you need them. This is especially true of coupons and warranties.

Cutting Back on Coupon Clutter

"Eighty percent of American shoppers do use coupons from time to time, but few of them do it in an organized way," notes self-described "coupon queen" Susan Samtur in *Cashing In at the Checkout*. Indeed, coupons are easy to save and trade, but they can also add up to a mountain of paper. The important thing to remember is that once you clip or download coupons, you must keep them in their proper place until you use them. It's easy to throw them in a folder or drawer, but you'll waste a considerable amount of time trying to find the ones you need when you need them. Here are some better ways to deal with them.

Get the right receptacle

Coupon organizers come in a variety of shapes, sizes, and prices. Some cost $10 or more. You can make your own organizer from a manila folder. Cut the folder in half so that it measures 5 to 6 inches wide by 8½ inches high. Staple the edges so that the coupons can't fall out. Slide in dividers (made from the unused half of the folder) to create compartments. This organizer will work just as well as one that you buy.

Arrange by aisle

As with your shopping list, separate your coupons according to the supermarket aisles in which the products are found. This makes finding a particular coupon easier, especially if you're in a hurry.

Make a trade

Most grocery stores have bins where you can put coupons that you don't need and pick up those that you do. This is a good way to get rid of coupons that you don't need and that haven't yet expired.

Clean out periodically

Go through your coupon organizer once each week and throw away coupons that have expired. This takes only a minute or so, and it will save you the embarrassment of trying to use a coupon that is no longer good.

Continue to compare

A product doesn't automatically become a good value just because you have a coupon for it. You still need to compare prices. Even with a coupon, a name brand may cost more than a store brand.

Where Oh Where Is That Warranty?

A warranty is your insurance against a defective product. Electronics, appliances, and similar items usually come with limited warranties. The manufacturer or retailer may offer to extend the coverage for a fee.

Should you purchase an extended warranty? In many ways, that depends on the warranty itself. Always read the fine print and make sure that you'll use a product enough for the extended warranty to pay for itself in the event that repairs are required.

You probably own a lot of items with limited or extended warranties. Here are some suggestions for keeping any hardcopy documents organized and using them to your advantage.

Put them in one place

Keep all warranties together in a folder or notebook. Then when you need to refer to one, you can find it fast. This is especially important for expensive items such as electronics and appliances. But even some clothes and other personal goods come with lifetime warranties.

Pair them with receipts

Sometimes a receipt is the only proof you need to get warranty work done on an item that you own. Get in the habit of keeping receipts and warranty information in the same place. You may want to put all of the documents in a fireproof cabinet or safe-deposit box for safekeeping.

Throw out the old ones

Toss warranty cards (as well as owner's manuals) for items that you no longer own. These documents can contribute to clutter and take up valuable space that you could be using to store something else.

Refuse to play the name game

When you fill in a warranty card and return it to the manufacturer, the information that you provide may end up in the hands of other companies. They, in turn, may add you to their mailing lists. To prevent this—and the ensuing avalanche of junk mail—attach a note to your warranty card saying that you want all the information about you to be kept confidential. You can do the same when registering your warranty online.

Go with what you get

Limited warranties are free of charge and are usually valid for one year after the date of purchase. Chances are that if an item has a serious defect, you'll learn about it within a year. Then you can just get a replacement. All an extended service contract does is take money out of your pocket, because you have to pay for it. You're better off putting that money in the bank.

'Tis the Season to Be Buying

Stock up on fresh fruits and vegetables in season, when they're at their cheapest. Then freeze or can them for use in the months ahead. Here's what to buy when, though of course seasons may vary based on where you live.

January, February, March, And April

Apples	Corn
Grapefruit	Melons
Oranges	Strawberries
Pears	

May

Asparagus
Pineapple
Strawberries
Tomatoes

June

Asparagus
Cherries

July

Berries
Cherries
Corn
Grapes
Lemons

August

Apples
Corn
Grapes

Remember the resale rule

If you frequent flea markets and yard sales, keep in mind that the warranties on resold items are not transferrable and therefore no longer valid. So don't expect a refund or replacement—at least not from the manufacturer—if the item that you buy doesn't work properly.

Let them know how you feel

If you're not satisfied with an item that is still under warranty or with the service that you receive for it, notify the manufacturer. Often, the manufacturer will send you a refund or gift certificate just to stay in your good graces. For an item that's no longer under warranty, the manufacturer may offer free maintenance as a gesture of goodwill.

It's in the Mail

Not everyone has easy access to a mall. But you have easy access to the Web. That's all you need to shop from home.

You certainly can't beat online ordering for convenience. But if you're not careful, you can run up quite a tab. The following strategies will help you order wisely so you save not only time but money, too.

Keeping Good Company

Not all online or mail-order companies operate alike. Here's how to identify the ones that will serve you best.

Sail without shipping

Perhaps the primary distinction between online purchases and regular retail purchases is that you usually have to pay shipping and handling for the former. These charges can run up your bill if you're not careful. Some online companies have a flat rate for shipping and handling, no matter how much you buy. Others offer discounts if your purchases total a certain dollar amount. Either way, you'll keep shipping and handling costs to a minimum.

Ensure happy returns

If the item that you order is the wrong size or color, you'll have to send it back. Make sure that return postage is guaranteed, so you're not charged twice for shipping an item that you've decided not to keep.

All Is Not Lost

You ordered an item weeks ago, and it still hasn't arrived. What do you do? For starters, try these strategies.

Demand action

Many times, a delay in shipping results from simple human error. A phone call to the vendor can ensure that your package is sent out that very day, often at no charge to you.

Ponder payment methods

A mail-order or online company won't send out a package until it receives payment from you. So while you're sitting around wondering why you haven't received your order, the company is sending you a letter saying that the charges to your credit card have been denied. If it is a credit problem, call the card's issuing company to get it straightened out. And consider paying for future mail-order purchases by check or money order. (Keep in mind, though, that you can pay this way only when ordering by mail.) Alternatively, pay online via paypal or other funds transfer services.

Request a carrier

When you place an order, you're entitled to choose the carrier that you want to deliver the package. Most online companies ship through United Parcel Service, USPS, or Federal Express, but perhaps you'd prefer someone else. The most important thing to remember when choosing a carrier is to pick one that services your area often and that issues a tracking number for each order. The number makes finding a lost or incorrectly delivered package much easier, especially around the holidays.

Get confirmation

When you order an item over the phone, the customer service representative may offer you a confirmation number. If she doesn't, ask for one. Jot the number down and keep it in a safe place. Then should your package get lost, the company can use your confirmation number to locate it. You may never need your confirmation numbers, but it's better to be safe than sorry. Online vendors usually send you a confirmation number by e-mail.

Gift Giving Made Easy

You know the old saw about gift giving: It's the thought that counts. It may seem trite, but it still holds true. So often folks get hung up on how much to spend that they lose sight of why they're giving a gift in the first place—namely, to commemorate a special occasion or as a goodwill gesture. If you can just keep this in mind, you may find that the best gift of all costs nothing, except maybe a bit of your time. What could be simpler?

Perfect Birthday Presents

Because a birthday is such a personal event, you want the gift to be special, too. These tips can help you find just the right thing without a lot of hassle.

Give the gift of time

Instead of buying a gift, wrap up an IOU for babysitting services, yard work, or general household maintenance—whatever you're good at. This saves you money while giving the recipient a welcome break to do something else she enjoys.

Guerrilla Grocery Shopping

Saving money on your grocery bill is easy if you shop smart. These tactics can help you spend less—and get you into and out of the supermarket fast.

- Avoid shopping on weekends. Stores tend to be most crowded then.
- Go by yourself, if possible. Kids, especially, can distract your attention and persuade you to buy more than you really need.
- Look at the "price per unit" label. It's usually posted on the shelf below each item. This tells you how much an item costs per ounce or other unit of weight or volume. Use the price per unit to compare brands—or various sizes of the same brand—and choose the best value.
- Always look for or ask about advertised and unannounced specials.
- If you're buying just a few items, pay in cash to cut down on receipts.
- If you're paying by check, have the grocery store's name and date already filled in. Then when you're at the register, simply write in the dollar amount and your signature.

Don't return—recycle

If you receive something for your birthday that just isn't to your taste, pack it away instead of taking it back. Then when someone else's birthday rolls around, you may already have the perfect gift on hand. Just be careful not to give the item to the same person you received it from in the first place. So you remember, write down the person's name and place it with the item.

Buy well in advance of the big day

There's no law saying that you must wait to purchase a present until the week immediately before someone's birthday. So even though your mom's special day isn't for another six months, go ahead and buy a gift if you see one that you like at a good price. When you get home, make a note of your purchase and put it in the appropriate month's tickler file so you don't forget about it.

Send light when sending far

Mailing packages to faraway family members and friends can add up in terms of postage. So instead of buying big, give a magazine subscription or a gift certificate to the person's favorite store. Sending it will cost you just the price of a stamp.

How Complex Can It Get

This, Too, Shall Pass: Don't be surprised if you suddenly have difficulty locating a product that you've been using for years. The average life span for products is decreasing. Less than one-third of those available 10 years ago are still on the market today. In some product lines, upgrades and improvements typically occur every three months or less. This rate is expected to speed up within the next few years.

Surviving Holiday Shopping

Shopping for gifts during the holidays is complicated by the fact that everyone else is out there crawling the malls with you. Then, too, some retailers raise their prices in an effort to make up for mediocre sales the rest of the year. All this can make for a very frenzied, frustrating shopping experience—unless you play it smart. Here's how.

Give up on gifts

Make a pact with other adult family members not to exchange gifts this year. You can use the money that you save to treat your family to a holiday vacation or other fun activities. Besides saving yourself a lot of hassle,

Gifts Are for Kids

If you've ever wandered into a toy superstore, you know how mind-boggling the array of merchandise can be. This table can help you choose a gift that's sure to please, whether you're shopping for a toddler or a 10-year-old.

Age Group	$15 And Under	Around $30
Toddlers	Soft balls and toys, stuffed animals	Foam-mat floor puzzle, wooden blocks
Preschoolers	Markers, rubber stamps, sewing cards	Fisher Price Kid-Tough Tape Recorder, Duplo building blocks
6–8	Simple musical instrument (such as a recorder) with instruction book	Easy-to-operate camera, indoor tent, sleeping bag
8–10	Boxed set of magic tricks, scrapbook	Craft kit, board game, globe

you'll have an opportunity to spend more time with those you love.

Simply Stated

Remember that time is money.
                    —Benjamin Franklin,
                    American statesman

Shop after the season

The last thing that most people want to do on December 26 is head for a mall. Yet this is the perfect time to find the best prices on seasonal merchandise. This is true for most holidays, not just Christmas. Prices on decorations take a dive the day after a holiday, as merchants make room for new items.

Foil phone solicitors

During the holidays, telemarketers may bombard you with sales pitches for everything from fruit baskets to videotapes. Avoid succumbing to this temptation unless you've made purchases from the same company in the past. It's never a good idea to buy something over the phone from a company with which you're not familiar.

Beat the December rush

The people who get all of their holiday shopping done by October are several steps ahead of the gift-giving game. The longer you wait to start your shopping, the more aggravating an experience it will be. The amount of time that you spend in the mall will be so excessive that when you finally find the perfect gifts for the folks on your list, you may not even like those people anymore.

The Simplest of the Simple

Living within your means is a hallmark of simplicity. Employ these tactics when making purchases, and you'll make the most of every dollar.

- Buy secondhand clothing, especially for growing kids.
- Organize your grocery list by supermarket aisle.
- Buy store brands instead of name brands.
- Use coupons when possible.
- Shop early for the holidays.

Chapter 16   Family Finances

Balancing Your Budget
without Bending Over Backward

Did you know that the vast majority of American millionaires made their money in one generation? According to Thomas Stanley, co-author of *The Millionaire Next Door*, two-thirds of all millionaires are self-employed, usually in blue-collar businesses. Why do these people fare so much better than the white-collar workers and old-money families whom we normally associate with wealth? The self-employed tend to live below their means.

The reality is that having a higher-paying job usually means having a higher standard of living, which leaves less income for saving. Self-employed folks have the ability to control how much they save, and they adjust their lifestyles to leave as much or as little for saving or investing as they like. By creating a well-planned budget that allows for investing sensibly and living comfortably but not extravagantly, virtually anyone can become a millionaire.

Okay, so maybe you have less lofty goals. Perhaps you want only to establish a budget and stick with it. Living within your means is an essential component of simplicity. So let's look at what you can do to get your finances on track.

Facing Your Financial Future

When people are polled about their financial goals, they most often cite buying a new home, providing for their children's higher educations, or having a productive, prosperous retirement. Yet longitudinal data from the Social Security Administration reveals that such goals are probably closer to wishes or fantasies.

Life spans are increasing, as are medical costs. Most older people require home care or spend from three to five years in nursing homes, with average annual costs of $32,000. By age 65, 75 percent of Americans are dependent on relatives or charity. Meanwhile, Social Security benefits are decreasing.

These numbers paint a fairly dismal financial picture. They're intended to persuade you to establish a budget so you can begin saving now. Otherwise, you'll forever be at the mercy of money.

Go with the (Cash) Flow

Ever since Lyndon Johnson financed the Vietnam War without raising taxes, we as a country haven't been able to live within our means. Unfortunately, this philosophy appears to have taken hold on a personal level as well.

Resolve now to live within your means. First and foremost, take steps to establish and maintain a positive cash flow. Here's how.

Assess your situation. Determining if you currently have a positive cash flow is simple. First, add up all your income for a typical month. Then add up all the expenses you have in a month. Include mortgage payments, insurance premiums, medical expenses, household expenses, and so on. Are you in the black (a cash surplus) or in the red (in debt)?

Accent the negative

As in a business, underestimating your income and over-estimating your expenses makes good sense. It keeps you in a financial safety zone.

Bank the surplus

With a positive cash flow, you can readily identify how much money you can save each month. Some people will spend any cash surplus that they have. Hopefully, you're not among them. If you find that you can't hold on to a surplus, have the money automatically deposited in your savings account each month.

Save Where You Can

Regardless of whether you're currently ending each month with surplus funds, you can do more to squeeze savings from your monthly income. A dollar here and a dollar there quickly add up. Here's what you can do.

Eliminate unnecessaries

If you think you can afford the lifestyle you're living, ask yourself this: How much money are you keeping after taxes and basic living expenses? Cutting back on little things or taking the time to find better bargains can make a big difference in your long-term savings. Decide which parts of your lifestyle are really important to you, and cut out the expenses you can do without. It will add up.

Pare down indulgences

Sure, splurging on an expensive pair of shoes or a new tool feels good. Eventually—in a year, or even a month—your purchase will be out of style or obsolete. Meanwhile, the money you spent could have been earning interest for you.

Financial security may mean making a small sacrifice—say, shopping at Wal-Mart instead of Bloomingdale's. That may be hard to swallow at first, but remember, your family's future is at stake.

Pocket your payments

Once you've paid off a car loan or a credit card balance, continue making the monthly payments to your savings account. You're already accustomed to not having access to that money, so you don't have to do anything different.

Pay yourself first

Every week (or whenever you get paid), take a small amount of money from your paycheck or checking account and invest it. You can put this money in a savings account, mutual fund, or stocks, just as long as you are contributing to your future well-being. No matter how small, every investment will help you fare better in the future.

Practice restraint

If you suddenly receive a significant amount of money that you weren't expecting, you may have the urge to treat yourself. Saving the money will reward you more in the long run.

Be prepared for disaster

Losing your job can turn your money situation topsy-turvy and lead to mountains of debt. Be sure that you always know where you stand financially, and don't underestimate the importance of a nest egg. At the least, you need to put away two to three months' worth of paychecks as a safety net in the event you lose your job or experience some other emergency that leads to loss of income. Six months worth of paychecks is better. Of course, the more you save, the better off you'll be.

Keep an Eye on Expenses

Saving money is only half of the cash flow equation. The other half is spending money. You will always have some unavoidable expenses for goods and services you can't live without. But every dollar that you spend is a dollar that you haven't saved.

Watching over your own finances is much easier than watching over the finances for an entire family. One option is to put every family member—including the kids—on a budget. Instruct everyone to keep track of what they buy and spend.

Here are some other ways to curb family expenditures so that money stays where it belongs: in your pocket.

How Complex Can It Get

Seems Like Over(s)kill: Shenandoah Life Insurance Company once identified 144 different skills required of workers and then estimated how much time is necessary to master each one. By the company's calculations, learning all 144 skills would take the average person about 321 weeks. The easiest skills can be mastered in a week, the most difficult, in 16 weeks.

Create a spending plan

"Spending is the key to saving," says Paul Richard, executive director of the Institute of consumer and Financial Education. "Everyday spending decisions, especially credit-based ones, can have a far greater negative impact on your financial future than most investment decisions you're ever likely to make."

Let the urge pass

How often have you seen something you wanted but been without your credit card, debit card, or checkbook and been unable to buy it? Afterward, you probably realized that you didn't really need the item anyway.

This is a good tactic to use all the time: when possible, travel without your impulse-buying tools. Then if you see something you want, you'll be forced to go home for your credit card or checkbook. You'll have time to decide whether or not you really need the item. If you have the resolve to go back to the store, perhaps the item is worth purchasing.

Review receipts

When making purchases, be sure to check that you've been charged the right price. For example, watch the scanner at the grocery store. Does the scanned price match the price on the shelf? Little things like this add up to big savings.

Eyeball your bills

Although you're a busy person, you may save money just by reviewing your monthly bills. That's the only way you'll catch mistakes. And they do happen—especially on power bills and phone bills. Cable service and credit card bills may also contain errors.

Use energy-efficient appliances

Pressure cookers and slow cookers use less energy than ovens and burners. Appliances that radiate heat waste energy and money.

Simply Stated

It is said that the world is in a state of bankruptcy, that the world owes the world more than the world can pay . . .

**—Ralph Waldo Emerson,
American essayist and poet**

Find out your insulating options

Your community may have programs to help you insulate your home without paying a lot for it. Your utility company may be able to tell you more about what is available to you.

Warm yourself, not your home

By turning down your thermostat just a few degrees during the day and a few more at night, you can save a lot of money on your energy bill each month. You can compensate by wearing warmer clothes and thicker socks during the day and adding more blankets to your bed at night.

Use fluorescent lights

Fluorescent lightbulbs may cost more than incandescent bulbs. But they also are more energy-efficient and last longer, which will save you a bundle in the long run.

Cutting the Big Bills

Two expenses that nearly all households have in common are insurance and taxes. You can't avoid either one entirely. You may, however, be able to reduce them considerably.

Insuring Is the Best Policy

Most people put off buying life insurance because they don't want to contemplate their own demise. Buying life insurance is seen as a type of personal validation that they will, in fact, die someday. It's the same with disability policies and other types of coverage.

You need to be sure that you have enough insurance—not just life but also health, disability, auto, and personal-liability insurance. These are relatively affordable and offer valuable protection against financial loss.

To keep your insurance premiums affordable, give these measures a try.

Deduct the maximum

You can save money on your health insurance premiums by signing up for larger deductibles on your policies. The amount saved increases if you carry a family policy. This may not be an option, however, if you have a chronically ill family member or if you don't have enough savings to cover the deductible in the event of a medical emergency.

Wait longer

Most employers offer disability insurance. It is up to you to decide how long of a waiting period you want before payment of benefits begins in the event of disability. Calculate how long you can afford to live without benefits, and set that as your waiting period. Oftentimes, the longer the waiting period, the lower the cost of the coverage.

Go for term

Always buy renewable term-life insurance. Do not buy whole-life insurance or any of the 200 other names that it's called—universal life, life plus, and so on. You want a renewal term-life policy and nothing else.

With renewable term-life, you pay a small premium each year in exchange for pure insurance coverage. You can cancel the policy at any time. Whole life, on the other hand, has an insurance component and an investment component. If you want to cancel, you may face a substantial penalty, depending on the terms of your contract.

So rather than purchasing a whole-life policy, invest the difference between the term-life and whole-life premiums (term life is cheaper) as you wish. You'll make a lot more money this way.

> ### Money in the Bank
>
> Putting your money in a savings account is better than stashing it somewhere in your home. At least it's safe, and it earns a small amount of interest.
>
> If only Yousouf Ishmaelo had followed this advice. In 1898, Ishmaelo, a renowned Turkish wrestler, made a small fortune touring and competing in major cities throughout the United States. Leery of banks and of money in general, he converted all of his winnings to gold ingots. He kept the ingots in a huge money belt that he wore at all times.
>
> When Ishmaelo was on his way home to Turkey, his ship, the *Burgoyne*, hit a reef and became stranded below the water line. Ishmaelo was unable to keep himself and his gold afloat. He was the only passenger to go down with the ship.

Make Your Taxes Less Taxing

You may not think you can do a lot to reduce your tax bill. In truth, you can—especially if you pay property taxes. For starters, follow this advice.

Analyze your assessment

As of 2003, according to the National Taxpayers Union, based in Washington, D.C., an estimated 60 percent of all taxable property in this country is overassessed. If you feel that the taxes you owe on your property are too high, contact the appropriate government office for a reassessment.

Befriend the assessor

Your local tax office of assessment can tell you how much your neighbors are paying in property taxes. You may discover that they are paying less for similar houses. Also, look into the description of your house on which your taxes are based. An error in square footage or number of rooms could result in a much higher—and inaccurate—assessment. Your assessor can help you find out how to file an appeal if you believe your current property taxes are unfair.

Taking Charge of Your Credit

How much debt can you reasonably handle? Here's an easy way to find out.

1. Determine your monthly take-home pay (what you retain after taxes and other deductions).
2. Add up all of your monthly credit payments, including car loans, student loans, and credit cards. Do not include monthly mortgage payments or rent.
3. Divide your total monthly credit payments by your monthly take-home pay. Suppose your monthly credit payments are $540 and your take-home pay is $3,600. Your debt-to-income ratio is 0.15, or 15 percent.

Now find your percentage in the list below.

Less than 10 percent	You're in excellent shape, debt-wise.
10 to 15 percent	You're okay, as long as you stay under 15 percent.
16 to 20 percent	You're perceived as too much of a risk. Work to reduce your debt-to-income ratio to less than 15 percent.
More than 20 percent	Take action now. Find ways to increase your income or pay off some of your debts. Aim to live within your means.

Getting the Best of Your Bank

Your bank plays a major role in your financial picture. It likely offers a variety of services that can make managing your money easier. By all means, take advantage of them. Just beware of any hidden charges and fees.

Not on Your Account

Many people believe that banks advertise their best rates. Perish the thought. If you have enough leverage or chutzpah, everything is negotiable.

Shop around

Not all banks are created equal. Neither are all checking accounts. Many banks will forego any checking account fee if you have a savings account with them. Also, many banks will offer free checking if, for example, you agree to maintain a minimum balance in your account. Some also provide free checking for senior citizens or students.

Earn interest

If your checking account does not bear interest, you're losing money if you deposit more in the account than you need. By maintaining a checking balance just above your expenses, you'll free up money that you can put into your savings or another interest-accruing account.

Simply Stated

Speak not of my debts unless you mean to pay them.

—George Herbert, English clergyman and poet

Stop that bounce

Most banks charge $30 and up to cover a bounced check. This can add up quickly if you don't catch your mistake in time. Overdraft protection will eliminate the charge, but the amount the bank deposits in your checking account to cover checks is usually subject to a finance charge.

If you're not familiar with overdraft protection, here's how it works. Suppose you have insufficient funds in your checking account to cover a check. Your bank will deposit a set amount in your account. So even if the check was for $25, the bank could put, say, $100 in your account. The finance charge, or interest, on the "loan" begins accruing immediately—perhaps before you even know that you've had an overdraft.

Overdraft protection may seem like a nice perk, but keep in mind that the bank offers it in order to make a profit from it. Avoid using overdraft protection whenever possible—and when you can't, be sure to pay off the loan as soon as possible.

Know your ATM allowances

Some banks now charge a fee for automatic teller machine (ATM) transactions or allow you a maximum number of free transactions from their own ATMs. You likely will be charged an additional fee if you use an ATM at a rival bank. Find out your bank's policy, and avoid using other banks' ATMs.

Keeping Checks in Balance

You can earn more interest and write fewer checks just by managing your checkbook properly. What could be easier?

Look for cheap checks

If you ask, your bank may provide you with free checks. If not, then ordering checks directly from a check printer could save you up to 60 percent of what you would pay at the bank.

Save stamps

Many people still spend a significant amount of time each month writing checks and mailing bill payments. These days just about every bill can be paid directly from bank accounts. This is a simple way to save time as well as money on postage. Canceling a direct payment is as easy as notifying the company at least three days before the next due date.

If you opt for direct bill payment, keep in mind that you must have enough money in your account to cover all of the bills. Direct payments that you cannot cover will end up costing you a lot more in the long run.

Pay a little extra

If you're not using direct bill payment, occasionally overpay your monthly bills by $30, $40, or $50—whatever you can afford. When you receive the next month's bill, you will have that much to your credit. This gives you a wonderful sense of breathing space. If you are significantly ahead in cash flow, overpay each bill so that you'll have no checks to write the next month.

Loans You Can Live With

Whether you're making a purchase with a credit card or taking out a mortgage for a new home, you're borrowing money. And borrowing means paying back—virtually always with interest. This is another way in which banks and other financial institutions earn money. And it's another way for you to slip into debt, unless you're very careful. So study your borrowing options and make sure that you're getting the best deal in terms of interest and payments.

Best Options in Borrowing

If you want to take out a loan, you don't necessarily have to go to your bank to get one. Here are some other low-interest borrowing opportunities to consider.

Borrow against your investment fund

If you're participating in a 401(k) or 403(b) retirement investment plan, you may be able to borrow some of your funds from your employer for a low interest rate. You can usually get automatic access to these funds if you contributed after-tax money. If you contributed pretax money, rules vary from plan to plan. One major drawback of this kind of loan: The default penalties can be significant.

Borrow against your stocks

If you own stocks, you may be able to borrow an amount equal to up to 50 percent of their value. Your stockbroker will be able to help you investigate this option.

Borrow against your life insurance

If you have whole-life insurance, you may be able to borrow a certain amount of money at a low interest rate, based on the length of time that you've held your policies. Call your insurance agent to find out how your policy handles this.

Borrow against your savings

Most banks will let you borrow the equivalent of up to 80 percent of your savings account balance. And you'll pay an interest rate that may be as low as 2 percent above your account's interest rate.

Get a home-equity loan

A fixed-rate home-equity loan may carry a lower interest rate than a credit card, and often the interest is tax-deductible.

Managing Your Mortgage

If you have a mortgage, when was the last time you looked at it? More than two years ago? Get out those papers right now. You may very well be paying more than you need to.

Whittle away the interest

By paying even a tiny bit extra on your mortgage each month, you can save thousands of dollars in interest and close out your mortgage months or even years ahead of schedule. For example, on a 30-year mortgage of $100,000 at 8 percent interest, paying an additional $1 a day would save you more than $27,000 in interest and reduce the duration of the loan by more than four years.

> **Simply Stated**
>
> *By no means run in debt: take thine own measure. Who cannot live on 20 pound a year, cannot on 40: He's a man of pleasure . . . .*
>
> **—George Herbert, English clergyman and poet**

Eliminate mortgage insurance

If you put less than 20 percent down on your home, your lender may require you to buy private mortgage insurance against default on your payments. But once you reach 20 percent equity, you may be able to cancel the insurance. Ask your lender what the policy is.

Give Yourself Some Credit

Credit cards can pose the greatest threat to your financial stability. Although most people intend to pay their full credit card bills, this rarely happens. Credit card issuers know this, and they use it to their advantage.

Examine the credit card finance charges that you've paid in the past 12 months. If the total exceeds $100, you need to reassess your credit card usage.

Vanquish the card

As a general rule, avoid charging any item that you can pay for with cash. Reserve the card for use when an emergency arises and you can't borrow money from a family member. Adhering to this guideline protects you against having to pay interest every month.

Pare down on plastic

Try to limit yourself to just one credit card. And carry it with you only when you suspect you'll need it—like when you're traveling, for example. This alone can save you a bundle.

Be wary of fabulous deals

Increased competition among credit card issuers has led many companies to offer special interest rates and other deals. While these may appeal to you, be sure to read the fine print before you sign on. Don't get trapped by high interest rates and fees that may be charged down the road. If the initial rate seems too good to be true, something higher is coming.

Find the right card for you

When shopping around for a credit card, consider this: If you can pay off your balance in full each month, choose a card with no annual fee. If you can't pay off your balance each month, look for the lowest interest rate. Either way, you'll save money.

Simply Stated

Death and taxes are inevitable.

—**Thomas C. Haliburton,
Canadian judge and humorist**

Reject your rate

If a credit card that you already own carries a high interest rate, the issuing bank may lower the rate if you just ask. Call the bank, talk to a supervisor if necessary, and don't hesitate to say that you have a better offer from another bank. Often you can reduce your interest rate by at least two percentage points this way.

Pay no mind to minimum payments

Credit card companies allow minimum payments supposedly to make your life easier. But by making only the minimum payment each month, you significantly prolong and even increase your debt by allowing more interest to accrue. The faster you pay off your credit card debt, the less you pay in interest, period.

Pay off the biggest debt first

If you're still carrying more than one credit card, make a list of your cards in order of their interest rates (highest to lowest). Each month, pay only the minimum amount necessary for each card except the one with the highest interest rate. Put all of the money you can afford toward paying off that card. Once you pay off that card, do the same for the card with the next highest interest rate. Keep moving down your list until you have paid off all your credit card debts, and you will have avoided paying the greatest amount of interest possible.

Consider consolidation

A home-equity loan can consolidate all of your credit card bills into one. And interest on a home-equity loan is usually tax-deductible. Be aware, though, that consolidating your credit card payments requires that you refrain from charging anything until your debt is completely paid off. Charging after consolidation can show up as bad debt on your credit report. Locking up your credit cards will help motivate you to quickly pay off your loan and will save you a lot of money in the long run.

Don't give up

If none of the above options is available to you, you still have other opportunities to avoid high-interest credit card payments. Talk to your bank about taking out a personal loan, and shop around for the lowest credit card rate you can find.

Questions to Ask Your Financial Advisor

Finding a financial advisor with whom you feel comfortable can take some time. But it's more than worth the effort. After all, you want the assurance that your hard-earned money is in the hands of a competent, capable, trustworthy individual. Remember to ask any potential advisor these questions. If he seems angered by your inquiries or reluctant to respond, take that as your cue to look elsewhere.

- Do you have a disclosure statement that lists the names and backgrounds of your firm's management and staff, potential conflicts of interest, and methods of compensation?
- How long has your company been in the financial counseling business?
- Is your firm financially sound?
- What other types of resources and benefits are available through your firm?
- How long have you been in the profession?
- What financial certifications, designations, and licenses do you maintain?
- Have any of your licenses or certifications ever been suspended or revoked?
- What percentage of your earnings is from investment advisory, tax services and planning, real estate, and commissions?
- Do you have letters from any current clients for my review?
- Have you personally ever filed for bankruptcy?
- Has any client ever sued you?
- Have you ever been reprimanded by any professional society or state regulatory agency?
- What safeguards do I have if I do business with you?

On the Road to Financial Security

The key to simplifying your finances is recognizing that what you keep is more important than what you earn. It's developing systematic ways to save more and spend less. It's putting your money where it will work the hardest for you, so you have a secure financial future.

Keep Tabs on Your Credit

If you've had a problem with debt, it's important that you keep tabs on your credit report. You want to make sure that all of the information is correct and up-to-date. Otherwise, a past financial misstep could haunt you for the rest of your life.

In fact, even if you've had a positive cash flow all along, you ought to take a look at your credit report. Here's how to go about it.

Know whom to contact

Perhaps the best-known credit reporting agencies are Equifax and Experian. You can find other credit bureaus in your area by looking in the Yellow Pages under "Credit Bureaus" or "Credit Reporting" or googling those terms.

Check before you buy

Request a free copy of your credit report once a year or before making any major purchase. Also get a copy if you're planning to apply for a credit card, an insurance policy, a job, or even an apartment. These folks may want to examine your credit history, too.

Read every word

The credit bureau must have trained personnel on staff to explain the information in your credit report. So ask questions, and dispute any incorrect information that you see. Write to the credit bureau and be specific about what is wrong with your report. Thereafter, the credit bureau has to investigate your dispute and respond to you, usually within 30 to 45 days. Information that is inaccurate or cannot be verified must be corrected or taken off your report.

Getting the Best Advice

Naturally, you care about your money more than anyone else does. And only you should decide how it's invested and spent. Still, a financial planner can provide invaluable advice.

Simply Stated

Death and taxes and childbirth! There's never any convenient time for any of them.

—**Margaret Mitchell, American novelist, in *Gone with the Wind***

Seek someone who's qualified

The financial services industry is growing by leaps and bounds, so you can pretty much have your pick of professionals. Unfortunately, at times it can seem like hunting for the proverbial needle in a haystack.

To simplify your search, ask family members and close friends for recommendations. And use the following list to help you assess each candidate's qualifications.

- Certified financial planner (CFP): A designation bestowed upon an independent financial counselor. It's awarded by colleges accredited through the International Board of Standards and Practices for Certified Financial Planners, based in Washington, DC.
- Chartered financial consultant (ChFC): A program of study that consists of required courses and electives, plus exams. The program is administered by the American College in Bryn Mawr, Pennsylvania, and is also offered as a correspondence course.
- Master of science in financial services (MSFS): A degree awarded by the American College to students completing advanced courses in financial planning.
- Registered financial planner (RFP): A designation offered by the International Association for Financial Planning based in Amherst, Ohio, to members who prove that they have had full-time practice as a planner and have either a business degree plus a brokerage securities license or an insurance license.
- Registered investment advisor (RIA): Registration with the Securities and Exchange Commission, which signifies that the candidate has provided written information about fees, types of clients, investment specialties, education, industry affiliation, and compensation. There is no requirement for formal training.

Generally, it make the most sense to retain a certified financial planner who earns a fee based on services rendered, not commissions.

Take a hands-on approach

If you blindly trust someone else with your money, you could lose everything because of his carelessness. Heed the advice of a reputable professional, but don't let another person make mistakes for you.

The Simplest of the Simple

If you want to keep your finances straight without a lot of effort, try these ideas.

- Don't let excuses stop you from engaging in and establishing important financial goals. The longer you wait, the harder the task.
- Analyze your income and expenses to take control of your finances.
- Live below your means. Although this may be hard to put into practice, saving extra money instead of spending it will make a huge difference later in your life.
- Automatically invest every month by having money withdrawn from your paycheck and deposited in a savings account or elsewhere.
- Be prepared by keeping some money on hand in case of an emergency.
- Create a budget and stick with it.
- Don't fall into credit card traps. Investigate your options before choosing a card, and then use the one you get sparingly.
- The moment you climb out of debt, begin a savings and investment plan. Recognize that what you keep is more important than what you earn.

PART FOUR Simplify Your Professional Life

Chapter 17

The Easy Exit

Tactics for an Uncomplicated Commute

Simplicity in getting to and from work is important. If you find your daily commute to be a major ordeal, you're going to feel more stressed. More stress invariably increases worry, reduces performance, and generally complicates your life. The smoother your commute, the better your whole day will go.

Up and at 'Em

One of the keys to a stress-free morning commute is a relaxed but efficient morning routine. Far too many people allow themselves barely enough time to get ready and get out the door. If even one thing goes wrong—a run in a pair of nylons or a misplaced briefcase, for instance—it disrupts an already-tight schedule. You end up feeling tense and harried, and you haven't even gotten to work yet. Talk about starting off your day on the wrong foot! There's a better way.

Get a Good Night's Sleep

This may seem obvious, but it's worth mentioning: How you sleep at night affects how you feel when you wake up in the morning. The following tips can help you get your best rest ever so you start your day refreshed and invigorated.

Crash early

Once a week, go to bed by 9 PM. Let yourself slumber for 9, 10 hours— however long you need. Make getting a good night's sleep your only objective. Your body will thank you.

One Friday each month, go to bed right after work and don't get up until Saturday morning. If you want to experience a fabulous weekend, this is a good way to start.

Curb caffeine

Avoid caffeine for at least six hours before retiring. This means that if you're thinking about going to bed around 10:00 at night, have your last cup of coffee no later than 4:00 in the afternoon. Also avoid alcohol in the evening. It'll put you to sleep quickly, but it tends to dry you out and wake you up prematurely. Then you have trouble getting back to sleep.

Simply Stated

All men whilst they are awake are in one common world; but each of them, when he is asleep, is in a world of his own.

—Plutarch, Greek essayist

Try a light workout

Moderate exercise a couple hours before going to bed helps ensure sound sleep. If you are too active too close to retiring, you may take longer to become relaxed enough to doze off. Moderate intake of proteins, such as a glass of milk, also helps.

Retire on cue

Go to bed when you're tired, not when you think you ought to. Let your body talk to you. It'll tell you when it's tired. Perhaps the problem you've had in the past is that you have ignored the messages.

Turn down the volume

If you're kept awake by your spouse's snoring, or if you're the one who snores, you need help. Get a snore control device for the snorer to wear on the wrist while sleeping. Whenever the snoring reaches a certain decibel, the device will emit a gentle vibration that's sufficient to disrupt the snoring and return the snorer to quiet slumber. Though buying a new device may seem counterproductive when you're trying to simplify, sometimes a small device can make a big difference in the quality of your life.

Relocate the phone

Don't sleep with your head by a telephone. Remove the phone from your bedroom, or install an answering machine and switch off the phone's ringer. At 3 AM., a call is much more likely to be a wrong number than an emergency anyway.

Engage in Preemptive Planning

A little preparation and organization can go a long way in keeping your morning running like clockwork. Use these two strategies to plan ahead.

Beat the AM rush

Each evening, do a quick mental rundown of everything that you'll need the next day. Pack your lunch and put it in the refrigerator. Set your briefcase and any other necessary items by the door, where you can grab them on your way out. Getting ready the evening before will allow you to start your day without stress.

Carry coins

Stash at least one roll of quarters and one roll of dimes inside your car, within easy reach. Even if you never use them, knowing that you have them at least offers some security. You never know when you'll need to park your car at a parking meter.

Sound Choices

If your car is equipped with a CD player, you can turn your daily commute into a relaxation ritual or an educational experience. It all depends on what sorts of recordings you prefer to listen to. Certainly, there are plenty to choose from. For example:

- You can catch up on your pleasure reading with audio books, which are available at your local library or by subscription directly from the company.
- You can develop various personal and professional skills with self-improvement tapes from companies such as Dartnell, Nightingale-Conant, and SkillPath.
- You can learn a foreign language with programs produced by companies such as Berlitz and Sybervision.
- You can stay abreast of the latest business books and articles with audio summaries from Executrak and similar services.

Of course, you can always listen to music. Choose tunes that energize you for the day ahead or help you unwind during the drive home. Or, if you wish, turn off your recording and enjoy the sweet silence.

A More Comfortable Commute

Whoever coined the phrase "rat race" back in the 1930s must have foreseen the sheer pandemonium of the modern-day commute. Twice every workday, millions of Americans slide behind the wheel of their cars and battle traffic, construction zones, and other elements to reach their destinations. The experience is enough to test anyone's patience and resolve. No matter how long or how far you have to drive, you can take steps to make the experience a lot less stressful.

Creating the Ideal Driving Environment

One of the most important aspects of being a commuter is keeping your car in tip-top shape. Take it in for servicing if you even suspect that something is amiss. It's one thing to be stalled in traffic because some turkey's car conked out and is blocking 10,000 others—it's another thing to be that turkey.

Assuming that your car is running smoothly, you want it to provide a relaxed, comfortable atmosphere for your a.m. and p.m. drives. Here's how to ensure that it does.

Listen up

Installing an MP3 or CD player in your car allows you to safely control your environment as you travel to and from work. If you listen to something that relaxes you while you drive, it can make quite a difference in how your day goes.

Learn something

Educational audio books can turn your car into a mobile classroom. If your one-way commute averages 25 minutes, you could listen to the equivalent of a college-length course in just 11 weeks, with no quizzes, term papers, or final exams. A company called Knowledge Products offers programs on American history, economics, and politics narrated by the likes of the late Walter Cronkite and George C. Scott. For a brochure, write to P.O. Box 305151, Nashville, TN 37230.

Keep your ears on the road

Whatever you choose to listen to while you drive, be sure to keep the volume down. Those 1,000-megawatt car stereos that can implode eardrums from a half-mile away hamper driving skills by interfering with information processing. When the driver's eyes are on the road but his ears are on the radio, his senses get scrambled. At least you can hear these menaces coming in plenty of time to get out of their paths.

Reflect on the day

Wean yourself from the habit of flicking on the radio (or MP3 or CD player) the moment you get into the car. Instead, take some time to think about what you'd like to accomplish while at work or about how your day has gone. And when you do turn on the radio, steer clear of "shock jocks," those radio disc jockeys who offer little to improve your life.

Tune out the noise

During warm weather, drive with the windows closed and the air conditioner on. You'll get at least the same miles per gallon as you do with the windows open and the air conditioner off. Plus, your ride will be quieter with the windows closed.

> **An Accident Waiting to Happen**
>
> According to preliminary research from the Rochester Institute of Technology in New York, your risk of being involved in an automobile accident is much greater if you have a cell phone in your car than if you don't.

'Pool with pals

If you're a member of a car pool, make sure you're riding with people with whom you enjoy conversing or simply spending time. Otherwise, you're just adding to the stress of your commute.

Remember, one thing at a time

"The incidence of people doing double duty while driving is increasing," says Thomas Havrilesky, PhD, professor of economics at Duke University in Durham, North Carolina, who has studied the impact of time pressure

> **How Complex Can It Get?**
>
> **No Place to Go:** If you think that traffic is congested now, imagine what it will be like in a few years. According to the League of American Wheelmen, 50 percent of urban space in the United States is devoted to roadways. Eventually, we're going to run out of room for expansion—never mind the cost of such projects and the impact on the environment.

on people's lives. He has seen people attempt to shave, eat breakfast, and put on makeup while operating cars. They erroneously believe that they'll arrive at their destinations having saved time, when they're more likely to arrive in a frenzy, without having a handle on the day. And of course, they're putting themselves and others in danger by not being in control of their vehicles. Avoid such dangerous practices—including conversing on a mobile phone—while driving.

Be Wise behind the Wheel

According to *U.S. News and World Report*, car travel has increased by almost 40 percent since 1986. In that same period of time, highway capacity has increased about 1 percent. As most commuters already know, this has led to increasingly bad traffic problems, especially during rush hour. These tips can make your drive a little safer and easier.

Keep 'em clean

Spotless windows enhance your view and, therefore, your ability to drive safely. Countless accidents occur because of something as preventable as dirty windows. Besides, driving a clean car feels invigorating.

Carry a kit

A first-aid kit can come in handy if you happen upon an accident and someone needs medical assistance. And you never know when you might need some ibuprofen or acetaminophen to head off a traffic-jam headache. You can buy a prepackaged first-aid kit, or you can put together your own in a small fishing-tackle box.

Watch every which way

Although the age-old rule of keeping your eyes on the road makes sense, there's more to driving than that.

One of the best ways to avoid an accident is to constantly survey your surroundings. Frequently glance in your side-view and rearview mirrors, checking for motorists who are driving crazily. While you may be an excellent driver, assume that everyone else on the road is not.

See red

When you drive, don't just focus on the car in front of you. Watch several cars ahead, especially if traffic is heavy. Looking for brake lights farther down the road allows you extra stopping time, which can be critical in preventing an accident—especially if the driver in front of you isn't paying attention and has to brake quickly.

Keep your distance

Tailgating is one of the most common causes of accidents in heavy traffic. To check whether you're following too closely, sight some landmark near the road, like a sign. Then count two seconds ("one, one thousand, two, one thousand") after the car in front of you passes it. If you pass the same landmark before you're finished counting two seconds, you're tailgating.

Illuminate yourself

Many people think that headlights are necessary only for them to see. However, they're just as important for allowing others to see you, especially during rush-hour traffic. Using your headlights is an important safety strategy, even when it's fairly light outside. In fact, most states require that you turn on your headlights whenever you're using your windshield wipers.

Shade yourself from the sun

Morning and evening rush hours can be the worst times of day for sun glare. Usually, the sun is low in the sky, which causes many problems. Wear good sunglasses, and be careful when you go from light to shadows. Your eyes need time to adjust to the change. Take off your sunglasses, and try to stay alert to what's going on around you.

What to Do When Accidents Happen

Despite all of the precautions, accidents can—and do—happen. Would you know what to do if you were involved in one? In this day and age, you must know how to act and react at the scene, especially to prevent yourself from becoming the victim of insurance fraud. Follow this advice.

Call the police

In the event of an accident, the first and most important step is to call the police, no matter how minor the damage to either vehicle. The other person involved may seem to be the nicest person you've ever met, and you may think that exchanging driver's license numbers and insurance information is enough. If you don't call the police, however, that leaves the door wide open for the other person to file huge insurance claims for damages and injuries that aren't your fault.

> ### Simply Stated
>
> *I feel about airplanes the way I feel about diets. It seems to me that they are wonderful things for other people to go on.*
>
> **—Jean Kerr, American author and playwright**

Account for everyone

In addition to the driver, take down the names and driver's license numbers of every person in the other car. You never know when someone who wasn't even in the accident might try to file a claim against you. Make sure everyone gets checked out by the police or paramedics, too.

Take pictures

Keep a disposable camera in your glove compartment. Photos can help in insurance claims and court cases. They can also be one of the best deterrents against fraud. Often, insurance scammers get into subsequent wrecks and try to pin the additional damages on you. Pictures taken at the scene of the accident will ensure that you pay only for the damages you caused, provided you're at fault.

Be on the lookout

Pay attention to details. Did that witness run up and support the other driver a little too quickly? Does the other car have damage that you don't think occurred in your accident? Does the driver seem to be faking any injuries? Take note of how everyone is acting, and continuously survey the scene. Details can be key to pinpointing fraud.

Alert your insurer

Your first instinct may be to keep the accident out of your insurance company's files. If you let your insurer know right away, the company will likely be much more open with you about things such as potential rate increases.

Putting Your Car in Park

Practicing safety in parking lots can be just as important as practicing safety during your drive. Once you arrive at your destination, be sure to do the following.

See the light

Park under a light or in a well-lit space, especially if you'll be returning to your car after dark. When you're ready to leave, walk to your car with your keys in hand, on the ready.

Survey the ground

Before you leave the parking lot, look around you for obstacles, such as posts and potholes, that could endanger your maneuvering. And always watch for pedestrians darting from behind cars or walls.

> ### Simply Stated
>
> *Half our life is spent trying to find something to do with the time we have rushed through life trying to save.*
>
> **—Will Rogers, in a letter to the *New York Times*, April 29, 1930**

Your Time, Not Overtime

If you feel as though you've been spending all of your waking hours on the job, you can begin reclaiming your private life simply by leaving the office at the appointed quitting time. This takes some getting used to, especially if you routinely work late. But it's important, if only to preserve your—and your family's—sanity. Here's how to get in the habit.

1. Get a good night's rest so you feel refreshed and energized for the day ahead.
2. When you arrive at the office, inform others of your plans to leave on time. Suppose your designated quitting time is 5 PM. Tell everyone that you have a personal commitment at 5:30. You can actually schedule something for 5:30, if that helps.
3. Mark on your calendar that you'll be leaving at 5.
4. Strike bargains with yourself at the start of the day and in the late morning, early afternoon, and late afternoon. Repeatedly remind yourself of your intent to leave on time.
5. View any intrusion as merely a regular part of your workday, not as a reason to stay late. Do your best to avoid adding items to your day's to-do list.
6. Eat a light lunch so you remain energized throughout the afternoon.
7. Imagine how you'll feel when you leave right at 5.
8. Ask a co-worker to stop by your desk at quitting time and leave the building with you.

Taking to the Air

Depending on your profession, you may be called upon to do some long-distance commuting—say, across the country or around the world. The quickest way to reach your destination is by airplane.

Everyone who has flown seems to have some horror story about lost luggage or delayed departures. While such incidents do indeed happen, they don't have to be the norm. You can take steps to protect yourself. (In fact, even if your job doesn't require travel, the tips that follow may come in handy when you plan your vacation.)

Problem-Proofing Your Flight

Flying, like driving, requires some preplanning. As you prepare for your trip, keep these strategies in mind.

Head for the emergency exit

When making your reservation, request exit-row seating. These seats often have even more leg room than first class. And since children aren't allowed in these seats, you'll have a lot more peace. Of course, sitting in these seats obligates you to open the door and help evacuate the plane in case of an emergency.

Pack less

Having less luggage to worry about and lighter bags to carry will make everything else easier for you. Pack as few clothes as possible, and use travel-size toiletries. If you can get a hair dryer or clothes iron at the hotel, don't take your own. Put the heaviest items on the bottom of your suitcase, with items that you'll need easy access to on the top.

Carry on when you can

Find out how many bags your airline will allow you to carry on, and try to stick with this limit. Then you don't

How Complex Can It Get?

Something for Everyone: These days, airlines offer special meals to accommodate almost any health need or palate. The selections vary from one carrier to the next, so if you're traveling anytime soon, ask what will be available on your flight. If you have a meal preference, it's best to indicate that when you make your reservations. The following are just some of the options that may be available to you.

Standard	High-fiber
Child	Vegetarian
Bland	Raw vegetarian
Diabetic	Asian vegetarian
Low-cholesterol	Asian
Low-fat	Kosher
Low-protein	Muslim
Low-sodium	Hindu
Gluten-free	Seafood
Lactose-free	

---

have to worry about your luggage getting lost, because you'll have it with you. What's more, you save time by not checking your bags, you have all your bags close by, in case you need something, and you protect your bags from being thrown around during loading and in flight.

Invest in wheels

It's a traveler's nightmare: Your flight lands late, and you're about to miss your connection. You're running across the terminal while trying to carry a suitcase filled with a week's worth of clothes. Imagine how much easier this would be if you could roll your luggage behind you. Make sure your suitcase has wheels as well as a long handle, so you don't have to hunch over to pull it. You might even make your flight.

Protect your laptop

More and more people are taking laptop computers on planes these days, and crooks know that. Never check in your computer as luggage. Always carry it on board. Keep it in a small, undistinguishable bag so you can fit it under your seat instead of putting it in the overhead compartment, where it could get damaged or stolen. Check whether your homeowner's insurance covers your computer, in case something does happen to it.

Break the code

Your airline may know well in advance whether your flight will arrive at its destination on time. How can you get this inside information? Ask your travel agent or reservations clerk for the last digit of the flight's computer code. The number signifies a flight's odds of arriving on time: five means a 50 to 59 percent chance that it will, eight means an 80 to 89 percent chance that it will.

Knowing this won't get you there sooner, but it may help you plan connections and meetings at your destination.

Join the club

If you frequently travel by air, look into joining an airline club. As a member, you have access to a variety of airport amenities, such as a lounge, free drinks, and perhaps a shower and locker room. If you usually have a lot of lay-overs, you may find this last option especially appealing.

A Primer for Passengers

On the day of your flight, do what you can to ensure that everything goes as smoothly as possible. Here are some suggestions.

Be the first

When you head for the airport, give yourself plenty of time for traffic, parking, and (if necessary) luggage check-in. If you're early, you will feel much more relaxed, and your entire flight will go better. Also, being early allows you to take advantage of any opportunities to choose a better seat.

Park away from the airport

Airport traffic is horrible, and avoiding it will save you time and energy. Most airports now have parking lots that are farther away, along with a shuttle service to the terminals. These parking lots are usually cheaper, and if they're fenced in, they're safer.

Give a gift to open doors

Flight attendants and desk clerks get as tired and frustrated as anyone else. Take small gifts, such as flowers or cookies, and give them to the people whom you think can help you the most, to show your appreciation. You will stick out in their minds, and you'll probably get their attention before anyone else does.

Improve your position

If the flight you're on isn't full, you may be able to upgrade your seating for little or no charge. Simply ask. The worst that can happen is that you'll be told no.

Change places

Once everyone has boarded, look around for an empty row of seats. If you spot one, ask a flight attendant if you can move. You and your seatmate will appreciate it.

Stay hydrated

The air inside a plane's cabin is extremely dry, so you'll need to take precautions to avoid becoming dehydrated. Drink lots of water and juice, even if you don't feel thirsty. And avoid alcohol since it dehydrates you even more.

Know your rights

Many people complain about airline delays, bungling, and foul-ups, but few people realize that most carriers provide some kind of compensation when something goes wrong. If you get bumped, you may receive a free ticket or other compensation. If your flight is canceled, request whatever you need to accommodate the delay—be it free phone calls, meals, or a hotel room. Also request a voucher for a future flight. Airlines want to keep your business. You'll be surprised what you can get when you ask.

Efficiency outside the Office

On any given workday, your job consumes at least half of your waking hours, if not more. Because your personal time is so limited but so very important, you need to use it wisely. Above all else, strive to maintain a healthy balance between your professional and private lives.

Getting Out of Work on Time

When you consistently work overtime or take business home with you, you begin to forget how having a free weeknight—or even a free weekend—feels. To get in the habit of leaving work on time, start with these steps.

Time Is on Your Side

When you work out of your home, the time you would normally spend traveling to and from your office becomes yours to do with as you will. As the following table shows, this "found time" can really add up over the course of a year.

Minutes Spent Commuting (Per Day)	Hours Spent Commuting (Per Yr.)	Weeks Saved By Telecommuting (Per Yr.)
30	120	3
40	160	4
50	200	5
60	240	6

Leave without guilt

Decide that on every Tuesday, for example, you'll leave the office at quitting time and take no work home with you. After freeing up Tuesdays for an entire month, try adding Thursdays. Continue adding a new day every month until you're leaving on time all week long.

Get focused

Once you've decided that each Tuesday will be a normal eight- or nine-hour workday and nothing more, you will automatically become more focused about what you want to get done on Tuesdays. Almost imperceptibly, you'll parcel out your time more judiciously over the course of the day. At midday, stop and assess what you've done and what else you'd like to get done. Near the end of the day, stop and assess what you can realistically get done in the amount of time that's left and what you need to leave for the next day.

Make a deal with yourself

It's 2:45 in the afternoon, and you have three tasks that you'd like to get done before the day is over. Ask yourself: "What can I realistically accomplish in the amount of time that I have left?" By narrowing down your to-do list in this way, you free yourself to feel good about leaving on time.

Accommodate changing circumstances

Suppose you have three tasks on your agenda for the afternoon. Then your boss waltzes into your office with a major project that she says needs your attention right away. Rather than calling your family and telling them that you won't be home for dinner, reevaluate what you can accomplish in the amount of time that you have left. You may take care of only two of the three previous tasks and a certain percentage of the new project. Or you may set aside all of the previous tasks and devote the afternoon to making sufficient headway on the new project. Again, your objective is to determine what you must do in order to leave work on time and feel good about it.

Managing Those Must-Do's

When you get to the point where you're leaving work on time every day, you don't want to spend all your newfound free time running errands and doing chores. Take advantage of businesses that make house calls, such as pharmacies and dry cleaners. When such services aren't available, and when other family members can't help out, use the following strategies to handle your tasks in the fastest, easiest way possible.

Set aside time

Designate one night each week as errand night, and do all your running around then. You may opt to go right after work since you're already in your car. Or you may want to go home and wait until rush-hour traffic subsides. Find the time that suits you best.

Whatever you do, avoid allowing your errands to stack up for the weekend—what self-help author Dennis Hensley, PhD, calls IDIOS syndrome, as in "I'll do it on Saturday." In many communities, you'll encounter more traffic on Saturdays and Sundays than on weekdays. And at least most folks are heading in the same general direction during the week—into the city in the morning, away from it in the evening. Weekend traffic tends to have a far more diffuse pattern.

> **Park It and Save**
>
> Telecommuting has a number of advantages. Among them: It significantly reduces the amount of wear and tear on your vehicle. According to Big Bucks Auto in Jamaica, NY, owning a car costs about $19,800 a year, on average. Including purchase, finance charges, insurance, maintenance, fuel, registration, license, parking, and tolls.

Don't put off until tomorrow

Handle tasks such as filling your gas tank, getting your car washed, and replenishing household items when they're not crucial. For example, stop for gas when your tank is one-quarter full rather than one-eighth or less. Yes, you may fill 'er up a few more times a month. But because you're not running on empty, you can look around for short lines and good prices. Give up the false economy of waiting until the last minute to fill your tank.

Go in circles

If you're starting your errand run from home, prepare for multiple stops in a circular route. If you're starting from your office, swing wide if you have to, all the while progressing in the direction of your home. List your stops in order on a self-stick note, then affix the note to your dashboard. Methodically cross off each item after completion to bolster your sense of accomplishment.

Put it in park

Crawling up to traffic lights, fighting for parking spaces, battling crowds of shoppers, and standing in long checkout lines do not give you a feeling of simplicity. If you encounter any of these circumstances on your errand run, just head home and try again at a different time—say, during off-peak hours.

Use a folder as a holder

Have a file folder or envelope ready and available for the various receipts, tickets, and sales slips that you collect on your errand run. Keeping these papers organized is a lot easier when you've accumulated them all in one place.

Clear the passenger seat

In general, the cleaner and more clutter-free your car is when you begin your errand run, the greater your chances of staying organized and efficient throughout your trip. If possible, keep the passenger seat clear for your new buys and pickups. Think of it as your portable desk or even your loading and unloading dock.

Be good to yourself

Give yourself a mental pat on the back for completing even the smallest or easiest of tasks, such as dropping off an item for dry cleaning, depositing a check, returning a video, and so on. You deserve it.

Get stamps by mail

Need stamps? Forget running to your local post office. You can order them by mail and have them delivered to your home. This postal service costs nothing, not even for the envelope you use to send in your order. The catch is that you have to anticipate when you might run out of stamps. Although "stamps by mail" has been available for more than two decades, hardly anyone knows about it, and of those who do, few actually use it. Also, you can order stamps online and even print your own!

Have You Tried Telecommuting?

As metropolitan areas keep expanding and daily commuting becomes more trying, a growing number of people are opting to work out of their homes.

Studies have shown that telecommuters can be just as productive as traditional office workers, if not more

so. The benefits to you, besides reduced commuting time, include savings on clothing and food, more flexible working hours, and potentially greater autonomy. The benefits to your employer, besides enhanced productivity, include lower office or "plant" costs.

Test the waters

At first, try telecommuting at least once a week. Rather than going to the office, communicate with your boss and co-workers via e-mail, telephone, or Skype. Working away from the office often enables you to engage in the creative, conceptual kinds of thinking that can be difficult in a busy, noisy environment.

Pause for pregnancy

Telecommuting is an especially attractive option for moms-to-be. If you're a woman who is pregnant, you may want to suggest to your boss an arrangement similar to one designed by a small California firm to accommodate an expectant employee. Early in her pregnancy, the woman worked from her home one day a week, communicating with her office via e-mail and phone. As her delivery date got closer, she gradually increased the number of days she telecommuted. About one month before she was due, the woman was working out of her home full-time, five days a week.

After the baby's birth, the company reversed the schedule. At first, the new mom telecommuted five days a week. Then she started going into the office one day a week, then two days, and so on, until she was back full-time.

The Simplest of the Simple

Do you commute? If so, here are the easiest ways to lessen the effects of the proverbial rat race and maintain your peace of mind.

- Get enough sleep. If you feel rested in the morning, you will probably be less stressed, and your whole day will go more smoothly.
- Organize everything you need for work the night before so it's ready to go in the morning.
- Keep your car serviced. Simple things like getting a tune-up, changing your oil, and making sure your tires aren't bald can save you a lot of grief.
- Never shave, apply makeup, or engage in similar activities while operating your car.
- If you're traveling by airplane, limit yourself to the number of bags that you can carry on board.
- If you often travel on business, invest in luggage with wheels and a good handle.
- Leave work on time at least one night a week. More often is better.
- Do your errands when you have time, but don't wait until they're urgent.
- Telecommute, if possible. Even if you work at home only one day a month, it will save you time and energy.

Chapter 18 | Office Efficiency

Putting Your Work Space to Work for You

Albert Einstein, the brilliant physicist who gave the world the theory of relativity, also ruminated on more mundane matters, such as work. He once explained his own work habits with three simple rules:

- Out of clutter, find simplicity.
- From discord, find harmony.
- In the middle of difficulty lies opportunity.

This wisdom rings true today more than ever, as working men and women try to maintain a sense of order and control in their fast-paced, technology-driven professional lives. Indeed, working efficiently has become a science in itself.

The great news is that you can simplify your workplace and office space in so many ways. We'll cover some key concepts here.

Secrets the Pros Know

Without question, working in these ultracompetitive times presents its challenges. It certainly keeps you on your toes. If you stay calm and organized, you can accomplish almost anything.

First Things First

When multiple tasks demand your attention, you must decide what gets done first. The following strategies can help you prioritize and prepare your workload.

Know what's important

Many business situations follow the 80/20 rule, according to Peter F. Drucker, PhD, author of *Managing for Results*. For instance, 80 percent of your sales are made to 20 percent of your customers, or 80 percent of the material you use is pulled from 20 percent of your files. Give priority to the 20 percent—those people or tasks that can help you attain your goals—and let go of the rest.

Put out fires when necessary

Your day may get off to a wonderful start, only to be overrun with "emergencies" by lunchtime. When a crisis occurs, take action—but don't overdramatize the situation. It may be genuinely urgent, or it may be merely important. Learn to recognize the difference. That way, you won't waste time and energy by losing sight of what needs to be done and when.

Deterring Distractions

Interruptions can throw a monkey wrench in an otherwise productive day. Allowing people to step into your office to "quickly run this by you" can end up costing you precious hours of your time. To cut down on distractions and keep your day on track, try these tips.

Set your limit

Be firm with an interrupter, telling her up front that your time is at a premium. Start the conversation with a definite, "I have only five minutes. How can I help you most?" Make the time limit visible by placing a clock on or above your desk.

If the interrupter offers to call you later, tell her, "No, I'll be busy later. How can I help you now?"

Send clear signals

When the time limit has elapsed, shuffle papers on your desk, stand up, or use other body language to indicate that the meeting has ended. You can ease the brush-off by maintaining a pleasant attitude and injecting a little humor ("Well, I better get back to this project before the paperwork starts to multiply"). Or you can simply say thank you, which officially closes any conversation.

Make your move

Another way to bring a meeting to an end: Make the interrupter aware that you have other commitments by having him wait a moment while you write a note about whatever you're working on. Eventually, he should take the hint.

If nothing else works, interrupt a lengthy discussion with a startled, "Wait, what time is it?" It's sure to terminate the conversation.

Don't Put Off until Tomorrow . . .

Procrastination can sabotage even the best-laid plans and turn them into a full-blown fiasco. If you tend to wait until the last minute to tackle big or difficult projects, the following suggestions can help you change your delaying ways.

Get it over with

Any time the order in which you tackle tasks or components of a task is at your discretion, opt for the seemingly unpleasant ones first. That gives you something to look forward to because you know more enjoyable endeavors lie ahead. If you do the opposite—taking care of what you like first and saving what you dislike for later—the likelihood that you'll procrastinate increases.

Clear the deck

If you're having a hard time getting started, try removing everything from the surface of your desk except the materials related to the task at hand. The fewer visual distractions that you have, the greater the probability that you can stay focused on what you need to do.

Recruit a cheerleader

A co-worker can help you get over the procrastination hump by giving you a little pre-project pep talk. Try to find someone who is a trailblazer—someone who has already tackled the task that awaits you.

Sneak a preview

If you have a project to tackle on a Monday, you may want to look it over the Friday before. Then when you return to the office after the weekend, you have some semblance of familiarity with the project's particulars. This strategy also works before you leave on vacation—or, for that matter, any time a few days or even a few hours pass before you can actually begin your work.

Take baby steps

It is certainly tempting to put off a big project. Procrastinating only makes the job—and your life—more difficult. Instead, divide the big project into mini-projects

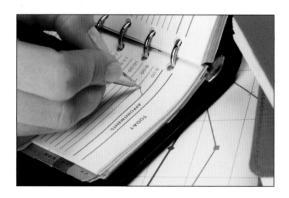

and focus on these individually, suggests Alan Lakein, a time management consultant to Fortune 500 companies and author of *How to Get Control of Your Time and Your Life*. By using this technique, which Lakein calls the Swiss cheese method because it punches holes in unwieldy tasks, the job won't seem so intimidating.

Write it for the record

When you document what you're going to do and by when, you reduce your likelihood of procrastinating. Sharing your deadlines with others helps even more: It breaks down any self-imposed barriers to getting started on time, and it brings you outside support.

Give yourself time

For many tasks, once you get started you'll want to follow all the way through to completion. You won't want to pack up everything because you've run out of time. Your best bet is to start early in the morning, on a day when you have nothing else scheduled. That way, you can devote as much time to the project as it requires. If you have the opportunity to complete your work in one day, you probably will. Just be sure to take periodic breaks so the work doesn't seem so onerous.

Keep the end in sight

Much of what you need to do to achieve a desired outcome may not please you while you're doing it. For instance, finding ways to cut costs in your department so that you're saving more and spending less won't necessarily make you feel good. When your department wins kudos for doing the best job on the smallest budget, however, you'll realize that your efforts, difficult as

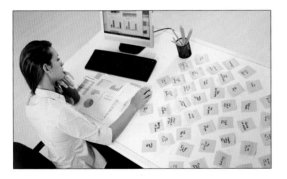

they may have been, have yielded a highly satisfactory outcome.

Give yourself a pat on the back

If you expect your project to last days, weeks, or even longer, reward yourself each time you meet a deadline or complete an especially difficult task. Treat yourself to a movie, a massage, or a meal at your favorite restaurant—whatever appeals to you. These reinforcements can help keep you motivated for the duration of the project.

Making the Most of Meetings

Some days, work seems like one meeting after another. You have no time left to attend to your own priorities. Meetings are necessary only for brainstorming ideas and for reaching agreements. Other discussions can be handled by phone or by e-mail.

When you must call a meeting, you can keep it short and sweet by being prepared. Have an agenda and stay within your own time limit. The following strategies can help, too.

Get it in writing

Take notes during meetings or ask someone else to do so. That way, you'll have an accurate record of what has been accomplished and what remains to be done.

Put attendees at ease

Find new ways to engage and energize participants during potentially boring meetings. Meeting leaders should tell jokes, blow bubbles, and sometimes act downright silly, suggests author Steve Kaye in his book *Meetings in an Hour or Less*. This relaxes the participants and allows them to feel comfortable suggesting even unconventional ideas.

Dramatize your mission

To persuade others in your meeting to use your time together efficiently, calculate how much the meeting will cost per minute. Include the participants' time, the facilitator's time, any supplies that will be used, and so on. Then begin the meeting by saying, "It's costing us $100 a minute to be here today, so I suggest that we make the best possible use of our time."

The Accessible Desk

When personal computers first became popular, experts predicted the advent of the paperless office, in which everything would be processed electronically. That day may come. For now, though, many folks continue to do their business on paper, most of which seems to find its way to your desk.

If you're buried under a backlog of memos, letters, and requisitions, take heart. You can take steps to banish the unwanted and unnecessary paperwork that is cluttering your professional life.

Purging Paperwork

Statistics show that the aggregate volume of correspondence encountered by professionals increases each year. Of course, this means more work—and more hassle—for you.

The best way to stay on top of the proliferation of paperwork is to keep only those documents that are of high importance. File them in a well-marked, properly organized folder. Toss everything else.

Apply the following guidelines to process papers quickly and efficiently.

Peruse to prioritize

When you go through your mail, give each document a cursory scan to assess its importance. Begin by checking the envelope and the letterhead. These may clue you in to what the document is about. You may be able to throw it away based on this information alone.

As you look over the document, ask yourself these basic questions: Who is it from? Am I the best person to handle it? Does it have a deadline? Is it important in the long run? Would something consequential happen if I ignored it? Is it nonessential but interesting? In most cases, your answers will help you decide whether to act on the letter immediately, file it, pass it on to someone else, or trash it. (Incidentally, this system also works for screening voice mail and e-mail.)

How Complex Can It Get?

Sorry to Bother You, but . . . Alvin Toffler, author of the landmark book *Future Shock,* once remarked that with all of its distractions, the modern office is a terrible place to get work done.

Write your reply

You have several options for handling letters that require immediate response, especially those from colleagues whom you know well (which means you can dispense with formal business correspondence protocol). For instance, you can stamp or label the document "Speed Reply," then write your response in the space at

---

The Right Stuff

No matter what your job, you can work with greater efficiency and confidence just by adhering to the Laws of Mental Prosperity. These 10 principles—identified by Tom Kubistant, EdD, an executive retreat specialist and an expert on individual performance and organizational productivity—drive professional satisfaction and success.

The Law of Self-Determinism: You become what you think about. If you improve the quality of your thinking, you will improve the quality of your life.

The Law of Dynamism: There is no neutral gear: Either you are progressing or you are regressing. If you aren't actively choosing to be positive, you are actually choosing to be negative.

The Law of Belief: Your beliefs define your realities. Focus on that which you can control.

The Law of Attraction: You are a living magnet. You attract that which you are. You also attract that which you need to become.

The Law of Correspondence: Your outer world is a mirror of your inner world—as within, so without. There are no crises, only gifts and opportunities.

The Law of Prospiros: Prosperity and spiritual awareness are intrinsically linked. (Dr. Kubistant coined the term prospiros from prosperity and spirit.) Purity of purpose is both the beginning and the end. Ethics before economics: Do the right thing at the right time.

The Law of Action: Whatever can be conceived and believed can be achieved. Do instead of try. Persistence is the hallmark of belief.

The Law of Work: Do what you love, and the money will follow. Every task is a test of your character. Going the extra distance is the only shortcut to success.

The Law of Service: The best way to find yourself is to lose yourself in the service of others. Giving something back is putting it back there for others. Service is the essence of humility.

The Law of Accumulation: Little things build up to become big things. Everything you do counts. How you do everything matters.

the bottom of the page. Use either a rubber stamp with oversize lettering and bright red ink or preprinted labels. You can order both from almost any office supply store. If necessary, make a copy of the document for your files before you send it back (but remember, you're trying to cut down on paper clutter).

Turn the page

For correspondence that requires a longer or more detailed response, write on the back side of the page. Make a copy of the document (front and back) for your own files, but only if you really need one.

Answer by number

Feel free to number the points in the correspondence you've received and address each point in your reply. This makes drafting a reply much easier and reduces the amount of time and energy required for the task. Otherwise, your response will go something like this: "Based on your statement in paragraph two, where you said X, I feel that Y. In paragraph four, you stated that Z . . ."

Ready to Respond

To prevent paperwork from eating up precious minutes of your workday, you can implement additional time-saving measures. Take advantage of any or all of the following shortcuts.

> ## Simply Stated
>
> *I wasted time, and now doth time waste me.*
> **—William Shakespeare,
> English playwright, in *Richard II***

Develop perfect form

Especially for in-house correspondence, create a standardized reply form. You may want to include a preprinted message like this one: "Excuse the informality, but I feel that responding promptly is important." Such a form may seem impersonal. But if you ask people how they feel when they receive one, and the vast majority will agree that they'd rather receive a quick, informal response to a question than wait weeks for a formal response that says essentially the same thing.

Many office supply stores carry books with predesigned business reply forms. They usually cost between $10 and $15, but they're well worth the expense. By

> ## Give Yourself a Break
>
> Sure, you have to get that project done. All work and no play, however, can make you downright miserable. You know you need to take a break when:
> - You yawn or sigh.
> - Your eyelids droop and your pupils appear dilated.
> - You feel the need to stretch or loosen your muscles.
> - You're hungry.
> - You must go to the bathroom.
> - You're daydreaming.
> - Your reflexes slow down.
> - You are mildly clumsy.
> - You experience mild numbness in your hands, elbows, feet, or elsewhere.
> - You feel fidgety.
> - You're preoccupied.

using the forms, you'll save enough time within a day or two to more than make up for the expense.

Return to sender

Clip the return address from the envelope of any letter that you receive. Then use glue or transparent tape to affix the address to the envelope in which you'll send your reply. That way, you avoid having to engage your computer and printer just to produce one label. Of course, this technique isn't appropriate for more formal correspondence. But it can serve you well in some situations.

Give out your address

When sending a reply to someone, insert one of your own address labels. This may prompt the other person to keep in touch with you. In fact, if you're expecting to have ongoing correspondence with the other person, you may even want to include extra address labels.

> ## Simply Stated
>
> *Politeness is as much concerned in answering letters within a reasonable time, as it is in returning a bow, immediately.*
> **—Philip Dormer Stanhope, fourth earl of
> Chesterfield, English statesman and author**

A High-Tech Survival Guide

Technology was supposed to simplify our lives. Instead, our lives have become even more complicated. Smartphones, tablets, and similar gizmos give others 24-hour access to our offices and our homes. Thankfully, there are ways to minimize the invasion and maintain some sense of order and control.

Calling All Callers

Perhaps no single piece of office equipment causes as much distraction as the telephone. You may spend an hour or more each day fielding calls and returning messages. Voice mail can help you manage your phone use more effectively. On the downside, you may spend one of every five minutes in voice mail just wading through menus.

With a little strategizing, you can make telecommunication work to your advantage. Here's how.

Reconsider call waiting

With call waiting, a series of beeps alerts you to an incoming call when you're already speaking to someone else. It's distracting, not to mention rude. Trade in call waiting for voice mail. Voice mail takes a message so you can complete one conversation before beginning another.

Be brief

When you create a greeting for voice mail (or an answering machine), keep it short and simple but include all pertinent information. Remind callers to leave detailed messages, especially their phone numbers and the best time to reach them. Let callers know that they can press certain numbers to bypass your greeting and leave their messages.

Better Now Than Later

Are you prone to procrastination? Read through the following list and decide which of the statements describes you. The more that do, the more you fit the classic procrastinator profile.

- You habitually file your taxes late.
- You send greeting cards too late for them to arrive on time.
- You shop for Christmas presents on December 24.
- You see your doctor months after you first suspect that something is wrong.
- You have desk drawers that are total disaster areas, and you've been "meaning to get to them."
- You begin some projects after their deadlines have passed—that kind of anxiety gets you going.

Rely on the old notepad

Keep a notepad or a phone log close to your phone so that you're prepared to take messages. Or outfit your computer with a pop-up message program, which you can quickly access by pressing certain keys or clicking on an icon. Avoid having to scramble around for a piece of scrap paper and a pen or pencil while trying to remember important information. And when messages become outdated, discard them. Don't be tempted to hoard them for later.

Simply Stated

Our inventions are wont to be pretty toys, which distract our attention from serious things. They are but improved means to an unimproved end.

—Henry David Thoreau, American author, in *Walden*

Reroute your calls

If you're on deadline or you're working on an important project, let voice mail take your calls for you. Many models of office phones have a "Do Not Disturb" feature, which routes incoming calls directly to voice mail. You won't even hear your phone ring. You can work uninterrupted, then return messages when you're ready. You'll accomplish a lot more this way than if you're grabbing the phone every few minutes.

E-Mail Essentials

With e-mail obviously you can send and receive messages faster than ever. You can't beat it for speed or convenience. If you're not careful, though, e-mail can become a huge time-waster. Here's how to use it wisely.

Separate business from pleasure. Establish individual e-mail accounts for professional and private use. Keep personal mail out of your office and business mail out of your home.

Check it sparingly. Going into your e-mail each time you get a new message wastes time. Depending on the nature of your job, you may be able to save time by checking your in-box once in the morning, perhaps once at midday, and once in the afternoon.

Can the spam. Use an e-mail program that can filter out and delete junk e-mail—or "spam." Most newer programs have filtering features that work fairly well.

Get organized. To save time, use the address book features that are built in to your e-mail program, rather than manually typing addresses. Also, create folders where you can file messages as soon as you've read them. If they require responses, act on them.

Keep it simple. A short e-mail message is a good e-mail message.

Leave a trail

If you're planning to be out of the office on business, change your voice mail greeting to indicate when you'll be back. You can have your calls forwarded to someone else while you're gone, or you can check your messages while you're on the road. Always make sure to leave a phone number where you can be reached in case of an emergency.

Venturing into Cyberspace

While exploring cyberspace can be fun, it can also eat up a lot of time.

Calling Hours

No more phone tag! You can increase your chances of actually reaching various professionals by contacting them at the times listed below.

Accountants	Any time of day (but remember that they're busiest between January 2 and April 15)
Bankers	Before 10 AM or after 3 PM
Builders and contractors	Before 9 AM or after 5 PM
Dentists	Before 9 AM
Department store heads, merchants, and store managers	After 10:30 AM
Doctors and surgeons	Between 9 and 11 AM or after 4 PM
Engineers	Between 4 and 5 PM
Executives and top managers	After 10:30 AM
Grocers	Between 1 and 3 PM
Home-based entrepreneurs	Mornings after 7:30 AM or after 5:30 PM
Housewives	Between 10 and 11 AM
Lawyers	Between 11 AM and 2 PM
Local, state, and federal government employees	At home, after work
Ministers, priests, and rabbis	Any time of day, Thursday and Friday
Pharmacists	Between 1 and 3 PM
Printers and publishers	After 3 PM
Professors and teachers	At home, between 6 and 7 PM
Secretaries, Administrative Assistants	At home, after work

Say the magic words

The way you phrase your search inquiries dramatically increases the percentage of accurate hits. Using the exact wording is your best bet. If you don't know it, then search by keyword or by date.

Resist temptation

Avoid exploring links that may lead you away from your original search. If you're tempted, bookmark it and return to it later. Much time is wasted in random surfing. Stick with your work, and leave the play for weekends.

Simplest of the Simple

To make the most of your time in and around your office, employ these strategies.
- Decide what's most important and focus your attention there.
- Don't allow others to get you off track.
- Clean off your desk. Keep only a handful of key documents at your fingertips. Stacks of paper sitting on your desk can make you feel even more stressed.
- Break big tasks into smaller ones so you derive a greater sense of accomplishment.
- Use meetings sparingly, and always stick to an agenda.
- Cancel your call waiting and use voice mail instead.
- Avoid phone tag by asking people to tell you the best time to contact them.
- Turn off the ringer on your phone when you need to concentrate.

It Keeps Piling Up

	COUNTRY	PAPER PER PERSON (LB.)
1.	Finland	707
2.	United States	676
3.	Canada	619
4.	Sweden	606
5.	Japan	549
6.	Denmark	534
7.	Holland	526
8.	Germany	483
9.	Switzerland	468
10.	UK	455

Source: **Earth trends, 2007**

Chapter 19

Reading Easy

Secrets to Survival in the Information Age

The typical professional spends between two and four hours of each work-day perusing reports, journals, and similar materials. Yet he probably feels anxious doing so, lest someone walk by his desk and see him "not doing too much." Likewise, the typical homemaker has to read more today than at any other time in history, just to perform routine tasks. Yet she may feel guilty for "wasting time."

Reading may be the only activity that is viewed by most people as a pastime despite the fact that it plays an integral role in day-to-day living. Whether you're reading for business or pleasure, you can make the time optimally productive and feel good about what you accomplish. If you frequently find yourself facing a backlog of books or magazines, you'll welcome the advice in this chapter.

More Than You'll Ever Know

We live in the Information Age. Thanks to the Internet—not to mention tele-vision, radio, and the print media—we now have access to more news and knowledge than ever before. As a result, many of us have developed a severe case of information overload. The only cure is to find ways to sift what we need to know from what we don't.

Identifying What is Important

Leaf through just about any publication and you're bound to spy at least one arti-cle or passage that piques your interest. Should you read it right away? Set it aside for later? Or pass over it completely? Use these guidelines to help you decide.

Select the right sources

Actively seek out those publications that supply the information you need. Then, do most of your reading from them. This saves you the time and trouble of wading through articles that are of little meaning or interest to you.

Skim the surface

Skimming involves perusing the first one or two sentences of a paragraph within an article to see if the information within that paragraph is useful to you. This technique enables you to quickly determine whether you should invest more time in that particular article or publication. If you have a pile of periodicals awaiting your attention, skimming helps you sift through them quickly and efficiently.

The Meaning of "Myth"

Books in Print lists thousand of volumes that feature the word myth in their titles. In one five-year period alone, publishers released 650 such books, including *The Myth of Psychotherapy, The Myths of Motherhood,* and *The Myth of Mental Illness.*

Why has myth become a book jacket buzzword? As readers grow more leery of the information that they're receiving from various media, many take refuge in books that reflect the skepticism surrounding particular topics. Perhaps this is a healthy trend of readers seeking a well-rounded perspective on issues and not relying on one source or the conventional view. It shows that they're wary of the complications that arise from buying into exaggerated, biased, and unsubstantiated claims.

Scan what's inside

While skimming works well for periodicals, scanning is better suited to books. This technique involves reviewing the table of contents, the index, any lists of charts and exhibits, and occasional paragraph lead-ins. From these elements, you should learn enough about the book to decide whether it meets your needs or interests. If you don't want to read the entire volume, you can simply photocopy the relevant pages or chapters. (Incidentally, photocopying a publication's pages for limited, personal use does not violate U.S. copyright laws.)

Skipping without Guilt

If you're accustomed to reading every single page of every publication that falls into your hands, the idea of disregarding certain materials can seem downright disconcerting. After all, what if you miss something important?

In all likelihood, you won't. These insights should help put your mind at ease.

Beware the information beast

Information feeds on itself. The more that you take in, the more that you seek to take in. Many folks allow far too much information to enter their awareness zones, and they feel overwhelmed as a result.

When weighing whether to read or reject a particular article or chapter, ask yourself, "What will really happen if I skip this?" You may be surprised—and pleased—by your honest response.

Evaluate relevance

Here's another way to assess the value of an article or chapter: Ask yourself whether it provides the sort of core knowledge that you need to advance in your profession, to serve your customers or clients better, or to further some other vital interest. In this context, you may realize that much of what you intended to read really has no benefit for you. So skip it in favor of information that is more germane.

Favor trends over fads

On balance, most of what you don't read won't affect you anyway. Why? Because in a world where a lifetime of information is generated every hour (soon to be every minute), almost anything you read will quickly become outdated. You're better off looking for trends or patterns that indicate the general direction in which your profession, industry, or special interest is heading.

Say Goodbye to Guilt

If saying no to certain reading material leaves you feeling guilty, remind yourself of the following:
- You probably won't be any worse off.
- You will likely see the material again in another form.
- Someone else on your team may already be on top of it.
- You can remember and act upon only a fraction of what you read anyway.

Tools and Techniques

Once you've decided what is essential and what is dispensable, you're ready to tackle some actual reading. Of course, you've already had a lifetime of practice, so you probably have the basics down pat. A few minor adjustments in your technique will have you perusing more proficiently and productively than ever.

Reviewing the Basics

Whether you're reading for purpose or for pleasure, make sure that you have the proper setting and the proper tools. Here are the basics.

Get the best seat in the house (or office)

Reading for pleasure can be done wherever you choose. Reading for purpose, on the other hand, requires a desk rather than a recliner, a couch, or even a table. Sitting at a desk puts you within reach of scissors, a ruler, pens, stationery, envelopes, and all the other office supplies that will enable you to clip, tear, send for, save, and file what you've read.

Give your eyeballs a break

Our prehistoric ancestors were hunters and gatherers. They used their eyes to peer into forests and across vast savannas in search of game and berries. Nature never anticipated that we humans would one day be focusing on the fine print in publications and on computer screens. Doing so for extended periods of time invariably causes eyestrain.

Be kind to your eyes by choosing large-print publications—even if you're not visually impaired. Your local library may carry large-print versions of magazines and books.

> **Simply Stated**
>
> *Reading is to the mind what exercise is to the body.*
>
> —**Joseph Addison,**
> **English essayist and poet**

Raise a glass

If a particular publication doesn't come in a large-print edition, you can enlarge the print yourself just by using a magnifying glass. This low-tech tool provides welcome relief for tired eyes, even if you're still a young 'un.

Pump up the point size

If you do most of your reading (or writing, for that matter) on a computer screen, increase the point size of the text as you see fit. You don't have to stick with the default type size, which is usually 12 point. While you're at it, select a font with serifs—those tiny lines at the ends of letters. They actually make reading easier because they establish better spatial relationships between letters.

Cruising while Perusing

If you're reading for purpose, your goal is to glean any information that you find useful from your selected sources. These tips will help you do a thorough but efficient job.

Use it or lose it

When you spot a magazine article or book passage that interests you, mark it with a paper clip or a sticky note. Then photocopy the pages you want and file them in a folder to peruse later on. This may seem like an annoyance while you're reading, but it sure beats allowing magazines and books to overrun your in-box.

Go on a tear

If you're the only person who needs to see a particular magazine, here's an even faster way to move it off your desk. As soon as you receive it, flip through it and tear out only those pages that you think may be of interest to you. Then recycle the rest.

Save for the future

Any time you come across information that you think may come in handy, put it in a folder or a bin marked "Check when I have more time." Periodically sort through these clippings, especially when they accumulate, and see if you can chuck anything without having read it. Then set aside time—weekly or monthly, depending on how quickly your pile grows—to peruse the articles that you've put in your temporary file.

Make your mark

Most people prefer to preserve their books in mint condition. Yet nonfiction books, in particular, are intended as references—sources of information. One consultant contends that when you finish a book, "no one else should want it." He suggests highlighting passages, dog-earing pages, and inserting clips and notes throughout. In other words, employ whatever tools and techniques you have available to get the most from your book. If they help you absorb and apply the information you've read, they'll do you a lot more good than pampering your pages.

Dispensing with Convention

Who says you have to read a book or magazine from front to back or even from left to right? Forget what your grade school teachers told you. When you're reading for speed and comprehension, tackle each tome or journal in the manner that works best for you.

Choose where to jump in

If you have trouble sticking with a book (or any publication) once you start it, turn to the table of contents and select a chapter or passage that appeals to you. Then begin on that page, no matter where it falls within the book. You can even read the book from back to front, if you prefer. You're not subject to the tyranny of linear page progression.

Peruse what interests you

Suppose you want to read a book on succeeding in the workplace. Certain topics covered in the book may not apply to your particular job situation. Instead of wading through that information to find what you really want to know, select key subjects from the index and read only those. Many books, including this one, aren't intended to be read from cover to cover anyway. Even for those that are, you can choose your own method of perusal. Remember: You control the book, not vice versa.

Know the cone

Reporters write their stories using what is called the cone method. They put the most critical information—the who, what, when, where, why, and how—at the beginning. Then they add details in descending order of importance. If you visualize this organization, it resembles a cone.

Why does this matter to you? Because you can save yourself a lot of time by reading just the first 10 to 20 percent of an article. You'll get the gist of what's being said without actually perusing the whole thing.

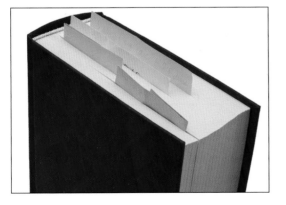

Wait until the last minute

Cramming may not have been such a good idea in high school or college. Trying to absorb a semester's worth of knowledge in three hours or less never quite makes the grade. But cramming does have its advantages in the real world. Suppose you're unexpectedly called into a meeting and you have exactly 20 minutes to acquaint yourself with the project being discussed. Don't panic. Instead, retrieve the appropriate file folder and read through it. The information will remain fresh in your mind, so you can handle the meeting like a pro.

To use cramming effectively, you have to devote your full attention to reading the relevant materials. Avoid losing precious minutes to phone calls, e-mails, and other interruptions. Protect your time against interlopers.

Shortcut to Success

To capture the essence of a full-length nonfiction book without spending hours reading it, follow these steps.

1. Read the entire book jacket, including the inside flaps.
2. Read the foreword, if there is one.
3. Read the introduction (but skip the preface).
4. Read the table of contents.
5. Read the first two paragraphs of every chapter.
6. Read the last three or four pages of the last chapter.
7. Glance at any reference list, resource list, or other back matter.
8. Photocopy the few pages that are relevant to you.

The Question Is . . . When?

The previous tip raises an important issue: Sometimes, the hardest part of reading is just getting around to it. So many other things demand your attention—at the office and at home—that reading consistently lingers at the bottom of your to-do list.

To find the time to read, you have to make it a priority. And why shouldn't you? After all, especially in terms of your job, staying on top of the latest developments and trends is just as important as returning phone calls and attending meetings.

Making Time, Saving Time

There are a lot of clever, convenient ways to fit reading into your day (or evening). For starters, try the following tactics.

Alternate between articles

When you have a lot of reading to do, you may get through it more efficiently if you mix complex items with simple ones, or must-reads with like-to-reads. Or tackle all of the tough stuff first and save the fun stuff for last, as a form of reward. Just avoid reading the fun stuff first: it will only spoil you for the longer or more involved items to come.

Seek peace and quiet

Interruptions account for half of the problems that people face when they try to concentrate on and comprehend reading materials at the office. So set aside time for reading when you know that you won't be disturbed. Do some of your reading early in the morning, before others arrive at the office and start making noise. Or find a quiet sanctuary where you can read at midday. In 20 to 30 minutes, you can plow through the pile of publications that has been accumulating on your desk for days.

Make nighttime the right time

Set aside one night each week for nothing but reading. Dig in right after dinner and continue until bedtime. Refrain from turning on the television or answering the phone or helping to find your spouse's glasses. The evening is yours to get all of your reading done.

Set a deadline

If you have a report, a magazine, or a book that you need to read and you've been putting it off for weeks, give yourself a specific amount of time to complete the task. For instance, allow yourself 20 minutes to glean everything you can from a particular book. Declare yourself done at the end of those 20 minutes. Whatever notes you've made, whatever pages you've decided to copy, whatever dossier you've created as a result of your review has to serve as the official wrap-up for the task.

Twenty minutes may not seem like a lot of time. Still, when you're devoting every second to a single report, magazine, or book, 20 minutes lasts for an eternity. You'll be pleasantly surprised when you realize how much information you can collect in that short of a time frame.

Count pages, not sheep

Rather than setting a time limit, decide in advance how many pages you'll read in one sitting. Again using a book as an example, you may choose to read 10 pages every night, or 5 pages every morning, or 15 pages every Saturday.

This technique can prove especially helpful when you have a deadline. Simply divide the total number of pages by the total number of available days to determine how many pages you must read per day. Let's suppose you have 25 days in which to finish a 250-page book. To meet your deadline, you should read 10 pages per day. This benchmark can be especially helpful when you have a voluminous amount of reading to do.

Reading on the Run

For some reason, most businesspeople feel compelled to carry reading materials with them wherever they go. If you're among them, these tips can help you make the most of your travel time.

Be a backseat reader

Whenever you're expecting to be a passenger for 10 minutes or longer, why not use that time to do some reading? As long as you don't get carsick and the driver isn't necessarily counting on you for conversation, spend those minutes flipping through magazines or reading three or four articles from your "Check when I have more time" file or bin.

Simply Stated

Those who make the worst use of their time are the first to complain of its brevity.

—**Jean de la Bruyère,
French moralist**

Simply Stated

If you spent 20 minutes a day reading, you would be able to read 15 200-page books per year.

—**Martin Edelston and Ken Glickman,
time-management experts**

Read while you wait

If you're going someplace where there's usually a wait, take with you a few articles from your "Check when I have more time" file or bin. Then if you find yourself standing in line at the bank, sitting at the doctor's office, or stuck in traffic, you can take the opportunity to read the items that you deem important. This is far more productive than standing around and doing nothing or sitting around and reading whatever happens to be available—if, indeed, anything is available.

Travel lighter

If you're taking a business trip, think twice about dragging along reading materials. The reason: When you read on the road, you'll inevitably create work for yourself—which means you'll have an even longer to-do list when you get back to the office. Unless you're reading for pleasure, leave magazines and books at the office, where you have the tools you need to actually act upon the information you collect.

Desperate Measures

If you find yourself struggling to stay on top of your reading despite the above measures, then you need to make more drastic changes. Some of the suggestions below will challenge old, established habits and force you to answer tough questions about what's really important to you. The process may be uncomfortable, but the results are definitely worth the effort.

Drawing the Line

If you want to cut down on your required reading pronto, the following steps will do the trick.

Cancel your subscriptions

Drop all of your subscriptions to publications that can be found on-line or in your local library and that primarily contain articles for which timeliness isn't a factor. Every few weeks or months, you can skim several issues of selected periodicals, copying or saving only those articles that you actually need.

Read the reviews

Instead of spending your money on books and trying to find time to read them from cover to cover, pick up the *New York Times Book Review* each Sunday. It offers lengthy profiles of 5 to 10 books, along with shorter profiles of several other books. Which tomes are covered? All the latest and greatest from the top publishers in the United States. The reviews are well-written and illuminating, and they'll give you enough information to be able to discuss the books intelligently at the office watercooler or a cocktail party.

If you don't have access to the *New York Times Book Review*, many other publications regularly run book profiles and critiques. Pick up a copy of the *New York Review of Books*, *Publisher's Weekly*, or the book review section of almost any major metropolitan newspaper such as the *Boston Globe*, *Chicago Tribune*, or *Los Angeles Times*. All have an online book review as well.

Befriend your local librarian

If your community has a library, ask the librarian if she knows of any other resources that may save you reading time. Many librarians have master's degrees in library science or related disciplines. They know what's out there, and they can introduce you to options that you probably have never explored. Besides, the librarian's services are free. (Actually, they're paid for with your tax dollars.)

Asking for Assistance

If you have a staff, you can appoint someone to pre-read material for you. This person can decide what you

---

Listen and Learn

If you want to keep abreast of business information, look into a service called Newstrack Executive Information Service. For a fairly hefty annual fee, Newstrack will send you a CD every month. The CD includes more than a dozen articles selected by the series editors over the previous few months and recorded by professional readers. A handy directory comes with each month's issue, telling you the title of the article, where it appeared, and how much time you'll need to listen to it. If you want more information about Newstrack's services, visit www.news-track.com.

Also, you can use your commuting time to listen to audio books; commercially produced CDs on self-improvement, leadership, career advancement, and sales; and audio summaries of the latest business books and articles visit www.booksontape.com.

Simply Stated

Intelligence is quickness in seeing things as they are.

—**George Santayana,
American poet and philospher**

need to see and what you should skip over. He can take care of the flagging and photocopying. He can also write brief summaries of articles or chapters, highlighting the most important points.

If you don't have a staff, perhaps your spouse, your teenager, or another relative would be willing to serve as your prereader. In this case, however, you may need to give the person a crash course in your business or special interest.

To guarantee the success of your reading partnership, pay attention to these details.

Get down to the nitty-gritty

Give your prereader clear instructions as to what information you're seeking. You may want to give her a list of key terms or themes that she should watch for. Also explain how you want the information presented. Perhaps you want copies of articles or chapters with the most important paragraphs highlighted. Or maybe you'd prefer a one-page list comparing the pros and cons of a certain

issue or procedure. Whatever format you decide on, make sure that you clearly explain your expectations to your prereader when turning over reading materials to her.

Have faith

Trust the ability and judgment of your prereader to highlight those articles and passages that you would select yourself. Of course, you're not limited to reading only what your prereader selects for you. But you'll find that you can go through the preread materials at record speed.

Ask around

Even if you don't have an "official" prereader, you can probably find one or two people who have already perused the same article or chapter that you need to read. Ask them to brief you on the information. If they're thorough, they'll save you from having to read the material yourself.

An Eye toward Efficiency

With a little ingenuity, you can probably come up with dozens of ways in which to cull the message from reading material in far less time and with far less effort. Take advantage of the many resources now available to get the information you want.

Going Straight to the Source

Imagine how much easier digesting information would be if you could hear it straight from the person who wrote it. After all, the author would most likely focus on the highlights of her article or book and skip over the less important details. This approach would save you a lot of time and trouble.

Well, you can get the lowdown directly from the author without hopping a plane to meet with her in person. Just turn on your television, as these tips suggest.

Take Notes

Use the Web to check your local television listings for *Book Notes*, a program on C-SPAN that features 60-minute, one-on-one interviews with prominent authors. During the show, the author usually reveals the essence of his book—how he came to write it, what difficulties he encountered when assembling it, and what he learned that surprised him.

Listen in on a lecture

C-SPAN airs a number of author lectures each week. Usually, the author is standing behind a lectern, speaking to patrons at a bookstore. The presentations tend to be candid, lively, and thoroughly good viewing.

Finding Facts Fast

Lots of people are feeling the crunch of the Information Age, and savvy entrepreneurs know it. They've introduced a variety of products and services designed to help you get the news and knowledge you want in a timely manner. Use these tools to your advantage.

Buy the abridged version

Book review services can reduce your reading time tremendously. For example, Audiotech Business Book Summaries offers MP3s of book excerpts and summaries. And Soundview Executive Book Summaries issues four- to eight-page executive summaries of business and management books. Other similar services are available as well. Check online for names and contact information.

Get your news in a letter

Newsletters are valuable sources of information. They're published by government agencies, political groups, industry groups, associations, and virtually every corporation. The best ones distill the most important information into a convenient, user-friendly format.

The *Oxbridge Newsletters Directory* categorizes several thousand newsletters by topic. *National Trade and Professional Associations* indicates which of the thousands of organizations listed issue newsletters.

Start your engine

To find a product, service, or other information on the Internet, head straight for one or more of the online search engines and initiate a search by keyword. Some search engines scour the entire Web, locating and indexing new sites as they appear. Others list only those sites that are submitted to them.

Most people don't realize that each search engine operates differently. When you find one that allows you to navigate comfortably, stay with it.

Identify indexes

Your local library should also have copies of the *Business Periodicals Index* and the *Magazine Index.* These can help you locate information specific to the topic that you're interested in.

Getting Information Online

Ninety-seven percent of people use the Internet to become better informed, while 81 percent use it to research products and services. Surfing the Internet can empower you as a consumer by putting an entire world of news and knowledge at your fingertips. The trick is searching quickly all of cyberspace to find what you're looking for. These two tips can help.

Simplest of the Simple

Productive reading boils down to these key concepts.

- Skim the first sentence or two of each paragraph in an article to make sure that it's really worth your while.
- In books, scan the table of contents and select the chapters that you think are most important. Read these first.
- Feel free to pass on certain reading materials. What you don't read most likely won't hurt you. If it's important, you'll find out about it another way.
- Read the articles you have to, then reward yourself by reading something for pleasure.
- Read in an environment where you won't be disturbed.
- If you find yourself waiting in line for an appointment, make use of that time by reading some of the shorter articles from your "Check when I have more time" file or bin.
- Ask someone else to scan reading materials for you, highlighting or photocopying key passages.
- Use the resources available to you. Librarians, book summaries, and search engines can help you get key information more quickly and efficiently.

Chapter 20

Connecting with Customers

In Business, Success Begins with Service

While you're trying to simplify your professional and private lives, remember that your customers and clients are doing the same in their own lives. How easily can they get in touch with you, deal with you, and buy from you? Your answer is important because it can affect your bottom line.

In this chapter, we'll explore the many simple ways in which you can enhance your company's marketing activities and customer service. You'll discover how to expand your customer or client base while keeping your business profitable and competitive.

Even if you don't own or manage a business (or a department within a business), you'll benefit from the information that is presented here. At least you may get some ideas that you can pass along to your boss. And you'll learn insider secrets that you can use to your advantage as a consumer.

It Pays to Advertise

Every company, no matter what products it makes or which services it offers, relies on customers for its survival. Larger corporations often spend top dollar on advertising campaigns designed to persuade people to buy their wares.

Of course, you don't have to do anything fancy or expensive to appeal to potential consumers. You simply need to make sure that they hear your message loud and clear.

Get Your Message Out

If you want to woo customers, keep your advertisements short and to the point. Remember, people don't have the time to wade through a lot of information. Why waste your time and energy telling them more than they want to know?

You'll spark the interest of customers—and stay a step ahead of competitors—just by applying these tricks of the trade.

Get thee to a summary

Pretend that your message has to be presented as an executive summary. You have just one side of a sheet of paper on which to tell a prospective customer or client everything you want him to know about your company's product or service. In such a situation, you could describe only the bare essentials: highlights, features, benefits. You'd come up with a product or service profile that is focused yet meaningful.

This exercise is extremely helpful for trimming the fat from promotional materials. Can you do it? Absolutely.

Tell a good tale

One of the simplest yet most effective methods of conveying a message about your product or service is storytelling. Donald Moine, PhD, a psychologist and sales and management–training consultant, studied the techniques of salespeople earning between $500,000 and $1 million a year in personal income. He found that the majority of them used some form of storytelling in their sales pitches. So use parables or anecdotes to get your point across, even if they're just three to five sentences in length.

Put them to sleep

Well, not literally. Nevertheless, Dr. Moine found that the stories sales professionals tell to customers have an almost hypnotic quality. Each tale creates such a strong mental image that the customer can't get the product out of his mind. He's thinking about it when he goes to bed that night—and when he wakes up the next morning.

How vivid a picture can you paint in the minds of prospective customers? Use this technique in your promotional materials to help boost your sales.

Choose the Proper Channels

You no longer need to rely on print and radio advertising to get the word out about your business. The Internet and other technological advances have opened up new avenues by which you can easily reach customers—and they can easily reach you. Here's how to make the most of what's available.

Become the mayor of Cyberville

People loathe spam e-mails, which contain messages that are of little interest to the vast majority of people who receive them. On the other hand, people like e-mails that they perceive as targeted to their interests. Consider establishing an electronic mailing list of customers who have like characteristics or needs. Then send a single, vital message to everyone in that community at once.

If you maintain a database of customers, you can easily identify various groups. For instance, you might create an electronic mailing list of all the people who have purchased a particular product or service or who have made inquiries to your company within the past six months.

Go the paper route

Then again, you may prefer to do your advertising the old-fashioned way: by regular mail. Send out a simple newsletter or even a one-page flyer. Update your customers on your business and any new products and services that you may have to offer. Most important, give them information or advice that you know they will find valuable.

Hold the bells, hold the whistles

Many people feel overwhelmed by the gadgetry that's supposed to simplify their lives. Survey after survey has shown that most folks don't use half the special features on the products they now own. Their cars and home electronics have knobs and buttons that they've yet to lay a finger on. Keep this in mind when marketing your product or service to prospective customers. Make your business as accessible and consumer-friendly as possible. If people can get what they want without jumping through a lot of hoops, they'll be happy.

The Perfect Follow-Through

Your relationship with your customer doesn't end at the completion of the sale. If you want him to continue patronizing your business, follow-through is essential. It lets your customer know that he's appreciated.

Day 1: Send a handwritten thank-you note.

Day 5: Call to determine that your customer has received the product or service. Ask whether he has any problems with it.

Day 15: Call again to determine whether the customer is still happy with the product or service.

Day 30: Send a small gift that is related to the customer's purchase and that has a high perceived value.

Many Happy Returns

Once you attract a consumer's interest, you want to make sure that she continues to patronize your business. The most successful companies reward regulars with special perks and privileges. These needn't be elaborate or expensive—in fact, the more clever and uncomplicated they are, the better. You can never overestimate the impact of reminding a customer that you value her and appreciate her business.

Identifying the Faithful

Too many companies direct their marketing campaigns toward new customers and all but ignore the folks who've already purchased their products or services. Yet studies have shown that acquiring new customers costs four to five times as much as retaining existing customers.

If you think that cultivating a relationship with your regulars can get too complicated, relax. The following strategies will show you how to do it—and why it's worth the effort.

Strive for 5 percent

According to an article published in the *Harvard Business Review*, a company can dramatically increase its profitability just by retaining 5 percent more of its customers. Said another way, you want one of every 20 customers to keep coming back to your company twice as long as usual or to order twice as often as usual. That one customer's contribution to the company's profits is

notable because the cost of generating the additional revenue is next to nothing.

Focus on the vital few

To streamline your marketing efforts, target the few customers who give you the most business. This lesson comes from an entrepreneur who had been producing and mailing a large catalog to thousands of customers each month. Analysis showed that 140 of those customers generated far more than 90 percent of total revenues. The entrepreneur realized that he could simplify his operations simply by severing ties with the people who never placed catalog orders.

Treat regulars like royalty

What do customers want in today's competitive world? In a word: responsiveness. If you're juggling too many balls, you simply can't attend to the needs of the customers you've already acquired. Eventually, they take their business elsewhere. Identify your top customers right now and initiate a campaign to let them know that you appreciate their business. Give them free gifts or discount coupons, or send them simple thank-you notes.

Keep in touch

In one study, nearly 50 percent of the customers of one large company were not contacted again by the company or called on by the person who made the initial sale. Presumably, the company or salesperson believed that the customers would renew or reorder on their own without prompting. They didn't, of course, and the company lost business as a result. Something as simple as

The Virtues of Not Being First

Your company doesn't necessarily have to be the first to offer a certain mix of goods or services to customers. Instead, aim to be the best or the most reliable in your line of business. If you examine history, you'll notice that many non-firsts have gotten credit for the success of certain ventures. Here are some examples.

- Thomas Edison didn't invent the lightbulb. He simply improved upon existing scientific principles. In 1815, Sir Humphrey Davy introduced the miner's safety lamp, a forerunner of the lightbulb. In 1860, Sir Joseph Wilson Swan devised a crude lightbulb. And Swan demonstrated a carbon filament lamp in New Castle, England, in 1878—10 months before Edison's "invention."
- The Wright brothers were not the first to fly. Nor, for that matter, were they the first to fly in a powered aircraft. The Wrights read everything about and by their predecessors, who included Samuel Langley, Otto Lilienthal, and Octave Chanute. They then improved upon what was already in progress to produce the first commercially viable aircraft. Hence, they deserve all the credit and acclaim that they've received.
- Johnny Carson was not the first host of *The Tonight Show*. He lasted the longest and was the most memorable.
- Richard Nixon was not the first to secretly record conversations in the Oval Office. In fact, John F. Kennedy installed the tape recorder early in his administration and used it extensively.
- Microsoft did not introduce the first DOS or Windows-type operating environment for computers. Bill Gates and company bought the rights to, borrowed, or emulated systems developed by Apple, IBM, Xerox, and others.

of your revenues, while 20 percent of your customers account for 80 percent of your revenues. Focus your resources on the 20 percent—the folks who will remain with you for the long haul. But don't ignore the 80 percent—the marginal customers who patronize your business on an infrequent basis. Whenever they contact you, handle their calls or correspondence in a highly professional, helpful manner. They may mention your company to other potential customers or eventually become regulars themselves.

Customers Worth Keeping

You want to cultivate a relationship with each of your regular customers because these folks are inclined to continue purchasing your products or services. They're valuable to your business for other reasons as well.

1. Regulars talk about your products or services with other potential customers. Word of mouth is generally the most effective form of advertising.
2. Regulars actually help you run a more profitable operation. They make key suggestions and offer valuable input and advice that you're not likely to get from infrequent customers.
3. Regulars are more receptive to your recommendations about other products and services. One of the reasons they may keep buying from you is that they see you as a creditable source of information and a trusted representative of the products and services in your industry.
4. Regulars can serve as sources of valuable market research. As their needs and interests shift, so may the needs and interests of less frequent customers.
5. Regulars are more likely to honor their debts. So your incidence of bad checks and delinquent payments will remain low, especially if you're unable to accept credit cards.
6. Regulars tend to order faster and with greater ease than first-timers. The net result for you is more sales per customer with less time and effort.
7. Doing business with regulars is easier and more rewarding than doing business with total strangers.

writing a letter or making a phone call will keep you in your customers' good graces.

Be discerning with data

With the widespread use of contact management software and database marketing, staying in touch with customers is relatively easy. Yet many businesses have allowed technology to overly complicate their marketing and customer service functions. In an attempt to broaden their customer bases, these companies shortchange their ability to stay in touch. Use your database as a tool for indicating who needs to hear from you, not as a dense depository of names with no meaning attached to them.

Take all comers

If you've read chapter 18, you may recall the 80/20 rule: 80 percent of your customers account for 20 percent

Making Your Presents Known

Many people equate gifts with appreciation. You can use gift giving to develop and affirm relationships with your customers without spending a fortune. Here's how.

Shower the spouses

Want to do something simple that will make you stand out in the customer's mind? Give a gift to the customer's spouse. This will get the two of them talking about you, and they'll remember you. Another option: Give gifts to the customer's children. For this to work, of course, you need to know whether a person is married or has kids. This is when a customer database comes in handy.

Let the customer choose

Send your customers a brief letter with a list of gifts that you're offering. Ask each customer to check off the gift that she would like to receive. This approach has several advantages: it ensures that the customer gets what she wants, it builds anticipation, and it makes your company stand out.

Double the goodies

Instead of giving the customer a choice, simply send her two gifts. You can spend the same amount on two items that you would have on one. And one of the items can clearly be of greater value than the other so the customer feels that he's truly being rewarded. Again, this strategy will make you memorable, as it's used by so few companies.

Send them somewhere

Give a gift certificate for a getaway—anything from dinner and a movie to a weekend stay at a resort. Treating a customer to fun and relaxation will definitely score a few points for your business.

Play the connection card

Think of a clever gift that a customer can get only from you. A former Capitol Hill staffer bought folders with notepads from the congressional supply store at the standard price of $5 each. The folders looked good, but what made them so appealing to the people who received them is that they had the official seal of the U.S. Senate. No place else in United States—or in the world—can anyone buy such a folder.

Monogram it

Have a customer's name inscribed on inexpensive items such as pens, pencils, or notecards. Most people appreciate seeing their names on items, especially when they don't have to pay for them.

Give him a head start

Offer a gift that the customer can add on to. For instance, start him off with one item in a set or series, then give him the opportunity to buy the rest. Encyclopedia publishers practice a variation of this by selling volume A at a bargain price.

Provide the paperwork

If your gift is a durable good, leave it in its original box with the warranty. You may even include the invoice and sales slip. This is no negative reflection on you. Even if the customer returns your gift for cash or for another item, you still get credit for offering the gift in the first place and for accepting the exchange.

Create your own reason

You can give gifts anytime you want—holiday or not. You can even choose your own special occasion, such as your company's anniversary, to reward your customers.

Always reevaluate

Like anything else, gift giving costs money. Once you start it, you need to periodically ask yourself, "Is this a simple but effective way for me, my department, or my company to stay at the forefront in the minds of those I wish to serve?"

How Complex Can It Get?

A New Word Record: Short messages have far greater impact than long ones. Abraham Lincoln delivered his Gettysburg Address in a few minutes, yet it remains permanently etched in American history. Here's how it compares with other less monumental documents in terms of the number of words they contain.

Gettysburg Address	272
Bag of Lay's potato chips	401
Box of California dates	676
Typical box of cereal	900
Federal purchasing guidelines	1,000+ for common items
Airline tickets	1,200+

Catering to Your Customers

Always look for ways to make life easier for your customers. In the long run, this will help you tailor your business to meet their needs and ensure that you turn a profit.

Consider the experience of Dave Yoho, a motivational speaker and management consultant in Fairfax, Virginia. In his early days, Yoho ran a roofing business with 22 branch offices. At the time, light-colored shingles were becoming popular. Yoho wondered how this trend would affect his inventory. With so many other colors available, stocking two or three dozen shades of shingle would prove costly—especially for 22 branch offices.

So Yoho devised a plan that would have one shade of shingle accounting for 90 percent of all his business. "Dawn grey blend" included speckles of green, yellow, red, and several browns. The blend coordinated well with an array of colors. And it made dirt on the roof less visible.

As Yoho's staff became more effective at selling dawn grey blend, they made it the only color that they would show to prospective customers. Yoho trained his people to say, "When looking at your house, I think this color would work well." Most people simply didn't have a preference.

Eventually, Yoho's business grew quite large. The simple one-color approach saved customers money because Yoho purchased the shingles in great quantity. He has often said that his business could not have grown at the same pace if he had maintained a substantial roofing inventory. Yoho kept things simple for himself, his staff, and his customers. As a result, he prospered. You can do the same.

Courting with Correspondence

In lieu of a gift, a personal note from you to your customer is a simple but effective marketing tool. You can maximize its impact by following these guidelines.

Be brief

To your customer, a short note means just as much as a long one. You may even want to purchase stationery specifically for simple notes. Your local office supply store or print shop probably sells inexpensive 4½- by 5½-inch sheets, folded once. With this size note, you have room for only two or three sentences, which is all you need to say anyway.

Share the spirit of the season

If someone is a good customer, you want your card to be displayed on her mantle during the holidays. People tend to remember whom they receive cards from. Some like to count the number of cards they receive.

Since other companies also send holiday cards, you want to make your card original so it stands out from the others. Send it earlier, or make it larger, more colorful, or more elaborate. As an alternative, send a Thanksgiving card. Only a fraction of the folks who receive Christmas cards ever receive Thanksgiving cards.

> ### Simply Stated
>
> *If I had my past life over again, I'd make all the same mistakes—only sooner.*
>
> **—Tallulah Bankhead, American actress**

Off-load the responsibility

If you don't have time to send handwritten notes or personally signed cards to your customers, there's no harm in assigning the task to someone else on your staff. Your customers aren't collecting signatures, nor are they saving your correspondence for any reason. What matters to them is that you took the time to send it. You may be the only manager or owner that a person has heard from in the past month or year—or in his lifetime as a consumer.

> ### Simply Stated
>
> *Forget mistakes. Forget failures. Forget everything except what you're going to do now and do it. Today is your lucky day.*
>
> **—Alfred Sloan, American industrialist and founder of General Motors**

Goodwill Bodes Well

While gifts and notes may score points from a marketing perspective, they can't replace good old-fashioned customer service. Taking care of people is what keeps them coming back to your business.

You've worked hard to establish your position in the marketplace. You've built a strong customer or client base. Now you want to make sure that you deliver on the promise of your marketing.

Serving after the Sale

One of the reasons that so many people shop at Nordstrom despite the department store's sometimes higher prices is the outstanding customer service. Most folks would rather pay a little more for a product or service if they know that it is of high quality, will last longer, will cause fewer problems, and will be easily corrected or replaced when a problem does arise. In their minds, less hassle is worth a higher price.

To show your commitment to customer service, incorporate the following measures into your company's standard operating procedure.

The Story on Storytelling

You may regard the storytelling sales technique as manipulative or unfair. Yet the salespeople who use it are doing nothing more than creating an environment in which the customer feels safe and responsive. By visualizing what a product or service can do for him rather than listening to a rundown of its specifications, the customer can identify with it in a pleasurable, compelling way. In essence, storytelling reduces complexity, giving the customer a simple but potentially clear understanding of how a product or service can benefit him.

Handle customers with consistency

Every employee should represent the company just as well as the employee who makes the original sale.

Customers want confirmation that they've made a sound decision in buying from your company. Likewise, they appreciate knowing that you care about them as much after the sale as you did before.

Speak with an unforked tongue

An old maxim in the consulting profession advises, "Only promise what you can deliver, and always deliver more than you promise." Your sales staff and staff assistants need to regard what they tell customers as though it were written in stone. If you want customers to think of your company in a positive light, make sure that you meet your stated shipping and delivery dates, immediately respond to requests for information, and otherwise conduct business in a manner that demonstrates that your word is your bond.

Anticipate the customer's needs

What is the life cycle of the product you sell or the service you render? In other words, after a customer buys one item, what else will she require for her continued satisfaction? What additional products or services will enhance the value of her original purchases? How soon will she need to replace her purchase with new merchandise, or how often will she have to replenish her supply of your product? What follow-up information and maintenance suggestions or instructions will she appreciate receiving? You can track these activities with contact management software.

Simply Stated

Giving presents is a talent; to know what a person wants, to know when and how to get it, to give it lovingly and well.

**—Pamela Glenconner,
British author, in Edward
Wyndhan Tennant: A Memoir**

Covering the Costs

For you, the most important aspect of running a business is getting paid. That's why you want to make paying as easy as possible for your customers. In return, you'll simplify your company's operations tremendously if you can avoid having to engage in bill collection.

To allow your customers flexibility while preventing bad debt, heed this advice.

Take credit

Have you ever considered how often you can use a major credit card for nonretail purchases? Plastic is now

accepted for everything from a pledge during a fund drive on public television to tuition for an adult education course at a local college or university. These organizations have realized that immediate payment with a credit card has its advantages. Perhaps most important, they're protecting themselves against late payment and nonpayment.

Unfortunately, many businesses become mired in the mess of bill collection. Some even have to close up because of it. The time and money spent trying to collect payments is bad enough. Some payments may be consistently late or altogether uncollectible, making matters worse. You can steer clear of all these complications simply by accepting major credit cards.

Pick up the points

Credit card companies collect interest—usually about 3 percent, or $3 on every $100 in purchases—from merchants that accept their cards. Pay these few percentage points so that customers can charge products or services. You'll simplify your business dealings—and your life— enormously.

Call in the pros

If a customer owes you a bundle of money, get help from an agency specializing in collection. Any businessperson who has attempted to collect payment himself can tell you that it's a difficult, time-consuming endeavor best left in the hands of a professional. In fact, bad debts have become a large enough problem to merit their own industry.

To find a collection agency, start by looking in the Yellow Pages. Consider independent operations as well as accountants and lawyers who specialize in collection and related litigation.

Consulting Your Customers

Dale Carnegie, traveling salesman turned public speaker and educator, first proposed this concept some 70 years ago: One of the simplest and most effective ways of getting people to notice and remember you—if not like you—is to ask them to do you a favor. The request naturally gets a customer's attention and plants your company's name in the customer's mind.

If you ask for feedback, you convey the message that you value the person's opinion. If you ask for a few moments of her time, you value her participation. Here are several effective ways to solicit favors from your customers.

Poll them in person

On-site and on the spot, ask customers about their preferences regarding product packaging, shelf arrangements, store displays, and so forth. Or ask for their input in addressing a particular business dilemma that you're facing. Maybe a product isn't selling and you'd like your customers to tell you what would make it more appealing.

Get them involved

Ask customers to participate in a brief demonstration or experiment. If you can cover the cost, offer a $5 gift certificate or an item of equal value as an incentive to

Purchase Plus

What else could you offer to your customers—without spending a fortune—that would enable you to stay connected with them? Here are some possibilities.
- 60-, 90-, and 120-day maintenance reminders
- Follow-up instructions
- Extra set of instructions
- Upgrades and enhancements
- New supporting products
- New supporting services
- Newsletter explaining how other customers use the product or service
- Three-month follow-up survey
- Personal letter from the chief executive officer

Any of the above items makes for an excellent reason to stay in touch with customers. This serves a twofold purpose: to truly serve them, and to remain prominent in their minds.

volunteers. (Truth be told, though, an incentive isn't usually necessary—people enjoy participating.)

Ask for their opinions

Make a comment box and put it in your place of business where people can access it. Create a sign for it that says, "Please do us a favor—give us your suggestions." Or write a brief, three- to five-question survey to quickly capture your customers' input. Set up a table where they can sit to complete the survey, and offer a free gift for participating.

The Simplest of the Simple

Customer service can make or break a business. Fortunately, you don't have to break your back—or your budget—to do it right. Simply follow the basic guidelines gleaned from this chapter.

- Keep your sales pitch as well as any other communication with customers short and to the point.

- Sell your product or service by presenting it in the context of a story. This creates a powerful image in the customer's mind.
- Instead of spending significant time and money trying to acquire new customers, focus on keeping the customers you already have.
- Analyze your sales to determine who your key customers are and then specifically target them.
- Stay in touch with each customer, even after making a sale.
- Send gifts, thank-you notes, or personalized e-mail messages.
- Always look for ways to make your customers' lives easier.
- Give your customers the option of using credit cards to purchase products or services, thus making payment easier for them and collection easier for you.
- Make your customers feel appreciated and needed by asking for their help and input through suggestion boxes, surveys, or personal communication.

PART FIVE   **The Personal Touch**

Chapter 21

Rewarding Relationships

*Get More out of Your Limited Time
with Lovers, Friends, and Family*

Simplifying your relationships doesn't mean they're going to become superficial or unrewarding. Relationships filled with angst, distrust, and poor communication complicate your life. On the other hand, relationships based on caring and honest communication are easier on your mind and much more rewarding. Let's focus on ways to maintain the quality of your relationships with less effort.

Friends, Dates, and Keeping Your Mate

When an instructor at Duke University in Durham, North Carolina, polled one of his classes, he found that most people—even the most good-looking and popular in the class—hadn't had a date within months. Without an abundance of free time, most people end up saying, "I'll meet you at Kristen's party," "I'll see you at the game," or "Let's meet at the library at 8:30."

Courting, it seems, is in peril. It's not that people don't care about getting to know one another or having a relationship unfold and finding their way toward marital bliss. Time being a commodity, many people would rather have a significant jump on the mating process by matching up with someone via computer, an ad, or a matchmaking service. From there, if things click, people hope everything else will fall into place.

If even college students don't have time for courting, how could older adults with jobs or children ever hope to have the time to keep their relationships vibrant? Here's the trap for the unwary: If you're in too much of a hurry to find time to court your mate, you are probably in too much of a hurry to do what it takes to stay happily married.

Keep Up the Chatter

A crucial component of a successful relationship is open and free-flowing communication. Here are some easy ways to keep the communication lines open.

Say you're sorry—in writing

On a single piece of paper, write down all the times you wished you had told your mate "I'm sorry." Have your mate do the same, then exchange lists. Remember the old saying "To err is human, to forgive divine." The longer the list of apologies, the greater your potential to receive forgiveness.

Declare your intentions

Write out your goals for your career, family, and other important matters, and have your mate do the same. Then exchange sheets. If you are comfortable

supporting one another on most of what each has written, your relationship is really cooking.

Play the match game

Make a list of goals specifically for your relationship. Ideally, your list and your mate's list will match up well here. If they don't, that's not necessarily a cause for alarm. Perhaps you'd be willing to add some of your partner's ideas to your list. And perhaps your partner will adopt some of your ideas as well.

The more items that make both of your lists, the more potential you have for a solid future together.

Get in sync

Start going to bed and getting up at the same time that your mate does. It may take a few days to adjust to this, but you'll soon be able to work it out.

Discover the Joy of Togetherness

When was the last time you felt supremely happy being with the mate you once tried so hard to woo? Here are some ideas for pumping life back into your relationship. These ideas are easily accomplished, so they should fit into even the most hectic schedule.

Give a caring caress

Scientists now think that people have a specific pathway of nerves that sends pleasure signals to the brain when the skin is gently stroked. Apparently, the pathway helps infants distinguish comfort from discomfort. It's been known for a while that human beings have separate nerve networks for detecting pain, temperature, and contact. Touch means much—have you hugged your partner today?

Trade weekends

One weekend, do all of the activities your spouse wants to do, and on the next weekend reverse it. Or spend one day of the weekend doing everything that your spouse wants, and give yourself the other day to do everything that you want. Attend to your spouse's every desire without crabbing or cutting corners. This extra attention will help you both to feel renewed and in control.

Name that tune

Record yourselves singing a few of your mutually favorite tunes. If one of you can't sing, then hum. If this sounds silly to you, then you'd better try it.

Lengthen your lovemaking

The next time you're together, spend an hour or more building up to you-know-what. Give yourselves the gift of peace and serenity with no thought about the clock. If you only do this once a month, it will still be a boost to your relationship.

Vary your routine

Whatever you do, keep it vibrant. Snuggle together under a blanket while watching a movie. Go buy something together that you've long discussed but have not yet splurged on. Disclose three secrets each. Play one-on-one basketball and let the shorter person get the ball after every basket made by either of you. Rediscover your photo album and reflect on all your most memorable times.

Find happiness in small things

One man described his idea of perfect happiness as sitting on the porch with his wife and watching the river flow by them. Quiet, simple moments like these can help you relax and enjoy the company of your loved one. What small things about your relationship can you find that make you happy?

In Search of Sane Parenthood

One fine day, a little tyke arrives, and then perhaps another. Your relationship with your children goes through many phases.

Moms, feel comforted. Are you a parent of small children? Don't attempt to do everything you want to do; only do what is possible to do. One woman sought to be the perfect wife, business owner, and mom at the same time. She ignored advice to sleep when her baby slept. She did chores instead, and during a late-night feeding, fatigue almost caused her to drop her baby. The baby doesn't care if the house is a mess, so take care of her and yourself, and handle the rest after you get rest.

Dads, take heart. If you're seeking advice on parenting, you're not alone. Men today are assuming more active roles in child rearing, but they are often left out of the postnatal information sessions that mothers receive. Now there are newsletters, online chat sessions and even an at-home dads convention to help dads swap advice and get support.

Stimulate Those Young Minds

Some experts regard boredom as an epidemic among children today, and they hold television, videos, and computer games responsible. These activities bombard children with fast-moving stimuli, but they do not give them the chance to slow down, reflect thoughtfully, or process new information. The antidote: reduce the amount of time that your kids spend on passive TV and noninteractive electronic games. Gee, have you heard that advice before?

Get theatrical

Show your children that there is life beyond television. Make puppets out of old socks and help your kids put on a show. Or make up a play-acting game based on one of your children's favorite books.

Strike up the band

Encourage your child's musical talents by making a flute from a paper tube (punch holes about an inch apart and cover the end with waxed paper). Or make a banjo from an old shoe box (cut a hole in the front and stretch five rubber bands across it lengthwise). Cover your ears and let him play. Better still, make your own and join in.

Simply Stated

Children have never been very good at listening to their elders, but they have never failed to imitate them.
—**James Baldwin, American author**

Challenge Your Children with Chores

Assigning household chores to your child has a couple of advantages. One, it helps to ease your workload. Two, it teaches your child responsibility.

Choosing the right chores is crucial. Of course, you want to challenge your child so she doesn't become bored. But if you give her a task that is confusing or too difficult for her age or her level of development, she'll lose confidence. Hence, you risk doing more harm than good. Also, avoid giving your small child a chore, such as ironing or possibly even vacuuming, that puts her in a potentially dangerous environment.

Sort the clothes

Your young child can help sort the colored and white clothes before washing. This is a good learning experience for your child. He can call out the colors while putting them in separate piles. After he sorts the clothes, look through the piles to see if some items need to be washed separately and to make sure everything is in the correct pile. After the laundry is done, let your child help to remove clothes from the dryer. (Make sure the machine has cooled first.) By helping with these laundry tasks, your child will learn that the house doesn't run by magic.

Tear up the food

Tearing lettuce for salads is an easy and fun task for kids. Show your child how to tear appropriate-size pieces and let her take as long as she needs to do this. (Remember, her coordination may not be as good as yours.) To save time, prepare other parts of the meal while your child is helping out. Later, enlist her help making simple meals or desserts and let her cut out cookies with the cookie cutter.

Do lunch

Let your child make his own sandwich for school or for a weekend lunch. He can fix it however he wants it (even with triple mustard and ketchup) and will better appreciate the effort when you prepare food for the family.

Try dish duty

Once your child is old enough to carry dishes or cups without dropping them, have her clear her spot at the table after every meal. Make sure you use dishes or cups that are unbreakable. Also, she can help clear plastic condiment bottles or other unbreakable items off the table. After everything has been cleared, she can wipe off her area at the table.

Turn over creative control

Make events like birthday parties less stressful for you and more fun for the kids by giving them a creative free rein. Buy a plain paper tablecloth and white paper plates and cups—which are cheaper than the decorated variety—and give each child a nontoxic felt-tip pen to decorate them with.

Alternatively, create an autograph tablecloth. Let each child sign and decorate his own space. You can reuse this each year, adding more and more friends.

Older Kids: Balancing Limits and Liberty

If you're having a trying time with your teenager, don't despair. Here are some tips for soothing the tension.

Stand your ground

Be tough. Stand your ground and show your kid where the limits are. Earn his respect before you allow discussions and compromises.

Drop back and punt

Sometimes it's important to keep your distance. Are you genuinely concerned over a particular issue, or are you micromanaging your child's affairs? Sometimes parents find fault with their children for behaviors they as parents dislike about themselves.

Let dreamers dream

Your child has her own life, with goals and aspirations you may not be able to comprehend—or if you do comprehend them, you may not value them. At the least, let your children be the unique individuals that they are, even though there will be a continuing need for parental guidance.

Celebrate Life Together

Be the family that plays together. Plan vacations or other group outings as a unit, letting even the youngest member contribute his ideas. By weaving traditions around work and play, the whole family will feel supported by each other and eager to participate.

Turn it into a tradition

Make chores as fun as holidays by developing traditions. Family members will gain a sense of belonging and comfort from activities that contribute to the greater good of the whole household. Set one meal aside each week to be the official family dinner, for instance, or take turns cooking for each other.

Treat some days like holidays

Don't wait for special days to find an excuse to spend time with your family. Young children, in particular, are always excited to have time alone with you. Think of special projects that you and your kids can work on together. For example, go on a nature walk to collect pinecones, then bring them home to paint them.

Store your memories

Keeping those special family moments stored in your head is no guarantee that they'll stay there. There are many ways to preserve memories that will last for more than just your lifetime. Videotape important occasions and give them as gifts to family members. Start scrapbooks and family albums to showcase photos, ticket stubs, theater programs, and the wonderful artwork your second grader brings home. Encourage everyone to keep a journal and tell family stories to pass on through the generations. Children love to feel part of the tradition, and later in life they will enjoy showing these keepsakes to their own families.

Let yourself laugh

Appreciate the humor and humility children can bring to your life. Your five-year-old's high-decibel belch at the supermarket checkout may seem the like end of your good reputation as well as your ability to ever appear in public again. However, nearly every parent within earshot is likely to understand. It's part of raising children. Savor the moment, even as you cringe.

Create a family mission statement

As your children grow older, involve them in what your family is all about. Gather up the whole crew. Ask all family members to write down what they believe is important to them and what represents the mission of the family. No one has to write a masterpiece—a short expression that inspires everyone to make a commitment to work and play together will do. Compare and consolidate the statements until you get a cohesive statement that everyone can support. Putting these important beliefs into words will reinforce their meaning and make the ideas visible and understandable to the whole family.

Facing the Critics

As a parent, a spouse, a worker, or in any other role that exposes you to other people, now and then, someone will negatively assess something you've done. This is human nature. Your ability to maintain viable relationships will depend on your ability to handle this criticism.

Keep Your Cool under Fire

Here are some strategies and specific language you can use when confronted by criticism, particularly unfair criticism.

Confess that you're an easy target

Television correspondent Barbara Walters knows how to handle criticism. In 1976, Walters became the first woman to anchor a major network's nightly news show when she joined Harry Reasoner as co-host of *ABC News*. The show earned consistently poor ratings, however. Eventually, Walters moved on to another assignment for the network, and she is still with ABC today.

Walters was asked in an interview why the ratings for her show had been so low and why the higher-ups at ABC were unhappy with her performance. Walters looked directly at her interviewer and said in a soft but commanding voice, "I guess I'm a pretty easy target these days." The response so disarmed the interviewer that, if he had intended to ask any other tough questions, he apparently let them slide.

Listen when it hurts

The next time you're criticized and you think that it's unfair criticism, listen carefully for any shreds of wisdom that may be helpful to you. Even the most vitriolic attacks may contain some insight worth mining.

However personal the attack may be, try not to *take* it personally. Try to remember that it's based on something you've done or behavior you've exhibited, and not on you as a person.

Acknowledge the source

Nearly all criticism is subjective. Someone who says you did a crummy job is voicing his opinion. Some aspects of the job you did might have been quite well done. Someone else may think that you did the whole job correctly. However, recognize that there are times, to be sure, when you've done a crummy job. If you can, let the other person finish. The temptation is to try to cut them off, but that only fans the flames.

Respond graciously

When a person is finished criticizing you, try to respond graciously. If you can't say something that's reasonably pleasant, at least say something that's not derogatory or belligerent. For example: "I'll give those thoughts the consideration they deserve," "Thank you for sharing," "I have received your message," "You're certainly entitled to your viewpoint," or "I promise you I've heard every word." Whatever you do, resist the temptation to make some sarcastic or sly remark back. Act as if the person criticizing you is making an honest attempt to give you constructive information.

Receive it like a champ

Look for the good in whatever criticism another person gives. Avoid attempting to listen between the lines—that is, to add meaning or implications where none were intended. Even if it's difficult for you to take, nod your head on occasion, maintain at least occasional eye contact, and give the other party some respect. If you have to, ask questions or seek added information. Maybe it's not as bad as it first sounded. Maybe the other person has some ideas or recommendations that will readily improve the situation.

State your intentions, sir

If you intend to act on anything that you've heard, let the other person know. If the other party is in a position to help you, ask for help. After all, if he understands the situation so astutely, he may be resourceful enough to lend a hand.

The Optimist Creed

The volunteer organization Optimist International believes that the world's future lies in the hands of its youth. To that end, Optimists sponsor service programs that touch the lives of more than six million young people each year. The organization's philosophy and mission are embodied in *The Optimist Creed*, presented below. We'd all do well to abide by these simple words of wisdom.

Promise yourself to:

1. Be so strong that nothing can disturb your peace of mind.
2. Talk health, happiness, and prosperity to every person you meet.
3. Make all your friends feel that there is something in them.
4. Look at the sunny side of everything and make your optimism come true.
5. Think only of the best, to work only for the best, and to expect only the best.
6. Be just as enthusiastic about the successes of others as you are about your own.
7. Forget the mistakes of the past and press on to the greater achievements of the future.
8. Wear a cheerful countenance at all times and give every living creature you meet a smile.
9. Give so much time to the improvement of yourself that you have no time to criticize others.
10. Be too large for worry, too noble for anger, too strong for fear, and too happy to permit the presence of trouble.

Don't play one-upmanship

Unless you have compelling information, don't attempt to play point-counterpoint with someone who is criticizing you. If you need to rebut some of what's said, pick the most important or compelling issue and stay with that. Do not respond with your own list of criticisms of the other person. Your criticisms will be irrelevant and unproductive. Also, don't shuffle your feet, fidget, turn away, or act as though you can't wait for this person to stop—even though that's how you really feel.

For That Rare Time When You're Wrong

Sometime, somewhere in the course of human events, you're going to face criticism that is just plain accurate. In that case, be the big person that you are.

Let the buck stop here

Take personal responsibility for whatever ensued. Say, "I accept responsibility for this situation, the ball is in my court, and I'll handle it."

Express regret

It isn't necessary for you to be sorry or apologetic. It is appropriate for you to regret whatever happened. This isn't skirting the issue; it's using the most appropriate language for the situation. For example, if someone ends up having to handle something because you were late, do you sincerely feel sorry about it, or do you simply regret it? Chances are you regret what happened. Save feeling sorry for when someone's grandmother passes away.

Accentuate the positive

State what you will do. Say, "To remedy this situation, I intend to do X, Y, and Z." Or, "Okay, good point. The next time this comes up, I'm going to do A, B, and C." You'll be amazed how this can smooth otherwise ruffled relations.

The Simplest of the Simple

If you do nothing else, these simple ideas will help a great deal when it comes to relationships.

- Devise common goals. Whether with your spouse or your whole family, establishing goals in your relationships will make them stronger.
- Work to keep your relationships vibrant. Do something out of the ordinary tonight. Don't be afraid to have fun.
- Let your child help around the house by finding safe, easy chores for him.
- Create lifelong memories. Take pictures, make videos, and keep scrapbooks.
- Be firm but understanding with your children. Don't hesitate to guide and teach them, but don't forget that your children are unique individuals.
- Listen carefully to criticism because there may be something worth hearing and learning.
- Don't rebut criticism.

Chapter 22	# Nutrition Know-How

Taking the Guesswork Out of Eating Right

So much has been written and rewritten about nutrition that anyone who wants to eat healthfully hardly knows where to turn. Almost every month, it seems, one group of researchers announces a breakthrough finding, only to have it refuted by another group of researchers. The situation is reminiscent of a scene in the 1973 movie *Sleeper* in which Woody Allen, awakening far in the future, learns that a hot-fudge sundae with nuts and whipped cream has been determined to be good for you. We should be so lucky.

This chapter sifts through the contradictions and controversy to present the fundamentals of good nutrition. You'll learn how to shape healthful eating habits by making smart food choices, monitoring portion sizes, challenging cravings, and—perhaps most important—listening to your body. These are tried-and-true dietary strategies that you can count on this year, next year, and for the rest of your life. They provide the simplest and most direct route to optimum health.

First, the Fundamentals

When life gets too complicated, turn back to the basics. So it is with nutrition. Despite all the new and often conflicting information about what we should and shouldn't eat, certain principles have remained relatively unchanged for years. These provide the driving force behind a healthy diet.

Good News on Dos

Feeding your body properly doesn't have to be complicated. Adhere to these key concepts, and you can't go wrong.

Fall for the pyramid scheme

The traditional Food Guide Pyramid that graces many a food label has become the standard for healthful eating. In a nutshell, the pyramid suggests that you get most of your daily calories from grains (including breads, cereals, and pasta), fruits, and vegetables. Relegate proteins—meats, fish, poultry, eggs, and dairy products—to secondary, side-dish status. And consume fats and sweets sparingly, if at all. By eating this way, you give your body the proper mix of nutrients to function efficiently.

Fill up on fiber

A diet high in fiber, an indigestible substance found in grains, fruits, and legumes, can decrease your risk of cancer, especially cancer of the colon. Researchers believe that the people of Sweden have very low cancer rates despite their high-fat diet because they consume a lot of high-fiber rye bread. Aim for a fiber intake of 25 grams per day.

Favor water

Make water your beverage of choice. It contains no calories, it rehydrates your body, and it satisfies your thirst. Amazingly, in any given week, the typical American consumes a larger volume of soft drinks than water. Soft drinks are heavily laden with sugar, sodium, preservatives, and a whole slew of stuff that your body really has no use for.

Learn from labels

Food labels reveal a wealth of nutrition information. Reading them is essential to making smart food choices. In particular, you can use labels to track the number of calories and fat grams that you consume each day. You can also use them to gauge serving sizes. For instance, if just 20 potato chips supplies 150 calories and 10 grams of fat, you know enough not to eat the whole bag. In fact, you'd be better off choosing another, more nutritious snack.

The Lowdown on Don'ts

As you read food labels, keep the following guidelines in mind. They'll help you steer clear of foods that have no place in a healthy diet.

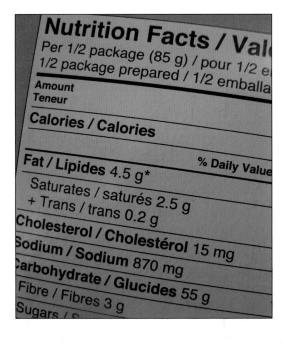

Dispense with dietary fat

The average American gets 34 percent of his daily calories from fat. Scientists have directly linked a high fat intake to an increased risk of cancer. In fact, for every 10 percent of calories from fat, the risk of cancer rises four to eightfold.

To reduce your fat intake, begin by cutting back on meats, whole milk products, and palm kernel oils. These foods contain primarily saturated fat, which weakens the immune system and helps tumors flourish. Stick with monounsaturated and polyunsaturated fats as much as possible. Sources include canola oil, flaxseed oil, and olive oil as well as cod and salmon.

Subtract the additives

Perusing the ingredients lists on food labels at times seems like reading a foreign language. Invariably, you'll come across unfamiliar, unpronounceable words such as "dipotassium phosphate" and "sodium stearoyl lactylate."

While the Food and Drug Administration has deemed such substances safe, they can cause side effects. For instance, some dyes, including Yellow #5, have been known to trigger allergic reactions, with symptoms such as hives, a runny nose, and shortness of breath. Other dyes, including Red #3, produce cancer in laboratory animals. Red #3 has been banned in cosmetics but not in all foods.

Your best bet is to eat a variety of foods to prevent prolonged exposure to potentially harmful additives, advises Barbara Deskins, PhD, professor of clinical dietetics and nutrition at the University of Pittsburgh. A varied diet also ensures that your body is getting the full range of essential nutrients.

Debate decadence

Thick steaks, premium ice creams, fancy mixed drinks, and other upscale foods can tip the nutrition scale against you if you consume them often enough. Still, they're experiencing a surge in popularity, with some of their manufacturers enjoying unprecedented growth.

Certainly, you're entitled to indulge. The trick is to do so in moderation. Allow yourself one bowl of premium ice cream each week or one mixed drink every other Saturday night. You decide what and when. Ignore the ads in magazines, on television, and on billboards that portray these foods as acceptable every day.

The Art of Eating

Now that you know what to eat, let's examine when, where, and how. All of these factors combine to create a sensible, satisfying dining experience.

A Relaxing Repast

From the moment you mastered the use of a knife and fork, your parents reminded you to eat slowly and to chew your food well rather than gulping it down. These are sound principles, and they still make sense now that you're grown up. Resist the urge to eat for speed. You're entitled to take time to enjoy a nourishing, satisfying meal. Also, adopt the following dietary habits.

For breakfast, take a seat to eat

Far too many folks eat breakfast behind the wheel on their way to work. Those who stay at home seldom fare much better in terms of where and how fast they devour their morning meals. If you don't have time to sit down at the table and eat breakfast each morning, start going to bed 15 minutes earlier each night. That way, you'll have a few minutes to spare for a decent, pleasurable meal.

For lunch, leave your desk

If you work in an office—even one in your home—make sure to eat your lunch elsewhere. Staying at your desk isn't likely to make you feel as though you've enjoyed your meal. Too many things can distract you. Besides, you don't make any gains, productivity-wise. You're better off taking 30 minutes to go where you can eat in semi-leisure, be it a cafeteria table or a park bench. And pack your lunch when you can, so you're assured of a nutritious meal.

For dinner, eat light and early

More than 200 years ago, Benjamin Franklin suggested that breakfast should be the heaviest meal of the day, followed by a medium-size lunch and a light dinner. And you know, old Ben was onto something: The less you eat in the evening, and the earlier you eat, the more energetic you'll feel the next day.

When you consume a large meal late at night, your body isn't as efficient at digesting and metabolizing the food. You end up feeling sluggish in the morning. Some studies have suggested that if you consistently have dinner after 7 PM, even if you eat the same volume of food every day, you'll gain seven pounds in a year.

On the other hand, if you consistently have dinner before 7 PM, you can actually lose weight. You're fasting for 12 hours, or from dinner until breakfast the next day.

A Day's Worth of Fiber

Here's an easy way to guarantee that you're getting enough fiber in your diet. Just be sure to eat the following every day.

- 2 to 3 cups of whole-grain foods such as breads, brown rice, and high-fiber cereals
- 1½ cups of beans and other legumes
- 4 to 5 cups of fresh vegetables, including leafy greens

This "menu" eliminates the need for counting grams of fiber. Plus, it helps you reach your daily fiber quota of 25 grams.

So for energy, your body has to burn the calories you've already taken in. That means fewer pounds on you.

Be chews-y

At every meal, chew your food slowly and thoroughly. Too many people eat too fast, chewing a bite of food far less than, say, 20 times. As a result, they miss out on the right mix of gastric juices and ground-up food particles, which makes for poor digestion and nutrient absorption.

By chewing each bite slowly and thoroughly, you ensure that the food is properly digested, the nutrients efficiently absorbed, and the waste quickly eliminated. Plus, your meal seems more satisfying.

Watch your speed

How fast you eat a meal significantly influences its net nutritional benefit. For example, if you plow through a plateful of fresh fruits and vegetables, barely taking the time to chew and taxing your digestive system, many of the nutrients literally go to waste. Conversely, if you slowly eat a burger and fries, thoroughly enjoying your meal and savoring every morsel, your body has ample opportunity to draw from these foods whatever nutrients it can. That's not to say eating fatty fare on a regular basis is okay. The point is to eat healthful foods—and eat them slowly.

Water Wise

How good is your tap water? The taste of it is usually a fairly good indicator. For a more official quality analysis, expect to shell out some bucks.

If your water comes from a well, annual analysis is recommended. A basic test for nitrates and bacteria is inexpensive. To find someone to administer the test, look on the Web or in the Yellow Pages under "Water Analysis."

Municipal water supplies usually must be screened regularly for 71 major contaminants and treated for any problems. You can request the results from your local water department. To interpret them, you'll need a copy of the Environmental Protection Agency's water quality standards. They're available by calling the Safe Drinking Water Hotline at 800-426-4791.

To check water quality on your own, you can start by examining your sinks and bathtubs. If they appear discolored or if the fixtures are pitted, your water may be leaching lead from the pipes. You can check the lead content of your water with a simple home test that's available in hardware stores and drugstores starting at $10. To remove lead, nitrates, and most other contaminants, your best option—short of replacing your pipes—is an under-the-sink reverse-osmosis water filter. This device forces water through a membrane that traps contaminants and sends purified water to a holding tank. The cost of the filter can vary widely, from $300 to more than $1,000.

The Right Dining Environment

Certain other factors can influence the overall healthfulness of your meal. Among them is the environment in which you eat, as these tips illustrate.

Choose earthy hues

According to researchers at Johns Hopkins Medical Institutions in Baltimore, bright colors actually increase your appetite. This is why McDonald's, Wendy's, Burger King, and other fast-food establishments use bright oranges, reds, and yellows in their color schemes. While you can't control their decors, you can choose less vibrant hues—dark greens, blues, and browns—for dishes and tablecloths at home.

Buddy up

Overeating is less likely when you have a companion than when you're alone. The presence of another person changes the dynamic of your meal. You converse a little, eat a little, converse some more, eat some more. On your own, you don't have this pattern to help limit the volume of food you ingest. If you want seconds (or thirds), you can easily help yourself.

Your Restaurant Survival Guide

Dining out presents the nutrition-conscious consumer with more meal options—and more dietary pitfalls. Because someone else controls the food preparation, you don't always know exactly what you're getting on your plate. You may end up taking in more calories and fat than you intended.

How Complex Can It Get

Appealing to the Appetite: Food vendors routinely pay out mind-boggling amounts of money to woo you away from their competition. They compensate for the expense, of course, when they set the prices for their products. In 2008, McDonald's global advertising expenditure topped $2 billion, making it the world's 14th largest advertiser.

Paring Down Portions

Consider the humongous portions served in many restaurants nowadays. While most of us know that dietary fat widens our waistlines and undermines our health, we don't realize that too-large portions of virtually all foods contribute to high calorie intakes and, ultimately, extra pounds.

According to government statistics, the average weight in the United States has increased every year for two decades. Not so coincidentally, as the average weight has increased, so has the typical portion size. From fast-food chains to five-star bistros, bigger plates and bigger bowls reign supreme.

The shift to mega-portions has been driven by several factors. For starters, restaurants compete with each other for patrons, so they serve more food at reasonable prices in an effort to convey high value. Then, too, some restaurants use oversize portions as a marketing gimmick, such as half-price desserts and free meals for kids. And food has simply become more available as technological advances enable farmers to raise more livestock and crops.

In any case, those inch-thick steaks, deep-dish pizzas, big vegetable servings, and hefty slices of pie all add up to gargantuan amounts of food being consumed by diners every day. You can easily stay out of this nutrition trap just by following these restaurant rules.

Take home half

Since restaurants probably won't change their portion policies anytime soon, launch a preemptive strike by telling yourself that you'll eat only half of the entrée that you order. That's probably more than enough for a meal. Set aside what you don't intend to eat, then request a to-go box at the end of the meal. Or, if you think you'll be too tempted to polish off the whole thing, ask your server to wrap up half of the entrée before she even brings it to your table.

Share your fare

If you and a dining companion are in a restaurant known for serving huge portions, suggest that the two of you share an entrée. Request an extra plate, and when the meal arrives, divide it in two. Some folks find that they can't even eat an entire half-portion. They end up taking home the leftovers.

Mix it up

Some restaurants allow you to order à la carte items instead of a complete dinner with appetizer, entrée, side dishes, and so forth. Create your own meal consisting of soup and a salad, or salad and an appetizer, or even two or three side dishes. The choice is yours, based on your appetite, your nutritional objectives, and the portions involved.

Defer dessert

If you can get out of a restaurant without eating dessert, you're way ahead of the game for several reasons. One, your meal costs less. Two, dessert portions tend to be quite large. Three, desserts usually supply hefty doses of fat and sugar. If you simply must have something sweet to round out your meal, choose fresh fruit or another healthful treat.

More Dining-Out Advice

In addition to the above strategies, the following can help guarantee a healthful, hassle-free restaurant experience.

Seek substitutions

Most restaurants will go to great lengths to accommodate patrons just to keep them coming back. Would you prefer a baked potato to french fries? A garden salad to coleslaw? Don't be afraid to ask. More often than not, the answer will be "No problem." And you may not have to pay extra either.

Beat the crowds

If local eateries are at their busiest between, say, 6:30 and 8:30 PM, make your reservations for 5:30 or 6. You get better service because your server and the chef have more time to accommodate you. And you don't feel rushed—in fact, you may get to enjoy a decent conversation with your companion. (Remember, too, that eating dinner early is actually healthier for you.)

If you're concerned about the ambiance at an early hour, relax. Other diners will filter in while you wait for your meal, and by the time you're done eating, the place will be hustling and bustling.

A Weighty Issue

Here's some food for thought: While 53 percent of women and 75 percent of men say that they eat low-calorie or reduced-fat products, 64 percent of the American population is overweight. No, this doesn't mean that we're a nation of compulsive liars. It does mean that a lot of us are confused about food. Unfortunately, our waistlines are widening as a result.

Smart Strategies for Slimming Down

Losing weight does take some effort. But it shouldn't leave you feeling hungry, deprived, or unhappy. A few simple changes in your eating habits can make all the difference when you step on the scale.

Adopt a new attitude

Starving yourself to lose those extra pounds is not only ineffective but also unhealthy. The key to slimming down successfully, researchers say, is changing your mindset. Instead of obsessing about calories and fat grams, focus on eating healthful foods such as grains, fruits, and vegetables. Think not of "dieting" but of taking care of your body. This simple shift in perspective will pare away pounds, slowly but permanently.

Never say never

Losing weight doesn't mean that you have to give up favorite foods because they're high in calories or fat. People who slim down successfully will tell you that they do indulge once in a while. They just wait until a special occasion to treat themselves. Then, boy, is it worthwhile!

Make one change at a time

As you cut back on calorie- and fat-laden foods, remember that you don't have to go cold turkey. Instead, make small, tolerable adjustments in your eating habits.

Consider the story of a Virginia man who wanted to slim down. He came up with the idea of cutting back or cutting out a particular food every three weeks. First he gave up butter, and he lost weight. Next he eliminated meats, and he lost even more weight. He continued this pattern of making a healthy dietary change every three weeks. After just 15 weeks, he lost a total of 35 pounds. That's when he began a new eating plan to maintain his healthy weight.

This weight-loss method works best for people who are moderately overweight but otherwise in reasonably good health. If you have been diagnosed with clinical obesity, you need to be under a doctor's care.

Who Knows Best?

Studies have shown that many consumers rely on their physicians as their primary sources of nutritional information. Yet in one study, researchers surveyed doctors about their nutritional knowledge, and more than half of the respondents incorrectly answered 50 percent of the questions.

These results, say the researchers, reflect the lack of nutrition courses in medical schools. The typical MD receives little instruction in nutrition during his entire education. In fact, doctors are advised to make use of other health professionals whose training in nutrition goes beyond their own.

Obtaining reliable nutritional advice doesn't have to be a hassle. Take advantage of the following resources.

Go to the pros. Nutritional doctors and registered dietitians (RDs) have the expertise to deal with dietary issues. Nutritional doctors may be a bit more difficult to find than RDs. In both cases, you can start your search by calling your local hospital, checking the Web or the Yellow Pages under "Dietitians" and "Physicians and Surgeons," or just asking around. Make sure the person you select has excellent credentials. If you have doubts during your first office visit, seek someone else.

Read it and reap. Any number of magazines and newsletters offer well-researched, well-balanced articles on the subject of nutrition. In fact, they're often written by nutrition experts. Visit www.eatright.org or check out the periodicals section in your local library for detailed information.

Consult the Center. The Center for Science in the Public Interest (CSPI) offers pamphlets on nutrition issues. They also publish a monthly newsletter called the Nutrition Action Healthletter. For more information visit www.CSPinet.org.

Simply Stated

I never met a calorie I didn't like.
—From a refrigerator magnet

Heeding Hunger's Call

When your body needs sustenance, it will let you know. The trick is to tune in to its cues and tune out the false alarms.

Pay attention

Constantly dieting and counting calories and fat grams can impair your natural response to hunger. Recognizing when you are genuinely hungry—and, just as important, when you've eaten enough—can help you maintain healthy eating habits without obsessing about food.

Simply Stated

He who does not mind his belly, will hardly mind anything else.
—Samuel Johnson, English author

To sharpen your awareness of hunger, try this exercise at your next meal. Before you take your first bite, rate your hunger on a scale of zero (not hungry at all) to five (famished). Eat one-quarter of the food on your plate, then rate your hunger. Wait five minutes, then rate your hunger again. As you repeat the sequence, you may discover that you feel satisfied before you even clean your plate.

Take your time

Depending on the situation, putting down your fork when you've eaten enough can be hard to do. This is especially true when you're at a social function where food facilitates your interaction with others. The problem is that your brain takes a while to catch up with your stomach. Up to 20 minutes can pass between the time you swallow a bite of food and the time your stomach says, "I'm full." By then, of course, you may have already polished off a second helping and be on your way to a third.

The solution is to eat slowly and listen to your body. When you begin to feel full, put down your fork. If you feel full but not satisfied, chances are you've eaten too many of the wrong foods or an unbalanced meal. Of course, you can't correct the problem by going back and eating the right foods. Instead, simply push yourself from the table—and next time, be more wary of your food choices from the beginning.

Up in Smoke

By now, most everyone knows about the health hazards of smoking. As reported by David Frost in The World's Worst Decisions, one unfortunate gentleman learned the hard way.

In August 1981, Frederick Burness was admitted to Colindale Hospital in London after being diagnosed with acute bronchitis. As part of his treatment, he was placed in an oxygen tent.

Shortly after settling in, Burness got the urge to smoke. He reached for a pack of cigarettes and a lighter, despite repeated warnings not to light up. What happened next is illuminating. In Frost's words, "The oxygen tent and Mr. Burness exploded together."

The lesson to be learned, of course, is that giving up smoking makes life a lot easier. Longer, too.

Set your own lunch hour

Just because it's noon doesn't mean that you have to eat. By all means take a break, especially if it is the midpoint of your workday. But wait until you're truly hungry to have lunch.

Mend your mood without food

Emotions sometimes masquerade as hunger. Stress or loneliness, for example, may persuade you to turn to food for comfort. If you find yourself snacking to soothe inner turmoil, stop. Try to identify what's driving this false hunger. Whatever the underlying problem, food isn't the solution.

Quelling a Craving

A craving is an irresistible urge to eat a particular food. It wouldn't be so bad, except for the fact that it usually involves something fatty, salty, or sweet. Here's how to ride the craving wave.

Lead yourself not into temptation

The sight or smell of food—when you pass by the cinnamon bun stand at the mall, for example—may trigger a craving. That doesn't necessarily mean you need sustenance. So resist the urge to indulge. Just continue walking until you're out of range of the goodies. Within a few moments, any craving should subside.

Nibble a little

If you simply must have chocolate, or ice cream, or some other sweet, go right ahead—but limit the portion. Even Dean Ornish, MD, one of the country's leading heart experts and a proponent of low-fat eating, suggests having a little of whatever you want. Dr. Ornish allows himself a bite-size serving of a treat two or three times a week. He finds that this small portion satisfies his craving and creates a lingering positive association with the food.

Heed chocolate's call

If you'd describe yourself as a chocoholic, you're in luck. These days, supermarkets carry an array of chocolate treats that are low in fat and taste good, too. Snackwell's low-fat chocolate brownies and cookies contain only a few grams of fat per serving but retain the rich, fudgy qualities of the real thing. Nonfat or low-fat chocolate ice creams and sorbets are also popular alternatives.

Studies suggest that folks—primarily women—crave chocolate because it triggers the release of endorphins, "feel-good" brain chemicals that boost mood. So when you find yourself reaching for a candy bar or another chocolate treat, ask yourself whether you're stressed or blue. If so, try taking a walk, watching a favorite movie, or calling a friend. These can make you feel just as good as chowing down on chocolate.

Food and Your Body

The whole purpose of eating, of course, is to supply your body with the raw materials that it requires to function properly. But food influences your health in other, perhaps more surprising, ways as well.

Is It Something You Ate?

Foods can cause as well as cure certain physical symptoms. If you've been bothered by a minor health complaint, consider what you have—or haven't—been eating. Then try the appropriate tip below to correct the problem.

Sip away leg cramps

If you often experience leg cramps, especially after exercising, you may be dehydrated. Your top priority is to drink more water. Most experts recommend eight 8-ounce glasses a day, and more when you exert yourself. Also, enjoy a postworkout banana or low-fat yogurt. It will help replenish the minerals that you've lost through perspiration.

Stymie stomach cramps

If you develop bloating, diarrhea, or gas after eating dairy products, you may have lactose intolerance. This means that your intestines no longer produce enough lactase, an enzyme required to break down lactose, the natural sugar in dairy products. Try eliminating these foods for a week or two. If your symptoms subside, switch to lactose-free dairy products or use a lactose supplement and consult a physician.

I'm in the Mood for . . . Lunch?

A steady diet of burgers, fries, and other fat-laden foods may have a startling effect on your personal life. A study conducted years ago at the University of Utah in Salt Lake City suggests that high-fat fare may curb the production of testosterone, the hormone that fuels sex drive in both men and women.

In the study, researchers measured the testosterone levels of eight men and then served them high-fat shakes. After four hours, the men's testosterone levels had fallen by 30 percent. This is the first time that researchers were able to link dietary fat to a drop in testosterone. Why the drop occurred remains a mystery. "It may be that fatty acids act on the cells that make testosterone, cutting down on production," speculates A. Wayne Meikle, MD, the researcher who headed the study.

For men, at least, the sex-dousing effects of a high-fat diet don't end there. For starters, "dietary fat is easily converted into body fat, and men with more body fat tend to have less testosterone," says Dr. Meikle. What's more, fat clogs arteries, including those that rush blood to the penis to produce an erection.

Know the signs

Long before the advent of the neighborhood drugstore, when a person ate a food that upset her stomach or gave her heartburn, she simply didn't eat it again. These days, folks seem more inclined to reach for an over-the-counter fix.

Your body knows what it can tolerate. It keeps giving you clues all the time. You just have to recognize them and take action. If you usually break out in a rash after eating avocado, skip the guacamole on your tortilla chips. If you usually experience intense gas after eating pepperoni, change toppings on your pizza. If you usually develop a migraine after eating a hot dog, opt for a burger at your next cookout.

Basic Mouth Maintenance

Every time you take a bite of food, your teeth go to work for you. Care for them properly, and they'll last a lifetime. Skip sessions of brushing and flossing and you could face costly (and sometimes painful) dental work down the road. These tips will help keep your chops in tip-top shape.

Brush promptly

When you eat dates, figs, raisins, and other sticky foods, brush your teeth as soon as you can afterward. Dentists have found that these foods not only contain a lot of sugar but also hang on to your teeth longer. Both factors increase the probability of future tooth decay.

Become a softy

The American Dental Association (ADA) recommends using a toothbrush with soft bristles. Hard bristles combined with too-vigorous brushing actually wears away tooth enamel and erodes gums. "The only time you should ever use a hard brush is to clean the whitewalls on your tires," according to Matthew Massina, DDS, consumer advisor for the ADA.

Learn good form

To brush your teeth properly, advises the ADA, begin by tilting your toothbrush at a 45-degree angle. That way, the bristles come into contact with your teeth and gums at the same time. Then gently move your toothbrush in small circles rather than vigorously scrubbing. If the bristles begin to splay—that is, branch out in various directions—you're probably brushing too hard.

Test your technique

Disclosing tablets, available in drugstores and from dentists, can show you whether you're brushing properly. Chewing a tablet after brushing releases a harmless dye, usually bright red, that temporarily stains any plaque left behind on your teeth. Use the tablets for a week or two, and you'll be able to identify the areas that you consistently miss. Make a point of brushing these areas. Pretty soon, you'll pass the tablet test with flying noncolors.

Chicken Soup for the Sinuses

Before there were decongestants and expectorants and suppressants, there was chicken soup. Even today, it remains one of the best cold remedies around.

Chicken soup offers a rich supply of antioxidants from cysteine (a component of chicken meat), garlic, black pepper, and other ingredients. Antioxidants fortify your body's immune defenses so they're better able to fight infection.

The more boiled down and hot and pungent the soup, the more potent its healing properties, says Irwin Ziment, MD, the now retired professor of medicine from the University of California, Los Angeles, School of Medicine. As the soup cooks, get a good sniff of the vapors. That'll help open your sinuses. Other foods that can help relieve congestion include chili peppers, horseradish, and mustard.

The Simplest of the Simple

Eating healthfully doesn't require a degree in nutrition or a calculator to tally calories and fat grams. Follow these basic guidelines, and you can rest assured that you'll be feeding your body properly.

- Build your meals around grains, fruits, and vegetables. Treat meat, fish, poultry, eggs, and dairy products as side dishes. Eat fats and sweets sparingly, if at all.
- Aim for a fiber intake of 40 grams a day.
- Substitute water for high-calorie beverages.
- Enjoy a hearty breakfast, a moderate-size lunch, and a light dinner.
- Eat slowly and chew foods thoroughly. Savor every bite of your meal.
- When served monster portions in restaurants, wrap up half to take home.
- Give in to your cravings occasionally, but keep the portions small.
- When you have a cold, clear up congestion with chicken soup.
- Listen to your body: When a food disagrees with you, avoid it in the future.

Chapter 23	# Effortless Exercise

Easy Ways to Factor Fitness into Your Life

Most everyone jokes about the couch potato label. In reality, being overweight and out of shape is no laughing matter. Both factors put a person at risk for a host of health problems, including heart disease, America's number one killer.

Getting fit and staying fit doesn't require a Herculean effort. You need not even break a sweat. Your goal is simply to engage in some form of physical activity for a minimum amount of time each and every day.

With the information presented in this chapter, you'll be able to create an exercise program that you can live with. We'll focus on simple ways to get your body moving, as opposed to complicated workout regimens that many folks start with good intentions and abandon within a week.

A Body Built for the Long Haul

During the 1912 presidential campaign, Theodore Roosevelt was shot at point-blank range as he prepared to deliver a speech. The would-be assassin's bullet struck Roosevelt in the chest, bounced off the eyeglass case in his breast pocket, and punctured his lung. Roosevelt simply covered the wound with his handkerchief, then proceeded with his speech. When he was done, he bolted off the podium to receive medical attention. The .38 slug remained inside him for the rest of his life. Roosevelt's experience illustrates an important point: Often we're much tougher than we realize. Our bodies can withstand tremendous stresses, provided we've taken good care of them. That's where regular exercise comes into play.

Taking Care of the Necessities

Before you begin a fitness program, make certain that you're ready for one, especially if you've been inactive. Here's what you need to do.

Start with a physical

Your first order of business is to get a complete physical exam. At the very least, you want to establish your baseline fitness level so you know where you stand and what you need to improve.

If you're under age 40 and in relatively good health, a checkup every two years should suffice. If you're 40 or over, a checkup every year is recommended. The reason is that certain conditions, such as breast and ovarian cancer in women and prostate cancer in men, become more prevalent with age. A routine annual exam can ensure that you have a clean bill of health.

Get the works

Blood tests have become standard procedure for wellness exams. They're easily done, and they reveal a great deal about your health. Even if your doctor orders a blood workup for you, insist on a comprehensive physical that includes a treadmill test. This provides you and your doctor with a more complete picture of your health status.

Set new goals

If your exam reveals (or you already know) that you face a particular challenge in terms of your health, use that challenge as the driving force behind your fitness program. Suppose, for example, that you have high blood pressure. Decide what you would like your blood pressure reading to be six months from now, then identify what you need to do to get there. Regular exercise certainly will move you toward your goal. Making dietary changes and taking supplements may also help. Many other health objectives are likewise within your grasp.

Shaping Up, Slimming Down

Americans have steadily packed on the pounds since 1960. A growing percentage of people are overweight and out of shape.

As the general population grows ever heavier, traditional height and weight charts have become all but useless. They're based on national averages, not on what experts consider healthy. For instance, according to a formula used by many doctors, a large-framed woman who stands five feet five inches tall should weigh about 137 pounds. Yet the Metropolitan Life Insurance Company height and weight chart, long considered the standard scale, lists a desirable weight range of 137 to 155 pounds. That's another 18 pounds.

If overweight among adults is cause for alarm, consider what's happening among kids. Data from the National Center for Health Statistics in Hyattsville, Maryland, indicate that American children are getting fatter, too. The percentage of youngsters between ages 6 and 17 who qualify as overweight has nearly doubled since the 1980s

after staying at the same level for two decades. Presumably, kids are eating more junk food and exercising less.

Obesity costs the United States $147 billion annually and causes the premature deaths of hundreds of thousands of people each year, according to Weight Watchers International. "There's indisputable evidence that being obese is unhealthy," says Linda Webb Carilli, general manager of corporate affairs for Weight Watchers International in Jericho, New York. She observes that the public often gets mixed signals about this serious health issue. While a tiny percentage of overweight people qualify as fit, far more are just plain out of shape. Carilli describes obesity as one of the most rapidly growing health problems in this country.

Many people begin working out specifically to trim and tone their bodies. Unfortunately, their efforts sometimes lead to frustration, primarily because they do too much too soon or they don't see results fast enough. Whittling your waistline (and other parts of your body) does take time. But if you go about it properly, you'll achieve lasting results. Use these ground rules to guide your efforts.

Identify your ideal weight

A realistic goal weight gives you something to aim for as you slim down. Many different formulas exist for determining how much you should weigh. Here's one of the simplest. Allow 100 pounds for your first five feet of height, and for every inch over five feet, add 5 pounds if you're a man and 4 pounds if you're a woman. The total is your ideal weight if you have a medium build. Add 10 percent if you're large-framed, or subtract 10 percent if you're small-framed.

For example, a medium-framed woman who is five feet five inches tall might weigh about 120 pounds. That's 100 pounds for the first five feet of height, plus 4 pounds for every inch over five feet (or 20 pounds). If she were large-framed, her ideal weight could be 132 pounds (120 plus 10 percent). If she were small-framed, her ideal weight would be 108 pounds (120 minus 10 percent).

Better Health, One Step at a Time

The 12 Steps of Alcoholics Anonymous, listed below, offer a simple yet effective means for confronting and overcoming just about any health challenge. Replace the word "alcohol" with your specific problem, and you may find these steps quite empowering.

1. We admitted we were powerless over alcohol—that our lives had become unmanageable.
2. We came to believe that a power greater than ourselves could restore us to sanity.
3. We made a decision to turn our will and our lives over to the care of God as we understood Him.
4. We made a searching and fearless moral inventory of ourselves.
5. We admitted to God, to ourselves, and to another human being the exact nature of our wrongs.
6. We were entirely ready to have God remove all these defects of character.
7. We humbly asked Him to remove our shortcomings.
8. We made a list of all persons we had harmed and became willing to make amends to them all.
9. We made direct amends to such people wherever possible, except when to do so would injure them or others.
10. We continued to take personal inventory and, when we were wrong, promptly admitted it.
11. We sought, through prayer and meditation, to improve our conscious contact with God, as we understood Him, praying only for knowledge of His will and the power to carry that out.
12. Having had a spiritual awakening as the result of these steps, we tried to carry this message to alcoholics, and to practice these principles in all our affairs.

Avoid overcompensating

Many people develop the mindset that if they vigorously exercise for 30, 40, 50 minutes or longer, they have permission to overindulge the next time they put food in their mouths. Of course, if you want to slim down, working out hard and then eating voraciously won't do the job. Your weight will simply hold steady. In order to win the battle of the bulge, you have to burn more calories than you ingest. That means not only exercising regularly but also eating healthfully.

A Whole New View

In the 1957 movie *The Bridge on the River Kwai*, Alec Guinness plays a British commander in charge of Allied prisoners being held in a Japanese prisoner-of-war camp in Thailand. The prisoners are directed to build a huge wooden span high over the River Kwai, providing a vital transportation link for the Japanese imperial forces. Guinness becomes so attached to the bridge that he forgets the reason for building it. Similarly, becoming attached to an unrealistic weight or fitness level can quickly make you lose sight of the reason for exercising: achieving and maintaining good health. If you don't see the results you expect, you may abandon your efforts in frustration.

Avoid getting tripped up by this stumbling block. Set reasonable goals, but focus on making fitness convenient and fun. You want exercising to become such an integral part of your life that any benefits you may experience seem like a perk rather than an expectation.

Making Fitness Fit

Above all else, fitness should never seem like drudgery. If it does, then you may need to choose another activity or find ways to make your workout more convenient. Otherwise, you'll find every reason not to exercise and few reasons why you should.

Only you know which activities you enjoy and feel comfortable with. If convenience is the issue, then these tips can help.

> ### Simply Stated
>
> *People who don't know how to keep themselves healthy ought to have the decency to get themselves buried, and not waste time about it.*
>
> **—Henrik Ibsen, Norwegian dramatist, in *When We Dead Awaken***

Use your time wisely

Most people think they need to set aside at least 30 minutes daily to work out. If you can do that, fine. If not, realize that any amount of physical activity, even a 15-minute walk around the block, makes a difference. Look for clever ways in which you can incorporate some form of exercise into a limited period of time. Your mission is simply to get your body moving as often as you can every day.

Become an opportunist

Pepper your daily routine with what fitness experts call opportunistic exercise. For instance, when you go to the supermarket or mall, park as far away from the entrance as possible so you'll have a longer walk to the store. Likewise, if you use public transportation, get off the bus or subway one stop before your destination and walk the rest of the way. If you work in a building with multiple levels, take the stairs instead of the elevator.

Doing What Comes Naturally

For sheer convenience, nothing beats walking. You can do it anytime and anywhere the spirit moves you. All you need is a pair of sneakers or walking shoes. As you prepare to perambulate, keep this advice in mind.

Move your feet, then eat

Get in the habit of walking before and after each meal, even if it's for just a couple minutes. This practice can actually diminish your appetite so you won't eat as much during the meal or feel hungry soon afterward. You may also avoid that familiar postmeal slump.

Stroll wherever it suits you

Take a couple laps around the block, morning or evening, and you'll get about 15 solid minutes of walking.

If you live near a mall, you can easily spend an hour walking around in there. Remember, though, that you want to stay in motion—no stopping to look at the merchandise.

Put a little swing into it

As you move your legs at a steady pace, get your arms pumping, too. Yes, it may look funny to some, but your cardiovascular system responds well to such activity. In fact, if you can raise your arms above your head while swinging them, so much the better. After all, orchestra conductors have longer-than-average life spans. Scientists postulate that all that time with the baton held high, arms above heart level, strengthens the heart muscle.

Simply Stated

Thou seest I have more flesh than another man, and therefore more frailty.

**—William Shakespeare,
English playwright, in *Henry IV***

Going on Location

Of course, circumstances won't always permit you to head for the outdoors or the nearest shopping center. That doesn't mean you should abandon your workout on those days. Simply tailor it to the situation. Here are some suggestions.

Move to the tube

If you're tempted to spend a rainy day camped out in front of the TV, why not work out while you watch? You can probably find an exercise program on some channel. If not, try doing calisthenics or strength training with hand weights. You may even want to invest in a treadmill, a stationary cycle, or another exercise machine for just such occasions.

Join the club

Becoming a member of a health club puts an array of fitness equipment at your disposal. The treadmills and stationary cycles are great because they allow you to start at a slow pace and cool down when you're done.

If the facility has mirrors along the walls, use them while you work out. They help you to maintain proper form and may prompt you to stay on a particular machine longer or to do more repetitions of a particular exercise. Likewise, if the facility has a sauna, steam room, or whirlpool bath, go ahead and enjoy it—but be careful not to overdo it. A prolonged sit or soak can actually drain your energy instead of recharging your batteries.

Speak Slower, Live Longer

Talking fast, which is often classified as a type A personality trait, may put you at greater risk for heart disease, according to a study published in the *Journal of Cardiovascular Nursing*. Researchers measured the blood pressures and heart rates of 111 heart patients as the patients read the US Constitution out loud, reading rapidly for two minutes, then slowly for two minutes. The fast readings triggered rises in blood pressure and heart rate, both risk factors for heart disease. Taking your time to speak tends to keep your blood pressure and heart rate on an even keel.

Perspire in unison

Recruit a friend to enroll in an exercise class with you. You can give each other motivation and support so you attend class more regularly and stay for the duration. Also, you may be more inclined to check out courses that you hadn't considered previously, such as aqua aerobics, belly dancing, and tai chi.

Take your show on the road

If you're traveling and you find yourself staying in a hotel with no exercise facilities, use the hallways or even your own room as a gym. Request a nonsmoking room or a nonsmoking floor—you want to work out in an environment in which nicotine has not infiltrated the carpets and curtains. Then run in place, do arm circles or squats, or engage in some other light activity. Turn on the TV, radio, or your iPod if you want. By working out for as little as 30 minutes, you'll feel much more energized for the rest of the day.

Working Out Stress

On especially hectic days, you may feel tempted to skip your planned workout. Yet that's when you most need to get moving. A workout releases tension and leaves you feeling calm and clear-headed. Just be sure to heed this advice.

Go easy on yourself

Taking out your stress on a stationary cycle or stairclimber is one thing. Beating up your body in the process is another thing entirely. Your workout should leave you feeling refreshed and invigorated. When you overdo it, you end up hungry and dehydrated, not to mention downright exhausted. You're in no condition to face a bear of a day.

During trying times, stick with a light regimen such as walking or doing calisthenics. You'll get a good workout without overexerting yourself. If you really need intensity, stay within 60 to 70 percent of your optimum performance level. In other words, trim your usual 60-minute aerobic workout to 35 to 40 minutes. Or instead of lifting 150 pounds during your strength-training workout, cut back to 90 to 105 pounds.

Get a grip

For on-the-spot stress relief, squeeze a hand gripper. It relaxes tense muscles in the jaw, neck, and shoulders. As a bonus, it strengthens your hands and wrists.

Pampering Your Body

Depending on the activity and the level of intensity, a workout demands a lot of your body. Prepare it to meet the challenge by sticking with these strategies.

Stay hydrated

Whenever you exercise, keep a sports bottle filled with water in hand or nearby. Sip from it constantly so you stay hydrated. Don't wait until you feel thirsty. At that point, your body has already experienced a prolonged water shortage because it has given up a lot of fluid via perspiration. It desperately needs replenishment. In fact, if you feel fatigued during or after a workout, it may mean that you're dehydrated. Try drinking lots of water (slowly, to avoid cramps). It may be enough to rejuvenate you.

Simply Stated

The preservation of health is a duty. Few seem conscious that there is such as thing as physical morality.

**—Herbert Spencer,
English philosopher, in Education**

Wash pain down the drain

To ease any postworkout soreness, take a comfortably hot shower for two minutes, then switch to cold water and let it run full throttle for 30 seconds. Repeat these two steps 5 to 10 times. As you switch from hot water to cold, your blood vessels actually widen and narrow. This flushes the lactic acid out of your muscles, making you less likely to feel stiff and sore.

Feeling Sore? Get on the Ball

A golf ball can come in handy even if you never step onto on a fairway. According to practitioners of reflexology, rolling the ball with the soles of your feet relieves pain not only in your feet but all over your body.

Reflexologists believe that the sole of each foot is like a map of the body. The points where the sole is tender indicate precisely where the body is weak or stressed. Applying pressure with the golf ball to a specific point on the sole triggers a response in the corresponding part of the body.

With your shoes and socks off and the golf ball on the floor, slowly roll each foot over the ball. It may hurt a bit when the ball comes into contact with tender points. Remember, though, that you want to relieve pain and tension throughout your body. So even though it hurts, continue to roll the ball back and forth with your foot until the discomfort subsides. Then switch to the other foot.

Sometimes, the ball may scoot out from under your foot. To prevent this from happening, you can use towels, books, or furniture to "fence in" the area where you're doing the exercise. Even better, roll the ball on carpeting.

For faster relief, use two balls instead of one, rolling both balls with one foot. Don't try to work both feet at once—it's too difficult and not as relaxing.

If you do this exercise on successive days, you'll begin to notice that any pain on the soles of your feet is subsiding. Take this as a good sign: It means that any pain in the corresponding part of your body is subsiding, too.

Let It Rain on Your Parade

If the TV weatherman predicts rain, you may want to time your workout for right when the showers end. A rainstorm floods the air with negative ions, which improve air quality and enhance the rejuvenating effects of exercise. You breathe easier, and you feel better, too.

The following chart compares post-rainstorm air with the air in various other environments. The lower the ratio of positive to negative ions, the better the air quality.

Environment	Positive Ions	Negative Ions	Ratio
Post-storm air	800	2,500	0.3:1
Rural air	1,800	1,500	1.2:1
Urban air	600	500	1.2:1
Clean mountain air	2,500	2,000	1.3:1
Air in an office with windows	200	150	1.3:1
Air in a light-industrial plant	400	250	1.6:1
Pre-storm air	3,000	800	3.8:1
Air in an office without windows	80	20	4.0:1
Air in a closed moving vehicle (car, bus, plane, or train)	80	20	4.0:1

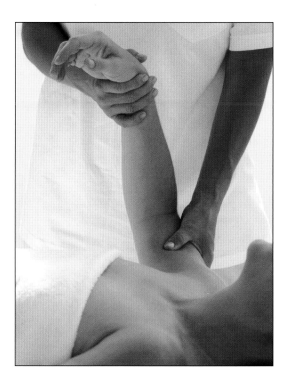

Relax with a rubdown

Consider getting a full-body massage from a certified massage therapist (CMT). A massage helps remove lactic acid from your muscles, reducing soreness. To locate a qualified CMT in your area, ask family members and friends for recommendations, or look online or in the Yellow Pages under "Massage Therapists."

The Simplest of the Simple

Working out doesn't have to be work. The following strategies can help you achieve optimal fitness with minimum effort.

- Before you begin an exercise program, get a comprehensive physical that includes blood tests and a treadmill test.
- Set a goal for yourself, such as a desired blood pressure reading or waist measurement.
- Look for little ways to engage in a few minutes of physical activity at various times throughout the day.
- Take a walk before and after each meal.
- Give your TV a higher purpose—work out while watching a show or DVD that you like.
- Find a friend to exercise with.
- When you're under stress, keep your workout light. Stay within 60 to 70 percent of your optimum performance level.
- Drink water constantly while you exercise.

Simply Stated

Look to your health; and if you have it, praise God, and value it next to a good conscience; for health is the second blessing that we mortals are capable of; a blessing that money cannot buy.

—Izaak Walton, English author, in *The Compleat Angler*

Chapter 24

At Your Leisure

Guaranteed Fun for Everyone

> *Oceanside amusement parks such as Coney Island catered to thrill seekers of the day. Hair-raising rides and games of ring toss with Kewpie-doll prizes were new "leisure time" activities—the phrase was coined in 1907—that beckoned after the workday began to grow shorter.*
>
> **—Carol Strickland, in *Civilization***

The responsibilities of job, home, and family all too often transform the daily routine into one big blur. Carving out quality leisure time becomes difficult.

True leisure means engaging in a pleasurable and rewarding activity without being preoccupied by other aspects of your life. You can't force leisure into an otherwise frenzied schedule and expect it to feel good. Sometimes, the strains you experience during the week make you place great emphasis on weekends and other days off. You hope to relax, but the pressure is enormous. You can't rest even when you have the time to do so. Your mind may not be free to enjoy it.

Make no mistake: Leisure is a fundamental component of your life. If you don't have frequent and rewarding leisure time, you're missing out.

Where do you weigh in on the leisure scale? This brief quiz can help you find out. Simply answer yes or no to each question.

1. I fully understand the value of leisure in my life.
2. I have at least one rewarding weekend a month.
3. I take care of errands during the week so I don't use up my weekends.
4. I plan and take an annual or semiannual vacation.
5. I engage in rewarding, relaxing hobbies or other interests.
6. I regularly exercise at a tennis club, pool club, spa, or another facility.
7. I can be comfortable doing nothing at all at selected times.
8. I can relax without the use of chemical substances.
9. I engage in regularly scheduled leisure-time activities.
10. I have achieved a reasonable balance between work and play.

Tally up your yes responses. If you have five or fewer, you definitely need more leisure in your life. The tips in this chapter will help you get it. If you have more than five, good for you! This chapter can show you some clever ways in which to enhance your leisure time.

Time Out for You

When time is at a premium, leisure activities are usually the first items to disappear from the daily schedule. One of the advantages of simplifying your life is that you'll have more windows of opportunity to do stuff just for fun. Think of leisure as your reward for all those little extraneous things that eat up precious minutes of your day.

Relearning to Relax

If you're unaccustomed to having free time, you may need a brief refresher course in choosing and planning leisure activities. Here are the basics.

Indulge your desires

Devote one afternoon or evening per week entirely to yourself. Use those hours to do something, anything, that you enjoy. Listen to your favorite music. Assemble a jigsaw puzzle. Dig in your garden. Do whatever you always wish you could but never seem to find time for. And do it where there's nothing to remind you of other obligations.

Get lost

If you find yourself constantly watching the clock while participating in a leisure activity, you're not truly relaxing. Let yourself go, to the point where you lose track of the hour. In this state of timelessness, you can derive optimum benefits from relaxation.

Opt for low-tech

The popular fascination with technological advances in all areas of life has diverted attention from the simple pleasures of many traditional pastimes. People think they must have the best, most up-to-date equipment available to enjoy themselves. When keeping up with trends becomes the focus, the sheer pleasure of leisure is lost. Let yourself have fun without trying to outdo your friends and neighbors.

Simple Ways to Unwind

Putting the needs of others before your own is unquestionably noble. Over time, however, such self-sacrifice begins to exact a toll. Unless you take good care of yourself, you won't have the mental or physical energy necessary to deal with the problems and demands of family and friends.

Remember, you need and deserve leisure time just as much as anyone else. So give yourself a well-earned break by trying one or more of these easy relaxers.

> **Simply Stated**
>
> *There is more to life than increasing its speed.*
> **—Mohandas Karamchand Gandhi,**
> **Indian nationalist leader**

Go for a soak

One of the best and simplest ways to relax—even for men—is to take a long, comfortably hot bath. Add bubble bath, bath oil, or mineral salts, or leave the water as is. Position a bathtub pillow so that you can lie back. Then just close your eyes and enjoy. To ensure solitude, lock the bathroom door and post a sign that says, "Don't You Dare Disturb."

Treat your feet

If you don't have time for a whole-body soak—even a short one—then take the plunge with just your feet. Fill a small basin with comfortably hot water and set it in front of your favorite chair. Then take a seat and submerge your feet. This keeps you in one place, so you can't easily interrupt your footbath to answer the door or the phone.

Follow your nose

Breathing deeply for just a few minutes can do wonders to help you relax. As you inhale, concentrate on completely filling your lungs. Allow your diaphragm (the muscle that separates your chest and abdominal cavities) to expand completely. Feel your chest rise and fall. By focusing on your breathing, you help send oxygen throughout your body and relax tense muscles. You also take your mind off any stress or anxiety that may be bothering you.

Humor yourself

Do something that is guaranteed to make you laugh. Watch a funny movie, read the comics section in the newspaper, or play a game with your spouse or kids. Laughter is great medicine. You'll be surprised at how much better it can make you feel.

Make a big deal of your midday meal

Busy day ahead? Set aside an hour or so to have lunch at your favorite restaurant, either alone or with a friend. Leave your work at the office (or at home), and if you're with someone, agree not to talk business. In this way, you can turn your lunch break into a mini-vacation.

Yes, an hour may seem like a huge chunk of time. But the relaxation you derive from a long, leisurely lunch will help you function more efficiently the rest of the day. This alone makes the hour time well-spent.

Beautify your bedroom

Some days, your bedroom may provide your only refuge from the outside world. By adding a few inexpensive decorative touches, you can transform it into an even more inviting retreat—a place of escape and relaxation. Simply outfitting your bed with soft sheets and a few extra pillows may do the trick.

Fun for the Whole Family

Balancing the need for true leisure with the reality of family life presents its challenges, particularly if you have children. The solution? Include your kids in the fun. Here are some activities for the whole family to enjoy.

Pet Therapy

Having a pet is a huge responsibility. Yet many people are willing to take on the task in exchange for the companionship that a pet provides. Humans benefit mentally and physically from contact with animals, according to an article in *U.S. News and World Report*.

Studies have shown that nursing home residents became measurably more alert in the presence of animals. Likewise, physically aggressive patients became noticeably more tolerant of people standing near them. The presence of animals also lowers heart rate, calms disturbed children, and encourages incommunicative people to talk.

No one knows precisely why pets have these effects. Scientists suspect that it has something to do with the fact that interaction with animals is uncomplicated—unlike interaction with other humans. "Animals are nonjudgmental, accepting, and attentive; they don't talk back, criticize, or give orders," states the article in *U.S. News and World Report*. "They give people something to be responsible for and offer a nonthreatening outlet for physical contact."

Visit the park

The kids are clamoring for something to do, but you'd rather not spend a lot of money. The community park is the perfect place for an afternoon of free fun. There's plenty to keep the kids busy: basketball courts, nature trails, swings, and more.

Plan a picnic

Whether you head for the park or hang out in your backyard, a picnic is a nice change from eating at the kitchen table. And it keeps the kids from spending time in front of the television.

Eat out for less

Entertainment Publications produces regionally oriented coupon books that can save you a bundle when you treat the family to dinner. Some coupons give flat discounts (usually in the 15 to 30 percent range), while others offer buy-one-get-one-free deals. The books are often sold as fund-raisers by nonprofit organizations. You can also contact Entertainment Publications directly. The phone number is available from toll-free directory assistance.

Simply Stated

He has spent his life best who has enjoyed it most.
—Samuel Butler, English author

Set your sights on the silver screen

While the price of movie admission continues to climb, matinees and twilight shows still cost a few dollars less than the evening shows. Or you can wait for a film to appear in second-run theaters, which charge even less.

Head for the great outdoors

With an inexpensive campsite and a few basic supplies, you and your family can commune with nature. No matter where you live, there's probably a campground less than an hour's drive away.

Getting Away from It All

Say "leisure," and most folks think "vacation." Indeed, spending quality time—whether a long weekend or an entire week—in the locale of your choice provides a welcome, rejuvenating break from the daily grind. Provided, of course, that everything goes as planned.

We've all heard the stories of dream vacations turned nightmares, thanks to canceled flights, botched hotel reservations, lost luggage, and destinations that don't quite live up to their brochures. Never fear: With the following strategies, you can avoid hassles and make your vacation memorable for all the right reasons.

Planning the Perfect Escape

When planning a vacation, first decide where and when you want to go and what you want to do. As you consider the possibilities, keep these factors in mind.

Remember the reason

The goal of a vacation is to relax. If you fill each day with activities and spend most of your time on the go, you and your family may arrive home feeling more stressed than when you left. Don't feel that you have to plan every minute of your vacation. If you enjoy sightseeing, allow yourself plenty of time at each stop. Don't feel obligated to see everything in one trip. After all, you can always go back. Likewise, if you prefer to spend your days lounging at the pool or on the beach, by all means do. That's what a vacation is for.

Time your trip right

Just because everyone else goes to the beach in July doesn't mean that you have to. Travel in the off-season, if your job allows. You'll avoid the crowds and save money, as many hotels offer reduced rates at nonpeak times of year. Avoid the weeks around the Fourth of July and Christmas because so many others take vacations then.

Find a home away from home

To avoid the cost of staying in hotels and the hassle of making reservations, consider a home exchange: Your family and another family swap houses for a defined period of time. If you're interested in this option, join a home-exchange club, which will provide you with guidelines and a directory. These clubs usually have quality control to make sure that all participants are reliable. You make arrangements directly with the other family, so you can pick and choose your situation. HomeLink International is an established home-exchange club. Visit www.homelink.org.

Travel Steals and Deals

If you already have a destination in mind, you may prefer to plan your vacation yourself. Finding the best deals takes some legwork, but knowing where to look and who to call can simplify the task substantially.

Tripping the Flight Fantastic

How are you going to travel? Flying gets you to your destination fastest. And these days, it's more affordable than ever. You can save even more on airfare by choosing flights scheduled for off-peak hours. In particular, flying in the middle of the day and in the middle of the week can mean huge savings for you.

Here are some more tips for finding the lowest airfare available.

Scan all sources

Airlines list flights and fares on the Internet. They also have toll-free numbers that you can call to hear fares.

Fly with the night owls

Most late-night flights ("red-eyes") don't fill up, so airlines often cut the rates for these flights significantly. Also, on Wednesdays, many airlines post drastically discounted last-minute fares via e-mail or the Internet. Call various airlines to find out more about their e-saver policies.

It's Official: Time Flies When You're Having Fun

Time perception was one of the first subjects to be examined by psychologists. In 1904, studies determined that a given interval of time seems shorter when you're active than when you're sitting around. In 1933, a Harvard University study concluded that when someone is "bored or feels despair, time seems long; when he is interested or eager, time seems short."

Be an early bird

Unless you're planning for a trip a few months down the road, never buy tickets at the airline counter in the airport. You won't get the best fares, and you likely won't get the seats you want. Instead, make your reservations in advance and have confirmation sent via email. And get your seat assignments as far in advance as possible, especially if you're traveling with someone and you want to sit together.

Aim for the aisle

On a short flight, when you won't be doing much sleeping, request an aisle seat at the front of the plane. You'll have more room to stand up and stretch. You'll also have better luck getting the attention of the flight attendants. On longer flights, where you sit depends on where you're most comfortable. Choose an exit-row seat if you want extra legroom and you don't mind opening the door in the event of an emergency. Choose an aisle seat if you intend to get up and walk around a lot. A window seat is okay if you plan to sleep for most of the flight.

Take names

Whenever you reserve a ticket with any transportation company, be sure to ask for the representative's name. This increases the probability that the representative will make sure that all parts of your reservation are correct. Also ask about the punctuality of the flights that you'll be taking. This information is readily available to reservation agents.

Preview your flight plan

Review the itinerary that indicates your scheduled arrival and departure times, any stops or layovers, and onboard food service (meals or snacks).

Sleeping for Less

When you're traveling, your hotel room becomes a home away from home. You want accommodations that are safe, clean, and comfortable, all for a reasonable price. Seems like too much to ask? Not if you heed this advice.

Bank on budget motels

We all like to be pampered now and then. Still, spending $150 a night to sleep seems ridiculous when budget motels offer rooms for one-third the price. You may have to do without a few amenities, but then again, you

probably won't be spending that much time in your room anyway. Look for the least expensive motels in the safest locations. For convenient comparison shopping, stop by your nearest bookstore or library and pick up a travel guide for your destination.

Book a bargain

You're likely to get a better deal on room rates by making reservations directly with a particular hotel rather than through a toll-free number that services an entire hotel chain. While you're on the phone, ask whether the hotel offers family, educational, government, or senior rates. This tactic may prompt the front-desk clerk to give you some kind of discount. Also, check your memberships: Automotive clubs, professional and civic associations, and other organizations often offer reduced hotel rates to members.

Overly Optimistic

If you routinely forfeit your leisure time because you have "more important things to do," you may be underestimating how much time those other things actually take. Most people routinely shortchange themselves on the amount of time required to complete a given task, according to research at an American Psychological Association conference. The problem is a failure to evaluate performance honestly. Folks generalize from those rare occasions when everything went perfectly.

If you want to get tasks done on time so that you can enjoy leisure activities, realistically calculate during a project's planning stages the hours that will be required. Then increase the time commitment by 25 percent to safely allow for unexpected delays.

Suitable Suitcases

Planning your vacation includes deciding what to take with you and what to leave behind. You want only the essentials. Of course, when you're spending several days away from home, everything seems essential. Just remember that the less baggage you have to tote around, the more hassle-free your vacation will be.

Packing Makes Perfect

Packing for travel is an underappreciated art form. Become a master by following these simple strategies for lightening your load.

Lighten up

Luggage that's heavy before you put anything in it will be a nightmare to transport when it's full. Invest in the lightest bags you can find. Your clothes and other personal items will more than make up for the difference in weight.

Carry on what you can

If you're flying, ask your carrier what you're allowed to take on board. Increasingly, airlines are restricting passengers to just one carry-on bag. If you can fit all your necessities in that one bag, do. Otherwise, you'll have to wait 20 minutes or so at baggage claim—provided, of course, that your bags actually arrive with you. Keep a cadré of frequently used personal items with you, just in case your luggage gets lost.

Take advantage of amenities

Pack as few toiletries and cosmetics as possible in the smallest containers possible. Don't take anything that you know your hotel will supply, such as soap and shampoo. When you make your reservation, ask what items are provided.

Mix and match

By selecting your travel wardrobe wisely, you can make many outfits from just a few articles of clothing. Two shirts and two pairs of shorts or pants could last you four

days with a little creative coordination. Accessories can increase your outfit options.

Pack with panache

When packing your suitcase, put shoes and other heavy items on the bottom. Next go lightweight items, followed by wrinkle-prone items on top. Use plastic bags to house and separate items and to hold dirty clothing on your return trip.

Soak Sensibly

If you've ever soaked in a hot tub, you know that it can make you feel relaxed. Elevating your body's temperature for more than a few minutes, however, could leave you feeling light-headed and woozy. Hot tubs are absolutely off-limits for children under age 14, women who are pregnant, and people who have or are at risk for heart disease. The heat dilates blood vessels, causing blood pressure to rise.

Identify yourself

Use luggage identification tags that include your picture. This tactic reduces the likelihood of someone making off with your bags. If you're traveling with a small child, buy him a picture ID bracelet. Most airport vendors sell them, as do discount stores and travel catalogs. Also carry a picture of the child in your wallet, in case he gets separated from you.

Ship souvenirs home

Take priority mail packs with you and use them to send home the stuff that you collect in your travels. You can pick up the packs at your local post office. One pack weighing two pounds costs $3 to ship, which is relatively inexpensive.

Luggage on Wheels

If you've spent any time in an airport, you know that rolling travel bags are the latest trend. They do make getting around easier because you don't have to carry your luggage. Instead, you just drag it along behind you.

Pardon the pounds

Although in general you want to buy the lightest luggage you can find, rolling travel bags are the exception to that rule. The best-made models of these bags are actually heavy. They roll so well, however, that you'll barely notice their weight.

Size up the spacing

The wheels of your bag should be positioned far apart so the bag doesn't tip over when you turn a corner. Also, avoid plastic wheels. They can snap off in a turn or over a bump, leaving you literally holding the bag. You're better off with wheels made of rubber or another highly durable material.

Restoring Nature to Our National Parks

For some of the visitors who jam Yosemite National Park on summer weekends, simply marveling at its granite domes and thundering waterfalls isn't enough. These folks want to go horseback riding, play tennis or golf, and then cool down with glasses of Chablis from their hotel mini-bars.

In 1994, Yosemite officials discontinued many of these amenities. Their decision reflects a new view of our national parks. Gone are the days of luring visitors by building hotels, cutting archways in redwood trees, and pushing bonfires off cliffs to create rustic fireworks. With support from the Clinton administration and Congress, park rangers aim to return the parks to a more natural state, maintaining them as wild sanctuaries rather than theme parks.

This welcome change has been provoked by overuse. National parks have become plagued by much of the urban frenzy from which people try to flee in the first place. Besides being the home of America's highest mountain, biggest glacier, tallest geyser, and longest cave, the park system has been plagued by some of the densest crowds, dirtiest air, ugliest architecture, and longest traffic jams. Environmentalists applaud the back-to-nature shift.

Man the handle

Get a rolling travel bag with adjustable handles that lock. Many of the better bags have this feature. It enables you to go forward and backward without interruption. You'll appreciate this when you're backing out of plane aisles and elevators.

Before You Leave . . .

Your plans are set, you're all packed, and you're ready to hit the road for some adventure, relaxation, and fun (not necessarily in that order). Before you go, you'll want to be sure to take care of these last-minute details.

Safeguarding Your Home While You're Gone

Crafty burglars look for houses left unattended by families on vacation. So before you leave, take these steps to make your home more secure and your absence less obvious.

Discontinue deliveries

Nothing clues in thieves to an absent homeowner like newspapers accumulating on the porch or in the driveway. Contact the circulation department of your newspaper and request that your papers be held until you return. The same goes for your mail. Or if you prefer, you can ask a family member or friend to collect your newspaper and mail daily.

Set your switches

You can buy outlet timers at any hardware or home improvement store. Set them to turn your lights on and off periodically throughout the day, then off for good at night. You can also put your television and radio on timers. This is a great way to create the appearance that someone is at home.

Find your hidden keys

Having a spare key hidden somewhere outside your home may be convenient in case you lock yourself out. But it's an unnecessary danger while you're away. Store your spare keys elsewhere, or give them to a family member or friend to hold on to. Don't help a burglar gain access to your home.

Spread the word—discreetly

Tell the police and your next-door neighbors that you're going on vacation, and ask them to keep an eye on your home while you're gone. Let them know whether you're expecting any deliveries or services during your absence. Leave a number where they can reach you in case they notice anything suspicious going on.

> **Simply Stated**
>
> *When you get older, time gets a lot more valuable. You start thinking about all the things that you wanted to do with your life that you could have done if you had used your free time a little more productively.*
>
> **—Mike Strehren, photographer and father of three**

Your Pre-trip Car Inspection

Driving a long distance with a trunk full of luggage demands a lot from a vehicle. If you're planning to travel by car, make sure it's up to the challenge. The following measures can reduce your chances of getting stuck along the road.

Update your oil

If you haven't changed your oil recently, now is a good time to do so. In fact, most automobile experts recommend changing your oil every 3,000 miles, regardless of whether you do a lot of long-distance driving. If you have changed your oil recently, check the dipstick before you go. And keep a couple of extra quarts of oil in your trunk, just in case you run low during your trip.

Check your fluids

Make sure your car has adequate amounts of other necessary fluids, such as antifreeze and transmission fluid. Often, quick-lube shops will top off your fluids for free with an oil change.

Look for trouble

Visually inspect all belts and hoses to make sure that they're in good condition. In fact, while you're under the hood, eyeball everything for potential problems. If

Check-In Checklist

When making hotel reservations, remember to inquire about the following:
- Special rates for families, club memberships, and so on
- Frequent flyer affiliations
- Shuttle service to and from the airport
- Early check-in/late checkout
- Express check-in/checkout
- Nonsmoking guest rooms (if applicable)
- Guest rooms without adjoining doors
- In-room coffeemaker

you're unfamiliar with the inner workings of your car, take it to a reliable mechanic for a tune-up before you hit the road.

Pump up your tires

Check the air pressure in your tires and fill them if necessary. Also, inspect the tread for wear and tear. You don't want to be driving on a rain-slicked highway with treadless tires.

Rent at the lowest rate

If you'll be renting a car during your vacation, reserve a compact model. Then when you pick up the car, inquire about an upgrade to a larger model. Many rental companies will give you the larger car at no extra charge simply because they have more of them. Remember to thoroughly inspect the car before driving it off the lot, so you're not held liable for preexisting damage.

Join the club

If you often rent a car when you travel, why not become a member of a rental car club? You'll avoid the long lines in airports, get the best discounts, and receive other benefits. All major rental car companies have such clubs—just call the company of your choice for more details.

Getting There Is Half the Fun

D-day (that's departure day) has arrived at last. You're on your way to your best vacation ever. These final few suggestions will help guarantee a journey that's relaxing and stress-free.

Onboard Basics

If you're traveling by plane, the following tips will guarantee a comfortable flight.

Loosen up

Wear loose, comfortable clothing for your flight. Remember, an airplane seat is confining. Heavy clothes, restrictive belts, and tight-fitting shoes will only make matters worse.

Stay hydrated

Carry your own water bottle on board so you don't have to ask the flight attendants for drinks. Also, you'll be able to wet your whistle during your meal (if one is served) rather than waiting a half-hour for the beverage cart to roll by.

Stretch your legs

An occasional walk while in flight is good for your circulation. If you're on a jumbo jet with two aisles rather than one, you can probably get up and move around fairly often without creating a bottleneck. On a plane with just one aisle, go for a walk every 45 minutes or so, if only to the restroom. Stay on your feet for a good 5 to 10 minutes or as long as you can without irritating the flight attendants.

Move to the back

In the rear of the cabin, you'll have enough room to do deep knee bends, arm circles, and other stretches.

The flight attendants can see what you're doing, but the other passengers won't. Besides, it's your body and your trip. Stretching on the plane will give you energy and endurance for when you're back on the ground.

For Snow-Lovers Only

If you're planning to take your vacation in the winter months to get away from the snow, you may want to avoid the following destinations. They have the highest annual snowfalls in the continental United States. Notice, too, that not all of them are up North.

Blue Canyon, California	240.8
Marquette, Michigan	128.6
Sault Sainte Marie, Michigan	116.7
Syracuse, New York	113.6
Caribou, Maine	110.4
Mount Shasta, California	104.9
Lauder, Wyoming	102.5
Flagstaff, Arizona	99.9
Sexton Summit, Oregon	97.8
Muskegon, Michigan	97.0

Don your nightcap

If you want to get some shut-eye, put on a baseball cap with a note that says, "Sleeping—Please do not disturb" pinned to the rim. If you want to work, change the note to, "On deadline—Please do not disturb." Either message will get you the peace and quiet you need.

Questions to Ask Travel Agents

If you decide to have a travel agent plan your vacation for you, keep in mind that agencies vary considerably in the spectrum and quality of services they provide. You can get a good read on a particular agency's commitment to its customers by asking the agent these questions, suggests Rob Sangster, author of *The Traveler's Tool Kit*. If the agent seems evasive or uncomfortable with your inquiries, take your business elsewhere.

- Are you a certified travel counselor? (This tells you that the agent has at least five years' experience in the travel industry and regularly participates in professional training.)
- Are you on salary or commission? (Salaried agents may make more of an effort to hold down costs.)
- How much travel have you done to the places in which I'm interested?
- Is your agency approved by the International Air Transport Association? (To be approved, an agency must be bonded. This means you'll be protected in case the business goes bankrupt.)
- Do you use ticket consolidators? (Consolidators sell unused airline tickets at a savings of 20 to 50 percent.)
- Will you maintain a computer file on me so I don't have to continually repeat my seating, meal, and other preferences?

Good Ideas for a Great Time

Once you reach your destination, these measures will make for a pleasurable stay.

Request the right room

If you're checking into a high-rise hotel, ask for a room between the third and sixth floors. Most thefts occur on the first and second floors, and fire truck ladders seldom reach past the sixth floor.

Eat cheap

When traveling, opt for meals that are healthful and energizing. They shouldn't cost you an arm and a leg. Unless you consider fine dining a necessity for a pleasurable vacation, choose reasonably priced restaurants and save your money for other aspects of your trip.

Make contact on your terms

If you must keep in touch with the office while on vacation, initiate the calls yourself. Set times for your calls before you leave, and limit your contact to only those times. Instruct your secretary or co-workers to get in touch with you only if an emergency arises and absolutely no one else can handle it.

The Simplest of the Simple

Leisure time is one of the rewards of simplifying your life. To make the most of every minute, stick with these ground rules:

- Set aside one afternoon or evening just for yourself. During this time, avoid anything that could remind you of your other responsibilities.
- Choose leisure activities that you enjoy—things that you do because you like doing them, not because you feel you should.
- Let yourself have fun without worrying about keeping up with the Joneses.
- If you take a vacation, avoid planning every minute so that you're doing something all the time.
- Book airline flights in advance. For the best rates, choose flights at off-peak hours.
- Make reservations with specific hotels rather than through national toll-free numbers that service entire hotel chains. You're likely to get better rates that way. Remember to ask about discounts.
- Pack as few toiletries and cosmetics as possible. Don't pack anything that the hotel will supply, such as soap and shampoo.
- Secure your home before you leave, and ask the police or your next-door neighbors to keep an eye on it for you.
- If you're traveling by car, have it serviced before you leave.
- Wear loose, comfortable clothing when flying.

What? Me Take a Vacation?

More than 20 percent of working Americans don't take the vacation days that they're entitled to. Compare that with other Western countries such as Australia, France, Germany, and Sweden, where workers wouldn't dream of giving up even a single day of their five- and six-week vacation allotments.

"Quality leisure is an experience that broadens, teaches, challenges, stimulates, and provides a sense of accomplishment," writes Joe Robinson, former publisher of *Escape Magazine*. "For those who haven't experienced the charge of exploring an unknown land, a battery of excuses bars the way—no time, no money, and no idea what to do."

Credits

"Avoiding Laundry Quandaries" on page 179 contains text adapted from *Solving Laundry Problems*, a pamphlet distributed by the Eureka Company.

"Time for a Tune-Up" on page 235 is adapted from "Time to Tune Up," an article that originally appeared in *Family Circle* magazine.

"In Case of an Accident" on page 245 is adapted from "Accident Data Form," an article that originally appeared in *Family Circle* magazine.

"The Optimist Creed" on page 371 is reprinted with permission from Optimist International.

The 12 steps of Alcoholics Anonymous on page 394 are reprinted with permission of Alcoholics Anonymous World Services, Inc. Permission to reprint the Twelve Steps does not mean that AA has reviewed or approved the contents of this publication, nor that AA agrees with the views expressed herein. AA is a program of recovery from alcoholism *only*. Use of the Twelve Steps in connection with programs and activities that are patterned after AA, but that address other problems, or in any other non-AA context, does not imply otherwise.

About the Author

Jeff Davidson is the internationally recognized expert on work-life balance and holds the registered trademark from the USPTO as the "Work-Life Balance Expert"®. He is the author of *Breathing Space; The Smart Guide to Winning Back Your Time;* and *Dial it Down, Live it Up* along with 61 previous books. His books, the *60-Second Organizer, 60-Second Self-Starter,* and *60-Second Innovator,* are popular titles in Japan, Malaysia, Indonesia, Russia, Turkey, Saudi Arabia, Italy, Poland, Spain, France, and Brazil.

Jeff is often interviewed, featured, or quoted in the *Washington Post, Los Angeles Times, Christian Science Monitor, New York Times,* and *USA Today,* and in *Businessweek, Forbes Travel, Investor Business Daily, Amtrak's All Aboard, American Way,* and *USAirways Magazine.*

Delivered with passion, Jeff presents his cutting edge, hands-on strategies for a balanced career and a balanced life to audiences from Singapore to San Diego, with clients as diverse as Novo Nordisk, Wells Fargo, Lufthansa, IBM, National Office Furniture, Re/MAX, Swissotel, and the National Association of Realtors. He has been a guest on *Late Night with Charlie Rose,* CNBC, *America in the Morning,* the Australian Broadcasting Company, and USA Today *Sky Radio.*

Index